本书的出版获得

教育部人文社会科学重点研究基地
北京大学中国考古学研究中心资助

谨致谢忱

北京大学中国考古学研究中心稽古系列丛书之一

北京大学中国考古学研究中心
那不勒斯东方大学亚洲、非洲和地中海系
地中海与东方学国际研究协会

异宝西来

考古发现的丝绸之路舶来品研究

主 编

葛 嶷

齐东方

CENTER FOR THE STUDY OF CHINESE ARCHAEOLOGY ,
PEKING UNIVERSITY

DIPARTIMENTO ASIA, AFRICA E MEDITERRANEO
UNIVERSITÀ DEGLI STUDI DI NAPOLI "L'ORIENTALE"

ISMEO

West and East
Archaeological Objects Along the Silk Roads

Edited by
Bruno Genito
and
Qi Dongfang

Shanghai Classics Publishing House

序一
Forward

　　中西交通的动力来自于不同文明间的相互吸引。中国境内出土的外国遗物，原中国社会科学院考古研究所所长徐苹芳先生曾经做过系统的整理，近年来又有不少新的发现。从保存的状况看，这些异域珍宝保存状态都比较好，即使是很薄的玻璃器，可见中国古人对其珍视的程度。这些来自远方的器物在中国都有具体的出土地点，我们可以借以了解这些文物的年代下限，也就是不晚于什么时间，但是，对于这些文物生产和制作的"原境"的研究，需要多方面的合作，才能够取得比较满意的成果，因为这些文物来自不同的文明，制作时间跨度很大。

　　意大利那不勒斯东方大学亚洲、非洲和地中海系跟北京大学考古文博学院计划通过长期的合作，深化学术界对中西交流的研究，《异宝西来：考古发现的丝绸之路舶来品研究》其中的一项阶段性成果。除了需要感谢两位主编葛巍和齐东方教授不懈的努力之外，北京大学考古文博学院的魏正中教授做了大量的基础性工作甚至是行政性工作，也是需要特别感谢的。尤其欣喜的是，通过这种长期的合作，一些年轻学者成长了起来，可以预见他们在未来的中西交通的研究中，都会成为中坚力量。

　　The attraction of a different culture was the driving factor in the communications between China and the West. Xu Pingfang, former dean of the Institute of Archaeology, Chinese Academy of Social Sciences, created a comprehensive catalogue of western antiquities found in China years ago. In recent years have seen the discovery of a large number of important sites and artefacts. Many of these treasures have been found in a good state of preservation, even fragile glassware, giving witness to the care with which ancient Chinese cherished them. These objects which are clearly imported from faraway locations have been found in concrete archaeological contexts in China, so that we can define the date before which they were made. As far as the issue of studying the original context in which they were created, there is a need of wider cooperation in order to obtain significant answers, since these objects came from several different civilizations over a long period of time.

　　Dipartimento Asia Africa e Mediterraneo of the Università degli Studi di Napoli "L'Orientale" and the School of Archaeology and Museology in Peking University have been planning to work together in this area for a long time, aiming at improving academic research about the communications between China and the West. "*West and East: Archaeological Objects along the Silk Road*" represents a significant academic achievement. Thanks must go to the two chief editors, Prof. Bruno Genito and Prof. Qi Dongfang for their unstinting efforts in the collection and coalition of this book. Special thanks are also due to Prof. Giuseppe Vignato of Peking University, for the support that he has provided throughout this process. This book has also allowed the young scholars involved in this process to understand the importance of international academic collaboration. They

就如美国学者谢弗在其名著《唐代的外来文明》中所揭示的那样，外来文明对中华文明产生过巨大而深远的影响；同样，中华文明也为世界文明作出过杰出的贡献。除了持续研究中国境内出土的外国遗物之外，我们也计划通过双方的友好合作，陆续开展外国境内所存中国文物的研究工作，期待这两方面的工作都能够不断有成果问世。

考古文博学院院长

杭 侃

will grow as a strong force in the field of communication between China and the West in the future.

Just as Edward Schafer suggested in his famous book, *The Golden Peaches of Samarkand*, western civilization had huge and extensive influences on China, while Chinese civilization also contributed a lot to the global civilization in general. In addition to researching western antiquities found in China, moving forward we must do more work on Chinese antiquities found in Western contexts. By moving forward in a spirit of collaboration we hope there will soon be more significant achievements on both sides.

The Dean of
School of Archaeology and Museology
Hang Kan

序二
Forward

    在历经数年共同开展卓有成效的合作研究之后，在此我非常荣幸地介绍由北京大学考古文博学院的齐东方和那不勒斯东方大学亚洲、非洲和地中海系的葛嶷共同编辑出版的这本书。

    2011年以来，我校与北京大学考古文博学院签署并不止一次更新协议，确立并发展了非常密切的考古学合作关系。

    我们非常清楚这类旨在整合不同学术背景的科研活动的艰难与复杂，近年来在赵辉教授和杭侃教授的领导下，北京大学考古文博学院在这方面拥有崇高声望。

    本书的题目《异宝西来：考古发现的丝绸之路舶来品研究》讨论了丝绸之路考古问题，也是探讨丝路历史复杂本质的现代尝试。

    特别鸣谢我们的校长埃尔达·默里奇奥教授，她一直支持并鼓励我校在考古学领域的此类合作，也非常感谢本书的两位编者——齐东方教授和葛嶷教授，以及为本书最终出版辛勤工作的所有人。

亚洲、非洲和地中海系主任

米凯莱·贝尔纳蒂尼

It is with particular pleasure that I present this volume edited by Qi Dongfang of the School of Archaeology and Museology, Peking University and Bruno Genito of the Dipartimento Asia Africa e Mediterraneo, Università degli Studi di Napoli "L'Orientale". Since 2011 our University and the School of Archaeology and Museology of the Peking University, have developed an intense relationship of archaeological collaboration.

This book is the product of an intensely complex collaboration which has brought scholars from a number of disciplines and backgrounds. This could not have been achieved without the prestige by the School of Archaeology and Museology, Peking University, directed in recent years by Prof. Zhao Hui and now by Prof. Hang Kan. Entitled: "*West and East: Archaeological Objects along the Silk Roads*", this book is related to the archaeological issues of the Silk Roads. It provides a modern approach the complex nature of the historiographic category of Silk Road.

Special thanks go also to our Rector, Prof. Elda Morlicchio, for his unstinting support of this collaboration. Special thanks also to the two editors of the volume, Prof. Qi Dongfang, and Prof, Bruno Genito, along with the other collaborators have worked hard to bring us this innovative work.

The Director of

Dipartimento Asia, Africa e Mediterraneo

Michele Bernardini

致 谢
Acknowledgements

这次中意考古合作自发端至今,七年时光匆匆而逝。因种种构想而促成意大利亚非研究院(IsIAO)也就是如今的意大利地中海与东方学国际研究协会(ISMEO)、那不勒斯东方大学(UNO)亚洲、非洲和地中海系与北京大学考古文博学院一同开始本书的编辑,也已经过去了相当长的一段时间。

我们不禁要对这些年来促使工作得以顺利开展的各方致以最诚挚的谢意:首先感谢中意双方所有的撰稿者,感谢北京大学考古文博学院,衷心感谢赵辉和杭侃两位院长以及考古系诸位同仁。他们的开放包容让这场前所未有的合作成为可能。

我们同样感谢亚非研究院和如今地中海与东方学国际研究协会及其历任主席:盖拉尔多·尼奥利、马可·曼奇尼和阿德里亚诺·罗西;感谢意大利外交与国际合作部(MAECI);感谢文化促进与交往总局第六办公室(DGPRC)在2008年至2015年期间给予我们资金支持;感谢意大利驻中国大使馆以及里卡尔多·谢飒和白达尼大使。

我们也衷心感谢多家意大利文化机构,没有他们的支持,项目成果将大打折扣。感谢那不勒斯东方大学及其中多位负责人帕斯夸里·奇列洛、丽达·维伽诺妮、埃尔达·默里

Seven years have passed since this Chinese-Italian archaeological collaboration started, and indeed, a rather long time has gone by, since the ideas and the concepts that led IsIAO (Istituto Italiano per l'Africa e l'Oriente) and now again ISMEO (Associazione Internazionale di Studi sul Mediterraneo e l'Oriente), UNO (Università degli Studi di Napoli "L'Orientale") the Dipartimento Asia, Africa e Mediterrano and the School of Archaeology and Museology of the Peking University, actually developed this editorial project.

We cannot refrain from expressing our deepest thanks for the work that it was made possible to carry out in these years: first of all to the Chinese and Italian contributors, to the School of Archaeology and Museology of the Peking University and their directors Zhao Hui, Hangkhan, and different colleagues, who were sufficiently open-minded to allow a collaboration never before experienced.

We are mostly grateful also to IsIAO and new ISMEO and its Presidents, Gherardo Gnoli, Marco Mancini, and Adriano Rossi, to MAECI (the Italian Ministry of Foreign Affairs and International Cooperation), to Office VI of its Directorate-General for Cultural Promotion and Relations (DGPRC); which from 2008 to 2015 wanted to give its financial contribution to the initiative, to the Italian Embassy in China and the Ambassadors, Riccardo Sessa and Alberto Bradanini.

Profound gratitude is also due to the various Italian Cultural attachés; without their support much less would have been achieved, and to UNO and their different Rectors Pasquale Ciriello, Lida Viganoni,

奇奥；感谢国际交流办公室及其负责人玛丽娜·圭代蒂、尼可莱塔·德·多米尼奇斯，感谢亚洲研究系以及现在的亚洲、非洲和地中海系及其历任负责人：阿尔贝托·文图拉、弗朗西斯科·斯菲拉、罗伯托·托托里和米凯莱·贝尔纳蒂尼，感谢相关工作人员、执行秘书安吉洛·福斯康托以及他们的同事卡梅拉·阿尔法诺、安娜·萨索和露西亚·科佐利诺，感谢真纳罗·达历山德罗。

意大利方面我们还非常感谢土耳其、伊朗和中亚考古、东西方交流以及亚洲、非洲和地中海关系等博士项目，感谢考古学跨学科服务中心（CISA）对项目的学术支持，特别是对"丝绸之路考古"系列会议的赞助，感谢我的同事露西亚·卡特琳娜，她一度是本项目的组织者之一，感谢法比娅娜·拉娅诺和安德烈·蒙泰拉宝贵且必不可少的组织及学术工作。

考古学跨学科服务中心、那不勒斯东方大学还从资金及技术方面支持了本项目，为此我们要感谢鲁道夫·法托维奇和法布里齐奥·佩萨多主席，以及伊莱奈·布拉甘蒂尼、罗塞拉·潘奈恩、安东内拉·圣尼诺、科技指导委员会的安德烈·德安德烈，以及罗萨里奥·瓦伦蒂尼。

最后还要特别感谢魏正中教授，是他最早建议中意学者进行此类合作。尽管没有直接参与本项目，但他提供了宝贵的人力和学术支持。

Elda Morlicchio, the office of the International Relationships and their different responsible Marina Guidetti, Nicoletta De Dominicis, to Dipartimento di Studi Asiatici and then Dipartimento Asia, Africa e Mediterraneo and their different Directors, Alberto Ventura, Francesco Sferra, Roberto Tottoli and Michele Bernardini and the related staff composed by and the Administrative Secretary, Angelo Fusco; to Carmela Alfano, Anna Sasso and Lucia Cozzolino of the same office and to Gennaro D'Alessandro.

We are also profoundly grateful from the Italian side also to Dottorato di Ricerca in *Turchia, Iran e Asia Centrale, Archeologia. Rapporti tra Oriente ed Occidente, Asia, Africa e Mediterraneo* and to CISA/Centro Interdipartimentale di Servizi per l'Archeologia, which have been the scientific sponsors for different initiatives specially the series of conferences dedicated to the *Archaeology of the Silk Roads*, and my colleague Lucia Caterina who was one oof the coo-organizer of the initiative, Fabiana Raiano, Andrea Montella for their precious and indispensable organisational and scientific work.

The financial and technical support from Italian side has also been granted by the *Centro Interdipartimentale di Servizi per l'Archeologia* (CISA), UNO and for that, many thanks are devoted to the Presidents Rodolfo Fattovich, Fabrizio Pesando, the colleagues Irene Bragantini, Rossella Pannain, Antonella Sannino, Andrea D'Andrea of the Directive and Technical-Scientific Committee, and Rosario Valentini.

Last but not least a special mention and thanks are deeply due to Prof. Giuseppe Vignato who first suggested this kind of collaboration to Chinese and Italian colleagues and who, although not directly involved in the initiative, did not miss his invaluable support and human and scientific support.

前 言
Preface

葛嶷、齐东方 撰，李雨生 译

Bruno Genito, Qi Dongfang, trans. by Li Yusheng

自从1877年被德国地理学家李希霍芬（Ferdinand Freiherr von Richthofen）首次命名以来，丝绸之路（Seidenstraße）一词的内涵与外延因层出不穷的考古新发现而被不断刷新丰富，并推而广之成为研究旧大陆古文明交流的专门领域。在中国考古学史上，丝路中国段发现的外来物品是中外考古研究的恒久课题，对这些外来物品的追根溯源也曾是中国考古学者了解域外考古成果的最初动力。如今，中国的丝绸之路研究更因国家经济发展战略的调整而得到了政府的大力支持。就像100多年前来自中国新疆的精美文物在欧洲所造成的轰动那样，今天丝绸之路在它所连接的遥远东方再度成为焦点，应接不暇的展览和精美印刷的图录被不断策划与出版，收入本书的49件器物也是其中当之无愧的主角。

这些器物因其独特的造型与纹样而备受中外考古学者关注，但长期以来，最了解这些器物发现背景的中国学者，因为中国国内域外考古传统的缺失，很难充分占有资料开展研究；而对中国发现外来器物兴趣浓厚的外国学者，又

Since first denominated by German geographer Ferdinand Freiherr von Richthofen in 1877, *Silk Routes (Seidenstraße)*, the signification of which has already been renovated and enriched by inexhaustible archaeological foundings, are extended to be a specialized field concerning with communications among different ancient civilizations of Old World. During the development of the Chinese Archaeology, the study of exotic objects unearthed along the *Silk Routes* in China were not only the eternal theme for Chinese and overseas scholars, but also the initial motivation for Chinese archaeologists to learn foreign archaeology. For now, due to the adjustment of national economic development strategy, *Silk Routes* study in China receives more powerful support from the government. Just like the great sensation in Europe caused by exquisite antiquities from Xinjiang a hundred years ago, in the distant East which was once connected by, *Silk Routes* come back again in a more fashionable way. New exhibitions and fine printed catalogues are being planned and published, in which the 49 objects of our book now are playing the well-deserved major roles.

Due to the unique shape and unparalleled decorative motif, these exotic objects have attracted so much attention of Chinese and overseas scholars. However, for such a long time, as the ones who know the context best, Chinese scholars have difficulties in collecting analogous findings abroad systematically because of the absence of foreign archaeological study tradition in China. On the other hand, foreign scholars, who always show great interests in exotic findings from China, also could not understand their original context comprehensively because of the language barrier etc.

常常因为语言等原因无法全面了解它们的出土背景。本项目的初衷便是试图通过推动中外合作来打破这种壁垒。具体来说，在前期广泛搜集资料并保持密切沟通的基础上，选取跟陆上丝绸之路关系最密切的、西北五省区出土的宋代以前的49件外来物品为研究对象，这些遗物包括了不同的材质和渊源，多数来自科学考古发掘，拥有可靠的出土背景信息，有的还有明确的年代下限。由中方提供出土背景及研究状况的详细资料，然后意方学者根据这些资料重新审视过往研究并撰写条目，最后再经双方讨论定稿。除此之外，项目收录了项目双方负责人的两篇论文，反映出中外学人各自对丝绸之路的独特理解。项目最终成果以中、英双语出版，方便中外学者参阅。器物的中文名采用中国国内学界长期以来约定俗成的称呼，而英文名则按照意方建议尽量从简。

本项目从刚开始的偶然提议到如今付梓在即，断断续续七年时光匆匆而过，其间由于早已为中国学者所熟悉的种种原因，意方学者一直希望的实物观摩环节始终无法成行，一定程度上限制了合作研究的进一步深入。但或许可以这么理解，缺憾本身即意味着未来更为广阔的合作空间，衷心希望我们这本小书的出版可以为将来开展更深层次的中外合作考古研究略尽绵薄之力。

The original intention of our project, therefore, was designed to break through the block by means of international cooperation. To be specific, based on the wide searching and close communication with each other during earlier stage, the Chinese and Italian scholars finally chose 49 objects unearthed from the five northwest provinces which held the closest relationship with the ancient *Silk Routes* before Song Dynasty. Different in textures and cultural backgrounds, most of these objects were obtained through scientific archaeological excavation, which means they owned explicit context, not only that, what is even more rare hence more valuable part, is that some of them had clear *terminus post quem*. Our project was first started from China, that is to say, Chinese scholars prepared detailed description of the context of the chosen objects and review of past research, based on this, Italian cooperators studied and wrote the items. In the end, there was a discussion between the Chinese and Italian scholars to finalize. In addition to this, there are also two papers written by the co-leaders from both sides, which also reflect the different comprehensions of *Silk Routes* between the Chinese and Western scholars. The project will be published in Chinese and English, which, from our point of view, will be beneficial for both Chinese and foreign academics. Another thing needs to note is about the names of the objects. For the Chinese ones, we used the calls which had been conventionalized for such a long time, while for the English names, we adopted our Italian cooperators' suggestion to denominate in a more simplified way.

Our project started from a very occasional proposal, since then till the forthcoming publication, seven years passed. Unfortunately, for various reasons which had already been familiar by Chinese scholars, the visiting and observation of the chosen objects, extremely wished by our Italian cooperators, could not been planned throughout, which, to some extent, limited our possible further cooperation. However, maybe the imperfection itself also means much wider cooperative space in the future. We sincerely hope the publication of our book could make its due contributions to the deeper archaeological cooperative research between Chinese and foreign academics in the future.

目　录
Contents

序　一

Forward ··· 1

序　二

Forward ··· 3

致　谢

Acknowledgements ··· 1

前　言

Preface ·· 1

丝绸之路研究的新视角

New Research Activities on the Archaeology of the Silk Routes ·················· 1

交流的价值——外来器物与中国文化

New Archaeological Discoveries along the Chinese Branches of the Silk Routes ················ 41

器物研究

Catalogue ·· 72

    1. 对翼兽铜环

      Copper Ring　*72*

    2. 青铜武士像

      Bronze Statue　*76*

3. 铜盘
   Bronze Tray *79*

4. 竖琴
   Harp *83*

5. 釉陶杯
   Glazed Pottery Cup *85*

6. 银杯套
   Silver Cup-Sheath *88*

7. 有柄铜镜
   Bronze Mirror *90*

8. 金项饰
   Gold Torque *93*

9. 铅饼
   Lead Ingots *95*

10. 印花棉布
    Cotton Cloth *100*

11. 裤子
    Trousers *103*

12. 红地罽袍
    Felt Caftan *107*

13. 玻璃杯
    Glass Cup *110*

14. 嵌宝石金戒指
    Gold Ring *117*

15. 金饰件
    Gold Ornament *121*

16. 玻璃杯
    Glass Beaker *123*

17. 玻璃高足杯
    Glass Goblet *128*

18. 印章
    Seal *133*

19. 印章
    Seal *136*

20. 金面具
    Gold Mask *139*

21. 带盖金罐
    Gold Covered Jar *144*

22. 金杯
    Gold Cup *146*

23. 金剑鞘
    Gold Sword Scabbard *149*

24. 银瓶
    Silver Vase *151*

25. 金饰件
    Gold Plaques *153*

26. 编织金带
    Gold Woven Band *155*

27. 金杯
    Gold Cup *156*

28. 金指套和护臂
    Gold Finger and Arm Guard *158*

29. 陶来通
    Rhyton *160*

30. 梳妆托盘
    Toilet Tray *164*

31. 三耳陶罐
    Pottery Jar *170*

32. 金戒指
    Gold Ring *173*

33. 玻璃碗
    Glass Bowl *178*

34. 对羊对鸟灯树纹锦
    Brocade *185*

35. 覆面
Brocade　*187*

36. 联珠鹿纹锦
Brocade　*190*

37. 金壶
Gold Pot　*192*

38. 鎏金铜盘
Gilded Bronze Tray　*195*

39. 印章
Seal　*197*

40. 鎏金铜覆面
Gilt Bronze Mask　*202*

41. 铜壶
Bronze Ewer　*206*

42. 玻璃瓶
Glass Bottle　*210*

43. 银带把杯
Silver Cup　*212*

44. 玻璃杯
Glass Cup　*216*

45. 兽首玛瑙杯
Rhyton　*218*

46. 玻璃瓶
Glass Bottle　*222*

47. 黄玻璃盘
Glass Dish　*226*

48. 蓝玻璃盘
Glass Dish　*229*

49. 玻璃杯
Glass Cup　*232*

结 语
Conclusions ·········· 235

图片出处
List of Illustrations ·········· 244

丝绸之路研究的新视角

New Research Activities on the Archaeology of the Silk Routes

葛嵋（那不勒斯东方大学）撰，童歆 译

Bruno Genito (UNO), trans. by Tong Xin

在古代中亚考古学文化的研究之中，中国西北是最值得关注的地理区域之一。它包括了新疆这个当代中国最大的行政区以及邻近的甘肃、宁夏、陕西和青海。许多带有异域风格的外来器物在这一地区都有发现[1]。

从2007年开始，意大利亚非研究院（IsIAO）和北京大学（PKU）签署协议（详见下文）。在协议框架下，一项意—中考古学合作项目得以开展。从那时起，我们就在分析这项国际合作的理论前提、项目实现的具体可能性以及与中国机构和学者合作最终所能达成的目标。主要的依据包括以下几点：

1. 那不勒斯东方大学在中国考古方面仅参与过一项工作，即从1997年开始，由意大利外交部（MAE）、那不勒斯东方大学（UNO）亚洲研究系、意大利亚非研究院（IsIAO，罗马）、意大利国立东方学研究所（京都）、龙门石窟研究院和洛阳市文物局共同合作，由露西娅·凯特琳娜（Lucia Caterina）教授和乔瓦尼·韦拉

The northwestern China is one of the most privileged geographical point of view to watch at the ancient Central Asian archaeological cultures. Xinjiang Uygur Autonomous Region, the largest in China, along with Gansu, Ningxia Hui Autonomous Region, Shaanxi, and Qinghai as well, located in that part of the country, constitute the areas where many particular and "exotic" objects and items are coming from[1].

An Italian-Chinese archaeological cooperation started in 2007 with an agreement between IsIAO and Peking University (see below), and since that time one was wandering which could have been the theoretical premises, the concrete possibilities of realization, and the scientific aims of eventual joint projects with the Chinese scholars and Institutions, taking in consideration, nonetheless, the following points:

1. In IsIAO there was only one study tradition of archaeological field work in Cina: the excavation activity (pure sinological in character) jointly with Ministero Italiano degli Affari Esteri (MAE), Dipartimento di Studi Asiatici dell' Università degli Studi di Napoli, "L'Orientale" (UNO), the IsIAO (Rome), the Italian School of East Asian Studies

---

[1] 多数器物属于铁器时代直至中世纪早期，带有浓厚的中亚、萨珊伊朗、伊斯兰和佛教文化因素。

Most part of these objects are datable back to the early and late Iron age and to the historical and early mediaeval age as well, and present a strong central-Asian, Iranian-Sasanian, Islamic and Buddhist cultural character.

尔蒂（Giovanni Verardi）教授领导，在已故的富安敦（Antonino Forte）教授的资助下，在奉先寺展开发掘。该寺位于中国河南省洛阳市南12公里久负盛名的龙门石窟西南（Visconti 2006；2010）。

2. 那不勒斯东方大学在伊朗、土库曼斯坦、乌兹别克斯坦、哈萨克斯坦、吉尔吉斯斯坦这些与中国距离最近的中亚国家有着悠久而扎实的田野考古工作和学术活动，但毕竟没有在中国进行考古工作的经验，对中国考古学也仅限于一些常识性了解。

3. 最有可能开展考古合作的地点，应在中国的西北地区，主要是新疆、甘肃、陕西、宁夏和内蒙古。

4. 可行的合作研究领域是铁器时代至中世纪欧亚草原的游牧民族、边界与帝国，以及关于丝绸之路的问题。

在意大利外交部的资助下，从2008年起至今的每一年，那不勒斯东方大学都组织考察团，与中国方面进行学术接触，这可以视为以往一系列考古研究工作的扩展，包括1983—2000年在匈牙利提萨河谷（Tisza valley）（Genito 1986；1988；1990；1992；1993a；1993b；1995；2008）(Genito ed, 1994; Genito a cura di, 2002; Genitocura di, 2002a; Genito a cura di, 2002b) (Genito, Madaras, eds, 2005)，1989—2004年在土库曼斯坦的穆尔加布河三角洲(Murghab delta)(Koshelenko, Gubaev, Tosi 1988)，1999—2002年在乌兹别克斯坦的泽拉夫善河谷（布哈拉绿洲），2008—2012年在该国的撒马尔罕地

(Kyōto), the Longmen Grottoes Academy (Longmen shiku yanjiuyuan 龙门石窟研究院) and the Bureau for Cultural Relics of Luoyang (Luoyangshi wenwuju 洛阳市文物局), headed by Profs. Lucia Caterina and Giovanni Verardi and sponsored by the late Prof. Antonino Forte in the Buddhist monastery of Longmen since 1997, was aimed at excavating the Buddhist monastic complex of Fengxiansi, whose remains lie southwest of the celebrated Longmen Caves, 12km south of the present town of Luoyang in the Chinese province of Henan (Visconti 2006; 2010);

2. Although IsIAO had a long and consolidated experience of field archaeological activity and academic presence in Iran, Turkmenistan, Uzbekistan, Kazakhistan and Kirghisistan, the nearest central-Asian countries to China, there was no scientific archaeological experiences in that country, and, basically, only a common knowledge of it;

3. the most concrete possibility to open an archaeological cooperation appeared, thus, that which could orient the research activities *versus* aspects and topics related to northwestern China and the related matters, mainly in Xinjiang, Gansu, Shaanxi, Ningxia and Inner Mongolia provinces;

4. It was decided to develop a possible ground aimed at dealing with the nomads, frontiers and empires in the Eurasian Steppes from Iron age to the Middle Ages and to the *Silk Routes* issues.

As a sort of a widening the archaeological research activities conducted years before in the Tisza valley in Hungary (1983–2000)(Genito 1986; 1988; 1990; 1992; 1993a; 1993b; 1995; 2008) (Genito ed, 1994; Genito a cura di, 2002; Genito cura di, 2002a; Genito a cura di, 2002b) (Genito, Madaras eds, 2005), in the Murghab delta (1989–2004) in Turkmenistan (Koshelenko, Gubaev, Tosi 1988), in the Zeravshan valley (Bukhara oasis, 1999–2002) in Uzbekistan (Samarkand region

区[1]，这些工作都与欧亚草原游牧和定居民族的早期文化有关[2]。

在欧亚考古领域，中国的学术机构已经在其境内进行了多种调查和发掘活动，包括其西部的甘肃、内蒙古和新疆北部地区。对意大利学术机构来说，对上述地理关系复杂、历史记载明确的地区的考古研究，可以为20世纪80年代以来的相关工作提供新的启示，从那时起，（意大利方面）进行了许多与中亚古代人类相关的科学研究（Genito 2010）。其中值得一提的有：

1. 举办了一次题为"草原考古：工作方法和策略"学术研讨会，文集收在1994年出版的亚洲研究文丛中（Genito ed, 1994），是我们与匈

2008–2015)[1], and related to the early cultures of the nomadic and sedentary peoples of the Eurasian steppes[2], IsIAO and UNO organized study tours and scientific and academic contacts with China with the financial support of MAE (since 2008).

In the field of Eurasian Archaeology, Chinese Institutions had carried out, from their own side, various activities related to surveys and excavations in the western province of Gansu, Inner Mongolia and the northern part of Xinjiang. These new perspectives for the Italian Institutions in this geographically complex and historically very articulated region, could be the crowning achievement to the archaeological research themes conducted since the 80s, when there were numerous scientific initiatives in relation to the themes of the ancient central-Asian peoples (Genito 2010). Among these, one may mention:

1. the Symposium *The Archaeology of the Steppes:*

---

[1] 意大利亚非研究院与博洛尼亚大学在乌兹别克斯坦开展的考古研究可以追溯到1999年。从2008年开始，乌兹别克斯坦科学院考古研究所与那不勒斯东方大学开展了一项新的考古工作，开始对撒马尔罕地区的阿契美尼德王朝时期遗存进行田野工作，具体选择了 Koj Tepa 这个地点，开始是探沟试掘，然后进行了大规模发掘。(Genito, Gricina 2009; Genito, Gricina 2010; Abdullaev, Genito 2011; Abdullaev, Genito 2010–2011; Genito, Raiano 2011; Abdullaev, Genito 2012; Raiano 2012; Raiano 2013; Cocca 2014; Genito *et alii* 2014; Raiano 2014; Abdullaev and Genito eds, 2014).
The archaeological Italian activity of IsIAO (and of the Università degli Studi di Bologna) in Uzbekistan dates back to 1999; since 2008, a new collaboration with the Institute of Archaeology of the Academy of Sciences of Uzbekistan (IAASU) and UNO led to start a field project related to the archaeological Achaemenid horizon in the Samarkanda area, with trial-trenches and extensive excavations effected at Koj Tepa (Genito, Gricina 2009; Genito, Gricina 2010; Abdullaev, Genito 2011; Abdullaev, Genito 2010–2011; Genito, Raiano 2011; Abdullaev, Genito 2012; Raiano 2012; Raiano 2013; Cocca 2014; Genito *et alii* 2014; Raiano 2014; Abdullaev and Genito eds, 2014).

[2] 苏联解体后出现的这些新兴国家开始关注自身的历史、文化和人民。对大部分西方学者来说，在若干年前对这些国家的了解仅限于一些地名。如今这里属于土库曼斯坦、哈萨克斯坦、塔吉克斯坦、乌兹别克斯坦、吉尔吉斯斯坦五个国家，它们与阿富汗以及中国新疆、甘肃共同组成了"丝绸之路"，不仅激发了人们对绿洲、商栈、形形色色的游牧人和大帝国、异国情调的人群和珍禽异兽的想象，而且公众对诸如中亚等遥远之地的着迷也重新唤醒了人们对这一地区朦胧不清的古今民俗的好奇心。
Since the Soviet collapse the emergence of new states helped to make attention on their history, culture, and people. For most of the western scholars, these were places whose names barely were known decades ago. Today they are independent states as Turkmenistan, Kazakhstan, Tajikistan, Uzbekistan, and Kyrghizstan, and in the more remote past, along with Afghanistan, Xinjiang, and Gansu, they evoked images of the ancient *Silk Routes* — oases, caravanserai, nomads, empires, fantastic and exotic beasts and people. The public fascination with these distant lands has rekindled a dormant curiosity in the obscure past and modern folkways of what we now call Central Asia — the lands which embraced the multitude branches of the ancient *Silk Routes*.

牙利科学院考古研究所以及前苏联科学院考古研究所（包括随后的俄罗斯方面在土库曼斯坦境内的工作）十年合作的工作成果。

2. 与上述资料收入同一系列的，还有1995年出版的一卷针对亚洲萨尔马提亚（Asian Sarmatia）地区铁器时代墓葬的社会分析，这是与俄罗斯科学院考古研究所的合作成果（Moškova, Genito eds, 1995）

3. 巴林特主编的一卷出版物（Balint ed, 2000），是匈牙利科学院考古研究所、意大利亚非研究院和那不勒斯东方大学的共同成果。

4. 1999年（VV.AA 1999）、2000年（VV.AA 2000）和2001年（Genitoa cura di, 2002），在那不勒斯国家考古博物馆举办了三次考古学展览。

5. 2005年出版了与匈牙利索尔诺克博物馆（Szolnok Museum）的合作成果（Genito and Madaras eds, 2005）。

6. 由那不勒斯东方大学组织、露西娅·卡特琳娜和所有参加者编辑出版的（2012—2013, 2014）以"丝绸之路考古：路线、图像和物质文化"为主题的三个系列讲座。这些讲座由那不勒斯东方大学东方学及非洲方向研究生院（主要包括土耳其、伊朗和中亚、东亚和南美洲等方向的博士），亚洲、非洲以及地中海间的跨文化研究院（主要包括东西方关系方向的考古学博士生），考古学跨学科研究中心（CISA）等机构的资助，目前已经上线（Caterina, Genito eds, 2012, 2013, 2015; 2016）[1]。

Work Methods and Strategies, published in the *Series Minor* of the Dipartimento di Studi Asiatici, (Genito ed, 1994) which followed 10 years of joint collaboration with the Institute of Archaeology of Sciences in Budapest, and with the Institute of Archaeology of the Academy of Sciences of USSR, and, then, Russia in Turkmenistan;

2. the publication in the same series, in 1995 of a volume on the social analyses of the Iron Age cemeteries in Asian Sarmatia within a joint collaboration with the Institute of Archaeology of Russian Academy of Sciences (Genito, Moškova eds, 1995);

3. the publication of a volume (Balint ed, 2000) in collaboration with the Institute of Archaeology of the Academy of Sciences in Budapest, IsIAO and the Istituto Universitario Orientale in Napoli (now Università degli Studi di Napoli, "L'Orientale") (UNO);

4. three archaeological exhibitions held at the Museo Archeologico Nazionale di Napoli, one in 1999 (VV.AA 1999) a second in 2000 (VV.AA 2000), and the third in 2001 (Genito a cura di, 2002);

5. the publication in 2005 of the joint volume within a collaboration with the Szolnok Museum (SE Hungary) (Genito and Madaras eds, 2005).

6. the organization at the Università degli Studi di Napoli, "L'Orientale" by the writer and Lucia Caterina of three series (2012–2013, 2014) of lectures on the theme *Archaeology of the Silk Routes: Paths, Images,and Material Culture*. The conferences under the scientific sponsorship of Scuole di dottorato di Studi Orientali e Africani (PhD: Turchia, Iran e Asia Centrale; Asia Orientale e America meridionale), di Studi Interculturali (PhD: Archeologia: Rapporti tra Oriente e Occidente), Asia, Africa e Mediterraneo, and CISA (Centro Interdisciplinare di Servizi per l'Archeologia), are now on line (Caterina, Genito, eds, 2012; 2013; 2015; *eidem* forthcoming 2016)[1].

---

[1] 题目的选择旨在阐明以下主题：1. 以往丝绸之路概念分类中的"路线、图像和物质文化"所反映的文（转下页）

中国西部地理概说

中国最大的省区新疆维吾尔自治区（面积达166万平方公里，约占中国的1/6），位于这个国家的西北部，与中亚地区的文化联系密切，因为从地理特征上说，它实际上是延伸至中国境内的中亚地区的一部分，包括被高原和山脉环绕的塔里木盆地。其地理范畴，西到哈萨克斯坦草原和帕米尔高原，北至天山和阿尔泰山，东至戈壁（包括蒙古国和中国的内蒙古自治区），南至喀喇昆仑山脉（图1）。

新疆既是中国西部与中亚交界的边境地区，也与西藏、青海、甘肃三省区以及蒙古国、俄罗斯、阿富汗、巴基斯坦、印度等国家接壤。塔里木盆地的河流主要汇入罗布泊，盆地的中央被塔

Geographic Outline of the Western China

Xinjiang Autonomous Uygur Region, the China's largest province (circa 1660000 sq.km, 1/6 of the whole country), is located in the northwestern part of the country and it represents the most suitable area where to find a large amount of Central-Asian cultural relationships, being as it is the geomorphological portion of the Central-Asian land mass in China, having the Tarim basin and the high plateaus and mountains surrounding it. The geographic boundaries of the land are the steppes of Kazakhistan and Pamir chain to west, the T'jan Šan' and Altai mountains to north, the Gobi desert to east, including parts of the Mongolian People's Republic and the Inner Mongolian Autonomous Region of China, and Karakorum range to south (Fig.1).

Tip of the western China to Central-Asia, Xinijang is bordering the Tibet Autonomous Province, Qinghai and Gansu province, the Mongolian People's Republic,

（接上页）化中心，但不仅仅是年代学意义上的；2. 陆上及海上丝绸之路路线的多元化；3. 丝绸之路以前即已存在或跟丝绸之路同时存在的交通路线（例如玉石之路、青金石之路、香料之路等），是从历史时代早期到中世纪晚期包括罗马、近中东、中亚和中国在内整个古代世界广泛和多样贸易领域的集中反映；4. 贸易中心及沿线的居住点、停驻点、军队要塞和戍堡的重要性；5. 居住点、商路、地质环境、土地使用、水的供应和管理之间的统一关系；6. 基于不同的水平和特色，将丝绸之路视为一种政治结构的表征，这催生了由市场而不是国家权力主导的现代经济。正因为此，商业活动可以灵活整合不同的经济体，例如中国、印度和西方等；7. 对于构建更为丰满的地理、历史和考古图景非常有必要的文献和铭文史料。2015年该系列的第四轮讲座已安排就绪。

The theme chosen is aimed at trying to clarify the following aspects of the topic: 1. the cultural centrality, not uniquely chronological, of "Paths, Images and Material Culture" that were previously categorized within the concept of *Silk Road*; 2. the plurality of routes and sea paths of the *Silk Road* that can only be updated with that now, more precisely, of *Silk Routes*; 3. the "precedents" and "contemporary" paths to the *Silk Routes* (e.g. *Jade Routes*, *Lapis lazuli Routess*, *Incense Routes* etc.) as determinants aspects of a much more broad and diverse ground embracing the whole ancient trade, between Rome, the Near and Middle East, Central Asia and China from the early historical times until the late Middle Ages; 4. the centrality and importance of territory settlements, parking stations, military garrisons and forts along the routes of trade; 5. the Unitarian relationships between settlements, trade routes and geo-environmental conditions, land use, water supply and control; 6. the *Silk Routes* as a phenomenon of political structure based on work at various levels and in various specialities, that virtually "invented" the modern economy, dominated by the market and not by the state power. Precisely for this reason, businesses are able to integrate with agility and dexterity in far more rigid state economies, such as Chinese, Indian and Western; 7.the Historical and Epigraphic sources, as necessary help to the construction of a rather ample geographic, historical and archaeological picture. A fourth and conclusive cycle ha been already realized for 2015.

图1   位于中国西部的新疆维吾尔自治区，图片采自 Google Earth
Fig. 1   Xinijang Autonomous Uyghur Region in western China, after Google Earth

克拉玛干大沙漠占据，它是世界第二大沙漠（图2）。吐鲁番地区地势低凹，最低点在海平面以下154米，是中国陆地最低点（图3）。从帕米尔高原往东南至喀喇昆仑山脉，以及喜马拉雅山脉和与其平行的外喜马拉雅山脉，构成了一个巨大的弧型分界线，将印度次大陆和亚洲内陆分开。

青藏高原本身是一个干旱的草原，其间点缀着一些很大的咸水湖（图4）。东南亚和中国的四条大的水系发源于高原的东部地区。南部的三条江即萨尔温江（怒江）、湄公河（澜沧江）和长江（金沙江），基本都流向南方和东南方，被一些连续性的高大山脉与印度支那隔开。第四条即黄河，它的上游与长江相距不远，然后向东和东北方向流向蒙古地区。

Russia, Afghanistan, Pakistan and India. The great Tarim basin running out into the Lopnur Lake, whose center is occupied by the Taklamakan desert, is to the vastness the second in the world (Fig.2). The depressions of Turfan, located at −154m. below the sea level and that of Hami (to −200m) are the lowest points of the whole China (Fig.3).

Extending southeast from the Pamirs the Karakoram range, the Himalayas, and the parallel Trans-Himalayas (the Kailas [Kang-ti-ssu] range) describe a huge arc curving eastward and forming the boundary between the Indian subcontinent and Inner Asia.

The Tibetan plateau itself is an arid steppe, dotted with large salt lakes (Fig.4). The four great river systems of southeast Asia and China have their sources in the eastern portion. The three southernmost — the Salween, the Mekong, and the Yangtze (Kinsha-kiang) — flow generally south and southeast, separated by high

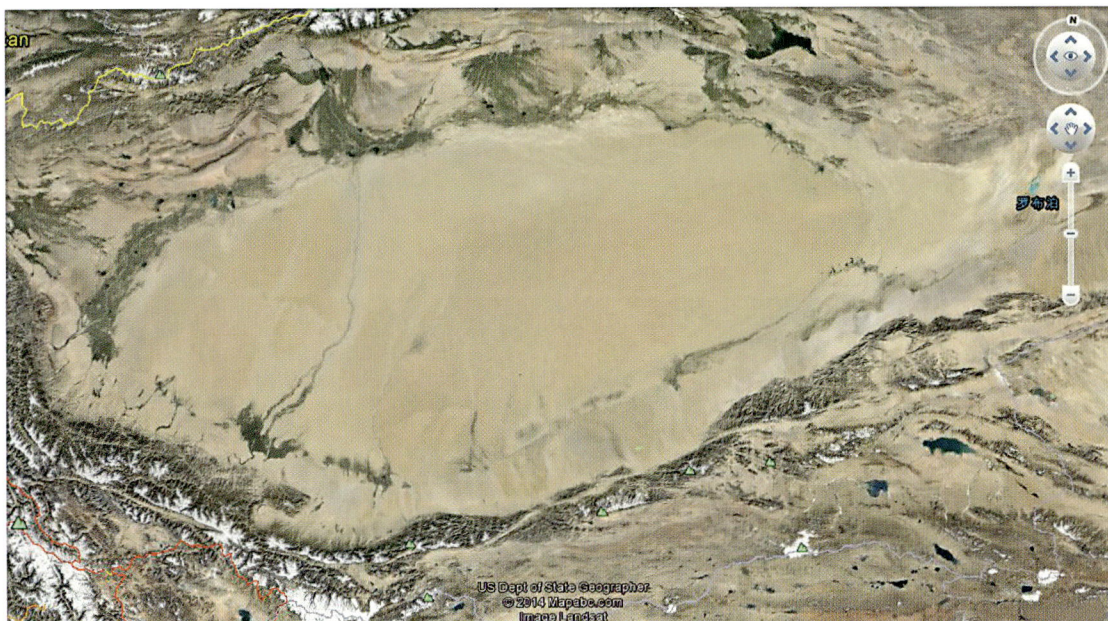

图2　新疆维吾尔自治区的南部,图片采自 Google Earth
Fig. 2　Southern border of the Xinijang Autonomous Uyghur Region in western China, after Google Earth

图3　塔克拉玛干沙漠北缘,吐鲁番附近的沉降区,图片采自 Google Earth
Fig. 3　Northern border of the Taklamakan desert in Xinijang Autonomous Uyghur Region in western China, the depression area in Turfan, after Google Earth

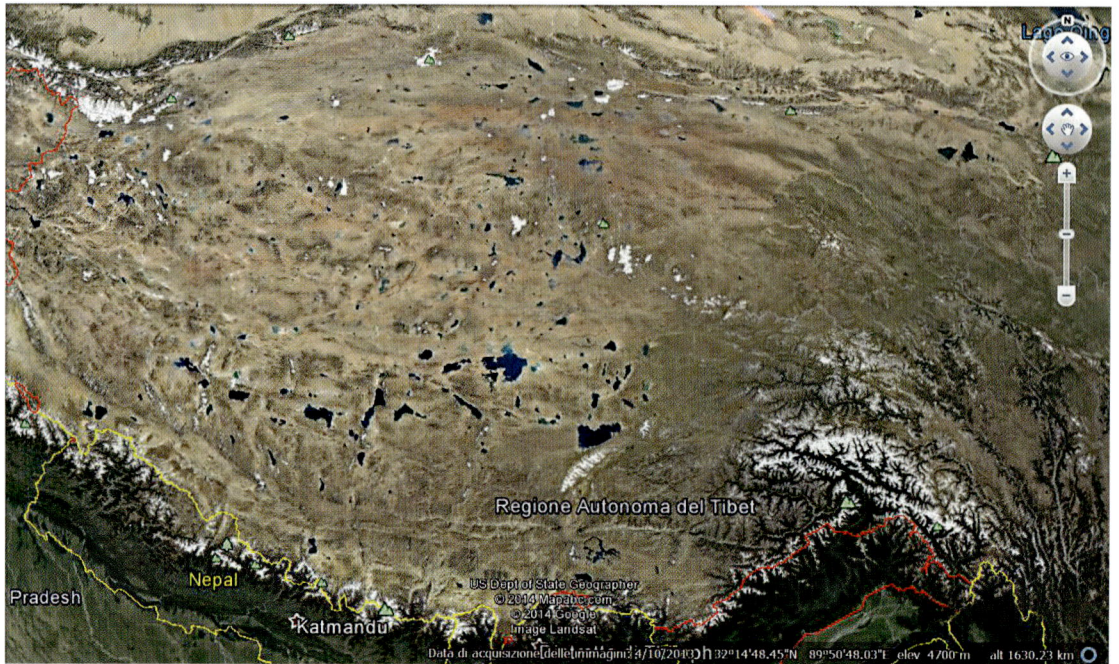

图4　青藏高原，图片采自 Google Earth
Fig. 4　The Tibetan plateau, after Google Earth

　　发源于喀喇昆仑山脉东段的叶尔羌河，与源于阿莱山脉及外阿莱山脉的喀什喀尔河汇合后，形成塔里木河，其水量最大的支流是发源于北部的天山山脉的阿克苏河。而塔里木河原来接纳的那些发源于昆仑山的南部河流，在汇入塔里木河之前就已消失在干涸的土地上。塔里木河往东流过沙漠最终汇入罗布泊，这里海拔730米。这个"游移湖"在1896年被斯文·赫定发现，1934年他再次造访之时，罗布泊已从原来位置向东北方向发生了移动。这种移动是频繁的，既反映出塔里木河流向的不规则变动，也反映出风力对于浅水的影响。盆地的主要城镇集中在古代丝绸之路的两条分支线路上，它们的西端都在喀什（海拔1230米）。

parallel ranges extending into Indochina. The fourth, the Yellow river (Huang He), follows the Yangtze closely in its upper course, then bends east and northeast toward Mongolia.

The Yarkand river, which rises in the eastern Karakoram, flows together with the Kashgar, which has its sources in the Alai and Trans-Alai ranges, to form the Tarim river, the main tributary of which is the Aksu, descending from the T'jan Šan' mountains to the north; all the former southern tributaries, which rise in the Kunluns, disappear into the dry earth before reach the Tarim. The river flows eastward through the desert to feed the shallow Lop Nor (elevation 730m), the "wandering lake" discovered by Sven Hedin in 1896 and again in 1934, when it had shifted to the northeast of its former position. The major towns in the basin are laid out along two branches of the ancient *Silk Routes* starting from Kashgar (elevation 1230m) at the

北线沿天山南麓而行,途经阿克苏(1010米)、库车、靠近博斯腾湖(890米)的焉耆(1090米)、吐鲁番(-50米),穿越山区抵达巴里坤(1720米)。南线沿着昆仑山的北麓而行,途经莎车(1200米)、和田(1410米)、于阗(1430米)、尼雅(1430米)和且末(1280米)。楼兰古城则位于罗布泊的西北方。

科克沙尔陶(Kok Shaal Tau)山脉从帕米尔高原往东北方向延伸,与天山相连,后者的走向基本与昆仑山平行。西天山位于塔什干以东70公里处,其主峰海拔超过3000米,一年大部分时间里被积雪覆盖,将富饶的费尔干纳盆地与南哈萨克草原分隔开。塔什干以东600公里处的一些北部山脉,其北部被分为昆格山脉和Trans-Ili Alatau(意指天山在中国境外的部分)山脉,南部则是泰尔斯凯山脉,这些山脉的侧面是伊克塞湖盆地(海拔1623米,深700米)。

有两条不大的河流发源于天山,即塔拉斯河和楚河,它们最终都消失在沙漠里。楚河是该沙漠和东部七河流域沙漠的一条边界河;七河得名于一些穿过阿拉套山最终注入巴尔喀什湖的小河流,该湖海拔340米,深达26米。

历史和考古学概说

在演变为浩瀚沙漠以来的许多年间,新疆地区几乎难以接近,也很难进行考古及研究活动。关于新疆历史的研究可以回溯到公元前2世纪,当时汉朝与匈奴之间发生冲突,中国的历史学者们开始注意到并记录下这个地区的地

western end. The northern branch followed the southern slopes of the T'jan Šan' through Aqsu (1010m), Kuça, Qarašahr (1090m) near the Baghrash Köl (890m), and Turfan (-50m), crossing the mountains to Barkol (1720m). The southern followed the northern slopes of the Kunluns through Yarkand (1200m), Khotan (1410m), Keriya and Niya (both 1430m), and Cherchen (1280m). The ancient city of Krorain (Lou-lan) was situated northeast of Lop Nor.

The Kok Shaal Tau branches off from the Pamirs to the northeast, linking them with the T'jan Šan', which run generally parallel to the Kunluns. Beginning about 70km east of Tashkent, the western T'jan Šan', the highest peaks generally exceeding 3000m in elevation and snow-capped most of the year, separate the fertile Fergana valley from the southern Kazakh steppes. About 600km east of Tashkent the northern chains divide into the Kungey and Trans-Ili Alatau on the north and the Terskey Alatau on the south, flanking the large basin of the Issyk Kul, 1623m above sea level and 700m deep. Two small rivers flowing from the T'jan Šan', the Talas and the Ču, vanish in its sands. The Ču forms the boundary between this desert and the Yetisu (lit., "seven rivers," Russian Semireč'e) desert farther east, which takes its name from a few small watercourses that cross it from the Džungarian Alatau and empty into the Balkhash Lake, 340m above sea level and 26m deep.

A Historical-Archaeological Outline

The area of Xinijang, for some time become largely desert, was for many years, almost inaccessible and it was very difficult to have related studies and archaeological activities. A few studies in the history of Xinijang can be traced back even to the 2nd century BC, during the conflict between the Han Dynasty and the Hsiung-nu, when Chinese historians began to reflect and record the geographical, historical, political,

理、历史、政治、军事和经济诸方面的信息。《史记》[1]的诸多章节被认为是最早的资料来源，此书由著名的历史学家司马迁（Records 1961; Memoires 1967）写成。直至中国帝制时代晚期的清朝，中国的历史学者在对新疆地区的记载上还保持着相似的叙事传统。余太山（1998; 2002）编著了直到突厥时代（7世纪）这个地区的几卷政治史，在涉及新疆的章节中（即西域），人们可以找到历史学家用以描述本地区的方法和准则，特别重要的是当地政治关系的历史（2004; 2006; 2010; 2011）。

从19世纪晚期至1940年

英国和俄国在中亚地区的扩张导致了19世纪晚期至20世纪40年代的研究活动受到半殖民地时期政治形势的强烈影响。尽管中国中央政府试图去控制它们的势力，但新疆地区实

military, and economic aspects of the region. The earliest sources can be considered the various chapters of the *Shi Ji*[1], written by the famous Sima Qian (Records 1961; Memoires 1967). Until the last Chinese dynasty — the Qing — Chinese historians continued the tradition of telling stories and descriptions about the Xinjiang region. Yu Taishan (1998; 2002) compiled different volumes on the political history of the region until the Turkish period (7th century AD), and in the chapters relating to Xinjiang (Serindia), one may find the description of methods and rules by which historians used to describe the region, among them particularly important is precisely the history of the political relations (2004; 2006; 2010; 2011).

From late 19th century to 1940

As for the research activities from the late 19th century until the 40s of last century, one may observe how they have been strongly influenced by the political situation during the semi-colonial period, because of the English and Russian expansion in Central Asia. Although the Chinese central

---

[1] 《史记》，英语书名写作 *Historical Records* 或 *Records of an historian*，其编写工作最初由司马谈进行，此后由他的儿子司马迁完成，时代在汉武帝统治时期（前140—前87）。《史记》有一百三十卷，基本是按照时间顺序编排，内容包括本纪，以编年的方式概括地记录帝国重大事件；表，它以表格的形式记录了周代列国的统治者和汉代诸侯、将相名臣的概况；书，它的每一部分都对应某一个领域，像礼乐、经济、仪式方面的内容；世家，则以详细的方式，记录了周代列国和汉代诸侯的故事；列传，常常很模式化，记录重要人物的事迹。《史记》的体例成为以后二十三部王朝正史的编写范本，唯一的区别在于君主世系方面——与这个王朝之前的时代存在的联系不再被记录——并以"志"取代了"书"。这部世界历史上的不朽著作的出现反映了汉帝国开疆拓土的野心，也促进了意识形态的形成。

Shi Ji or *Shiji*, known also as *Historical Records*, or *Records of an historian*, is a work initially compiled by Sima Tan and completed by his son Sima Qian, during the reign of Wu emperor (140–87 BC). The *Shiji* is composed by 130 chapters constituted in time by annals, giving a chronological profile of the most important events of the Empire, tables, containing, under the forms of table, a summary of the reigns and of the sovereigns under the Zhou dynasty and of the feuds under the Han dynasty, treaties, each of which deals with a single argument, as the music, economy and rites, hereditary families dealing, in a detailed way, with the stories of various states under the Zhou, and feuds under the Han, exemplar traditions, biographies, often extremely stereotyped, of eminent personalities. The structure of the Shiji was taken as a model for all the 23 subsequent dynastic histories, the only difference being that the section of hereditary surnames — linked to the pre-imperial era — was never recovered and the name *shu* changed in *zhi*. This monumental work, as world history, is presented to support the ambitions of domination of the Han Empire and contributed to the formation of ideology.

际上还是被分割为两个国家的势力范围:北部包括天山属于俄罗斯,南部属于英国。

这两个部分呈现出不同的地理环境条件:北部主要是游牧民族居住的草原,而南部则是生活着农业人口的沙漠和绿洲。考古活动起初伴随着充满激情和艰辛的地理探险,其中最著名人物之一的斯文·安德斯·赫定(1898a;1898b;1903;1937,r.1940,r. 1942,r. 1955;1943;1954)创立了新疆史地研究的基础。此外,基于大量文物和艺术史内容的发现,同时出于政治上的原因,俄国学者的大部分工作是在南疆即塔里木盆地进行的。

马尔克·奥莱尔·斯坦因(1907;1912;1921a;1921b;1925;1928;1932)、阿尔伯特·冯·勒柯克(1912;1922)、黄文弼(1934;1948;1951;1954;1958;1981;1983a;1983b;1990)[1]和保罗·伯希和(1934)[2],他们在众多学者中,留给我们关于古代防御体系、殖民点、寺庙以及题铭的最好、最重要的描述。

government managed to contain a portion of their strength, Xinjiang region was effectively split into two: the north with the mountains of T'jan'-Šan, to Russia and the south, to Great Britain.

The two sides present different geo-environmental conditions: the northern, made mostly of steppes, was inhabited by nomads, the south, consisting of deserts and oases, by farmers. The archaeological activity was in the first place, carried out together with intense and assiduous geographical exploration. One of the most famous geographer Sven Anders Hedin (1898a; 1898b; 1903; 1937, r.1940, r.1942, r.1955; 1943; 1954) established its research base in Xinjiang.

Furthermore, based on the large amount of antiquities, and art historical items found there and also for political reasons, most of the work of Russian scholars took place in southern Xinjiang, the Tarim Basin.

Marc Aurel Stein (1907; 1912; 1921a; 1921b; 1925; 1928; 1932), Albert Von Le Coq (1912; 1922), Huang Wenbi (1934; 1948; 1951; 1954; 1958; 1981; 1983a; 1983b; 1990)[1], together with Paul Pelliot (1934)[2], were among the scholars who have left us descriptions of the best and most important defense systems, settlements, temples, ancient inscriptions etc.

---

[1] 黄文弼(1893—1966),中国考古学家,也是中国现代考古学的奠基人之一。他参与了斯文·赫定在内蒙古和新疆(在戈壁沙漠中)的考察,主要关注罗布泊地区。他的考察日记于1990年出版(译者注:《黄文弼蒙新考察日记(1927—1930)》)。黄文弼后来供职于中国社会科学院考古研究所,并从1950年代起领导了在西域地区更多的考古工作,尤其是对古代高昌城的研究。
Huang Wenbi (1893-1966), a Chinese archaeologist and one of the founders of the modern Chinese archaeology, participated to the Swedish expedition of Sven Hedin in Mongolia and Xinjiang (in the Gobi desert) which focused on the Lop Nor area. His run on this expedition diary appeared in 1990. Huang Wenbi was a member of the Institute of Archaeology of the Chinese Academy of Sciences and led since the 50's further archaeological explorations in the "Western Regions" (Xiyu), in particular, the study of the ancient city of Gaochang.

[2] 保罗·伯希和(1878—1945),法国汉学家和中亚地区的探险家。起初为了进入(法国)驻外的办事机构,伯希和学习了中文,成为列维和沙畹的学生。伯希和在河内的法国远东学院工作,1900年被派往北京为学院的图书馆搜集中文图书,在那里他遇上了义和团运动,并被困在外国公使馆。被困期间伯希和对义和团发动了两次突袭:一次夺取了义和团的旗帜,另一次为那些被困困的人取得了新鲜水果。他的勇敢使他获得了法国荣誉军团勋章。伯希和22岁返回河内,成为远东学院的汉学教授,以后又当选为法兰西学院的教授。
Paul Pelliot (1878-1945), a French sinologist and explorer of Central Asia, initially intended to enter the (转下页)

1950年至今

自1949年起，中国建立了许多学术机构，承担了研究新疆古代文明的任务。作为这方面最高的官方机构，新疆自治区文物局负责其境内文化遗产和考古遗址的管理，包括管理当地博物馆的办公室和新疆文物考古研究所，后者是唯一有权可以对当地古代遗存进行发掘和保护的地方单位。学术框架下的研究工作从1950年展开，从1979年至今进一步发展，足迹遍布阿勒泰山到昆仑山几乎所有的山区。主要有两个方面的工作：北部的天山地区主要集中在欧亚草原，在南部则是绿洲文明。从1979年至1989年（参见《新疆文物考古新收获1979—1989》，1995）的工作可以分为8个主题：史前史、青铜时代、楼兰考古、塞人考古、车师考古、察吾乎沟口（文化）的研究（位于乌鲁木齐西南的天山北部）、回鹘考古、黑汗王朝考古。其中塞人考古和察吾乎沟口文化研究与欧亚草原研究关系密切。大部分考古发掘报告和研究文章发表在《新疆文物》这本最初作为内部流通的刊物上，许多另外的文章也发表在《文物》《考古》《考古与文物》等杂志上（参见《新疆文物考古新收获（续）1995》，

From 1950 to the present day

Since 1949 China had put up several academic institutions that were to be the official task of the study and research on the ancient civilizations of Xinjiang. As an official institution of the highest rank, the Office of the Xinjiang Cultural Heritage is responsible for the management of cultural and archaeological heritage in the Autonomous Region. It includes an office of local museums and the Institute of Cultural Relics and Archaeology, the only regional institution that has rights of excavating and conserving the ancient remains. The research and studies in the academic framework initiated as early as in the 1950, and has further developed since the 1979 to date, almost all the mountains of Altaj Kulun of Xinjiang. There are two main sections of operational work, at north of Tjan' Šan focusing activities related to the issues of the Eurasian steppes to the south, and those relating to the Oasis civilizations. From 1979 to 1989 (New Achievements 1995), the work performed were grouped into 8 main topics: Prehistory, Bronze Age Archaeology, Archaeology of Loulan, Archaeology of Saka, Archaeology of Jushi (or Cheshi, Chu-shih), studying the culture of Chawuhugoukou (CWHG) (southwest of Urumqï on the southern side of T'jan' Šan), Archaeology of the Uyghurs, Archaeology of Karakhanids. The Archaeology of Saka and the study of CWHG culture are close to the theme of research of the Eurasian steppes.

Most of the studies and reports of archaeological excavations and articles are published in the *Xinjiang Wenwu* (Cultural Relics of Xinjiang), seeking *XiYu* (Western

（接上页）foreign service, Pelliot took up the study of Chinese and became a pupil of Sylvain Lévi and Édouard Chavannes. Pelliot worked at the École Française d'Extrême Orient in Hanoi, from where he was dispatched in 1900 to Beijing to search for Chinese books for the École's library. While there, he was caught up in the Boxer Rebellion and trapped in the siege of foreign legations. Pelliot made two forays into enemy territory during the siege — one to capture an enemy standard and another to obtain fresh fruit for those under siege. For his bravery, he received the Légion d'honneur. At age 22, Paul Pelliot returned to Hanoi, where he was made Professor of Chinese at the École. He was later elected professor at the Collège de France.

1997）。也有一些独立的学者和组织对新疆草原特别是青河县的巨大古墓进行了研究与分析。

从1999年开始，新疆草原地区的考古工作开始得到快速发展。沿着伊犁河上游开展了大量考古发掘工作，另外还有配合大型农业水利设施所进行的工作。主要由新疆文物考古研究所、伊犁州文物管理局、西北大学联合承担，基本上可分为两个部分：一是沿着尼勒克县境内的巩乃斯河，另一是沿着巩留县、特克斯县境内的特克斯河、昭苏河。发现了不同类型的考古遗存，包括墓地、岩画和居址，时代从旧石器时代至公元8世纪不等。在尼勒克县穷科克首次发现了安德罗诺沃文化遗存，此外西北大学还特别关注穷科克遗址中居址、墓地和岩画之间的联系。

古代和中世纪丝绸之路概况

上古及中世纪时期人们对丝绸之路的研究、学习及分析主要基于古典作家的作品（弗拉罗斯Florus 1999；狄奥尼索斯Dyonisius Periegetes 2005；老普林尼[Pliny]的《自然史》，1962；普利斯库斯Priscus 1983；普洛科匹斯Procopius 1914；托勒密Ptolemy 1971；斯特拉波Strabo 1969）。这些作品提供了有关Seri人（当时生产丝绸的人群）的一些观点，尽管这些观点看来是奇异而不切实际的。到了伊斯兰时代，主要的信息来自伊本·白图泰（2006），他主要提到了在刺桐港（今天的泉州）的经历，此地在厦门以北，正对台湾，在12、13世纪极为繁

Regions, Serindia), which consists of editorial form, a kind of diary for internal circulation. Many other articles are also published in the journals *Wenwu* (Cultural Relics), *Kaogu* (Archaeology), *Kaogu yu Wenwu* (Archaeology and Cultural Relics) (New Achievements 1995–1997).

There were also some independent scholars and organizations that have made analyses and studies mainly in the Xinjiang steppe, particularly with respect to a gigantic Kurgan in Qinghe County.

Since 1999, the archaeology of the steppes of Xinjiang began to greatly grow, with the opening along the upper course of the Ily River, of large excavations and also with gigantic hydro-agricultural works.

The excavation work was carried out in collaboration with the Institute of Archaeology and Cultural Relics of Xinjiang, the Office for Cultural Heritage of Ily and NWU, Xi'an. The whole project was basically divided into two parts: one related to the areas along the Kaxs River, Nilka County, the other along the Tekes and Zhaozu rivers in the counties of Gongliu Tekes. They were discovered at that time different types of archaeological remains, including cemeteries, petroglyphs, and settlements. The topics which those findings were reported are mainly related to the Paleolithic until the 8th century AD. Remains of the Andronovo Culture, first in China, were discovered in Qiongkek, Nilka County. In addition, the North West University, Xi'an has devoted particular attention to the relations between the settlements, cemeteries and petroglyphs, always at Qiongkek.

The Ancient and Medieval Silk Routes Concepts

As far as the ancient times and early and late medieval time is concerning the research activities, studies and analyses on the topics related to the *Silk Routes* have been mostly based on the classical sources (Florus 1999; Dyonisius Periegetes 2005; Pliny 1962; Priscus 1983; Procopius 1914; Ptolemy 1971; Strabo 1969) which can offer an idea, although exotic and fantastic, of the people called *Seri* which were producing the tissue called silk. In Islamic time the most important source is represented

盛，不同国家的商人居住在这里，进行瓷器和丝绸的买卖。根据这位来自摩洛哥的旅行者的记载，这座港口"是世界上最大的港口……一座巨大的城市，此地生产的绸缎，也以刺桐命名"。

在中国方面，僧人玄奘（《大唐西域记校注》，1985年出版）在结束印度之行后返回中国，于公元644年将他在西域的见闻记录下来，目前这仍然是现代人了解当时朝圣者所经行的不同路线的重要资料。从那时起对丝绸之路各种问题的关注开始集中于佛教在中国的传播上。书中仅涉及于阗的部分就提及数以百计的佛教寺院，这些遗址后来逐渐湮没，直至1860年为农业生产修建从喀拉喀什河引水的水渠，当地人发现了陶器、金器、玉器，地方政权开始专门派出人员来这里淘金（译者注：即和田境内的约特干遗址）。以斯文·赫定（1896）和斯坦因（1901、1906）为代表的学者们重新识别出了整个遗址。

当人们说起"中亚"或"丝绸之路"，它们指代的其实并非同一事物，也不是可以互相替换的概念。"中亚"相对更容易定义，因为它有个大致明确的地理区域；"丝绸之路"以中亚为中心，但其含义却超越了单纯的地理概念，还包括了复杂的历史和文化意义。

地域上的距离以及对19世纪基于旧旅行记录形成的有异国情调的浪漫理解，都导致了西方关于中亚和其境内的丝绸之路的根深蒂固的扭曲印象，爱德华·萨义德在他的名著（《东方学》，1978）中对此做了精准的解构式讽刺。

当然，西方旅行者、学者和考古学家难以进

by the travel of Ibn Battuta (2006) who amongst many other things mentions the Citong harbor (present time Quanzhou), to north of Amoy, in front of Taiwan. In this extremely active harbor in the 12th and 13th century, different foreign merchants lived, buyers of porcelain and silks. For this traveller from Morocco, the harbor "*was the vastest harbor of the world ... a big, superb city, where tissues were produced ..... called zeitounyyah*".

From the Chinese point of view the record of the western regions written in 644 by a Chinese Buddhist monk in his travel to India and return to China, named Xuan Zang (1985) is still the basis to deal with the different itineraries crossed by the pilgrims at that time, starting to focusing all the matter of the Silk Road on the diffusion of Buddhism in China. Only in Khotan he was mentioning hundred Buddhist monasteries. The site covered up until 1860, till when following the work of canals for agriculture, to convey water from the Karakash river, the locals quickly began to report the discovery of pottery, gold and jade, and the authorities, began to send specialized teams in the place. The entire area was recognized and explored by archaeologists of the time beginning with Sven Hedin (in 1896) and Aurel Stein (in 1901 and 1906).

When one refers to "Central Asia" or *Silk Routes* is not referring to one in the same thing — they are not interchangeable terms and conceptions. Central Asia is relatively easily to be defined and it is roughly a geographic region, *Silk Routes* are centered on Central Asia, comprising, nonetheless, much more than geographic aspects and issues, including complex historical and cultural processes to be interpreted.

Both the distance from of the territory and the 19th century romantic and exotic notion based on the dated travel accounts, contribute to keep distort and rooted convincement which have been ably and devastatingly deconstructed only in the famous Edward Said's volume (1978).

Of course the difficulty of access for western

入这一地区,而俄国和中国著作仅仅以本国文字出版,都导致了关于这一地区详细的科学资料的匮乏。对于希腊的希罗多德和中国的司马迁各自生活的世界来说,中亚都是特殊而遥远的外围地区,因此也很难建立起一个与他们所了解的世界等量和自主的历史进程。周邻国家与中亚有关的书面材料出现得也相当晚。揭开失落在长期历史进程中的中亚的神秘面纱之责任,只能交给考古学,然而这已是相当晚近的事情了。

丝绸之路还反映出另外一系列问题,例如曾存在一条比运送中国的重要物资——丝绸早得多的"丝绸之路",在"丝绸之路"这个名词被创造出来之前,这条通道就存在很久了。第一批走出非洲的古人类在欧亚大陆发现了新的栖息地,他们之间一定程度上存在技术、工具和物品的交换。人类逐渐适应了在欧亚大陆大部分地方的生存状况,尤其是在距今15000年前末次冰期之后。在大约距今8000年前的新石器时代,现代人已经将欧亚大陆变成一个大的文化交流舞台,互相间存在许多直接或间接的往来。中国输出的丝绸只是从汉代开始成为主要产品,至唐代达到鼎盛。然而并不只是丝绸创造了"丝绸之路",这个连通欧亚的复杂联系网可以看作是今天常说的"全球化"现象的最早证据。

丝绸之路不是一个简单的时间和地点概念,不过它在传统上的含义就是由商队路线和绿洲构成的连通中国和黎凡特(Levant)的网络。而我们要研究的"丝绸之路",是一个抽象的、动态交互的过程。这条路不是历史演进的产物,也并非基于特定目的被刻意创造然后又

travelers, scholars, and archaeologists to the area and the fact that the Russian and Chinese works and publications have been written only in their respective languages have done practical unknown large part of the scientific documentation at disposal for the area.

What is more Herodotus for Greece and Ssu Ma Chien for China, were dealing with Central Asia as a particular and very far periphery of their respective worlds, and this did not help very much to construct an equidistant and autonomous historical perspective.

Written Central Asian documents appear relatively late in time compared to its better known neighbors. The duty of unlocking the mysteries of these long lost regions has fallen almost exclusively to archaeology, and even then, only relatively recently.

Silk Routes present another cluster of problems. There existed *Silk Routes* long before the material silk was actively traded by China, and there existed *Silk Routes* for long after that the term *Silk Route* was coined. The first humans out of Africa discovered to new Eurasian habitats, their adaptations and technologies with one another and traded with each other for tools and goods. Gradually, humans developed adaptations to most of Eurasia, especially in the wake of the melting glaciers in the last 15000 years. By the Neolithic, about 8000 years ago, modern humans had transformed the great Eurasia into a large cultural interaction sphere, which effectively connected, on many direct and indirect levels. The silk trade out of China only began to be a major factor in Han times and reached its full flowering in the Tang Dynasty. It was not the silk that created the Silk Road, however. It could be argued that the complex network of links across Eurasia was the first evidence of what we now call globalization.

Silk Routes are not simply a time or merely a place. While it embraces the traditional meaning of a complex network of caravan routes and oases linking China and the Levant, *Silk Routes* for our purposes encompass in addition more abstract processes and dynamic interactions. A road is not an historical artifact, a thing

走向消亡。在更广泛的意义上，丝绸之路是人类在许多实在和抽象方面进行互动和交易的副产品。作为一个概念，丝绸之路包含了史前史和现代人类到达欧亚大陆以后的历史。从这层意义上说，丝绸之路就等同于整个（欧亚）大陆，并且到今天依然积极影响人们的生活，这种影响的方式值得我们努力去确认和理解。

近年来历史学家和考古学家们已经建立起作为文化广泛互动空间的新的欧亚大陆概念，如果喜欢的话，可以用"世界体系"（world system）这个词，整个大陆的许多直接和间接的互动都可以回溯到5万至10万年前。在这种更广阔的时空背景下，丝绸之路是一个多方面互动的象征，其进程依靠不同民族和文明之间在物质文化、行为和信仰方面的交流。例如，不仅有贸易上的往来，还有深层的思想和技术的传播，还有迁移和征战、基因和时尚元素、艺术和文学、音乐和舞蹈、服饰和图像、食品和饮品等方面的交换。当然举出这些例子并不排除其他各种各样的可能内容。在这个更宽泛的意义上，丝绸之路作为族群和文化的交流中介的标志，不仅仅是简单的贸易往来的概念，其中有许多细节值得我们去探索[1]。

deliberately created, existed for limited purposes, and then died out. Rather, in our wider use of the term, the *Silk Routes* are a by-product of human interaction and exchange on many levels, concrete and abstract. As a concept, the *Silk Routes* embrace the prehistory and history of modern humans since their arrival in Eurasia. In this sense, the *Silk Routes* correspond to the entire continent, they still exist, and they are still active in transforming peoples' lives in ways which are worth our effort to identify and understand.

Recent historians and archaeologists have evolved a new model of Eurasia as an extensive cultural interaction sphere, a "world system" if you will, with direct and indirect interaction across the continents entire expanse on many levels going back 50000 to 100000 years. In this wider context of space and time, *Silk Routes* are a symbol of the manifold interactions and processes by means of which peoples and cultures influenced each other's material culture, behavior, and beliefs — for example, by trade and exchange certainly, but also by less direct diffusion of ideas and technologies, by migration and conquest, by genes and jeans, by art and literature, by music and dance, by costume and design, by food and drink. These examples are not meant to preclude other less or more obvious possibilities. And in this wider sense, *Silk Routes* as symbol transcend its traditional idea of oases and caravans transporting trade and exchange *via* intermediaries between dispersed peoples and cultures. There are more nuanced dimensions to the *Silk Routes* than simply trade and exchange which are worth our while to explore[1].

---

[1] 这一系列问题在近年多有争论，关于争论的最新进展可参照以下在线出版物：http://www.silkroadfoundation.org/toc/index.html; http://depts.washington.edu/silkroad/; http://www.livius.org/sh-si/silk_road/silk_road.html; http://idp.bl.uk/; http://www.silkroad-infosystem.org/specto/bin/view/home; http://www.unwto.org/silkroad/; http://www.unesco.org/culture/dialogue/eastwest/caravan/page4. htm/, 蒂姆·威廉姆斯（Tim Williams）的著作亦可通过互联网下载（2013; 2014）。
The whole set of issue has been for long debated in the last year and it is easy to give look to the last on line publications of the topic: http://www.silkroadfoundation.org/toc/index.html; http://depts.washington.edu/silkroad/; http://www.livius.org/sh-si/silk_road/silk_road.html; http://idp.bl.uk/http://www.silkroad-infosystem.org/specto/bin/view/home; http://www.unwto.org/silkroad/ http://www.unesco.org/culture/dialogue/eastwest/caravan/page4. htm/ and the volumes of Tim Williams also downloadable on line (2013; 2014).

与北京大学的合作

北京大学考古文博学院为意大利学者提供了一项新的合作研究计划，即从中国的墓葬及其他遗迹中发掘或收集到的但可以归属于中亚、伊朗、伊斯兰、佛教文化范畴的一些物品，在中国考古学者的大力帮助下，现在具备了研究出版的可能。他们熟悉这些发现的背景和完整的历史信息，这将对研究中亚粟特、伊朗、伊斯兰、佛教文化不同领域的西方专家们产生积极的影响。

2010年，在北京大学考古文博学院和意大利的不同研究机构，我们（中国方面有齐东方、杨哲峰、林梅村、魏正中等，意大利方面有卡列宁[P.F. Callieri]、丰塔纳[M.V. Fontana]、葛嶷[1]）就不同的议题举行了数次讨论并做了讲座[2]，2011年赵辉教授在那不勒斯参加了另外一次讨

The Collaboration with the Peking University

A new possibility of doing research activities and study in this topic has been offered to the Italians scholars by the Department of Archaeology and Museology of Peking University (PKU). Archaeological objects and items excavated and collected from Chinese tombs, and, nonetheless, attributable to Central Asian, Iranian, Islamic and Buddhist cultures can now be published together with a substantial help of the Chinese archaeologists. They know the original context of the provenance and the whole history of the findings and this facilitate to work on with a particular different perspective provided by different western experts of Sogdian, Iranian, Islamic and Buddhist cultures of Central Asia.

In the Department of Archaeology and Museology and in different Italian Institutions, in 2010 different meetings and seminars have been organized by the respective staff (Prof. Qi Dongfang, Yang Zhefeng, Lin Meicun, Giuseppe Vignato from the Chinese side; Prof. P.F. Callieri, M.V. Fontana, Bruno Genito[1], from the Italian), on various issues[2] and in 2011 in Naples by

---

[1] 2010年10—11月，我受邀在北京大学访问了一个月，其间做了如下的讲座和课程：第一场是《公元前2千纪中期至公元前1千纪的古代近东（米坦尼和赫梯帝国）》（10月19日，北京大学考古学系），第二场是《历史上的粟特：景观、起源和考古》（10月20日，北京大学考古文博学院），第三场是《草原考古：工作、方法和策略》（10月26日，中国社会科学院考古研究所，在丛德新、郭物和仝涛的陪同下），最后一场是《伊朗与中亚在文化和历史上的关联：铁器时代至萨珊时期的考古学证据》（10月27日，北京大学考古文博学院）。

I was invited for a month at the Peking University in October/November 2010 and I had the honor and the possibility to have the following lectures and lessons, the first on October 19th about *The Ancient Near East from the Half of the Second to the First Millennium* BC (Mitannian and Hittite Kingdoms) (School of Archaeology and Museology, Peking University), the second on October 20th about the *Historical Sogdiana: Landscape, Sources and Archaeology* (Department of Archaeology and Museology, Peking University), a third on October 26th, about *The Archaeology of the Steppes: Work, Methods and Strategies* Institute of Archaeology, Chinese Academy of Social Sciences, attended by the Deputy Director and Dr. Cong Dexin. Guo Wu, and Tong Tao, and the last on October 27th about *Iran and Central Asia: Cultural and Historical Connections, the Archaeological Evidence from Iron Age to the Sasanian Time*, Department of Archaeology, Peking University.

[2] 2010年12月，在意方的邀请下，北京大学考古文博学院组织了一个高水平的教授考察团（由杨哲峰、齐东方、林梅村、魏正中组成）赴意，以加强与意方在学术上的交流合作。12月10日，齐东方教授在博洛尼亚大学做了题为《唐宋金器》的讲座，14日林梅村教授在那不勒斯东方大学做了题为《蒙古山水地图：在日本新发现的中世纪丝绸之路地图》的讲座，16日杨哲峰教授在亚非研究院做了题为《关于汉墓研究的新视角》的讲座。　　（转下页）

论[1]。北京大学考古文博学院和那不勒斯东方大学的合作是很有成效的，他们邀请笔者及副校长朱塞佩·卡塔尔迪（Giuseppe Cataldi）教授于2011、2012年两次访问北京大学，我的同事帕特里奇亚·卡廖蒂（Patrizia Carioti）教授也在2011年4月访问北京，有效地巩固了我们的合作关系。

丝绸之路中国段在超过一千年的历史进程中，一直是个经济和文化变化频繁的通道。大量起源于中亚和伊朗的考古遗物在中国西部被发现，既有科学的考古发掘品，也有偶然发现。中国方面提议重新认识这些物品，并选择其中的涉及金器、银器、玻璃器、陶器和丝绸的49件进行更深入的研究。

由于复杂的历史原因，中国考古学家到目前为止还没有在中国以西的那些国家进行考古工作的足够经验，而西方考古家学们对于中国西部的许多考古发掘品也不够了解。这次研究选取的器物中有些之前被研究过，但直到现在所掌握的信息，可能只是来自一些简单的描述和不确定的评价，因而非常有必要在技术、风格、考古调查方面做进一步的工作，目的是为了全面理解这些器物的内涵，以促进丝绸

Prof. Zhao Hui[1]. The full availability of the School of Archaeology and Museology made easy for us to initiate a broader agreement with UNO which has allowed me to visit two more times PKU in 2011 and 2012 and the vice Rector of UNO Prof. Giuseppe Cataldi and Prof. Patrizia Carioti in April 2011 to consolidate at Peking very much the reciprocal institutional relationships.

The general theme of this scientific collaboration is the study and analyses of the Chinese section of the *Silk Routes* that for more than a thousand years have been the crossroads of intense economic and cultural exchanges. A large amount of archaeological materials from Central Asian and Iranian origin were found in western China, both during regular excavations and sporadic discoveries. The Chinese side has proposed among the materials newly recovered, to jointly publish 49 items, gold, silver, glass, ceramics, silk, selected for a more thorough examination and study.

Due to various historical reasons, the tradition of Chinese archaeologists has never, so far, acquired sufficient experience in the archaeology of the countries west of China, and western archaeologists enough knowledge of excavated materials in western China. The information on archaeological materials previously selected for this study were, until now, possible only through a brief description and provisional assessments; while it remains a strong need for further technical, stylistic and archaeological investigations in order to fully understand the meaning of these objects and contribute to understand the origin and development of economic, commercial and

---

（接上页）The School of Archaeology and Museology of Peking University has sent in December 2010 a delegation of high level Professors to Italy, formed by Zhefeng Yang, Qi Dong Fang, Li Meicun and Giuseppe Vignato, to consolidate the expansion of academic and scientific cooperation with Italy. In that occasion Prof. Qi Dong Fang had a conference at the Università degli Studi di Bologna, sight of Ravenna on December 10th with the title *Gold from Tang and Song Dynasties*, Prof. Lin Meicun had a conference at the Università degli Studi di Napoli, l'Orientale on December 14th with the title *Mongolian Landscape Map. A Silk Routes Map of Middle Age newly Discovered in Japan* and Prof. Zhefeng Yang had a conference in IsIAO on December 16th with the title *Han Tombs, New Research Perspectives*.

[1] 以北京大学与那不勒斯东方大学签署协议为契机，北京大学考古文博学院院长赵辉教授于10月25日做了题为《中国的新石器时代》的讲座。
In the occasion of the signature of the agreement between UNO and PKU the Director of the School of Archaeology and Museology of PKU had a lecture on October 25th about *Neolithic in China*.

之路的经济、商业和文化路径的起源和发展方面的合作研究。在这样的合作中，中国方面将会提供这些器物的原始和直接的背景知识，意大利方面将会提供它们可能的原产地文化背景的确切解释。这些物品可能是在原产地生产，然后被运往东方的（作为高档礼品）。也有的是中国工匠模仿中亚的产品，或作为新的时尚而制造的仿品。

意大利和中国的考古学传统有所不同，在处理考古记录和艺术史材料方面有不同的方法论，双方必将从这个项目的有效开展中获益，去讨论、分享和寻找到反映丝绸之路关键性问题的最佳方式，正如丝绸之路鼓励不同语言、文化和习惯进行直接沟通的传统一样。为了使双方学者受益，这次研究的成果希望能在2017年完成出版。项目在策划之初即受意大利外交部的支持，并遵循2010年与北京大学签署的协议。

在研究西方文化向东传播特别是对中国的影响方面，铁器时代的游牧人（斯基泰的各个分支），希腊化时代的巴克特里亚、贵霜和粟特（阿富汗、乌兹别克斯坦、印度次大陆西北，1—7世纪），伊朗（主要属于帕提亚和萨珊时代，1—7世纪），伊斯兰（玻璃和釉陶生产，7—10世纪），佛教（石质雕刻等，1—7世纪）等文化的遗物是关注的重点[1]。

cultural paths through *Silk Routes*. In this collaboration, the Chinese will provide an original and direct knowledge of the archaeological contexts in which these materials were found, and the Italians will provide a decisive contribution to the interpretative approach to the original cultural context in which they were supposed to have been made and produced. Those objects were possibly realized, and transported (high level gifts) to east. Other possibilities of interpretations are also both related to an original Chinese production imitating central-Asian items, and to a local Chinese production as a "fashion" of the time.

The Italian and Chinese traditions, with their different methodological approaches in the archaeological record and art history, will certainly benefit from the effective development of this project, to discuss, share and find the most beneficial ways to reflect on the many significant issues related to the *Silk Routes* which is known to have allowed and encouraged a long tradition of direct channels of communication, in spite of languages, cultures and habits: the results of the study will be published for the benefit of both scholars, hopefully within the year 2017.

The project has operated on the basis of the Italian activities already planned in the last years with the support of MAE, and since 2010 in accordance with the agreement just signed with the Peking University.

The contribution of main groups of cultures, the nomadic of Iron and late Iron age (Scythian, Saka, Sai,), the Greek-Baktrian, Kushan and Sogdian (Afghanistan and Uzbekistan, north-west Indian sub-continent, 1st–7th century AD) the Iranian (mostly Parthian and Sasanian, 1st–7th century AD), the Islamic (glass and glazed pottery production, 7th–10th century AD), the Buddhist (stone reliefs etc., 1st–7th century AD) must be emphasized as the differing aspects of the western cultures spreading over east and basically China[1].

---

[1] 哈萨克斯坦、吉尔吉斯斯坦、乌兹别克斯坦、塔吉克斯坦（亚欧草原的中心地区）、俄国、伊朗、阿富汗、巴基斯坦和印度，塞人、斯基泰、突厥、大夏、贵霜、粟特、伊斯兰、突厥、佛教，一直以来都是意大利亚非研究院和那不勒斯东方大学的学者们在考古研究领域的主要兴趣所在。2008年1月26日，北京大学与意大利非洲与东方研究院签订了一项有关学术合作的谅解备忘录，商议出版一套"欧亚丛书"，在这个协议下，已由魏正中、萨尔吉于2009年出版两部著作：《梵天佛地》和《探寻西藏的心灵：图齐及其西藏行迹》。2011年10月25日，北京大学 （转下页）

纵横于伊朗、中亚和中国西部间的丝绸之路：对一类史学概念的考古学解读[1]

自马可·波罗[2]记述了沟通东西方的商路之后，直到近现代[3]，有关这些贸易通道的记录一直不绝如缕。这些记录包括了碑铭题刻、文学作品、历史重构、地图、传说、绘画以及旅行家、探险家、商人、僧侣、科学家和艺术家们的日记。除此之外，来回穿行于地中海—中东—巴格达—中亚—中国西部—西

Silk Routes, between Iran, Central Asia and Western China. An Archaeological Reading for a Historiographical Category[1]

In medieval and modern times there are many epigraphic, literary, historical reconstructions, maps, legends, drawings and diaries of travelers, explorers, traders, religious, scientists and artists, since Marco Polo[2] who spoke or described the trade routes between East and West[3]. It is documented as well, that ambassadors, missionaries, soldiers and sailors have crossed the set of paths that departed from the Mediterranean Sea, passed through the Middle East, Baghdad, Central Asia, crossing

---

（接上页）考古文博学院又与意大利那不勒斯东方大学签署了一些建立学术交流的协议，计划在下一个阶段进行系统的合作，主要是在田野考古学和文物学方面。这些是在朱佩赛·尼奥利（G. Gnoli）教授、达仁利（Francesco D'Arelli）教授、赵辉教授、魏正中（Giuseppe Vignato）教授、齐东方教授、笔者本人以及其他人的努力下促成的。Kazakhstan, Kyrgyzstan, Uzbekistan, Tagikistan (the central areas of the Eurasian steppes) and Russia, Iran, Afghanistan, Pakistan and India as well, where the ancient cultures of the Saka Scythian, palaeo-Turkish, Graeko-Bactrian, Kushan, Sogdian, Islamic, Turkish, and Buddhist peoples were located as well, have represented and still represent some of the major archaeological research areas of interests of the Italian scholars of Istituto Italiano per l'Africa e l'Oriente, (IsIAO), Rome and of the Università degli Studi di Napoli, "l'Orientale" (UNO), Napoli. PkU with a *Memorandum of Understanding* for an Academic and scientific collaboration signed the 26th January 2008 with IsIAO [(up to now two are the scientific results of that agreement and others are in preparation: a volume in a new series entitled *EurAsia Series* have been published in 2009 by Giuseppe Vignato and Saerji (2009a; 2009b) on the basis of this agreement, *Indo Tibetica* (*Fantian Fodi*) and a second volume with the title *Seeking the soul of Tibet* (*Tanxun Xizang de Xinling*)], and another *Agreement of Education and Exchange and Academic co-operation* signed the 25th October 2011 with the *Università degli Studi di Napoli, l'Orientale* (UNO) has put the basis for a new season of scientific collaboration mostly in the field of archaeology and the antiquity as well. These initiative have been possible thanks specially to the generous and unique efforts of the late Prof. G. Gnoli, Prof. Zhao Hui, Prof. Giuseppe Vignato, Prof. Francesco D'Arelli and last but not least Prof. Qi Dong Fang and myself and others.

[1] 以下内容基本源于笔者2012年在那不勒斯的系列讲座。
This part and the next are more or less following an article of the author in the series of lectures at Naples (2012).

[2] 马可·波罗（1254—1324），意大利商人、旅行家和大使。他和他的父亲尼科洛（Niccolò）及叔叔马特奥（Matteo）是文献记载最早一批来到中国（马可·波罗称作"Chatai"）的西方人之一。他的旅行经历被热那亚监狱中的狱友鲁斯蒂谦（Rustichello da Pisa）用法语记录下来，并集结成一本叫做《马可·波罗游记》（*Deuisament du monde*）、也叫做《百万》（*Million*, 1954, r. 1981）的书。
Marco Polo (1254−1324), Italian merchant and traveler, ambassador, together with his father Niccolò and his uncle Matteo, was among the first documented westerners to go to China, which he called Chatai. The chronicles of his journey were transcribed in French by a writer Rustichello da Pisa, a fellow prisoner in Genoa. They were collected in a book called *Deuisament du monde*, better known as *Million* (1954, r.1981).

[3] 同类的人物还包括利玛窦（Matteo Ricci）、乔瓦尼·卡博托（Giovanni Caboto）、弗拉维奥·焦亚（Flavio Gioia）、乔瓦尼·达·韦拉扎诺（Giovanni da Verrazzano）、郎世宁（Giuseppe Castiglione）等等。
One can also mention Matteo Ricci, Giovanni Caboto, Flavio Gioia, Giovanni da Verrazzano, Giuseppe Castiglione and many others.

安一线的外交使节、传教士、士兵和水手们也都留下了各式各样的记载。长久以来，这些商路或多或少都被考古发现所证实。有鉴于此，我们就不能仅限于讨论丝绸之路研究所提出的传统问题，而应当扩大视野，特别是关注晚近学者，如费迪南·冯·李希霍芬（Baron Ferdinand von Richthofen，1877；1883；1886；1903；1907）、斯文·赫定（Sven Hedin 1898a, 1898b）[1]以及尼古拉·米哈伊洛维奇·普尔热瓦尔斯基（Nikolai Mihajlovic Przhevalsky 1870–1873）[2]的研究。他们提出并强调了中亚草原的游牧人群在丝绸之路

the western China and ended in Xi'an and vice versa of course. The same paths for ages long, are widely more or less archaeologically attested. In this perspective, certainly much larger than that which traditionally has always referred to the issues related to the *Silk Routes*, one should remember, of course, the role and the importance of more recent scholars like Baron Ferdinand von Richthofen (1877; 1883; 1886; 1903; 1907), Sven Hedin (1898a, 1898b)[1] and Nikolai Mihajlovic Przhevalsky (1870–1873)[2], again to name a few, and stress at the same time, the role of the nomadic peoples of the Central Asian steppes, which have always maintained cultural contacts between East and West, from at least the Iron Age. The phenomena can be glimpsed behind the historical and geographical concept of *Silk Routes*, all marked by the growth, no longer controlled by the traditional Great

---

[1] 就在沙皇俄国和大英帝国间的"大博弈"正如火如荼地进行时，瑞典探险家斯文·赫定决心跟随李希霍芬和普尔热瓦尔斯基的脚步，在19世纪与20世纪之交开启了一段动人心魄的探险旅程。他探访了中国的西北部，其中绝大多数区域在当时鲜为人知或无人涉足。在穿越塔克拉玛干沙漠时，他发现了许多重要的考古遗迹和遗物，并且曾一度接近拉萨。即将出版的两卷本图书值得一读。

At the height of the "Great Game" between the Russian and the British empires, the Swedish explorer Sven Hedin decided to follow the footsteps of Ferdinand von Richthofen and Nikolai Mihajlovic Przhevalsky, embarking on an epic journey spanning the end of the 19s and the beginning of the 20s century, through the regions of northwestern China, for the most at that time unknown or little explored. Through the Taklamakan desert, he makes important archaeological finds and also comes very close to Lhasa. The books that will ensue (2 volumes) are interesting and fun to read.

[2] 在沙皇俄国向中亚急速扩张期间，波兰裔的地质学家、探险家尼古拉·米哈伊洛维奇·普尔热瓦尔斯基上校受沙俄政府委托，接受了一项勘察蒙古、中国西藏以及中国其他地区并绘制相关地图的任务。随后他召集一众朋友，从青海湖出发。考察持续了多年，其间他们发现了多个先前不为人知的新物种。考察途中，普尔热瓦尔斯基听闻蒙古西南部某座城市有野马，这个消息不可谓不重大，因为在瑞典博物学家林奈（Linnaeus［1758]）著名的自然分类系统中，马类下面并没有包括野马。在随后由普尔热瓦尔斯基率领的第二次和第三次考察中，他得到了一个由边境警卫提供的野马头骨，并且在戈壁沙漠附近的塔钦沙拉努鲁（Tachin Schara Nuru）中见到了两群野马。根据林奈分类系统的命名法，新物种的名称要冠以发现者之名，因此这种野马就被称作普尔热瓦尔斯基氏野马，简称普氏野马。

During a time when Russia is rapidly expanding into Central Asia, the geologist/adventurer and colonel Nikolai Mihajlovic Przhevalsky, of Polish origin, welcomes a mission entrusted to the Russian government, to explore and map the regions of Mongolia, Tibet and China. Gathers some friends and embarks on his journey to the shores of Koko Nor, also known as the Qinghai Lake. All this holds for many years abroad and has led to the discovery of several previously unknown animal species. Having the great Swedish scientist Linnaeus (1758) not included in its system *naturae* the horse, made a great stir the news that during his travels Przhevalsky had heard of wild horses in the city's south-western Mongolia. In a second trip the colonel led, reflecting the fact, a skull of a wild horse that he had been given by a border guard and during a third trip he saw two herds of the animal in the mountains of Tachin Schara Nuru near the Gobi desert. Then as in the system *naturae* the name of a new species was provided to give the name of the discoverer, this wild animal received the complicated name of Przhevalsky.

上所扮演的重要角色。至迟从铁器时代开始，游牧民族就一直是东西方文化交流的纽带。结合丝绸之路的历史和地理的背景，这一现象的出现一方面得益于游牧人摆脱了传统帝国（罗马、波斯和中国）的控制，社会经济不断发展，另一方面则得益于地理上的中间位置，广阔地域内分布着众多政治实体，游牧人在社会、政治方面又具有特殊的联合性。他们的重大贡献远非仅仅维持游牧群体所提供的商贸路线这么简单，这些族群包括铁器时代伊朗语文献中提及的萨迦人（Saka），即汉文文献中所称的塞人；晚期有着不同种族起源的匈奴和乌孙，甚至是种族不甚明了的月氏等等。远在丝绸生产、运输和交易之前，不同种类的商品贸易便已存在，例如玉石[1]，尤其是在中国西部的新疆地区；或者是阿富汗与美索不达米亚之间呼罗珊大道（*Khorasan Road*）上的青金石[2]，都是原史时期长距离贸易的代表商品。作为中国与阿富

empires (Roman, Persian and Chinese), of new socio-economic realities on one hand, and geographically intermediate, numerous political entities, including their role held by the combined socio-political character of nomadic type on the other. Their decisive contribution not only was to fulfill the maintenance of these trade routes just offered by the nomadic peoples in the Iron Age, like the Saka, as they are called from the Iranian sources, or Se, as they are from the Chinese; or others, of a later period, of different ethnic origin, like the paleo-Turkish Xiognu and Wu Sun, or even those of more problematically uncertain ethnicity of Yüeh-chi, and others. But trade of different products, as is known, existed prior to the production, diffusion and distribution of *silk* and by the time it is the case of such materials as jade[1], especially in western China, the Xinijang, or as lapis lazuli[2] especially in the so-called *Khorasan Road* between Afghanistan and Mesopotamia, elements of a proto-historic trade of a middle and long distance. The commercial roads of jade and lapis lazuli, are some of the most well-known antecedent of the *Silk Routes* between China and Afghanistan. And it is difficult, here and on this occasion, forget other commercial roads, lived and used in other times and different geographical contexts, such as the so-called *Route of the Spices* considered as an intermediary between Europe and the Indies (Miller 1974; Keay 2007),

---

[1] 玉石与中国文明有着千丝万缕的联系。千百年来，中国人将玉石视作无价之宝并顶礼膜拜，然而在古代"中国"的范围内，这种矿物并不常见，它们基本是以原石状态从西域，即今天的新疆地区输入的。
The "jade" is inextricably linked to the Chinese civilization. From forty centuries the Chinese have given to this beautiful stone an invaluable value, and have bestowed a cult. Paradoxically, this mineral does not exist in ancient China itself, and has always been imported, almost in its entirety, from its western part, the present Xinjiang.

[2] 青金石是历史最悠久的宝石之一。关于它最早的记录可以回溯至公元前5000年，当时在法老时期的埃及被广泛用于制作珠宝。青金石为深蓝色，并由此得名。它的名字由拉丁文 lapis（石头）和 lazuli 组成，其中 lazuli 是属格名词，起修饰作用，其源于中世纪拉丁语 lazulum，而 lazulum 又是从阿拉伯语 al-lazward 和波斯语 lāzhward 而来，意为"蓝"。参见 Tosi (1974), Hermann (1968), Hermann Moorey (1983) 以及 Casanova 关于伊朗和中亚中长距离贸易的论述 (1994, 2000)。
Lapis lazuli is one of the precious stones considered the longest in history. His earliest documentation dates back to the 5th millennium BC, when it was widely used for the manufacture of jewelry found in tombs in the Pharaonic Egypt. The color is intense blue, and from this derives its name, made from the Latin *lapis* (stone) and *lazuli*, genitive of medieval Latin *lazulum*, derived in turn from Arabic (*al-lazward*), and from the Persian *lāzhward* that means "blue". See articles of Tosi (1974) and Hermann (1968) and Hermann Moorey (1983) and Casanova for business in the middle and long distance between Iran and Central Asia (1994, 2000).

汗之间丝绸之路的前身，玉石之路和青金石之路是最为著名的商路。此外，出现并通行于不同时期、不同地理背景中的商路也应多加留心，比如作为联系欧洲和东印度群岛的所谓的香料之路（Miller 1974；Keay 2007），从罗马时期就开通的连接阿拉伯半岛（阿曼和也门）和地中海的熏香之路，以及盐之路、琥珀之路和香水之路等等[1]。

对以上贸易之路的研究，无论是从时代跨度上还是在历史文化方面，都极大地拓宽了丝绸之路的内涵，而且其本身便是丝路研究的不同方法。人们逐渐认识到，这些可能在公元后逐渐定型的商路是特定历史时期特定地域内宗教信仰传播的通道，如佛教、景教、摩尼教和祆教，沿途不同种族、不同文化传统的人群也具有类似的社会经济生活条件。当然，这些商路绝非单线发展，在各个自然环境迥异的区域中它们有着纵横交错的支线。在一些地区，比如中国西部塔里木盆地中的塔克拉玛干沙漠，冬季极冷、夏季极热，对身处其间的人和动物来说都是严酷的考验。商队由于暴露在不同人群的攻击之下，也承受着巨大的风险。这些人群所扮演的角

or the *Route of Incense* linking the Arabian peninsula (Oman and Yemen) to the Mediterranean, in use since Roman times, to which could yet others be added, such as the *Route of Salt*, the *Route of Amber*, the *Route of Perfume* etc.[1].

These general considerations led to an expansion both in a chronological and the historical-cultural sense, of the meaning of *Silk Routes*, and become itself a methodological tool to deal differently with it. It is increasingly clear, in fact, to look further those roads were not only the means of transmission of ideological-religious beliefs of Buddhist, Nestorian Christian, Manichean or Zoroastrian élites, in a given historical period, in key areas and the center of articulated and complex geo-political and geo-economic matters. It seems increasingly plausible, rather, to imagine the routes, may be only better physically recognizable at the turn of the Christian era, as a century, if not millennia trade, between ethnically and culturally diverse peoples, with which they shared, often homogeneous socio-economic conditions of life. These trade-routes, presented, of course, different branches for many geo-morphological and geo-climatic conditions within the crossed regions, placed by the nature, that have always hindered certain linearity. The climate is very cold in winter and hot in summer, p. example, in the depressions of the Taklamakan desert in western China, and it could not put a strain on men and animals. The caravans could also run serious risks, as they were exposed to attacks of different population groups. The role of these populations, which has been already widely emphasized, was, in fact, inherently ambiguous, depending on historical circumstances, and sometimes it was an invaluable mean by which it was necessary to treat the transaction; sometimes, however, it became an insurmountable barrier not without through also

---

[1] 所有相关问题参见Betts, Kidd (2010)。书中提到了从史前到伊斯兰时期不同的贸易路线，使得我们十分有必要从新的"考古学"角度去研究"丝绸之路"，特别是目前考古发现中出土了大量青金石，以及汉以前的欧洲和公元前两千年的中亚发现了"丝绸"，如德国的哈尔施塔特文化（Hallstatt culture），雅典凯拉米克斯遗址（Keraimikos）的墓葬，以及中亚Sapalli Tepe遗址（Good 2010, 35, 36）。
For all these problems see the recent Betts, Kidd (2010) in which different items, ranging from prehistory to the Islamic period (all listed below), which is strongly raised the issue of a new "archaeological" approach to the concept of "Silk Road", especially in the light of numerous findings of "lapis lazuli", but also "silk" in the pre-Han period in Europe, particularly in the Hallstatt culture in Germany, and in the cemetery of *Keraimikos* in Athens, but also at Sapalli Tepe in Central Asia in the second millennium BC (Good 2010, 35, 36).

色已被广泛注意，其作用因不同的历史环境而有较大差别，有时他们是贸易正常进行之必需，有时又因军事武力所导致的永久冲突而成为无法逾越的阻碍。陆上丝绸之路的衰落，是因为一条与之相比更快捷、更安全的新商路崛起，即西方与印度、中国的海上交通。商路为东亚（特别是中国）与近东、地中海及途经地区的文明交流提供了机会，这些地区地处里海与黄河之间，是亚洲的腹地。中亚东边的中国，其最西面的新疆地区通过甘肃天然的河西走廊与内地，特别是以陕西西安为中心的区域连通。

中国以西，公元前6世纪阿契美尼德王朝建立，随后偏东的区域出现了不同的政治实体，如巴克特里亚（主要分布在阿富汗的西北部），粟特（主要分布在泽拉夫善谷地，包括塔吉克斯坦和乌兹别克斯坦）：前者作为双峰骆驼的原产地而闻名，后者则拥有从东伊朗到古突厥世界中最精明的商人。中亚地处中国和伊朗、地中海的古典世界之间，其间草原与沙漠交错，山脉阻隔，各种不同的生活方式各自发展又相互碰撞，互动交流[1]，北部区域居住着游牧人群，是训练有素的居于帐篷中的骑士和牧人，有着印欧和

military permanent conflicts. The decline of the *Silk Routes* began with the competition from a new market road, faster and more secure than the land routes: India and China, began in fact to be reached by sea from the West, and vice versa. The caravan routes were an opportunity for meeting between civilizations of East Asia (especially China) and the countries of the Near East and the Mediterranean and the crossed territory; they were the heart of Asia, between the Caspian Sea and the Yellow River. To the east of Central Asia the Chinese empire, with its extreme western regions from Xinjiang to Gansu Province, crossed by the famous Hexi corridor, constituted a natural passage leading to Central Asia and vice versa.

To the west of China from the 6th century, the Achaemenid empire was established, and was followed by further east political entities of Bactria (mainly in the north-west Afghanistan), Sogdiana (mainly in the Zeravshan valley, including Tadžikistan and Uzbekistan): the first, famous, among other things, because being the original area of the camel (*camelus Bactrianus*), the second because land of clever merchants, between the eastern Iranian and the starting paleo-Turkish world. Between the Chinese empire, the Iranian and the classical Mediterranean world, there was Central Asia, a steppic and deserted region, interrupted by mountain ranges, where different and opposite ways of life flourished, intended to interact each other[1]. The northern regions were, in fact, inhabited by nomadic peoples, while in the south sedentary civilizations agricultural populations lived, destined to become autonomous, where urban entities and state formed and made prosperous its intense commercial traffic. The men of the north were skilled horsemen and herders living in housing units and furniture, and belonged,

---

[1] 从粟特地区的撒马尔罕出发，可以南下经过阿富汗北部的巴尔赫（Balkh），马可·波罗可能曾在此停留，而根据传说，亚历山大大帝甚至在这里迎娶了波斯国王的女儿。再向南进入位于喀布尔（Kabul）西北的巴米扬（Bamiyan）地区，此处以两尊大立佛像而闻名于世。继续向西，就可以到达赫拉特（Herat）。这里的男人都剃头并包裹白色头巾，女人则将整个头部盖住仅露出眼睛。马可·波罗对伊朗的城镇和文化水平大加赞赏，其中对克尔曼（Kerman）、伊斯法罕（Isfahan）、大不里士（Tabriz）、巴格达（Baghdad）以及摩苏尔（Mosul）等地的描述也许有所夸大。大不里士是一个活跃的贸易中心，再向西就进入到威尼斯和热那亚商人控制的区域。巴格达城的西面没有城墙，而东面由于储放了大量的金银财宝，防御最为坚固。从美索不达米亚出发，人们可以选择不同的路线前往西欧。其中一条是古代以来的传统商路，即途经杜拉欧罗普斯（Dura-Europos）、帕尔米拉（Palmyra）或安条克 （转下页）

突厥两个不同的语言和种族来源；而南方则是自治的农业定居文明形成城市与国家，商贸繁盛。

贸易路线

中亚一直以来都是古代商路的必经之地，这些商路既是游牧部落的贸易路线，也是千百年来不同社会政治群体间的商贸交换的重要通道。得益于经济发展以及公元后产生的政治实体的刺激，一系列重要的贸易路线得以开辟，后来被统称为丝绸之路。它们中的一些随着时间而改变，而另一些却保持了几个世纪。根据中国史书，特别是《汉书》(1962, 3872; 1979)、《后汉书》(1907, 1965)的记载，其中一条商路就是从中国当时的首都长安（现陕西省省会西安）发端，向西北延伸穿过中亚。这条道路在敦煌附近分成两支，分别沿塔里木盆地和塔克拉玛干沙漠（死亡之海）[1]南北两缘，即北道和南

however, to different linguistic and ethnic families: the Indo-Germanic and Turkic.

The Routes

Central Asia was always crossed by ancient caravan routes, which were utilized both as paths for trade of nomadic tribes and commercial routes established thousands of years old, for communities of differing socio-political level. Enriched by new economic potential, and energized by the political authorities not existing before the Christian era, the related regional areas were found to be crossed by a series of itineraries and routes, which were significantly, gave the name of the *Silk Routes* to. The routes taken by the travelers had to change over time, but some of them remained unchanged for centuries. Based on the written testimonies of important Chinese royal annals, particularly in the Han Shu (1962, 3872; 1979), Hou Han Shu (1907, 1965), one of these routes started right from China and its capital Chang'an (the present-day Xi'an, capital of the present Shaanxi Province), and stretched north-west penetrating Central Asia. Near Dunhuang the route forked in two main branches passing along the northern (bei dao) and southern (nan dao) limits of the Tarim Basin and the Taklamakan desert (the place of no return)[1],

---

（接上页）(Antioch)或阿卡(Acre)，然后进入地中海，或者可以从克里米亚(Crimea)经黑海或东土耳其前往君士坦丁堡，最后经海路至意大利。

Moving on to Samarkand in Sogdiana, you could descend along the northern part of Afghanistan, Balkh, where would have stopped Marco Polo and even where, according to legend, Alexander the Great had married the daughter of the king of Persia, Bamiyan famous for the presence of two colossal statues of the Buddha, located to the north and west of Kabul. Continuing west, one could reach Herat. Here men shave the head and wrapped in a piece of white cloth, the women covered their heads, leaving only a slit for the eyes. Marco Polo testifies, p. example, with regard to Iran, the urban and cultural quality, though perhaps a bit exaggerated, of Kerman, Isfahan, Tabriz, Baghdad and Mosul, much later. Tabriz was an active center of trade, and beyond it entered the territory controlled by the Venetians and Genoese merchants. As well as Baghdad, whose western part of the city was without walls, while the eastern, given the large amount of gold and precious stones contained there, was most probably fortified,. Starting from Mesopotamia one could choose different directions to reach Western Europe. One could follow the trade-routes of classical antiquity, through Dura-Europos, Palmyra or Antioch or Acre, and then cross the Mediterranean, or even Constantinople, which could also be reached from Crimea, and from eastern Turkey, before crossing the Black Sea, to reach, by sea, Italy.

[1] 马可·波罗这样描述他所途经的塔克拉玛干沙漠："罗不(Lop)是一大城，在名曰罗不沙漠之边境，处东方及东北方间。此城臣属大汗，居民崇拜摩诃末。前此已言凡行人渡此沙漠者，必息于此城一星期，以解人畜之渴。已而预备一月之粮秣，出此城后，进入沙漠。此沙漠甚长，骑行垂一年，尚不能自此端达彼端。狭窄之处，须时（转下页）

道，然后在喀什汇合。这一路线有效地避开了敦煌以西浩瀚的戈壁沙漠[1]。

北道从敦煌（甘肃）出发，途经哈密、吐鲁

and then reunited in Kashgar. This route was necessary in order to avoid the huge desert gravel west of Dunhuang[1].

The northern route from Dunhuang (Gansu province)

（接上页）一月，方能渡过。沿途尽是沙山沙谷，无食可觅。然若骑行一日一夜，则见有甘水，足供五十人或百人暨其牲畜之饮。甘水为数虽不多，然全沙漠中可见此类之水。质言之，渡沙漠之时，至少有二十八处得此甘水，然其量甚寡。别有四处，其水苦恶。沙漠中无食可觅，故禽兽绝迹。然有一奇事，请为君等述之。行人夜中骑行渡沙漠时，设有一人或因寝息，或因他故落后，迨至重行，欲觅其同伴时，则闻鬼语，类其同伴之声。有时鬼呼其名，数次使其失道。由是丧命者为数已多。甚至日间亦闻鬼言，有时闻乐声，其中鼓声尤显。渡漠情形困难如此。"（汉译摘自冯承钧译《马可波罗行纪》，上海书店出版社［上海］，2001年，页106—107）位于盐湖罗布泊绿洲地区的楼兰遗址，可能由于干旱缺水，在公元400年左右遭到废弃。在楼兰遗址，考古学家发现了大量产自中国和西欧的丝绸和其他织物。得益于本地区极度干旱的环境，考古学家还找到了一些木乃伊，年代不仅是汉唐时期，甚至更早。从罗布泊出发，南道穿过了若羌、且末、和田、叶尔羌的绿洲地带，到达塔克拉玛干沙漠西端、帕米尔高原下的喀什。罗布泊到和田之间是世界上最荒凉的自然环境之一。西行求法的玄奘在公元645年由印度返程时，留下了这样的记载："从此东行，入大流沙。沙则流漫，聚散随风，人行无迹，遂多迷路。四远茫茫，莫知所指，是以往来者聚遗骸以记之。乏水草，多热风。"（季羡林等校注《大唐西域记校注》，中华书局［北京］，1985年，页1030—1031）

Marco Polo, who travelled the desert described it this way (1954/1981, XLV, 47–48): *Lop è una grande città ch'è all'entrata del Gran Diserto, che si chiama lo Diserto di Lop, ed è tra levante e greco; e sono al Gran Cane, e adorano Malcometto. Quegli che vogliono passare lo diserto si riposano in Lop per una settimana, per rinfrescare loro e loro bestie; poscia prendono vivanda per un mese per loro e per le loro bestie. E partendosi di questa città, entra nel diserto: ed è sì grande, che si penerebbe a passare un anno; ma per lo minore luogo si luogo si pena lo meno a trapassare un mese. Egli è tutto montagne e sabbione e valli, e non vi si truova nulla da mangiare. Ma quando se' ito un dì e una notte truovi acqua, ma non tanta che n'avesse oltra cinquanta o cento uomeni co' loro bestie: e per tutto il diserto conviene che uomo vada un dì e una notte, prima che l'acqua si truovi: e in tre luoghi o in quattro truova l'uomo l'acqua amara e salsa, e tutte l'altre sono buone, che sono nel torno di ventotto acque. E non v'ha né uccelli né bestie, perché non v'hanno da mangiare. E sì vi dico che quivi si truova tale maraviglia: egli è vero che, quando l'uomo cavalca di notte per lo diserto, egli avviene questo: che se alcuno rimane adrietro degli compagni per dormire o per altro, quando vuole poi andare per giungere gli compagni ode parlare ispiriti in aiere, che somigliano gli suoi compagni, e più volte è chiamato per lo suo nome proprio, e è fatto disviare talvolta in tal modo che mai non si truova; e molti ne sono già perduti: e molte volte ode l'uomo molti stormenti in aria, e propriamente tamburi. E così si passa questo Gran Diserto. Or lasciamo del diserto, e diremo della provincia ch'è all'uscita del diserto.* Near the site of the lying salty Lopnor oasis of Loulan, was abandoned in 400 AD perhaps because of the drought. Among the ruins of Loulan archaeologists have found numerous fragments of silk and other fabrics made in China and Western Europe. They also found the remains of some human beings, thanks to that particular phenomenon of natural mummification due to the severe drought in the region, the desert Loulan, in fact, returned the dried bodies of individuals not only dating back to the Han and Tang periods, but even during very oldest. From Lopnor, the southern route went through the oasis of Ruoqiang, Qiemo, Khotan, Yarkand, to reach Kashgar, located at the western end of the Taklamakan Desert, at the foot of Pamirs. The landscape between the Lopnor and Khotan is one of the most inhospitable imaginable. The Chinese pilgrim Xuanzang in 645 AD on his return from India describes *A great desert of shifting sands. The masses of sand have a monstrous extension: at the whim of the wind come together and separate. Travelers do not find evidence of human and many of them are lost. From all over the desert stretches to the horizon, and no one knows which way to go. The travelers crowded therefore, to show the way, animal bones. Is not no water or vegetation, and often fiery winds* (1985, 1030–1031).

[1] 从敦煌分支的两条商路中的南道，向西南穿过干涸的罗布泊荒漠，因为风和洪水沉积经常改变着地形地貌。

Of the two caravan routes which branched off from Dunhuang, the south west across the desert Lopnor, a semi-lake dried up, because the winds and flood deposits have frequently changed the contours and location.

番[1]、伊犁河谷及北疆, 到达哈萨克斯坦的草原地带。由西向东的路线则必定经过费尔干纳 (现在乌兹别克斯坦和吉尔吉斯斯坦境内) 到达喀什[2]。另一条路从印度河谷出发, 最终到达敦

and through Hami and Turpan[1], the Ili River valley, and Zungaria reached the steppes of Kazakhstan. A western route was definitely that from Ferghana (now in Uzbekistan and Kirghisitan) which reached Kashgar[2]. Another route again, finally reached Dunhuang, starting

---

[1] 马可·波罗和玄奘都到访过哈密的绿洲。威尼斯商人曾在这里居住并讲述了在此地的冒险奇遇, 以及绿洲人民的风俗习惯和日常消遣:"哈密 (Camul) 州昔是一国, 境内有环以墙垣之城村不少, 然其要城即哈密。此州处两沙漠间, 一面是罗不大沙漠, 另一面是一广三日程之小沙漠。居民皆是偶像教徒, 自有其语言。土产果实不少, 居民恃以为生。其人爱娱乐, 只知弹唱歌舞。"(汉译摘自冯承钧译《马可波罗行纪》, 上海书店出版社 [上海], 2001 年, 页 118—119)。这一描述与哈密地区的实际完全相符。在《马可波罗行纪》中提到的"唐古忒州"先前为西夏王国 (1038—1227), 包括了今天的宁夏回族自治区和甘肃省。继续向西北行进约 800 公里, 就到达绿洲盆地吐鲁番, 它是北道上最重要也最古老的商业中转站。在汉代, 汉王朝将其营建成控制中亚的据点之一。当地居民是中亚古老突厥民族的后代, 而周围的文物古迹则见证了绿洲历史漫长的发展过程。其西面是交河故城遗址, 当年曾作为汉代的军事前哨。东面则是靠近所谓"火焰山"的高昌故城, 以及佛教石窟遗存柏孜克里克。该地区另一个重要的地点是离高昌不远的阿斯塔那古墓群, 由于干燥的气候, 墓中出土了大量的丝绸。
The oasis of Hami was visited by Marco Polo and Xuanzang. The Venetian merchant tells of the adventures of this place and lived there, describing the habits and past times of the people of the oasis (XLVII, 50, 51) *Camul (Kamul) è una provincia, e già anticamente fu reame, e havvi ville e castella assai. La mastra città ha nome Camul. La provincia è in mezzo di due deserti: dall'una parte è il grande diserto, dall'altra è un piccolo diserto di tre giornate. Sono tutti idoli, lingua hanno per sè, vivono de' frutti della terra, e hanno assai da mangiare e da bere, e vendonne assai; e sono uomeni di grande sollazzo, che non attendono se non e suonare istormenti e a cantare e a ballare.* The description is entirely consistent with the reality of the area of Hami. The province of "Tangut" mentioned in the "Million" (XLVI, 48) indicates the Xixia Kingdom (1038–1227), whose territory included the Ningxia Hui Autonomous Region and Gansu Province today. Continuing the road to the north-west for about 800km, the caravan routes reached the deep depression of the oasis of Turfan, its most important and earlist of all those of the northern route. During the Han Chinese people made it one of their strongholds in Central Asia. The inhabitants are descendants of ancient Turkic peoples of Central Asia and its surroundings are rich in places of great historical and artistic interest, where are the monuments that bear witness to the ancient past of the oasis. To the west lie the impressive ruins of Jiaohe, a military outpost in the Han period. Equal suggestive power exercise the ruins of Gaochang in the east, near which, on the side of the so-called "Mountains of Fire", you can see what remains of the complex of Buddhist caves of Bezeklik. Another place of importance in the area is the cemetery of Astana, where inhabitants were buried not far from the famous city of Gaochang; inside the graves were found many silks, preserved thanks to the dry climate of the area.

[2] 从喀什开始, 根据商人们的需求不同, 丝绸之路会走向不同的方向。商路在翻越了帕米尔高原后, 会继续向印度、伊朗和更西方延伸。喀什绿洲十分广阔, 有村庄同时也有大型城镇。虽然远离当时中国的边境, 但喀什时常处于中原政权的政治和军事控制之下。为了保证与西方的交流畅通, 中原王朝与中亚突厥民族反复斗争以取得对喀什的控制权。从 10 世纪开始, 喀什成为活跃的穆斯林中心, 到 18 世纪才重新回到中原政权的管辖范围, 不过伊斯兰风格的建筑仍随处可见。土壤呈砂石质的绿洲的一大特点就是露天市场, 几个世纪以来甚至直到今天, 来自东西方的产品都在这里交换, 如骆驼、织物、马、驴、水果和山羊等。
From Kashgar on, the Silk Routes could take different directions depending on the needs of the merchants. The caravan routes, having crossed the steps of the Pamir, continued in other locations to India, Iran and the West. The Kashgar oasis was extensive, there were villages that were, at the time, major cities. As far from the borders of China, Kashgar was sometimes placed under the political and military control of the Chinese, who fought against the Turks of Central Asia to retain possession of this place, and so check the connections with the West. From the 10th century Kashgar became an active Muslim center, in the 18th century it returned to Chinese control, but still features of Islamic architecture are found there. One of the characteristics of the oasis, where the soil is sandy and stony, are open-air markets, where, as in past centuries, even today eastern and western products are exchanged: camels, textiles, horses, donkeys, fruit, goats.

煌。这一路线从喀喇昆仑山脚下开始，穿过旁遮普（Punjab）和斯瓦特（Swat）的山地，然后继续沿着印度河经过吉尔吉特（Gilgit）和罕萨河谷（Hunza valley），之后穿过海拔5000多米的明铁盖达坂（Mintaka pass），最后一路东下到达喀什。各个方向上的支线并不发达：一些路线经齐拉斯（Chilas）上至帕苏（Passu）和明铁盖达坂，一些沿着萨特帕拉河谷（Satpara valley）和卡彭鲁（Kapunlu），另一些到达拉达克（Ladakh）、旁遮普河谷（Punjal valley）和亚辛（Yasin），连接吉尔吉特（Gilgit）和吉德拉尔（Chitral）。这些支线上有很多古老的人类活动遗迹，时代不同、风格和艺术形式各异的题铭，展现了五千多年来不同人群及其文化的发展历程。北部地区有众多的考古圣地，齐拉斯就是其中之一，从青铜时代的岩画到阿契美尼德王朝、帕提亚时代以及犍陀罗时期的文化遗存应有尽有。犍陀罗地区的艺术风格不断演进，发展出更加复杂的形式，包括对佛塔以及佛教神祇的塑造。这些道路除了用于商贸以外，还为沿途地区文化、宗教以及语言的交流提供通道，形成了多元文化碰撞融合的大熔炉。这些陆上交流的网络，两千多年来连接着东西方文明，从古都西安到地中海，途经现在的中国、俄罗斯、哈萨克斯坦、塔吉克斯坦、吉尔吉斯斯坦、乌兹别克斯坦、土库曼斯坦、阿富汗、伊朗、伊拉克、亚美尼亚、叙利亚、土耳其、希腊、埃及等国家。

伊朗和中国

众所周知，汉代军事战备的需要，是东西

from the Indus valley. The route began at the foot of the Karakorum, in the hilly areas of Punjab and Swat, and continued along the Indus, through Gilgit, Hunza valley, up to 5000meters of the Mintaka pass, before descending to Kashgar in Chinese Turkestan. Arteries are less developed in every direction: some paths from Chilas went up to Passu and Mintaka, others along the Satpara valley and Kapunlu, others reached Ladakh, the Punjal valley and Yasin, linking Gilgit with Chitral. In these arteries much more ancient are the traces of the human passage. Depictions carved in rock, calligraphy, inscriptions, in a historical sequence and in various styles and art forms, recall the history of different peoples and their cultures have developed over a period of about five thousand years. In the northern territory, the most important archaeological stations begin with Chilas, where there are numerous representations dating back to the Achaemenid (6th century BC), the Parthian (2nd century BC) and the period of the culture of Gandhara (2nd century AD), without forget, however, that there are significant examples of Bronze Age petroglyphs. Artistic styles change up to evolve into more sophisticated forms of Gandhara areas and those of the depictions of stupas and Buddhist deities. These pathways, in addition to trade, constitute, as you can imagine, a backgrounds of crossroads of cultures, religions and languages, a "melting pot", where very different cultural experiences met and mingled. They have provided an extraordinary network of contacts originally terrestrial, which for over 2000 years have been a link between the eastern and western civilizations, from the ancient city of Xi'an, to the Mediterranean, through China, Russia, Kazakhstan, Tadžikistan, Kyrgystan, Uzbekistan, Turkmenistan, Afghanistan, Iran, Iraq, Armenia, Syria, Turkey, Greece, Egypt, etc.

Iran and China

It is commonly known that one of the reasons for the development of trade routes between China and the West, is traced back to the new military demands of the

方之间丝绸之路发展的重要原因之一。新商路的开辟使得人们可以安全地到达更远的地方；西方的商人得以出口典型的西方产品，如马、骆驼、兽皮、皮草、西瓜、核桃、芝麻、无花果、苜蓿、石榴，甚至还有酿制葡萄酒的方法，而东方的商人则可以出口重要的奢侈品原料，如象牙，以及塔里木盆地山脉中蕴藏的丰富玉石矿，当然还有相当珍贵的丝绸。

这种具有超前性的世界市场在很短的时间内便促进了沿线地区的普遍繁荣，也无疑促进了新商路沿途地区商品交易税收的有益平衡。在第一位中国人到达费尔干纳之后，更多的使者被遣往西方，其中一批时代在公元前115年至公元前105年，相当于伊朗的帕提亚时代。有关这一事件的某些记述也许有夸张的成分，但两国间的互遣使节由此而始，成为当时中国与波斯之间建立新兴商贸关系的基础。

公元1世纪末，由印度—斯基泰人和希腊人组成的贵霜王国崛起并开始控制中亚。有人认为贵霜人就是亚历山大大帝东征遗留在印度的军队的后裔。尽管时间不长，但作为新兴政治力量的贵霜还是有效控制了塔克拉玛干盆地以西绿洲、印度河谷、中亚以及咸海等地的商贸道路。由此，四大政治军事力量，中国、贵霜、波斯和罗马开始争夺丝绸之路上的霸主地位。几个世纪前令中国人恐惧的游牧式袭击及其他军事手段，给伊朗世界带来相同的灾难，然后直奔罗马。应对这些新战术所生产的武器也具有新的功能要求：箭头、铠甲、各色马具、弓，甚至是金属马镫。杜拉·欧罗普斯（Doura

Han Dynasty. The opening of new trade routes offered the chance to ride safely on roads never traveled so far; merchants from the west were able to export typical western products, such as horses, cattle, hides, furs, watermelon, walnut, sesame, figs, alfalfa, pomegranate and, perhaps, also the method of making wine, while those from east had the ability to export important luxury goods, such as ivory and jade from the rich deposits contained in the mountains of the Tarim Basin and, of course, silk, which became a very precious material.

This kind of global market *ante litteram* determined in a short time, a widespread prosperity in all the regional involved areas, promoting undoubtedly positive balance of new taxes imposed on new caravans of goods crossing the vast territories of the area. After the first Chinese travel in Fergana, there were many other ambassadors sent to the west, one of which is chronologically located between the 115 and 105 BC, possibly, during the Parthian Iran. All this could have led to a mutual exchange of ambassadors and this event, maybe legendarily magnified, can only emphasize the fact that they were, at that time, the basis for new established commercial relations between China and Persia.

At the end of the 1st century AD, a new power, formed by the Indo-Scythians and Greeks, descendants, according to some, of the Alexander the Great's army in India, began to practice forms of political control over Central Asia, the Kushans. Become a new political force on the *Silk Routes* to the western oases of the Taklamakan basin, in the Indus basin, Central Asia and the Aral Sea, the Kushans took, albeit for a short time, the role of new lords in controlling these important commercial roads. With their arrival on the new commercial artery, four political/military powers become to contend a sort of supremacy, the Chinese, the Kushan, the Persian and Roman. The raids and other techniques of military nomad assaults who had already scared the Chinese centuries ago, will lead to the same apprehensions in the Iranian world, first and Roman later. The objects that are beginning to be produced in order to adapt them to these new military tactics have the effect

Europos）的涂鸦，蒙古和中国的图像遗存以及萨珊波斯的石刻等，无不在展示着新的军用装备的划时代意义，从铠甲到束带都是典型的 *catafractarii*[1] 传统，并开启了之后中世纪锁子甲的发展。

当然现实情况远为复杂，以上插曲仅向人们展示了物质交换和文化交流的必要性。另一方面，在罗马人多次被帕提亚人击败后，后者成为了新的统治者，得以完全控制丝绸之路。公元3世纪初，本土的萨珊王朝控制了波斯西南部的法尔斯省。224年，首位萨珊国王阿达希尔（Ardashir, 211–241）击败帕提亚人，控制了波斯全境。在其子沙普尔（Shapur, 241–272）的辅助下，开启了一个政治、经济、文化的新时代。由此萨珊时期的丝绸之路格外繁荣，而新王朝严格控制丝路贸易并开始征收重税，使沿途各国得以分享利益。

在东方，萨珊王朝控制着撒马尔罕地区，纺织技术不再为汉朝垄断，当地的粟特人发展了丝织业。这些产品有少部分抵达欧洲，而另一些则出现在塔里木盆地的佛教洞窟中。它们的设计与风格影响了后来中国、拜占庭和伊斯兰

of novel functional requirements: arrowheads, armor, items of horse harnesses, bow, and, finally, even the metal stirrups. From the graffiti in Doura Europos, those in Mongolia and China, the Sasanian rock sculptures, one can see how the new military clothing, from armor and strip, typical heritage of the *catafractarii*[1], and the anticipation of later medieval vintage chainmail is obsessively played on various media iconography, just to show the sign of a great epoch-making change.

The reality was, of course, more complex, and the episode shows us how the contacts and the exchanges were, by now acquired, a necessity. On the other hand after the repeated defeats of the Romans suffered by the Parthians, these last ones became the new lords able to exercise full control over the *Silk Routes*. At the beginning of the 3rd century AD, the province of Fars in the south-western Persia fell under the political control of the local dynasty of the Sasanians. From 224 AD, the first Sasanian king Ardashir (211–241 AD) defeated the Parthians and exercised, in turn, control over all Persia. With the help of his son Shapur (241–272 AD), Ardashir started a new political, institutional and cultural era. In this way along the *Silk Routes* flourished particularly during the Sasanian period, and the strict control exercised by the new dynasty on trade from which they passed, the Sasanians produced the imposition of new considerable taxes, which favored a redistribution of welfare which enjoyed all the involved countries.

To the east, the Sasanians shared the role of controllers over the Sogdians of the Samarkand region, developing industrial activities related to the silk production, because,

---

[1] *Catafractarii* 是罗马帝国时代的重装甲骑兵。模仿帕提亚的铁甲骑兵，他们从脖子到脚趾都被鳞片形铠甲（*lorica squamata*）覆盖，通常双手执一种长矛（*contus*），有时也持弓。此外他们还会佩剑。在一些情况下，他们的战马同样也会披着同样的鳞片形铠甲。罗马军队中重装甲骑兵的出现，是为了与东部边境的帕提亚和潘诺尼亚的萨尔马提亚铁甲骑兵相抗衡。
The *catafractarii* were the heavily-armored cavalry of the Imperial Roman army. Modeled on the cataphracts of Parthia, they were covered from neck-to-toe by lamellar (scale) armor (*lorica squamata*), and normally armed with a *contus* a long lance held in both hands, although sometimes they carried bows instead. In addition, they were armed with swords. In some cases, their horses were covered in scale armor also. Cataphract cavalry was developed by the Roman army to counter Parthian formations of this kind on the eastern frontier and Sarmatian cataphracts in Pannonia.

的纺织艺术。

除了丝绸，欧亚大陆上其他不同种类物资的交换与传播也展示了新商路日益增加的重要性。丝绸之路沿线广泛交易的产品有银器、玻璃器[1]以及"萨珊"风格的带具，这些物品使得萨珊世界成为当时东西方文化交流最好的展示地。它们不仅刺激了新风格与新设计的出现，同时对各国间的商贸与外交关系，乃至军队装备——即骑士装的发展来说都意义重大。这些产品与广袤且多元的曾被称为外伊朗的区域有关，跟这一称呼相比，"欧亚草原"要简略且局限得多。正如我们今天说中国以外一样，这种阐述并不奇怪。目前我们了解到的装饰有狩猎或宴饮场景以及用不同工艺制成的银器，都表现出萨珊时期的特有风格。

大部分发现于中亚，包括粟特地区甚至远东的器物，都普遍被认为是萨珊王朝官方外交活动所赠予的礼品。目前这些器物的原始功用与目的尚不明确，然而它们无疑传播了萨珊艺术风格的主题和图像，并刺激了众多的地方仿制品和创新品的出现，如粟特、花刺子模或是希腊—巴克特里亚王国和远东地区等。萨珊岩刻中描绘的带具，则直接反映了草原骑马民族的影响，它们的广泛使用在一定程度上展示了4—6世纪军事战术与战略发生的重大变化。

in the meantime, the weaving techniques were no longer protected by the Han Dynasty. Very few examples of silk products made their way to Europe, while others have been discovered in the Buddhist caves in the Tarim Basin. Their design and style influenced the designs of later Chinese, Byzantine and Muslim fabric.

In addition to the sources, the increasing importance gained by new trade routes is indicated by the presence and spread throughout Eurasia of particular classes of materials. These products widely traded along the *Silk Routes* were the silver plates, glass vessels[1] and belt fittings of "Sasanian" type, and which evoke, in a way, the Sasanian world, perfects indicators of the cultural interaction between East and West. These classes of materials are both significant for new styles and iconography, and trade and diplomatic relationships, on one hand, and military costume — chivalrous, on the other. These productions are related to the vast and diverse world, once called outside Iran, since the concept of the Eurasian steppe was perhaps a simplistic and limiting meaning. It would not be absurd today, according to the logic to speak about an outside China as well. It is known how the production of plates and silverware decorated with hunting scenes, or investiture banquet and manufactured according to different techniques, has been considered peculiarly characteristic of the Sasanian period.

Most of these objects, found in Central Asia, including Sogdiana, and even in the Far East, have been widely regarded as a gift offered by the Sasanian dynasty in official and diplomatic missions; of these objects remains uncertain at the moment, the original function and purpose. No doubt they have helped to widespread themes and iconography of a stylistic repertoire, inspiring a number of local productions, among them especially those of Sogdiana, Chorasmia or the Greek-Bactrian kingdom and the Far East. The belt fittings, instead, refer to functional

---

[1] 这些风格突出、设计雕刻精美的容器由厚的透明玻璃制成，远到日本都有发现。

These are the characteristic containers made from thick clear glass, with elaborate carved designs found up to far Japan.

如果说草原文化所带来的社会经济影响导致了技术的实质性变革，那么骑士装备以及相应马具的变化，则只是接下来马背战争一系列新技术与新功能发展的开端。作为最常见的物质遗存，带具是骑士阶层典型的身份标志。此外，由于制作技术、装饰以及风格的不同，人们还可以利用它们来重建当时的历史文化背景，并据此寻找社会等级划分的蛛丝马迹。然而尽管目前已经发现了数量庞大的墓葬和随葬品，但却很少能依据墓葬遗存所提供的身份、地位、财富等信息来进行复原古代社会的研究。一般认为，草原艺术所反映出的亚洲最后部落迁移的时代已经结束，但目前的研究似乎并不支持这一说法。"大迁徙"时代不断增长的多民族、多文化复杂性并不直接继承于前代。如果将草原艺术归为游牧—畜牧背景下的创造，那么我们就应当认识到那些大量发现于公元500年至1000年之间，跟匈奴、阿瓦尔、哈扎尔等民族相关的器物，其实都属于相同的产品系统（Genito 2002a; 2002b）。尽管以最简单、最基础的形式表达，并且逐渐摘掉"大迁徙时期游牧艺术"的标签，这个产品系统却创造并发展了一系列其他装饰形式，如几何蔓纹装饰等相关体系。与先前的器物相比，它具有更强的民族意味，但却又是前者最终的艺术表现形式。由此看来，认为这些产品是当时定居区域（拜占庭、波斯、中国等）工匠制作的观点有待商榷，而且只有最为广袤、最为强大和最为持久的帝国文明，才有可能对中世纪游牧艺术

and symbolic aspects directly related to the world of the horsemen of the steppes, whose echo was already present in the representations of the Sasanian rock reliefs. Their wide use does not reflect but, on a small scale, the metamorphosis took place in tactics and military strategies between the 4th and 6th centuries and which is attributable to the very cultural contribution of the nomads of the steppes.

If the socio-economic changes brought by the cultures of the steppes had led to a substantial adaptation of these techniques, are now just the knights, with their clothes and all the elements related to the horse' harness, to be harbingers of the new features, both technical and functional, a new way of being and fight on horseback. As is known, the belt-fittings, between the most common material remains, characterize the typical trousseau of the knight of rank and beyond; based on their technical productive aspects, decoration and style, it is possible to make reconstructions of the cultural and historical grounds of the period, also trying to find some sort of social hierarchy. There are few, however, those studies of mortuary analysis that can, on the basis of the indices of status, rarity and wealth etc., try to reconstruct the society of those communities, whose grave goods were found in abundance in numerous tombs. With the migration of the last Asian tribes the period of reference of the Steppe Art, recognized, now, as an appendage chronologically extreme, and certainly much less expressive, is traditionally considered to have finished. The multi-ethnic and multi-cultural growing complexity of this period, defined not by chance *Migration Period*, does not, however, to see a direct continuation of the previous eras. If to the category of art of the steppes is attributed the sense and the expressive value of a production of a nomadic — pastoral background, one can and must recognize that the enormous amount of objects found between the middle and the end of the millennium AD, and attributed to different peoples like the Huns, the Avars, the Khazars, can only belong to the same sphere of pre-existing production figurative (Genito 2002a; 2002b).

具备如此高还原度的理解。在中世纪早期，定居文化与游牧文化依然有着密切的互动与交流。这套产品系统的装饰风格，并没有失去前代的艺术气质与活力，其中心依然流行动物纹，只是增添了新的几何纹样。近年来专家们对草原风格图像文化的研究有了新进展。他们的研究一方面有效遏制了"民族主义"的解释趋势，即将一种物质文化和装饰风格与特定的族群联系，但同时却忽视了游牧艺术风格的周边产品与其他中心文化间的二元解读，认为存在独立的工匠技术集团，没有考虑到其他文化的特有贡献。同前代文化一样，中世纪早期草原民族的物质文化还有待进一步研究与解释。这一时期的新产品蕴含着许多前所未有的图像学意义，为了更好地理解它们，就需要了解近几十年来各个学者所作出的不懈努力，无论是风格细节分析还是更为综合的研究。

结论与视角

在广阔的西部地区，尤其是那些地理特征主要以草原为主的区域，如中国新疆地区，仍然是考古学的处女地，无论对中国学者还是外国学者都是如此。可能会在不久的将来，在不同的国际合作框架之下，中国社会科学院考古研究所、中国国家博物馆、西北大学、吉林大学、南京大学等单位将在新疆开展新的考古活动，这些探索性的考古活动将与欧亚大陆尤其是丝绸之路中国段密切相关。在国际合作的大前提下，在新疆进行考古工作的前景充满希望，而且

Perhaps reductively labeled as *Nomadic Art of the Age of Migration*, even if expressed through the basic forms, but much more simplified than the last, this production creates and develops, however, a number of new coherent systems of decoration defined by others, such as geometric tendril ornamentation. This production, which is recognizable as stronger ethnic connotation than the previous one, is, in a sense, the ultimate stylistic outcome of the first. The idea that such objects have been achieved, as well as has been claimed, at the artisan workshops of contemporary sedentary (Byzantines, Persians, Chinese, etc.), does not appear, in this sense, very convincing, and only the largest and most apparent state-imperial consistency of those peoples may have contributed to have such a reductive perception of the artistic nomadic production of Middle Ages. The phenomena of interaction between the sedentary and nomadic cultures continue with the same intensity along the Early Middle Ages, although their nature is now radically different from the previous. The figurative expression, with at the center still prevalent the animal representation, but enriched with new decorative trends of geometric type, did not lose the elegance and the dynamism of the first. Specialist studies have contributed in recent years to shed light on new aspects of the figurative culture once again "steppic" in character. Their contribution, prevented the development of that "nationalistic" interpretative trend aimed at identifying a material culture and decorative items with a particular group of people on one hand; it has, at the same time indicated autonomous schools and technical trends of production, which escape the duality of interpretation between an artistic nomadic peripheral production and another central, with which one risks to set zero one or another of the several specific contributions on the other. The material culture of the peoples of the steppes of the early Middle Ages is still waiting to be inserted into interpretive categories, similar to what happened with the earlier period. The new products of this era bring many unexpected and figurative meanings; to better understand

会变得更加频繁。

这类考古调查的主要动机源自对由沙漠、荒漠、草原和山脉构成的独特的地理环境的关注。这些新的学术活动将进一步支持和推动自公元前一千纪以来有关新疆的研究传统，同时追寻着公元一千纪以来欧亚草原游牧民族的足迹。众所周知，这些活动在天山及其东西地区的人群的主要特征是游牧，他们不曾留下永久性的居住遗址，但随葬品中金银器等器物上流行雕刻动物形象，也就是所谓动物纹传统，包括鹿、豹、虎、狮、羊，这些东西存在着区域性特征，作为交流媒介，也许便是这些文化中能对其他文化产生影响的诸多领域中最有趣的一个方面，并因情感跟品位的不同而变化着。

them needs to be collected the considerable efforts made in recent decades by various scholars and propose, from time to time, stylistic detailed and more general analyses.

Conclusions and Perspectives

The vast western regions, especially where is predominantly the steppe character, and in particular Xinjiang is still a virgin land for archaeology, both for Chinese and international scholars. It is possible that in the near future, new archaeological activities in Xinijang with the Department of Archaeology and Museology of PkU, the Institute of Archaeology of the Chinese Academy of Social Sciences, the National Museum, the North-west University in Xi'an, Jilin University, the University of Nanjing, the Institute of cultural Relics of Urumchi etc. in the frame of different international cooperation will be opened. The pioneer activities will be those related to the Eurasian and especially the Chinese section of the Silk Routes. The future of archaeology in Xinjiang seems promising in the framework of the international co-operations with increasing frequency.

The very reason of this archaeological investigation lies in a very unique environmental landscape, made up of deserts, grasslands, steppes and mountains. These new research activities opportunities will help and develop very much the tradition of studies in Xinijang related to the first millennium BC, tracing the path of the nomadic peoples of the Eurasian steppes and to the first millennium AD. As is known, the main characteristic of these populations which inhabited the space between the T'jan' Šan mountains to the west, east China, is the pastoral nomadism. This cultural feature left no traces in permanent settlements, but above all, in the funerary objects. They include wooden decorations in gold or silver or other finely carved with zoomorphic representations typical of the traditional "Animal Style", including deer, leopards, tigers, lions, goats, made in its regional variants of the area, perhaps one of the most interesting aspects of these cultures able to act as a catalyst for many other cultures, recasting them according to moods and tastes.

Sources

Florus: Epitome of Roman History (1929) Text and Translation on Lacus Curtius by E. S. Forster, *Loeb Classical Library* edition Oxford.

Dionysius Periegetes (2005) *Descrizione della Terra abitata*, Bompiani,Torino.

Han shu, Ban Gu (ed) (1962) *Zhonghuashuju*, Beijing.

Han shu, Hulsewe, A.F.P. (1979) *China in Central Asia: the Early Stage: 125 B.C.–A.D. 23. An annotated translation of chapters 61 and 96 of the History of the Former Han Dynasty, with an introduction by M.A.N. Loewe*, 273. Leiden: Brill.

Hou Han shu, Fan Ye (ed) (1965) *Zhonghuashuju*, Beijing.

Hou Han shu: Chavannes, E. (ed) (1907) Les Pays d'Occident d'apres le Heou Han chou, *T'oung Pao*, series II, vol. VIII, 149–234, and Chinese text.

Ibn Battuta (2006) *I viaggi*, Einaudi.

Pliny, *Natural History*, Eichholz, E. (ed, trans. and comm.) (1962), *Natural History*, libri XXXVI–XXXVII, vol.X, 344. Cambridge (Mass.). Harvard University Press.

Memoires (1967) *Les memoires historiques de Se-ma Tsien* traduits et annotés par Edouard Chavannes. Paris, A. Maisonneuve.

Polo, M. (1954, 13-esima edizione 1981) *Il Libro di Marco Polo detto Milione* (nella versione trecentesca dell "ottimo", a cura di Daniele Ponchiroli. Torino.

Priscus, Blockley, R.C. (ed, trans.) (1983) *The Fragmentary Classicising Historians of the Later Roman Empire. Eunapius, Olympiodorus, Priscus and Malchus II: Text, Translations and Historiographical Notes*, (ARCA, 10), 222–400. Liverpool: Francis Cairns.

Procopius, Dewing, H.B. (ed, trans.) (1914) *The History of the Wars*, I, 583. Cambridge (Mass.): Harvard University Press.

Ptolemy, (1971) *Geography*: Ronca, I. (ed, and trans.), Ptolemaios, *Geographie 6,9–21. Ostiran und Zentralasien, Teil I*, (IsMEO, Reports and Memoirs, XV,1, IsMEO, 118,Rome.

Records (1961) *Records of the Grand Historian of China* (trad. Burton Watson). New York, Columbia University Press.

Strabo (1969) *Géographie*: Aujac, G. (trans.), Livre II, 197. Paris: Les Belles Lettres.

XuangZang, Bianji (1985) *Da Tang Xi Yu Ji Jiao zhu*, Ji Xian lin (recensed). Beijing.

References

Abdullaev, K., Genito, B. (2010–2011) Arheologičeskie raboty na Koj tepa (Past dargomskij rajon, Samarkandskoj oblasti, ijun.ijul' 2011) *Arheologičeskie Issledovanija Uzbekistane*, 8, 9–22. Samarkand.

Abdullaev, K., Genito, B. (2011) *Trial Trenches at Kojtepa, Samarkand Area (Sogdiana)(Third Interim Report 2011)*, with contributions by Davide Lunelli, Fabiana Raiano, *Newsletter di Archeologia CISA*–2, 7–72, http://www.unior.it/index2. php?contentid=6572&content_id_start=1

Abdullaev, K., Genito, B. (2012) *Trial Trenches at Kojtepa, Samarkand Area (Sogdiana)(Fourth Interim Report 2012)*, with contributions by Davide Lunelli, Fabiana Raiano, Li Yusheng and Francesco Franzese, *Newsletter*

di Archeologia CISA–3, 9–85 http://www.unior.it/userfiles/workarea_231/file/NewsletterArcheologia%20
numero%203/1_%20Abdullaev-Genito.pdf.

Abdullaev, K., Genito, B. (eds) (2014) *The Archaeological Project in the Samarkand Area (Sogdiana): Excavations At Kojtepa (2008–2012)*. Napoli.

Balint, C. (ed) (2000) *Kontakte zwischen Byzanz, Iran und der Steppe, Varia Archaeologica*, X, Budapest-Rome-Naples.

Betts, A.V.G. and Kidd, F. (hrgs.) (2010) Preface, *Archäologische Mitteilungen aus Iran und Turan*, band 42, *New Directions in Silk Road Archaeology, Proceedings of a Workshop*, held at *ICAANE V*, 2006, 1. Madrid.

Casanova, M. (1994) Lapis Lazuli beads in Susa and Central Asia: a preliminary study, Parpola, A., Koskikallio, P. (ed) *South Asian Archaeology 1993,Annales Academiae Scientiarum Fennicae*, series B 271, 137–146. Helsinki.

Casanova, M. (2000) Le lapis-lazuli d'Asie Centrale a la Syrie au Chalcolithique et à l'Age du Bronze, Matthiae, P., Enea, A., Peyronel, L. (eds) *Proceedings of the First International Congress on the Archaeology of the Ancient Near East*, May 18th–23rd, 1998, 171–183. Rome.

Caterina, L., Genito, B. (a cura di) (2012) *Archeologia delle "Vie della Seta": Percorsi, Immagini e Cultura Materiale*, I ° Ciclo di Conferenze, 14 Marzo–16 maggio 2012, edizione online nel settore *Conferenze e Contributi* all'interno del sito del CISA,

http://www.unior.it/cisa/pubblicazioni/viedellaseta/ICiclo/ViedellaSetaI.htmlNapoli.

Caterina, L., Genito, B. (a cura di) (2013) *Archeologia delle "Vie della Seta": Percorsi, Immagini e Cultura Materiale*, II ° Ciclo di Conferenze, 7 Marzo–22 maggio 2013, edizione online nel settore *Conferenze e Contributi* all'interno del sito del CISA.

http://www.unior.it/cisa/pubblicazioni/viedellaseta/IICiclo/ViedellaSetaII.htmlNapoli.

Caterina, L., Genito, B. (a cura di) (2015) *Archeologia delle "Vie della Seta": Percorsi, Immagini e Cultura Materiale*, III ° Ciclo di Conferenze, 12 Marzo–14 maggio 2014, edizione online nel settore *Conferenze e Contributi* all' interno del sito del CISA.

http://www.unior.it/cisa/pubblicazioni/viedellaseta/IIICiclo/ViedellaSetaIII.htmlNapoli.

Caterina, L., Genito, B. (a cura di) (2016) *Archeologia delle "Vie della Seta": Percorsi, Immagini e Cultura Materiale,* IV ° Ciclo di Conferenze, 12 Marzo–14 maggio 2014, edizione online nel settore *Conferenze e Contributi* all' interno del sito del CISA.

Cocca, E. (2014) Kojtepa 2013: The Use of 3D for the Drawings of Excavation: A Methodological Approach, *Newsletter di Archeologia*, CISA—Volume, 5,1–20, http://www.unior.it/ateneo/11491/1/volume–5–anno–2014. html.

Genito, B. (1986) The Italian Archaeological Activity in Hungary (1985/86), *Is.M.E.O. Activities, East & West*, 36, 4, 367–375. Rome.

Genito, B. (1988) The Archaeological Cultures of the Sarmatians with a Preliminary Note on the Trial-Trenches at Gyoma 133: a Sarmatian Settlement in South-Eastern Hungary (Campaign 1985), *Annali dell'Istituto Universitario Orientale di Napoli*, Vol. 48, 2, 81–126. Napoli.

Genito, B. (1990) The Late Bronze Age Vessels from Gyoma 133, S.E. Hungary, The Stratigraphical Evidence, *Communicationes Archaeologicae Hungariae*, 113–119. Budapest.

Genito, B. (1992) The Endröd 19 Project, the 1988 Season, *Cultural and Landscape Changes in South-East Hungary, Archaeolingua*, I, 336–368. Budapest.

Genito, B. (1993a) Trial-Trenches at Gyoma 133: a Sarmatian Settlement in South-East Hungary: a Second Interim Report (The 1986–1987 Campaigns), *Annali dell'Istituto Universitario Orientale di Napoli*, 53, 1, 35–53. Napoli.

Genito, B. (1993b) Some Evidences from Iran: On the Iranian and Central-Asiatic Connections with East Europe, *Acta Archaeologica*, 45, 153–158. Budapest.

Genito, B. (1995) The Asiatic Nomad Peoples into Carpathian Basin: A Western Backwater of the Eurasian Steppes between the 1st Mill.B.C. and the 1st Mill. A.D, Seaman, G. & Marks, D. (eds), *Foundations of Empire, Archaeology and Art of the Eurasian Steppes, Vol. III, Proceedings of the Soviet-American Academic Symposium in Conjunction with the Museum Exhibition, Nomads: Masters of the Eurasian Steppe*, Los Angeles, February 3–5 1989–Denver, June 8–11, 1989, Washington, D.C., November 16–17, 1989, 105–110. Los Angeles.

Genito, B. (a cura di) (2002) *Pastori erranti dell'Asia, popoli storia e archeologia nelle steppe dei Kirghisi*, Museo Nazionale Archeologico *(3 maggio–31–agosto)*. Napoli.

Genito, B. (2002a) Archeologia, popoli e storia delle steppe: tra l'Iran e la Cina, Genito, B. (a cura di) *Pastori erranti dell'Asia, popoli storia e archeologia nelle steppe dei Kirghisi*, 83–92, Museo Naz. Arch. *(3 maggio–31–agosto)*. Napoli.

Genito, B. (2002b) Premessa alla Mostra, Genito, B. (a cura di) *Pastori erranti dell'Asia, popoli storia e archeologia nelle steppe dei Kirghisi*, 19–24, Museo Nazionale Archeologico (3 maggio–31–agosto). Napoli.

Genito, B. (2008) The Archaeology of the Steppes: the Excavations at Endröd 19 (S E Hungary) a Particular Viewpoint, *Acta Archaeologica Academiae Scientiarum Hungaricae*, 59, 353–372. Budapest.

Genito, B. (2010) *The Western Scythian Identity: a Territorial and Archaeological "Puzzle"* International Conference, *Iranian Identities in the course of History*, 119–144. Roma.

Genito, B. (2012) Vie della Seta, tra Iran, Asia Centrale e Cina Occidentale. Una lettura Archeologica per una Categoria Storiografica, Caterina, L., Genito, B. (eds) I ° Ciclo di Conferenze: *Archeologia delle Vie della Seta, Percorsi, Immagini e Cultura Materiale*. Napoli. http://www.unior.it/cisa/pubblicazioni/viedellaseta/ICiclo/ Viedella Setal.html   P=14.

Genito, B. (ed) (1994) *The Archaeology of the Steppes: Work Methods and Strategies, Proceedings of the International Symposium*, held in Naples, November 1992. Naples.

Genito, B. *et alii* (2014) Trial-Trenches at Kojtepa, Samarkand Area (Sogdiana). Fifth Interim Report, *Newsletter di Archeologia,* CISA — Volume 5, 197–317, http://www.unior.it/ateneo/11491/1/volume–5–anno–2014. html

Genito, B., Moškova M.G. (1995) (eds) *Burial Customs of Early Nomads of the Eurasian Steppes, I. Statistical Analyses of Burial Customs of the Sauromatians 6th–4th Centuries B.C.* Napoli.

Genito, B., Madaras, L. (eds) (2005) *Archaeological Remains of a Steppe people in the Hungarian Great Plain: The Avarian Cemetery at Öcsöd 59. Final Reports.* Naples.

Genito, B., Gricina, A.(2009) The Achaemenid Period in the Samarkand Area (Sogdiana): with contributions by Luciano Rendina, Maria D'Angelo, *Newsletter Archeologia (CISA)*, 0, 122–141, Naples. http://www.unior.it/userfiles/workarea231/file/Articoli/Genito,%20Gricina%20et%20alii,%20UZB%20122–141. pdf.

Genito, B., Gricina, A.(2010) The Achaemenid Period in the Samarkand Area (Sogdiana): Trial Trenches at Kojtepa 2009 Campaign, with contributions by Luciano Rendina, Maria D'Angelo, *Newsletter di Archeologia CISA*–1,

113–161, Naples, http://www.unior.it/index2. php?contentid=5429&content_id_start=1

Genito, B., Raiano, F.(2011) *Ceramics from KojTepa (Samarkand Area-Uzbekistan): A Preliminary Study Report (2009–10), assieme a F. Raiano, Newsletter di Archeologia CISA*–2, 103–177,http://www.unior.it/index2. php?contentid=6572&content_id_start=1.

Good, I. (2010) When East met West. Interpretative problems in assessing Eurasian contact and exchange in Antiquity, Betts, A.V.G. and Kidd, F. (hrsg.) *Archäologische Mitteilungen aus Iran und Turan*, band 42, *New Directions in Silk Road Archaeology, Proceedings of a Workshop*, held at *ICAANE V*, 2006, 23–46. Madrid.

Hedin, S.A.(1898a) *Durch Asien Wünsten. Von Stockholm nach Kaschgar* (1893–1895). r. Erdmann 2001.

Hedin, S. (1898b) *Durch Asien Wünsten. Von Kaschgar nach Peking* (1895–1897). r. Erdmann 2001.

Hedin, S.A (1903) *In Asia*, 1927–1928 explorations, with addition in the English ed. of chapter "Lop-Nor, the Wandering Lake" 360–392, and a note from July 1931 on further Lop Nor exploration in early 1931. Mentions a film by Paul Lieberenz, who accompanied the expedition: "With Sven Hedin Across the Deserts of Asia".

Hedin, S.A. (1937) *Den vandranesjön.* Stockholm. Bonniers.

Hedin, S.A. (1940) *The Wandering Lake.* New York: E.P. Dutton, (Tr. by F.H. Lyon from Swedish).

Hedin, S.A. (1942) (German ed) *Der wandernde See.* 9. Aufl. Leipzig. Brockhaus.

Hedin, S.A. (1943) *History of the Expedition in Asia 1927–1935.* 4 v. Stockholm, 1943. Parts 1–3 written in collaboration with Folke Bergman: I. 1927–1928; II. 1928–1933; III. 1933–1935. IV. General Reports of Travels and Fieldwork, by Folke Bergman, Gerhard Bexell, BirgerBohlin, GöstaMontell. (=*Reports from the Scientific Expedition to the North-Western Provinces of China under the Leadership of Dr. Sven Hedin—The Sino-Swedish Expedition. Publications* 23–26).

Hedin, S.A. (1954) *Mot Lop–Nor. En flodf ärdpå Tarim.* Stockholm: Bonniers.

Hedin, S.A. (1955) Xu Yunshu (trans.) *Luobuzhuoer Kao Cha Ji* (*The expedition of Lop–Nor*).Taipei.

Herrmann, G. (1968) Lapis Lazuli. The early phases of its trade, *Iraq*, 30, l, 21–57, pl. 13–16.

Herrmann, G., Moorey, P.R.S (1983) Lapis Lazuli, Edzard, B.D.O. (ed) *Reallexikon der Assyriologie und Vorderasiatischen Archäologie*, 489–492, 6, München.

Huang Wenbi (1934) *Collection of pottery in Gaochang*, Published by Chinese — Swedish Scientific Mission to North-Western China, Beiping (Beijing).

Huang Wenbi (1948) *The Archaeological Record of Lop Nur*, Published by Institute of History of the National Academy of Peiping and Chinese Scientific Mission to North-Western China, Peiping (Beijing).

Huang Wenbi (1951) *Collection of Bricks in Gaochang* (revised and enlarged book), Published by Chinese Academy of Sciences, Beijing.

Huang Wenbi (1954) *The Archaeological Record of Turfan*, Published by Chinese Academy of Sciences, Beijing.

Huang Wenbi (1958) *The Archaeological Record of Tarim Basin*, Sciences Press, Beijing.

Huang Wenbi (1981) *Studies on History and Geography of North-Western China*, Shanghai People's Publishing House, Bejing.

Huang Wenbi (1983a) *An archaeological tour of Xinjiang* (*1957–1958*) Cultural Relics Publishing House, Beijing.

Huang Wenbi (1983b) *The Historical and Archaeological Memoir of Huang Wenbi. The 30 Years' Archaeological Research in Xinjiang.* Urumqï.

Huang Wenbi (1990) *Investigation Diary in Inner-Mongolia and Xinjiang by Huang Wenbi,* Cultural relics publishing house, Beijing.

Keay, J. (2007) *La Via delle Spezie*. Milano.

Le Coq, Von, A. (1912) *Türkische Manichaica aus Chotscho*, I, *Phil.-hist. Klasse. 1911. Anhang. Abh. VI.* Vorgelegt von Hrn. Müller in der Sitzung der phil.-hist. Klasseam 19. Oktober 1911, Zum Druck verordnet am gleichen Tage, ausgegeben am 25, April 1912, 393–451.

Le Coq, Von, A. (1922) *Die buddhistische Spätantike in Mittelasien — Die Plastik*. Berlin.

Linnaeus, C. (1758) *Tomus I. Systema naturae per regna tria naturae, secundum classes, ordines, genera, species, cum characteribus, differentiis, synonymis, locis*. Editio decima, reformata. Holmiae. (Laurentii Salvii): [1–4], 1–824.

Miller, J. Innes (1974) *Roma e la Via delle Spezie*, Torino.

New Achievements (1995) *New Achievements in Archaeological Research in Xinijang during the Time Span (1979–1989)*, Compiled by Xinijang Institute of Archaeology Xinijang People's Publishing House.

New Achievements (1997) *New Achievements in Archaeological Research in Xinijang during the Time Span (1990–1996)*, Compiled by Xinijang Institute of Archaeology Xinijang People's Publishing House.

Prževalskij, N.M. (1870–1873) *Auf schleich wegen nach Tibet*. r. Erdmann 2001.

Raiano, F. (2012) Ceramics from Koj Tepa (Samarkand Area — Uzbekistan): Second Interim Report 2011 — *Newsletter Archeologia CISA, Volume 3, 2012*, 337–373. http://www.unior.it/userfiles/workarea231/file/ NewsletterArcheologia%20numero%203/7_Raiano_2012. pdf.

Raiano, F. (2013) Ceramics from Koj Tepa (Samarkand area — Uzbekistan): Third Interim Report (2012), *Newsletter di Archeologia*, CISA — Volume 4, 303–340, http://www.unior.it/ateneo/8917/1/volume–4–anno–2013. html.

Raiano, F. (2014) Hellenistic and post-Hellenistic Pottery from Kojtepa, *Newsletter di Archeologia*,CISA — Volume 5, 455–477, http://www.unior.it/ateneo/11491/1/volume–5–anno–2014. html.

Richthofen, Von, F. (1877) *China: Ergebnisse eigener Reisen und darauf begründeter Studien. Vol. I*, Berlin.

Richthofen, Von, F. (1883) *Aufgaben und Methoden der heutigen Geographie*, Leipzig.

Richthofen, Von, F. (1886) *Führer für Forschungsreisende*, Riemer, Berlin.

Richthofen, Von, F. (1903) *Letters by Baron von Richthofen 1870–1872*, second edition, Shanghai, North Herald China Office.

Richthofen, Von F. (1907) *Tagebücher aus China*, Vol. I, E. Tiessen (eds). Berlin.

Said, E.W. (1978) *Orientalism*. London.

Stein, Aurel M. (1907) *Ancient Khotan: Detailed Report of Archaeological Explorations in Chinese Turkestan*, 2 vols. Clarendon Press. Oxford.

Stein, Aurel M. (1912) *Ruins of Desert Cathay: Personal Narrative of Explorations in Central Asia and Westernmost China*, 2 vols. Reprint: Delhi. Low Price Publications. 1990.

Stein, Aurel M. (1921a) *Serindia: Detailed Report of Explorations in Central Asia and Westernmost China*, 5 vols. London & Oxford. Clarendon Press. Reprint: Delhi. MotilalBanarsidass. 1980.

Stein, Aurel M. (1921b) A Chinese Expedition across the Pamirs and Hindukush, A.D. 747, *Indian Antiquary*, 1923

Stein, Aurel M. (1925) Innermost Asia. Its Geography as a Factor in History, *Geographical Journal*, May-June, 1–55.

Stein, Aurel M. (1928) *Innermost Asia: Detailed Report of Explorations in Central Asia, Kan-su and Eastern Iran*, 5vols. Clarendon Press. Reprint: New Delhi. Cosmo Publications. 1981.

Stein, Aurel M. (1932) *On Ancient Central Asian Tracks: Brief Narrative of Three Expeditions in Innermost Asia and Northwestern China*. Reprinted with Introduction by Jeannette Mirsky. Book Faith India, Delhi. 1999.

Stein, Aurel M. (1921) *The Thousand Buddhas: ancient Buddhist paintings from the cave-temples of Tung-huang on the western frontier of China*.

Tosi, M. (1974) The lapis lazuli trade across the Iranian plateau in the 3rd millennium BC, Forte, A., Remaggi, L.P., Taddei, M. (ed) *Gururajamaiijarika. Studi in onore* di Giuseppe Tucci I., 3–22. Napoli.

VV. AA. (1999) *L'Uomo d'Oro- La Cultura delle steppe del Kazakhstan,dall'età del Bronzo all'epoca delle Grandi Migrazioni*, 10th April-10thJuly (Neapolitan edition), Rome.

VV. AA. (1999) *L'Uomo d'Oro*, Roma.

VV. AA. (2000) *Museo Nazionale di Teheran in Fotografia*. Naples.

Vignato, G., Saerji (2009a) *Indo Tibetica (Fantian Fodi)*. Beijing.

Vignato, G., Saerji (2009b) *Seeking the soul of Tibet (Tanxun Xizang de Xinling)*. Beijing.

Visconti, C. (2006) Architectural Decorations and Other Finds from the Excavations of the Fengxiansi Monastery in Longmen, *Supplemento n. 96 agli Annali (sez. Orientale)*, Vol.66.

Visconti, C. (2010) The Chinese-Italian Archaeological Mission to Longmen, *Newsletter di Archeologia, CISA*, Volume, 1, 163–176. Napoli.

Williams, T. (2013) *The Silk Roads: Thematic Study WORKING REPORT*, Institute of Archaeology UCL London.

Williams, T. (2014) *The Silk Roads*: an ICOMOS *Thematic Study* on the Behalf of ICOMOS. Charenton-le-Pont.

Yu, Taishan (1998) *A Study of Saka History, Sino-Platonic Papers*, Number 80, July,Mair,Victor H. (ed), *Department of East Asian Languages and Civilizations University of Pennsylvania Philadelphia*, PA 19104–6305 USA.

Yu, Taishan (2000) *A Hypothesis about the Source of the Sai Tribes, Sino-Platonic Papers*; Number 106, September, Mair, Victor H. (ed) *Department of Asian and Middle Eastern Studies, University of Pennsylvania, Philadelphia*, PA 19104–6305 USA.

Yu, Taishan (2004) *A Hypothesis on the Origin of the Yu State, Sino-Platonic Papers*, Number 139, June, Mair, Victor H. (ed) *Department of East Asian Languages and Civilizations University of Pennsylvania, Philadelphia*, PA 19104–6305 USA.

Yu, Taishan (2006) *A Study of the History of the Relationship Between the Western and Eastern Han, Wei, Jin, Northern and Southern Dynasties and the Western Regions, Sino-Platonic Papers*, Number 173, October, Mair, Victor H. (ed) *Department of East Asian Languages and Civilizations, University of Pennsylvania, Philadelphia*, PA 19104–6305 USA.

Yu, Taishan (2010) *The Earliest Tocharians in China, Sino-Platonic Papers*, Number 204 June, Mair, Victor H. (ed) *Department of East Asian Languages and Civilizations University of Pennsylvania, Philadelphia*, PA 19104–6305 USA.

Yu, Taishan (2011) *The Origin of the Kushans, Sino-Platonic Papers*, Number 212 July, Mair,Victor H. (ed) *Department of East Asian Languages and Civilizations, University of Pennsylvania, Philadelphia*, PA 19104–6305 USA.

Weggel, O. (1985) *Xinjiang/Xinkiang. Das zentralasiatische China. Eine Landeskunde*, Hamburg.

交流的价值——外来器物与中国文化
New Archaeological Discoveries along the Chinese Branches of the Silk Routes

齐东方（北京大学考古文博学院）撰，王倩 译

Qi Dongfang (PKU), trans. by Wang Qian

没有外来文化的参照，我们很难看清自身，了解不同文化之间的差异与共性，不同文化之间的借鉴乃至融合，古人为我们提供了经验、教训和方向。无论是古代还是现代，不同的文化享有许多共同的美、共同的人性。交流的价值在于影响人们的思想、行为，任何一个民族、国家，外来文化不仅是补充，还将激发出创造和发展的活力。

中国汉唐时期有很多外来文物，自身制造的一些器物中有些造型、纹样，原本也来自外来文化，最终融入了人们的生活之中。分辨它们的渊源流变，会发现交流使社会的物质文化不断推陈出新，精神资源也不断丰富发展，交流给人类社会进步带来了巨大影响。

从"溥天之下莫非王土"到"丝绸之路"

"溥天之下，莫非王土，率土之滨，莫非王臣"[1]，曾是中国早期的政治地理概念。中国东临浩瀚无际的太平洋，北接荒芜人烟的西伯利亚，西北是苍茫险峻的塔克拉玛干大沙漠，

It's difficult to get a clear knowledge of ourselveswithout taking in due account comparisons with foreign cultures. Our ancestors' experiences and teachings help us to understand diversities and similarities, borrowings and integrations between different cultures and to give us a sense of direction. Different cultures, no matter if ancient or modern, share an appreciation for beauty and for life. The value of exchange rests in the fact that it influences people's thinking and behaviors; for any people, another culture is not only complementary, but also stirs up creative and innovative energies.

Between the Han and Tang periods large quantities of foreign artifacts flooded into China, while artifacts produced in China present evident exotic forms and patterns: foreign influences became progressively assimilated into people's lives. If one tries to distinguish the origins and evolutions of these elements, he will find out how much exchanges affect society, constantly renovating material culture at the same time enriching and developing the spiritual culture, continually impacting the progress of the humanity.

From "All the land under Heaven belongs to the emperor" to the "Silk Road"

The concept of "All the land under heaven belongs to the king; all people are the king's servants" (*Shijing, Xiaoya, Beishan*) was an early Chinese geopolitical concept. China

---

[1]《毛诗注疏》卷一三《北山》，上海古籍出版社（上海），2013年，第1141页。

Maoheng *et alii* (2013), vol.13, Beishan (North mountain), 1141.

西南为耸入云端的喜马拉雅山。当人们无法跨越这些地理障碍时，这种自然环境带来的消极观念，影响和限制了人们对外部世界的了解。封闭的环境，使早期的政治地理概念，又被孔子（前551—前479）发挥为"天无二日，土无二王，家无二主，尊无二上"的大一统观。

公元前2世纪发生的"张骞通西域"事件[1]，动摇了这一传统观念。张骞（约前164—前114），历经千辛万苦的西方之行，直接原因是要联合大月氏攻打匈奴，然而却成为一次放眼看世界的突破，意外的收获是，使中国改变了过去把异态文明看作是自身敌人、采用一些极端的方式加以对付的做法，而是开始逐渐勾画沟通

faces the vast Pacific to the east; neighbors the desolate Siberia to the north; the boundless Taklimakan desert lies on its northwest and the soaring Himalayas Mountains mark its southwest. At the time when people could not overcome these geographic barriers, their acquaintance with the outside world was impacted and limited by a negative perceptions generated by the natural environment. This condition of closeness, an early geopolitical concept, was expounded as the principle of Great Unity by Confucius (551–479 BC) "Heaven cannot support two suns, nor earth two kings; a home cannot allow two masters, nor state two rulers".

Zhang Qian's Mission to the Western Regionsin the 2nd century BC undermined this traditional concept. Zhang Qian's (164–114 BC) expedition was originally a tentative to establish an alliance with the Darouzhi in the fight against the Huns, yet unexpectedly it became an epoch-making event that broadened China's view of the world. China

---

[1] 大月氏曾居住在敦煌、祁连间，被匈奴打败后迁到西域。汉朝强盛后为消除匈奴的威胁，想与大月氏建立联合。建元三年（前138）张骞"以郎应募，使月氏"。但出使中途即被匈奴截留10余年，逃离后西行到了大宛（今乌兹别克斯坦共和国境内）、康居（今哈萨克斯坦共和国东南）、大夏（阿姆河流域），找到了大月氏。这时臣服于大夏的大月氏，已无意东还与匈奴为敌。张骞逗留了1年多只好归国，途中又被匈奴拘禁1年多。公元前126年，乘匈奴内乱脱身回到长安。张骞出使时带着100多人，历经13年后，只剩下他和堂邑父两个人回来。张骞回来以后，向武帝报告了西域的地理、物产、风俗情况，为汉朝开辟通往中亚的交通提供了宝贵的信息。元狩四年（前119年），张骞第二次奉使西域，率领300人组成的使团，每人备两匹马，带牛羊万头，金帛货物价值"数千巨万"到了乌孙，游说乌孙王东返，没有成功。他分遣副使持节到了大宛、康居、月氏、大夏等国。元鼎二年（前115年）张骞归来，乌孙派使者几十人随同到了长安。此后，安息等国的使者也不断来长安访问和贸易。从此，汉与西域的交通建立起来了。

According to the source, the Yuezhi people once lived in an area between Dunhuang and Qilian, who migrated to Xiyu (Serindia) after defeated by Xiongnu. In order to eliminate the threat from Xiongnu, the Han dynasty intended to set up alignment with Yuezhi. Zhangqian was recruited as the envoy to Yuezhi area in 138 BC, yet was imprisoned on his way by Xiongnu for more than ten years. After escaping he went to Dawan (Fergana), Kangju (southeastern part of now Kazakhstan), Daxia (Bactria) and eventually found Yuezhi, who, at this moment, had no intention to withstand Xiongnu back to the east. After one-year-stay, Zhangqian had to return, who was imprisoned again on the way by Xiongnu for another year. When he escaped back to Chang'an in 126 BC, comparing with more than one hundred people setting off with him, there was only one attendant coming back with him after thirteen years. Zhangqian reported to Emperor Wudi about the basic situation of the western region, such as geography, products and customs, which provided precious information for the government to communicate with central Asia. Zhangqian's second diplomatic mission happend in 119 BC, he set off to to meet king of Wusun with three hundred people with two horses for each person and thousands of flocks and herds, the goods taken along with the diplomatic mission worthed thousands of millions. But he failed to persuade the king to return east, in the meantime, he also sent other envoys to visit Dawan, Kangju, Yuezhi and Daxia. Zhangqian returned back to Chang'an in 115 BC with dozens of Wusun envoys. After this, Parthian envoy also visited Chang'an and from then on Han dynasty's communication with the western region had been set up.

欧亚的蓝图,此后不断派出的庞大使团,不再完全以政治军事为目的。许多国家的使者也纷纷来到中国。"张骞通西域"开创的与西域诸国政府间的往来,使对异国满腹孤疑的防范心理逐渐变为试图了解和求知的渴望。一代代肩负重任的使者,穿梭于异常艰难的戈壁沙漠通道,寻找着东西方文明对峙中的调解办法。

东、西方使团互访,常常带着各种礼品,有的以使团的名义出行,实际目的却是纯粹的商业活动。人们通过商品交换逐渐增加了对对方的了解,进而开始了文化方面的交流。

文献记录与考古发现不同,文字记录主要赞扬武力战争,对将士进行歌颂。考古却发现的是精美的外来艺术品及其背后代表丝绸之路盛况的商贾和驼队。文字记录通常记录的是一些事件和特例,考古发现的多是日常生活的器物,更反映了当时的社会风貌。

西汉(前202—8)以后,西域各国、各民族前来中原王朝的次数巨增[1]。途中主要用驼马等运送物资,因此胡人牵引的满载货物的骆驼成为那个时代具有特色的形象,反映了东西交往的盛况(图1)。

在汉代张骞之后,值得一提的是隋炀帝(569—618),他是中国历史上亲自西巡的君王,曾率众历时半年到达张掖[2],会见了西域

began to plan systematic communication with Eurasia, and from then on, large diplomatic missions were frequently sent to the Western Regions, not only for political or military reasons; China changed the way it viewed cultures different from itself as enemies, and also the extreme ways it used to deal with them. Many foreign embassies also came to China one after another. Zhang Qian's Mission to the Western Regionsbegun the intergovernmental contacts among the countries of the Western Regions, and the continuous contacts favored a change from an attitude of suspicion to a desire of knowledge and curiosity. Generations of embassies shouldering heavy responsibilities marched through the threatening desert to mediate pacification among eastern and western civilizations.

The eastern and western delegations exchanged visits, always taking along various gifts, sometimes undertaking commercial activities under the cover of diplomatic exchanges. After people knew more about each other through a long-time commodity exchanges, cultural exchanges began to take place.

There are differences between written sources and archaeological discoveries. The documents mainly glorify wars, generals and soldiers. Archaeology unearths exquisite foreign artworks, silently recalling experiences of merchants and caravans along the Silk Road. The written records often depict extraordinary events, while archaeological findings are usually daily-use utensils, reflecting more directly the social landscape of the age.

In the period succeeding the Western Han Dynasty (202 BC–9 AD), countries of the Western Regions and different ethnic groups came to the royal court in Central China more and more frequently (Yu Taishan, 1995; Huang Lie, 1981). Camels and horses were the main

---

[1] 黄烈:《魏晋南北朝时期西域与内地的关系》,《魏晋隋唐史论集》(第一辑),中国社会科学出版社(北京),1981年,页58—90。余太山:《两汉魏晋南北朝与西域关系史研究》,商务印书馆(北京),2011年,页94—281。
Huang Lie (1981), 58–90; Yu Taishan (2011), 94–281.

[2]《隋书》卷三《炀帝上》,"经大斗拔谷,山路险隘,鱼贯而出。风霰晦冥,与从官相失,士卒冻死者太半"。中华书局(北京),1973年,页73。
See Wei Zheng et alii (eds.) (1973), vol. 3, 73.

图1　汉唐时期墓葬中出土的骆驼俑
Fig.1　Camel statues unearthed from the Han and Tang Tombs

二十七国的君主或使臣,场面十分隆重[1]。后来诸番酋长又会集洛阳进行交易,"相率来朝贡者三十余国"。隋炀帝命整饬店肆,陈设帏帐,陈列珍货,大设鱼龙曼筵之乐,会见西方宾客。盛会昼夜不歇,灯火辉煌,终月而罢[2]。这犹如一次"万国博览会",是中国史无前例的创举,对中外交流是一次大促进。

唐代(618—907)在中国政治史上更为成功,它的前半段,对内一个稳固的专制帝国,通过强化控制防止了内部的冲突,对外则积极主动地开展外交活动。与"张骞通西域"相比,统治的观念进一步发生变化。唐初在一次宴会上,太上皇李渊令突厥、南蛮首领共同歌舞,高兴地说"胡、越一家,自古未有也"[3],感慨各族人聚集一堂,四海一家。唐代第二个皇帝李世民,击败了西部劲敌突厥人后,曾兴奋地对来自中亚安国(故地在今乌兹别克斯坦共和国布哈拉一带)的人说:"西突厥已降,商旅可行矣!""诸胡大悦。"可见即便发生了残酷战争,和平通商和友好交往是最终的目的。

东西方之间的中亚地理环境恶劣,气候变化莫测,当时只有骆驼才能穿越令人生畏的沙漠戈壁。汉唐文物中骆驼被重点表现,在塑像、绘画等艺术作品中大量出现,反映了人们对骆驼的

means of transportation, and therefore artworks of foreigners pulling fully loaded camels vividly reflect the blossoming trade between the East and the West (Fig.1). After Zhang Qian, another worth mentioning person is Emperor Yang of the Sui Dynasty (569–618 AD), who personally, as a sovereign, went to the Western Regions. Leading a group of people, he travelled over a long distance for more than half a year and finally reached Zhangye City (*Suishu*, 73). In Zhangye, he met with the monarchs and embassies from 27 countries of the Western Regions, a very spectacular event (*Suishu*, 1580). Later, the western monarchs from more than 30 countries gathered in Luoyang for a trade fair, and in succession came to pay tribute to the court. The Emperor Yang ordered to mend stores, display stalls and precious goods and prepare entertainments for western guests. The grand feast continued round the clock for a whole month, the nights brilliantly illuminated (*Suishu*, 1841). This was an unprecedented activity in Chinese history, like a "World's fair" that greatly boosted international exchanges.

The Tang Dynasty (618–907 AD) was a still more successful dynasty in Chinese political history; in its early period it was a stable autocratic empire; tough control was employed to avoid interior conflicts, while at the same time it positively engaged in foreign exchanges. Compared to the period of *Zhang Qian's Mission to the Western Regions*, the concept of government changed further. In the early Tang, during a official banquet the retired emperor Li Yuan ordered the chiefs of the Turk and Southern Barbarian to dance together and he said happily "all peoples belong to one family; it's unprecedented in

---

[1]《隋书》卷六七《裴矩传》"皆令佩金玉、被锦罽,焚香奏乐,歌舞喧噪。复令武威、张掖士女盛饰纵观,骑马填咽,周亘数十里,以示中国之盛"。中华书局(北京),1973年,页1580。
  See Wei Zheng *et alii* (eds.) (1973), vol. 67, 1580.
[2]《旧唐书》卷六三《裴矩传》,中华书局(北京),1975年,页1841。
  See Liu Xu *et alii* (eds.) (1975), vol. 83, 1841.
[3]《资治通鉴》卷一九四"十二月,甲寅,上幸芙蓉园"条,"上皇命突厥颉利可汗起舞,又命南蛮酋长冯智戴咏诗,既而笑曰:'胡、越一家,自古有也!'"中华书局(北京),1956年,页6103—6104。
  See Sima Guang *et alii* (1956), vol. 194, 6103–6104.

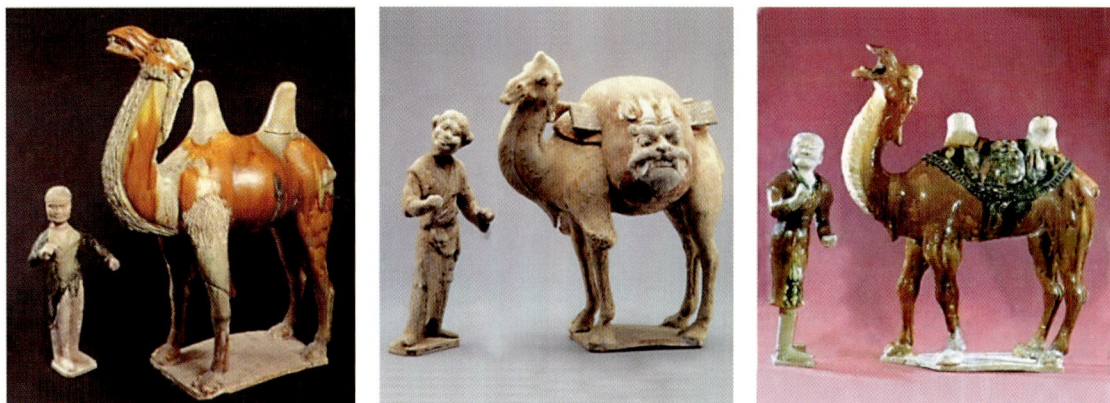

图2 唐墓中出土的胡人牵驼俑
Fig.2 Camel statues with foreign merchants unearthed from the Tang Tomb

钦佩、崇敬之情，和对丝绸之路上的勇者的开拓精神的歌颂。而且骆驼与商胡常常是一个固定的组合，展现了杜甫诗中"东来橐驼满旧都""胡儿制骆驼"的具体形象。商胡几乎都是深目高鼻，满脸浓密的络腮胡，或秃头顶，或卷发，身穿翻领长袍，足蹬高靴，带各种胡帽（图2、3）。具有高超技术的艺术家们对各国来的客人有深刻了解，在陶俑上塑造出了各种各样生动的容颜。这些见多识广的胡人也是中西文化的传播者。

汉唐骆驼形象的变化轨迹，表现出了中外交往的不断深入。汉代骆驼较少，而且显得有些稚拙，蹄子与马蹄无异，形象塑造与真实的骆驼存在差距，似乎对骆驼并不十分了解（图4）。北朝时期的骆驼多以驮载物品为特征，点明骆驼的运输用途（图5）。唐代胡人牵引载货骆驼如同是天经地义的造型选择，把骆驼和对外交往、交通贸易紧密地联系在一起。除了时代变化，还有一个有趣的现象，中国西北出产骆驼的地区，骆驼的形象塑造并不精致，反而越靠

the history" (*Zizhi Tongjian*, vol.194). Li Shimin, the second Tang Dynasty emperor, after defeating the Turks, the strongest enemies in the West, excitedly declared to the people coming from the Central Asian Country of An (Bukhara, Uzbekistan), "the Western Turk has surrendered, merchants and visitors can travel without trouble", and the barbarians were quite delighted at this news. Therefore, peaceful commerce and friendly exchange was the ultimate goal, even though sometimes achieved through cruel wars.

Central Asia, the link between East and West, is characterized by the harsh geographical environment and unpredictable weather. In ancient times, the camels were the only animal capable to pass through the formidable desert. During the Han and Tang Dynasties, camels were meticulously depicted in many artworks, such as sculpture and painting, reflecting people's praise for the pioneering spirit along the Silk Road. What's more, camels were always attended by foreign merchants portrayed with deep eyes, high-bridged noses, full beards, and bald head or with curly hair; worn long lapel gowns, high boots and various kinds of hats (Figs.2, 3). Skilled artists had a profound knowledge of the foreign merchants and portrayed them lively; it was those experienced foreign merchants who

图3　唐墓出土胡俑细部
Fig.3　Details of foreigner statues unearthed from the Tang Tomb

图4   汉墓中的骆驼形象
Fig.4   Camel images or statues Unearthed from the Han Tomb

图5   北周李贤墓出土骆驼俑   图6   西域出土骆驼俑
Fig.5   Camel statue from Li Xian's   Fig.6   Camel statues from the northwest China
tomb, Northern Zhou Dynasty

东方不生存骆驼的地区，骆驼形象塑造越多，制作越生动（图6、7）。即在越不熟悉骆驼的繁荣地区，骆驼形象刻画得越精美，这显然是在向往、猎奇后的创作，把骆驼作为一种符号，用来象征当时"丝绸之路"的兴盛。有些塑像抓住了骆驼习性中精彩的瞬间，刻意表现了骆驼与自然抗争、勤劳顽强的特点，勾画出"无数驼铃遥过碛，应驮白练到安西"的美妙图景，充满动感，极为传神（图8）。

汉代开通丝绸之路，开拓了人们的视野；

created a cultural bridge between East and West.

The changes in the plastic representation of the camel form the Han to the Tang Dynasties demonstrate the constant deepening of Sino-foreign exchanges. In the Han Dynasty, there were fewer artistic representations of the camel, and they were clumsy: the hooves of camels were represented as those of horses and on the whole the resemblance was not accurate, a fact suggesting that the artisans at that time were not familiar with the camel (Fig.4). During the Northern Dynasties, camels were mainly depicted with loads of goods on their back, suggesting that camels were regarded as means of transport (Fig.5). In the Tang Dynasty, loaded camels

图7　中原地区出土骆驼俑
Fig.7　Camel statues from the eastern China

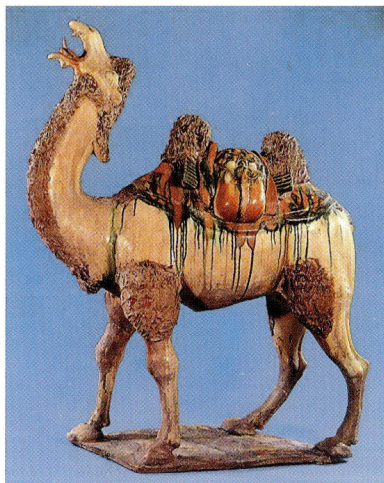

图8　隋斛律彻墓出土骆驼俑细部
Fig.8　Detail of the Camel Statue unearthed from the Hulv che the tomb of Sui Dynasty

唐代坚持宽容、开放的治国方略，在古老传统和外来文化影响的漩涡中寻找自己前进的方向。胡人与骆驼的大量出现，反映了对丝路贸易的重视已不是政府和统治阶层独有的崇尚，丝路贸易、对外开拓的精神成为社会普遍的追求。到了唐代，出现了"九天阊阖开宫殿，万国衣冠拜冕旒"的盛况，首都长安如同世界的大商场，举行着永不谢幕的国际博览会，改变了人与人的关系和不同文化之间的关系。

商品的魅力与东西方的碰撞

对异域物产的惊奇和需求，是商贸交往的最初动力。在重农抑商、自给自足的农业中国，商业的繁荣对传统产生了冲击，然而商贸过程中带来的公平意识，却影响了人们对生活其他方面的态度。

pulled by foreign merchants were much common, thus indicating that camels were closely connected with the international exchanges and trades. In addition to these chronological differences, another phenomenon can be observed: in northwest China, where camels lived, their artistic representations were quite rough, while moving progressively east, where no camels lived, their representations were more vivid (Figs.6,7). It's obvious that the production of camel images in the eastern regions reflected deep curiosity, and camels were regarded as the symbol of the prosperous Silk Road. Some of the camel images seized vivid postures, representing their industrious, tenacious characters in their struggle with nature (Fig.8).

The opening of the Silk Road in Western Han Dynasty widened people's worldview. The Tang Dynasty kept an open attitude towards the Silk Road, seeking a path between traditional culture and the acceptance of foreign influences. The numerous artistic representations of foreigners and camels suggests that the Silk Road trade was no longer exclusive enterprise

新疆乌恰深山的一个石缝中曾发现大量的金条和947枚萨珊银币[1]，通向楼兰的黑山梁也发现过970多枚唐"开元通宝"铜钱。与其他考古发现不同，这些荒芜之地的发现，显然都是过路商人因突发事件而埋下的，也证明了东西方之间大规模地相互购买货物的事实（图9）。丝路贸易的繁荣，使波斯萨珊银币、东罗马金币和唐"开元通宝"成了跨区域的通用

图9　丝绸之路中国段沿线出土的外国金银币
Fig.9　Foreign gold and silver coins unearthed along the silk road in China

of the government and ruling class, but the pioneering spirit had reached all the levels of the society. During the Tang Dynasty, the capital Chang'an had become an international "shopping mall", holding long-lasting international fairs and a hub of international relations.

The Charm of Commodities and the Collisions between East and West

Commercial exchanges are born of people's wonder and desire for exotic things. In ancient China agriculture was encouraged and business restricted, therefore the prosperity of commerce was a blow to the traditional way of life.

In a rock fissure in the Wuqia Mountain, Xin Jiang, many gold bars and 947 Sasanian silver coins were discovered (Li Yuchun, 1959, 482–83); in Heishan Liang, on the way to Loulan, more than 970 bronze coins of the Tang Dynasty (Kaiyuan Tongbao) were unearthed. Supposedly, these archaeological finds in remote and deserted areas were buried by merchants in time of emergencies, demonstrating that there was large scale trade between East and West (Fig.9). The prosperous Silk Road trade made it possible for Sasanian silver coins, Eastern Roman golden coins and Tang Dynasty "Kaiyuan Tongbao" bronze coins, to become cross-regional currency; what's more, a fixed exchange rate between foreign gold or silver coins and Chinese bronze coins was established.

Goods contain cultural traits; the enjoyment of foreign products triggers a desire for knowledge of the objects' exotic culture. Chinese people gradually gained knowledge of the outside world through foreign goods, in the same way westerners became acquainted with China through the beautiful silk items. In the Tang Dynasty, people no longer blindly held a patronizing attitude towards foreign countries, to the point that

---

[1]　李遇春：《新疆乌恰县发现金条和大批波斯银币》,《考古》1959年第9期,第482—483页
　　　Li Yuchun (1959), 482–483.

货币,外来的金银钱与中国的铜钱还出现了明确的换算关系。

商品中包含着文化内涵,人们在享受外来物质的同时,会产生对另类文化的了解欲望,如同西方诸国通过美丽的丝绸等认识了中国一样,中国也通过外来商品逐渐认识了外部世界。通过商品的沟通,到了唐代,人们不再一味地用居高临下的态度描述其他诸国,某些近乎诋毁的语言也大大减少,商贸之路成了东西方文明的对话之路,频繁的商贸活动成功地转化为文化的交融。

驼背满载的织物、丝束,形象地述说着丝绸流向西方,驼背上携带的长颈瓶、胡瓶、扁壶等,也表明了外来物品的传入。这些物品穿过荒芜的戈壁滩和茫茫的沙漠,由大大小小的商贸队伍带来,为中外经济贸易留下了永久的记忆。驼背上详细刻画的扁壶和胡瓶,对异域器物惟妙惟肖地进行了塑造,在考古发现的实物中也有发现(图10)。

中国考古发现的最早的输入品中,战国到东汉时期常常发现的玻璃珠是重要的一类。由

denigrating words were greatly reduced. Consequently, trade routes became also a path for dialogue between eastern and western civilizations, and frequent commercial activities successfully facilitated cultural interaction.

Chinese renowned silk was commonly seen in the Western Regions, meanwhile foreign flask, 'Huping' and flat vessels were imported into China. These items were brought into China by large and small caravans after having passed the remote and vast deserts, and left permanent memories on Sino-foreign economy and trade. Among the objects carried on the back of the camel 'Hu ping' and flat vessels are often seen, a plastic representation of these exotic goods, which were also found in excavations (Fig.10).

Among the earliest imports discovered in China, from the Warring States to the Eastern Han Dynasty, glass beads were a conspicuous item. Since their surfaces were decorated by circles of various colors, they were called "dragonfly eyes". Sodium and calcium were the main chemical elements of most "dragonfly eyes" beads, elements which had appeared in Egypt in the 13th or 12th century BC and quickly spread over Central and West Asia. In China, "dragonfly eyes" beads were found in many provinces and cities; the earlier ones were unearthed in aristocratic tombs, while

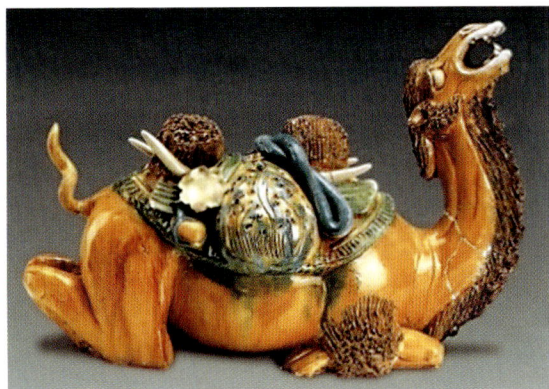

图10　驼俑背上的外来器物
Fig.10　Exotic goods on the back of camel statues

图11　战国至东汉墓葬中出土的蜻蜓眼玻璃珠
Fig.11　Dragonfly-eye glass beads unearthed from the Warring States to the Eastern Han Tombs

于表面有各种色环，被称为"蜻蜓眼"。许多
"蜻蜓眼"玻璃珠的化学成分主要是钠钙玻璃，
这在公元前13、前12世纪的埃及就已经出现，
很快遍布中亚、西亚。中国许多省市都有发现，
较早的出土于贵族墓中，稍晚的在中小型墓中
也有，出土时位于尸体的颈部和胸部，多的达千
枚以上（图11）。

外国输入的玻璃器皿，是采用型压、无模吹
制或有模吹制而成，成分主要为钠钙玻璃。产
于罗马地区的玻璃器皿主要在广州、洛阳、南京
及辽宁地区出土。这批玻璃器的质地、器形以
及堆贴玻璃条、磨花等装饰技法，是罗马玻璃常
见的特点（图12）。萨珊玻璃器皿广泛出土于
中国的新疆、宁夏、陕西、北京、河南、湖北等地。
萨珊玻璃擅长在表面用挑勾和磨琢的方法制出
乳钉或凹凸圆形的装饰（图13）。伊斯兰玻璃
纹样以几何刻纹最多见，陕西扶风县法门寺唐

in the later period they also appeared in medium or
small size graves. They were found on necks and chests
of the skeletons, numbering from a few to more than
one thousand (Fig.11).

The foreign imported glass wares were made
by mould forming, blown with or without molds;
the main elements were sodium and calcium. Glass
wares of Roman origin have been mainly unearthed
in Guangzhou, Luoyang, Liaoning and Nanjing; they
display features of the Roman glass production in
their quality, shape and techniques of applied and
polished decorations (Fig.12). Sasanian glass wares
have been widely discovered in Xinjiang, Ningxia,
Shaanxi, Beijing, Henan and Hubei. These glasses
are characterized by nail design and concave-convex
circular ornamentation (Fig.13). A rare collection
of well-preserved exquisite Islamic glass plates and
bowls were discovered in the underground treasure hall
of Tang Dynasty Famen Temple in Fufeng, Shaanxi
Province; these treasures were decorated with the
typical geometric patterns commonly seen on Islamic
glasses (Fig.14).

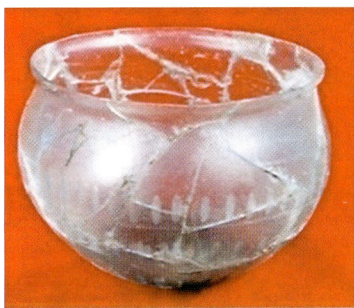

图12　中国发现的罗马玻璃器
Fig.12　Roman glass productions discovered in China

图13　中国发现的萨珊玻璃器
Fig.13　Sasanian glass wares discovered in China

图14　陕西扶风法门寺唐代地宫出土的伊斯兰玻璃器
Fig.14　Islamic glass plates and bowls Unearthed from the underground palace of Famen Temple in Fufeng, Shaanxi Province, Tang Dynasty

代地宫中出土了一批盘、钵，保存完好，制作精美，是伊斯兰玻璃中罕见的珍品（图14）。

　　输入品中还有金银器，广州西汉南越王墓的银盒，制作技术采用锤揲方法，做成凸起的纹样，犹如浮雕，富有立体效果（图15）。江苏邗江甘泉二号东汉墓出土一批掐丝、焊金珠、镶嵌绿松石和水晶的金饰品，都来自外国（图16）。汉代以后罗马银盘、萨珊银盘、中亚的银碗和银壶等也纷纷传入（图17）。

　　中国发现的外来文物，许多都是举世无双的，而且至少具备五个特点：有准确的出土地点；经过科学发掘获得；器物制作年代下限明

Some gold and silver wares were also imported. For instances, silver boxes found in the tomb of Western Han Nanyue King in Guangzhou City, were adorned with convex decorations, like the high-relief (Fig.15). A batch of foreign gold ornaments with filigree, welded golden beads, inlaid turquoise and crystal, were unearthed in Eastern Han Tomb 2 at Ganquan, Hanjiang County, Jiangsu Province (Fig.16). After the Han Dynasty, Roman silver plates, Sasanian silver plates, Central Asian silver bowls and flasks became a common import in China (Fig.17).

Most of the exotic artifacts discovered in China are unique because of these five characteristics: accurate context; obtained through scientific excavation; associated with an epitaph that defines the *terminus ante*

确（有墓志伴出）；同其他器物有组合关系；器物保存完好。这在地中海地区、西亚、中亚等地也是少见的。这些珍贵的器物表明了中国与西方诸国的往来十分密切。

quem; associated with other artifacts; well-preserved. These situations are rarely seen in the Mediterranean area, West and Central Asia. Those precious artifacts suggest close exchanges between China and the Western Regions.

图15　广州西汉南越王墓出土银盒
Fig.15　Silver box found in the tomb of Western Han Nanyue King, Guangzhou

图16　江苏邗江甘泉二号东汉墓出土金饰品
Fig.16　Foreign gold ornaments with filigree, welded golden beads inlaid turquoise and crystal, unearthed from Eastern Han Tomb no 2 at Ganquan, Hanjiang County, Jiangsu Province

图17　中国发现的外来银盘和银碗
Fig.17　Exotic silver plates and bowls discovered in China

各国派往中国的使节或商人带来的外来土特产与新技术令人耳目一新，首先在技术层面对中国产生了影响。中国古代玻璃器、金银器早期多采用铸造技术，没有显示出玻璃、金银材料制造器物的优越性。外来物品的输入，使玻璃逐渐采用吹制法，金银逐渐采用锤揲工艺，掐丝、粘金珠技术也很快被中国工匠掌握，汉代的金灶、金龙，就是用这种技法制成的。

古代器物除实用性之外，也包含着精神文化的内容，作为商品输入后，也会潜移默化地改变人们的思想。中国最初对外来事物的借鉴，通常是吸收和改造。齐王墓随葬坑出土的银盒，看上去像"豆"。但器物下面的座及上面的钮是青铜的，为后来安装（图18）。材质虽然不协调，原有器形改变后，反而符合了中国人的审美和使用习惯。同样的做法也出现在欧洲，他们将中国的瓷器加上把手（图19）。西安南郊何家村唐代遗宝中有一件极为奇特的玛瑙兽首

It was refreshing to come across foreign products and new technologies brought to China by embassies or merchants from different countries. First of all, the new technologies exerted a strong effect on China. In China, glass, gold and silver wares used to be made by casting technique, with the result that these objects failed to reveal their superior quality of the material. The appearance of foreign items brought with itself technologies such as glass blowing, gold and silver hammering, filigree and beads welding, which were rapidly mastered by Chinese artisans, and in the Han Dynasty these techniques were used in the manufacture of local products, such as gold stoves and gold dragons.

Apart from their practical aspect, ancient artifacts also contained spiritual elements; imported commodities slowly and unconsciously influenced people's mind. Initially, China absorbed and transformed foreign items. For instance, the silver box unearthed from the burial pit of the tomb of Western Han Qi Prince (179 BC) in Linzi, Shangdong Province, looked like a 'dou', but its bottom and knob were made of bronze and were attached later(Fig.18). Although the materials lacked harmony and the original shape was altered, it met Chinese aesthetic

图18 山东省淄博区西汉齐王墓1号随葬坑出土银盒
Fig.18 Silver box unearthed from the burial pit of the tomb of Western Han Qi Prince in Linzi, Shangdong Province

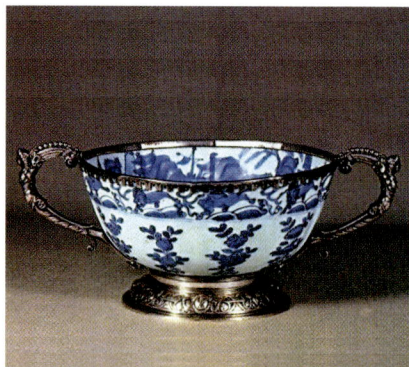

图19 欧洲收藏的带把手中国瓷器
Fig.19 Chinese porcelain with handles in Europe

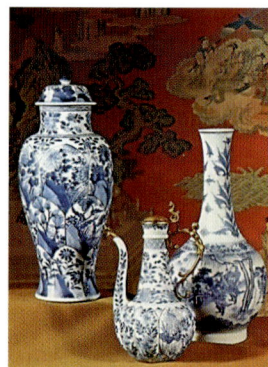

杯，早在西亚的亚述（Assyria）、波斯阿契美尼德王朝（Achaemenid）已经出现，在西方被称作"来通"（rhyton），多是角杯形，底端有孔，液体可以流出，用途与中原人生活习俗无关（图20、21）。令人惊异的是这类器物传到中国后，陶瓷器中出现了仿制品（图22），而且还出现在唐代表现贵族生活的壁画场景中[1]。仿制品还保持着角杯状、底部有兽首的形态，由于生活习俗不同和对西方文化的生疏，底部都没有泄水孔，已

standards and practicality. The same practice can also be seen in Europe, in the case handles were added to Chinese porcelain (Fig.19). Among the cultural relics of Tang Dynasty found at Hejia County, southern suburbs of Xi'an, there is a peculiar rhytonagate cup which appeared in West Asia as early as Assyria and the Persian Achaemenid Dynasty. It was called rhyton in the West: it was horn shaped with a hole at the bottom from which liquids could flow out (Figs.20, 21). There was no tradition of using the rhyton in Central China. When the rythons spread over China, it was reproduced in ceramic (Fig.22) and even represented on the mural paintings recounting aristocrats'

图20　西安南郊何家村窖藏发现的兽首玛瑙来通
Fig.20　Rhyton agate cup found at Hejia County, southern suburbs of Xi'an

图21　西亚亚述和波斯阿契美尼德王朝来通
Fig.21　Rhytons of Assyria and the Persian Achaemenid Dynasty

[1]　陕西省博物馆、文管会：《唐李寿墓发掘简报》，《文物》（北京），1974年第9期，第71—88页。
　　　Shaanxi Provincial Museum, Bureau of Culture (1974), 71–88.

图22　中国发现的唐代陶瓷来通
Fig.22　Ceramic Rhytons discovered in China, Tang Dynasty

经失去了原本的实用性。追求新奇导致对异类文化的关注，即便滥用外来文化成分，却也是思想上的解放。

外来物品及其文化，使中国传统的艺术表现也出现了变化，随着丝绸之路的畅通，西方艺术中的植物纹冲击了汉代的龙怪、云气独霸的现象，生动活泼的忍冬、葡萄等植物纹样立刻被接受，迅速流行，成为中国考古、美术史上的一次大变化。

中国古代帝王和官修史籍的编撰者都认为自己是世界的中心，周边邻国为"蛮夷"，商贸活动用所谓"朝贡"来表述，事实上通过"朝贡"而得到的"赏赐"，本质上仍体现了通商贸易关系。商品的魅力和移植在物品上的文化，最终使商贸活动转化为文化的交融。

模仿借鉴与文化的馈赠

中国历史上的民族关系，古人既有"五胡乱华"的诋毁，也有"胡越一家"的感慨。但无

lives of the Tang Dynasty (Shaanxi Provincial Museum, Bureau of Culture, 1974). The imitations kept the horn shape and animal head, but the bottom hole was not bored, and the object lost its original practical usage. The search for the new expresses a concern for different cultures; even the abuse of foreign cultural elements was actual ideological liberation.

Chinese traditional artistic expression changed under the influence of foreign objects and their cultures. The floral patterns of western art impacted the dominated animal and cloud design of the Han Dynasty; vivid floral and grape motifs were immediately accepted and rapidly prevailed in the decor, a significant shift in the history of Chinese archaeology and art.

In the eyes of ancient Chinese emperors and compilers of historical records, China was the center of the world and the surrounding countries were "barbarians;" commercial activities were regarded as "pay tributes to the emperor." In truth, the reward for the tributes paid was a commercial transaction. The charm of commodities and the cultures they convened finally converted commercial activities to cultural blending.

Imitations, borrowing and the Gift of Culture

In the history of relationships with other peoples, China

论如何,文化的碰撞都会使后人享受恩惠。古代文物展示出的各民族的交融,形象、深刻地揭示了交流中人们观念和生活的改变。

外来器物的新颖造型和纹样,激起了人们的创作热情,因而出现了一些精巧化、多样化、无固定模式、自由随意创作的器物群体。中亚粟特盛行一种带环形把手的杯,唐代进行了仿造(图23),开始时还直接仿造器体的棱面饰联珠纹、把手带指垫和指錾环、指垫上饰胡人头像等充满趣味的细节(图24)。后来融入的创新成分是将外凸的八棱改为内凹的八瓣,分界处的联珠变做柳叶,指垫做成多曲三角形,杯腹的主题纹饰也换成浓郁唐式风格的狩猎图和仕女游乐图(图25)。这种杯最初与其说是实用品,不如说主要用于观赏,但由于

did not only view them as the "Five Hu bringing turmoil to China", but also considered that "all people belong to one family". No matter how another culture was approached, in the end cultural interaction would benefit later generations. Ancient art crafts display the mutual influence in thought and life emerged from the cultural blending among different nations and between East and West.

Exotic artifacts' novel forms and decorative patterns sparked people's creative enthusiasms; exquisite and varied items came to life. For example, the cups with ring handle which prevailed in Sogdian Central Asia were copied during the Tang Dynasty (Fig.23). At the beginning, imitations directly counterfeited the original in detail, such as the pearl medallion motives on facets, ring handles with finger pads decorated with bust of foreigners (Fig.24). Later, innovative elements were incorporated: eight rounded petals were replaced by eight bilobed, the boundary decoration changed from the pearl medallion motives to a willow leaves pattern, the finger pads were

图23　粟特式带把杯
Fig.23　Cups with ring handle in Sogdian style

图24 唐代何家村遗宝中的仿制带把杯
Fig.24　Imitations of cups with ring handle, Hejia Village Treasure, Tang Dynasty.

图25 唐式带把杯及其装饰细部
Fig.25　Cup with ring handle and its detail

图26 瓷带把杯
Fig.26 Ceramic cups with ring handle

图27 多瓣银碗
Fig.27 Silver bowl in multi-petal shape

带把给使用带来便利,最终扩展到陶瓷器的制造上,并开创了后代带把器物的流行(图26)。中亚地区多瓣造型的器物传入中国后[1],也很快融汇演变成瑰丽唐式作风,凸瓣、细密水滴状瓣形变为桃形莲瓣装饰(图27)。器物形态与生活习俗有关,直接仿制外国的器物很难流行,只有进行重新搭配和改造,才能够被人们接受。唐人具有很高的艺术修养,在欣赏西方艺术的同时,把富于变化的多曲形改造成了适合中国人使用的创新产品,并呈现出花朵般的造型设计,既体现了对异域文化的取舍和改造,也融入了东方的审美情趣(图28),演变后新的样式又成功地得到推广,后来花瓣形的杯、碗和高足花口杯成为中晚唐乃至宋代器皿的主流(图29)。西方器物的传入,也一定程度上引起了人们生活方式的变化,陕西房陵公主墓壁画中仕女手持的器物有许多是外来的器形,应是贵族生活的真实反映[2]。

in a multi-curved pattern, and the decorative patterns in the main body were typical Tang-style hunting scenes and the representation of court ladies (Fig.25). Initially those cups were not so much object of daily use as they were mainly ornamental; however, for practical use, they were eventually made in ceramics (Institute of Archaeology of Chinese Academy of Social Sciences, 2001) and inaugurated the tradition of utensils with handles popular in the later ages (Fig.26). Other multi-petal shaped artifacts of Central Asia (Fig.27) were rapidly incorporated into the Tang style; after entering China, pointed lotus-petals patterns replaced the water-drops designs (Qi Dongfang, 1999). The forms of artifact reflect lifestyle patterns, so that direct imitations of foreign items rarely become the prevalent trend. Only by matching and transforming foreign elements can be accepted and come into vogue. Based on their high artistic accomplishments, the people of the Tang Dynasty changed exotic multi-curved artifacts into innovative objects suitable for Chinese lifestyle. The new floral design not only reflected the selections and transformation of exotic cultures, but also fulfilled the oriental aesthetic taste (Fig.28). New styles were successfully popularized in later ages, and petal-shaped

---

[1] 参见齐东方:《中国发现的粟特银碗》,《唐代金银器研究》,中国社会科学出版社(北京),1999年,页333—344。
    See Qi Dongfang (1999), Sogdian silver bowl found in China, 333–344.
[2] 安峥地:《唐房陵大长公主墓清理简报》,《文博》(西安),1990年第1期,页2—6。
    An Zhengdi (1990), 2–6.

图28　何家村遗宝出土金碗　　图29　晚唐花口碗
Fig.28　Gold bowl from the Hejia　Fig.29　Bowls in flower-shape, Late Tang period
Village Treasure

唐代"胡瓶"的出现和流行更是对外来器物的直接接受。胡瓶器身椭圆形，细长颈，流口作鸟啄形，带盖，口部到腹部有弯曲的把。文献记载它来自东罗马等地，形状奇特[1]。唐代的吐蕃人、安禄山等都向朝廷进献过"胡瓶"。日本奈良正仓院保存一件银平脱漆胡瓶，书于天平胜宝八年（756）的《东大寺献物帐》上称之为"漆胡瓶一口"[2]（图30）。胡瓶虽然不是中原汉人的发明，但使用起来方便，很快成为唐人生活中新崛起的器类，并以陶瓷制作来满足广泛的社会需求，走进了寻常百姓家（图31）。

比器物更为重要的还有家具的变化。中国古人原本席地而坐，相配合的家具是低矮的几、案之类（图32），后来从西域传来一种便于携带的轻便坐具"胡床"[3]，即今天还在使用的轻便

cups, bowls and goblets with the flower-shaped spout prevailed from the middle and late Tang Dynasty to the Song Dynasty (Fig.29). To some extent, imported western artifacts caused changes in the Chinese lifestyle. For instance, there is a vivid depiction of many maidservants holding exotic artifacts in the fresco of Princess Fangling's tomb in Shaanxi, which are believed to be a true reflection of aristocratic life (An Zhengdi 1990).

'Huping' were directly accepted during the Tang Dynasty; they had oval-shaped bodies, long narrow necks, bird shaped lids and spouts, and curved handles from the upper rim to the abdomen. According to historical records, the oddly-shaped 'Huping' came from East Rome and other places (*Taiping Yulan,* vol.758). During the Tang Dynasty, the Tubo people (Tibetan), An Lushan and others offered these foreign objects in tribute to the royal court. In the Shosoin Repository of Nara (a treasure house of the Todai-ji Shrine), Japan, is collected a lacquer 'Huping' with sliver inlaid, recorded as "lacquer Huping One" in *the*

---

[1]《太平御览》卷七五八器物部"瓶"条引《前凉录》，十六国"张轨时，西胡致金胡（瓶）瓶，皆拂菻作，奇状，并人高，二枚"，"拂菻"是指东罗马，西胡泛指中、西亚。中华书局（北京），1960年，页3365上栏。
　　See Li Fang *et alii* (eds.) (1966), vol. 758, 3365.
[2] 奈良国立博物馆：《正仓院展六十回のあゆみ》，天理时报社，平城二十年（2008），页84。
　　Nara National Museum (2008), 84.
[3]《三国志·魏书》卷一六《苏则传》载：魏文帝行猎时"槎桎拔，失鹿，帝大怒，踞胡床拔刀，悉收督吏，将斩之"，中华书局（北京），1979年，页493。易水：《漫话胡床——家具谈往三》，《文物》（北京），1982年第10期，页82—85。椅子起源于古代埃及、西亚一带。新疆和田的尼雅古城发掘到一把汉代高脚靠背的木椅。这种椅子的形制可能影响到印度，使印度佛教造像如犍陀罗式雕像中出现了垂脚而坐的佛像，后来更出现了坐高脚靠背椅说法的佛像。黄正建：《唐代的椅子与绳床》，《文物》（北京），1990年第7期，页86—88。
　　See Chen Shou (1979), vol. 16, 493; Yi Shui (1982); Huang Zhengjian (1990).

图30　日本奈良正仓院
藏漆胡瓶
Fig.30　Lacquer *Huping*
from the Shosoin
Repository of Nara

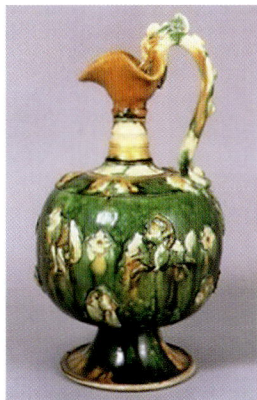

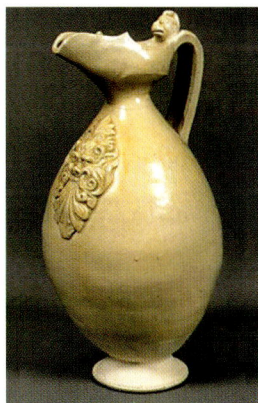

图31　中国发现的陶瓷胡瓶
Fig.31　Ceramic *Huping*
discovered in China

图32　北齐徐显秀墓壁画中的几案
Fig.32　Low and small tables and desks showed in the
wall painting of Xu Xianxiu's Tomb

list of offerings to the Todai-ji Shrine in 756 AD (Fig.30, Nara National Museum, 1990). Although 'Hupings' were not typical object of Central China, they became quickly popular during the Tang Dynasty thanks to their practicality. Finally, 'Hupings' were ceramic produced to meet the broad social demands and entered common people's home (Fig.31).

　　Changes in furniture were still more significant. Ancient Chinese sat on the floor; and the most suitable pieces of furniture were low and small tables and desks (Fig.32). Later, a kind of portable lightweight seat, called 'Huchuang', was introduced from the Western Regions (*Sanguo Zhi*; Yi Shui, 1982; Huang Zhengjian, 1990); this kind of seat is similar to the folding stools still in use today, also known as 'ma zha'er'. After the Sui Dynasty, the 'Huchuang' were renamed as "crossed stool",

图33　唐代壁画中的胡床
Fig.33　*Huchuang* showed in the wall painting, Tang Dynasty

的折叠凳，也就是俗称的"马扎儿"。胡床在隋代以后改名为"交床"，使用时下垂双腿，双足着地（图33）。又受佛教的垂脚坐式的影响，最终出现了高腿椅子（图34）。高背椅子在唐代叫绳床或倚床，宋代有人作了明确的解释，说是一种可以垂足靠背的坐具[1]。唐末木字旁的"椅"字正式出现。宋代以后人们终于改变了跪坐的习惯。

　　起居方式的变化会引发生活习俗的一系列变革。高腿家具与席地而坐迥然不同，与椅子配套的是桌子，不光使人们在居室内自由走动更加随意，视野开阔，日常生活器皿形态、装饰也发生了变化。晚唐和宋代以后作观赏用的图案花纹，也由仅仅装饰在器物外表，进而装饰内部。由于伏案姿势的变化，甚至连人的着装、书

seats where people sat in the European style (Fig.33). Influenced by the European style sitting of the Buddha, high-leg chairs appeared (Fig.34). In the Tang Dynasty high-backed chairs were called 'Shengchuang' (rope bed) or 'Yichuang' (leaning bed) and in the Song Dynasty they were explicitly expounded as a kind of seats on which one could lean against the back with straight legs in front (*Zizhi Tongjian*). At the end of the Tang Dynasty, the Chinese character for chair was created. After the Song Dynasty, Chinese people finally changed the habit of kneel-sitting.

　　Lifestyle changes can trigger a series of innovations. Using high-legged furniture was a major change from squatting on one's heels. Complementary to the high-legged chairs were high-legged tables and desks which not only allowed people move around more freely in the living room, but also propelled changes in the forms and decorations of many daily utensils. For instance, in the late Tang period and the Song Dynasty, ornamental patterns also appeared inside utensils, and

[1]《资治通鉴》卷二四二穆宗长庆二年"十二月，辛卯，上见群臣于紫宸殿，御大绳床"条，引程大昌《演繁录》："交床、绳床，今人家有之，然二物也……绳床以板为之，人坐其上，其广前可容膝，后有靠背，左右有托手，可以搁臂，其下四足着地"。中华书局（北京），1956年，页7822。
See Sima Guang *et alii* (1956), vol. 242, 7822.

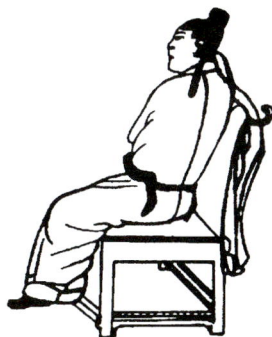

图34　唐代高腿椅子
Fig.34　High-leg chairs of Tang Dynasty

法的艺术追求也发生了改变。起居方式的改变也出现人际交往礼仪的新要求，儒家礼学大师认为"古人坐席，故以伸足为箕倨。今世坐榻，乃以垂足为礼，盖相反矣"，"若对宾客时，合当垂足坐"[1]。家具的变化不是一场轰轰烈烈的政治革命，却比较彻底地改变了人们的生活和思想观念。

　　音乐、舞蹈、服装等方面与外来文化的交

not only on the outside. With the change of the sitting posturechanged, garments and the way of writing calligraphy also changed. Moreover, lifestyle changes brought about new standards in interpersonal relations and etiquette. According to Confucians, the ancients sat on mats, so stretching out legs was regarded as impolite; but during the Song Dynasty sitting on couches with dropping legs was regarded as a decorous posture (*Zhuzi Yulei*, vol.91; *Jilei Bian*, vol.2). The change in furniture was not a vigorous political revolution, but had a deep

[1] 《鸡肋编》卷下 "唐有坐席遗风" 条，中华书局（北京），1983年，页126。《朱子语类》卷九一 "问盘坐于理有害否" 条，中华书局（北京），1986年，页2332—2333。

　　See Zhuang Chuo (1983), vol. 3, 126; Li Jingde (1986), vol. 91, 23322–2333.

融，在文物中得到明确的体现。唐初"以陈、梁旧乐杂用吴、楚之音，周、齐旧乐多涉胡戎之伎，于是斟酌南北，考以古音，作大唐雅乐"[1]。稍后增订完成了十部乐，分为燕乐、清乐、西凉乐、天竺乐、高丽乐、龟兹乐、安国乐、疏勒乐、康国乐、高昌乐。广泛吸收了各民族和外国音乐、乐器的精华，打破了传统文化的单调。外来的舞蹈，通过绘画、装饰的方式保存下来。以快速、热烈、刚健为特色的中亚胡旋舞，出现在一些器物的图案装饰上，如北魏时适于马背上携带的游牧民族喜爱的扁壶，上面有深目高鼻的胡人和乐队表演胡腾舞（胡旋舞）（图35）。唐人十分明确地指出，这种舞蹈源自中亚粟特[2]，最初

impact on people's life and ideas.

The absorption of foreign elements in music, dance and costume are vividly represented in the art crafts. In the early Tang period, "(Officers) composed the ceremonial music of Tang after having considered the music of the Chen and Liang Dynasties, which were a mix of Wu-Chu melodies; the music of the Zhou and Qi Dynasties, which contained tunes from the borderland of China, as well as having analyzed classical music"(*Jiu Tangshu*, 2710). Later, theTen-parts Music was completed: it included Yan Music (music and dance for banquet entertainment), Qing Music (the traditional court music of the Han nationality), Xiliang Music (from the present Gansu Province), Tianzhu Music (from the present India), Gaoli Music (from the present Korea), Quici Music (around the present Kucha), Anguo Music (from the present Bukhara area of Uzbekistan), Shule Music (around the present Kashgar), Kangguo Music (from the present Samarkand area of Uzbekistan), and Gaochang Music (from the present Turpan). Those melodies extensively absorbed ethnic and exotic music, breaking the monotony of traditional culture. Exotic dances can be admired in the paintings and also in decorations. The 'Huxuan Dance' from Central Asia, characterized by speed, liveliness and energy, appeared in the decorations on some artifacts, such as in the 'Bianhu' (flat vessel) of the Northern Wei Dynasty nomads: on their sides were depicted barbarians with deep eyes and high-bridged noses performing the 'Huxuan Dance' (Fig.35). Tang Dynasty people clearly knew that this kind of dance originated from Sogdia, in Central Asia, and

图35　北齐范粹墓出土扁壶上的胡旋舞装饰
Fig.35　*Huxuan* Dance depicted on the *Bianhu*, Fancui's tomb, Northern Qi Dynasty

[1]《旧唐书》卷七九《祖孝孙传》，中华书局（北京），1975年，页2710。
See Liu Xu *et alii* (eds.) (1975), vol. 79, 2710.

[2] 例如刘言史《王中丞宅夜观舞胡腾》："石国胡儿人见少，蹲舞尊前急如鸟。织成蕃帽虚顶尖，细氍胡衫双袖小。手中抛下蒲萄盏，西顾忽思乡路远。跳身转毂宝带鸣，弄脚缤纷锦靴软。四座无言皆瞪目，横笛琵琶遍头促。乱腾新毯雪朱毛，傍拂轻花下红烛。"参见《全唐诗》中华书局（北京），1960年，第十四册，页5323—5324。胡腾舞或胡旋舞的舞姿粗犷，要在铺设的小地毯上旋转、踏跳、腾跃。白居易形容是"左旋右转不知疲，千匝万周无已时"，参见《全唐诗》，第十三册，页4692—4693。岑参描写为"回裾转袖若飞雪，左铤右铤生旋风"，《全唐诗》，第六册，页2057。
See Peng Dingqiu *et alii* (eds.) (1960) book no.14, 5323–5324; no. 13, 4692–4693; no. 6, 2057.

图36　敦煌莫高窟初唐220窟壁画中的胡旋舞图
Fig.36　*Huxuan* Dance in the wall painting of early Tang Dynasty Cave 220 in Mogao, Dunhuang

流行于胡人之中[1]，后来几乎遍及中国。莫高窟初唐220窟中几乎完美地描绘出了这种技巧难度很大的舞姿（图36），宁夏盐池唐墓甚至将之刻在了石墓门上[2]（图37），湖南长沙窑还把这种形象装饰在瓷器上（图38）。唐代的音乐舞蹈出现的雄强之气，是与此前不同的新的精神面貌，其中得益于对外来艺术的借鉴。以外来乐舞为参照完成的更新改造，满足了新时代人们追求精神享乐的渴望，而且中国古代乐舞大多带有"功成作乐"的性质，与礼仪制度有关，是礼仪制度层面对外来文化的吸收。

　　表现人体自然之美，是古希腊罗马的艺术追求。借丝绸之路的畅通，一批西域画家将之东

initially prevailed among the barbarians (*Jiu Tangshu*, 6413), successively spreading almost all over China. This difficult dance was perfectly depicted infrescoes of the early Tang Dynasty Cave 220 in Mogao, Dunhuang (Fig.36); and was also carved on the stone door of a Tang Dynasty tomb in Yanchi, Ningxia (Fig.37, Ningxia Museum, 1998); besides, it was also a common decorative element on the ceramic wares of Changsha Kiln in Hunan Province(Fig.38). Influenced by foreign arts, the music and dance of Tang Dynasty were characterized by an unprecedented powerful spirit. The innovations in music and dance gratified people's aesthetic desire in a new era. Most ancient Chinese music and dance were a 'triumphal melody' in nature, related to ceremonial system; seen from this perspective, these innovations can be regarded as the absorptions of foreign cultural elements at the ritual level.

Expressing the physical beauty of the human body

---

[1]《旧唐书》卷二九《音乐志》记载康国舞"舞急转如风，俗谓之胡旋，乐有笛二、正鼓一、和鼓一、铜钹一"，中华书局（北京），1975年，页1071。《新唐书》卷二二五上《安禄山传》记载安禄山臃肿肥胖，"腹缓及膝"，却能跳胡旋舞，"乃疾如风"，中华书局（北京），1975年，页6413。
　　See Liu Xu *et alii* (eds.) (1975), 1071; Ouyang Xiu, Song Qi *et alii* (eds.) (1975), 6413.

[2]　宁夏回族自治区博物馆：《宁夏盐池唐墓发掘简报》，《文物》（北京），1988年第9期，页43—56。
　　Ningxia Museum (1988), 43–56.

图37　宁夏盐池唐墓石墓门雕刻的胡旋舞装饰
Fig.37　*Huxuan* Dance carved on the stone door of a Tang tomb in Yanchi, Ningxia

图38　湖南长沙窑瓷器上的胡旋舞装饰
Fig.38　*Huxuan* Dance depicted on the ceramic wares of Changsha Kiln, Hunan Province

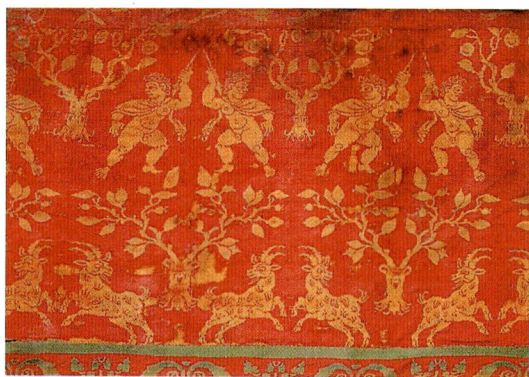

图39　新疆尉犁营盘墓地汉晋时期墓葬中出土的织物
Fig.39　Fabric unearthed from the tombs of Han and Jin periods in Yingpan, Yuli, Xinjiang

传。新疆尉犁县营盘汉晋时期古墓中发现的织物上可见异域风格的人物（图39）。北齐时从中亚移居而来的曹仲达，画人物"其体稠叠，衣服紧窄"，像水湿过似地贴在身上，后世有"曹衣出水"之说，隋唐时这种艺术风格被广为接受。在陶俑的变化中，有从唐初闲雅而潇洒，到盛唐的丰丽而浪漫，再到晚些时候舒展而放纵的演变（图40）。汉魏时期传统的褒衣博带式装束在唐

was the quest of Greek and Roman art, which spread over eastward along the Silk Road. On the fabric unearthed from the tombs of Han and Jin periods in Yingpan, Yuli, Xinjiang, there were exotic style characters (Fig.39). In the Northern Qi Dynasty, Cao Zhongda, a painter from Central Asia migrated into China, and became famous for his style of painting figures with adherent clothes, described like wet clothes clinging to the body. His artistic style was widely accepted in the Sui and Tang Dynasties.

代受到了新奇而大胆的胡服所冲击。女性服装的变化中,最有趣的是幂离、帷帽、胡帽的更替。幂离是在帽下垂布帛将全身遮蔽(图41)。帷帽为下垂布帛到颈。胡帽不垂布帛。最初由遮掩全身防止窥视转变为靓妆露面时,受到了唐高宗的严厉斥责,认为"过为轻率,深失礼容",被视为轻佻之举,但这种服装新潮流并没有因为皇帝反对而改变,在60年后的唐玄宗时期,不仅受到了诏令认可,还进一步要求妇人"帽子皆大露面,不得有掩蔽",鼓励妇女靓妆露面(图42)。

通过丝绸之路,西方各国和各民族的人大量来到内地,着装奇特的胡人、胡姬带来了异域的审美倾向,唐代女性服装由全身障蔽到窄狭贴身,再到坦胸露肌的动态变化过程,使缺乏对人体美的追求的中国古代造型艺术发生了改变。这种在西方文化影响下出现的反传统现象,其社会意义更为重要,应该是社会风尚、观念的深层变化。

During the Tang Dynasty, the long-established tradition of terracotta figurines experienced a series of evolutions. At the beginning of the dynasty they were characterized by an elegant and unconventional taste; in the prophase of Great Tang they exhibited a splendid and romantic feeling, and finally in the anaphase of the Great Tang turned into a luxurious flavor(Fig.40). The traditional dress style, a robe with very wide sleeves and long scarves of the Han and Wei periods, was impacted by the novel 'foreign fashion' during the Tang Dynasty. The most interesting change in women's attire can be seen in the style of the hat, with the successive use of the 'Mili', 'Weimao' and 'Humao'. The 'Mili' hat had a dropping piece of cloth covering the whole body(Fig.41); the 'Weimao' hat included a piece of cloth dropping to the neck; while the 'Humao' hat was without cloth. The women's custom of showing their faces with pretty makeup instead of covered them with some fabrics was severely rebuked by Emperor Gaozong of the Tang Dynasty, considering it a frivolous behavior. However, this fashion was not interrupted because of the emperor's opposition. After 60 years, during the Xuanzong Era, this custom was fully accepted; imperial edicts indicated that

图40　唐代陶俑的演变
Fig.40　Evolutions of terracotta figurines of Tang Dynasty

图41 唐代陶俑所见的幂离
Fig.41 *Mili* found in the pottery figure, Tang Dynasty

图42 靓妆露面的唐代女俑
Fig.42 The showing face female statue, Tang Dynasty

结 语

古代文物呈现了一个跌宕起伏、精彩变幻的世界。器物的制造、演变中每个充满趣味的细节，不仅凝塑着古人的智慧和情感，从中还可以看到与外来文化的交融。汉唐时期的移民与征服、交往与贸易，产生出的文化的相互馈赠往往超出最初的设想。在这个动态的过程中，人们接受外来文化的态度不断转变，突破国家、民族、地域的限制，放弃"非我族类，其心必异"的陈腐观念，以宽容与开放的心态主动善意与各民族交往，极大地促进了中国文化新的整合和盛世辉煌的出现，也加速了东西方文明的共同发展。

women were required to show their faces and encouraged to use cosmetics (Fig.42).

Through the Silk Routes, a large number of peoples from the Western Regions arrived in Central China with their fancy costumes and brought along a taste for exotic aesthetic. During the Tang Dynasty, women's costume changed from the traditional covering of the whole body to tightly fit clothes, to the décolleté. These changes deeply influenced the Chinese plastic art tradition which disregarded physical beauty. This counter-tradition phenomenon, influenced by western cultures, had a deep impact on society, and brought profound changes in social custom and ideology.

Conclusion

Ancient art works reveal a wonderful and changing world. The manufacturing of artifacts and their evolution, even of their smallest details, are not simply a concrete rendering of the ancients' wisdom and emotion, but also illustrate the integration among foreign cultures. Immigrations and conquests, exchanges and trades from the Han to the Tang Dynasties generated cultural reciprocities beyond imagination. In this dynamic process, people constantly changed their attitudes toward foreign cultures, overcame the limitations of the boundaries of their countries, and gave up the stereotypes of "any person of another race has a heart different from mine". The ancients positively make contacts with other nations with a tolerant and open mind, which brought to a new integration of Chinese culture and a period of prosperity, and also speeded up the common development of Eastern and Western civilizations.

Sources

Chen Shou (1979) *Sanguo Zhi (Records of the Three Kingdoms)*, Zhonghua Book Company, Beijing.

Li Fang *et alii* (eds) (1966) *Taiping Yulan (Imperial Readings of the Taiping Era)*, Zhonghua Book Company, Beijing.

Li Jingde (1986) *Zhuzi Yulei (Thematic Discourses of Master Zhu)*, Zhonghua Book Company, Beijing.

Liu Xu *et alii* (eds) (1975) *Jiu Tangshu (Old Book of Tang)*, Zhonghua Book Company, Beijing.

Maoheng *et alii* (2013) *Maoshi zhushu (The Collating Notes on Mao Shi)*, Shanghai Classics Publishing House, Shanghai.

Ouyang Xiu, Song Qi *et alii* (eds) (1975) *Xin Tangshu (New Book of Tang)*, Zhonghua Book Company, Beijing.

Peng Dingqiu *et alii* (eds) (1960) *Quan tang shi (Complete Collection of Tang Poems)*, Zhonghua Book Company, Beijing.

Sima Guang *et alii* (1956) *Zizhi Tongjian (Comprehensive Mirror to Aid in Government)*, Zhonghua Book Company, Beijing.

Wei Zheng *et alii* (eds) (1973) *Suishu (Book of Sui)*, Zhonghua Book Company, Beijing.

Zhuang Chuo (1983) *Jilei Bian*, Zhonghua Book Company, Beijing.

Zhou Zhenfu (2002) *Shijing Yizhu*, Zhonghua Book Company, Beijing.

References

An Zhengdi (1990) A Brief Report of Fangling Princess's Tomb of Tang, *Wenbo (Relics and Museology)*, 1, 2–6, Xi'an.

Huang Lie (1981) The Relationship Between Inland and the Western Regions during Wei, Jin, Southern and Northern Dynasties, in *Collection on History of Wei, Jin, Sui, Tang Dynasties*, Vol.1, China Social Sciences Press, Beijing.

Huang Zhengjian (1990) Chairs and Shengchuang of Tang Dynasty, *Wenwu (Cultural Relics)*, 7, 86–88, Beijing.

Institute of Archaeology of Chinese Academy of Social Sciences (ed.) (2001) *Necropolis of Tang Dynasty in Xingyuan, Yanshi*, China Social Sciences Press, Beijing.

Li Yuchun (1959) Discovers of Gold bars and lots of Persian silver coins in Wuqia County, Xin Jiang', *Kaogu (Archaeology)*, 9, 482–483, Beijing.

Nara National Museum (2008), *Sixty Shoso-in Exhibition in Perspective*, Nara.

Ningxia Museum (1988) A Brief Report of Tang Dynasty Tombs in Yanchi, Ningxia, *Wenwu (Cultural Relics)*, 9, 43–56, Beijing.

Qi Dongfang (1999) *Researches on golden and silver wares of Tang Dynasty*, China Social Sciences Press, Beijing.

Shaanxi Provincial Museum, Bureau of Culture (1974) A Brief Report of Li Shou's Tomb of Tang Dynasty, *Wenwu (Cultural Relics)*, 9, 71–88, Beijing.

Yi Shui (1982) The story of Huchuang - the History of Furniture 3, *Wenwu (Cultural Relics)*, 10, 82–85, Beijing.

Yu Taishan (2011) *Researches on the History of Relationships Between the Western and Eastern Han, Wei, Jin, Southern and Northern Dynasties and the Western Regions*, The Commercial Press, Beijing.

器物研究
Catalogue

1. 对翼兽铜环

收藏单位：新疆维吾尔自治区博物馆。

出土信息：巩乃斯河流域（位于伊犁哈萨克自治州新源县境内）出土。巩乃斯河是伊犁河的一条支流，从东南向西北注入伊犁河。这件铜环于1983年出土（《文博》1985.6），地点与1958年新疆生产建设兵团农四师在修渠时发现两件铜刀的地方很近（详见史树青，1960）。在1983年的一次农田水利建设中，发现了一批青铜器，包括铜武士俑一尊、铜环两件（这件和下面要提到的另一件）、铜铃一件、铜釜一件，以及一件已残损的承盘（见下文）。

器物概括描述：环首两只翼兽相对而卧，原来可能是一件项圈。

材质、工艺及保存状况：青铜或铜，铸造。

尺寸：直径42.5厘米。

器物详细描述：从对兽的头部类型看，像"斯芬克斯"一类，短鬃，双角后翘，背侧有双翼。

图像详细描述：铜环中空，横截面呈C形，看上去像轮盘的护套。表面比较粗糙，有一些凸棱。

风格分析：（铜环的）一边有两个带鬃毛、双耳和双角、有着猫科动物脸型的斯芬克

1. Copper Ring

Location: Xinjiang Uygur Autonomous Region Museum.

Context of Origin: Künes River basin (Xinyuan County, Ili Kasak Autonomous Prefecture); the river is one of the branches of the Ili River, entering into the main river from southeast to northwest. The ring was found in 1983 (Zhang Yuzhong 1985, 6), in a place very close to that where two bronze knives were found in the construction work (building an irrigation channel) by the 4th Division of Xinjiang Production and Construction Corps in Xinyuan, 1958 (Details of these finds are in the essay Shi Shuqing 1966). The find of 1983, contained 1 warrior-shape bronze statue, 2 bronze rings (this one and another see below), 1 bronze bell, 1 bronze pot and 1 bronze tray (see below).

Brief Description of the Object: ring with two winged beasts facing each other, may be worn as a necklace.

Material, Technique and Conservation: bronze/ copper, casting.

Measurements: diameter, 42.5cm.

Detailed Description of the Object: from the type of the heads the animals look like sphinxes, presenting short bristles, horns curving backward, wings on the back.

Detailed Description of the Iconography: the ring, hollow in the inner side, with a cross section C-sh, looks like a sheath for a steering wheel. The surface is little bit rough with burls.

1. 对翼兽铜环 Copper Ring

斯[1]，它们的脖子十分粗壮，肩部都有翅膀。前肢和前爪伸向前方，躯体则与环体连接。

地域、文化、年代属性及对比：发现地点在最初的考古简报中有描述，1984年6月20日至9月1日再次进行了发掘。这是一块南北长约200、东西宽约80米的台地，清理了房屋、灰坑遗址和6座墓葬。发现地点被认为属于乌孙人的遗存，但发掘简报中却未提及遗址区里发现的这批重要青铜器。对此，张玉忠（1989）提出了疑问，认为有关铜器的报道与发掘简报在时间和空间上存在矛盾，他指出后来发掘的墓葬与陶器的一些特征，与其他地点的塞人文化相似，他建议对这一地点及其周围地带进行深入的调查和发掘。景骞（李滔）（2003）谨慎地提出青铜项圈是斯基泰人绞杀牺牲的刑具。

Stylistic Analysis: on one side, the two sphinxes[1] have the mane, two ears and horns, and a feline face as well. Their necks are quite strong, under which the animals present two wings coming from the shoulders. Forelegs and claws extend to the front. Then, the main bodies connect with the ring.

Comparing and Geographical, Cultural and Chronological Attribution: the specific place of the find described in the original archaeological report was excavated again from Jun 20th to Sep 1st, 1984. It was about 200m long N to S and about 80m wide from E to W. Houses, pits and six tombs have been identified in the area and were considered belonging to the Wu Sun people. In the archaeological report, nothing was said about these important Bronze Wares. Zhang Yuzhong (1989) advanced the hypothesis that there were contradictions between the find of these bronze wares and the archaeological report, both temporally and spatially. He pointed out that the characteristics of the tombs and

---

[1] 李零（2004）认为所有的有翼神兽都可以被视为格里芬。尽管确实都带有翅膀，但由于不同的历史背景和遥远的空间距离，有翼神兽应有完全不同的起源。
Prof. Li Ling (2004) regards all the fantastic beasts with wings as griffins. Although wings are the commonness, they have completely different origin, because of the different historical backgrounds and far distances.

原报道（1984）认为这批铜器"可能属于秦到汉初的乌孙或塞种人"，而学者们一致把它们视为战国前后活动在伊犁河流域的塞人文化遗物，伊犁河流域自古就有游牧民族存在。20世纪80年代以来在这里不断有新发现，尤其是青铜艺术品。根据汉文史籍记载，西汉以前塞人曾在伊犁河谷有较长时间的活动，在这一地区发现了不少属于塞人文化的遗存，如尼勒克县发现了一处相当于东周时期的曾被塞人开采冶炼的铜矿遗址，新源、昭苏、特克斯、尼勒克等县境内发掘清理了不少土墩墓，时代相当于战国到汉代前后的墓群，其文化属性也可能与塞人有关。景骞（李滔）（2003）结合希罗多德《历史》中对于斯基泰人信仰活动的记载，谨慎地指出这批青铜器可能与斯基泰人对希腊神祇，特别是战神阿瑞斯的信仰活动有关，这些器物发现的地点可能是一处祭坛。林梅村（2006）引述了景骞观点，进一步指出这批斯基泰风格的青铜器是中亚希腊化时期的产物。

the pottery found in the following excavation showed similarities with other Saka remains. He suggested further that survey and excavation should have been conducted in the site and the surrounding region. Jing Qian (Li Tao) suggested that the ring was an instrument of torture for hanging cattle. In the original report (1984) it is proposed that the find "might belong to Wu Sun or Saka people from Qin to early Han Dynasty". Scholars unanimously regard them as remains of the culture of Saka of the period of Warring States in the Ili River basin, where they lived as nomads since ancient times. Since 1980s there have been consecutive discoveries, notably some bronze art objects. According to Chinese historical records, Saka people inhabited for a long time in the Ili river basin before the western Han Dynasty. Large numbers of Saka remains were widely discovered in this area, such as an abandoned copper mine in Nilka County going back to the period of the eastern Zhou Dynasty. Graves with mounds were also excavated in Xinyuan, Zhaosu, Tekes and Nilka counties, Xinjiang, whose period ranged from the Warring States period to the Han Dynasty. Culturally these mounds are related to the Saka people. Comparing these bronzes found in Künes river basin with the presumed religious activities of the Scythians described in *The Histories* of Herodotus, Jing Qian (Li Tao) suggests that they are in relation with the worship of a Greek god, basically Ares and that the spot where these bronzes were excavated may be an altar. Lin Meicun (2006) further points out that these bronzes could be the products of the Hellenistic Age in Central Asia.

参考文献　References

1. 巴依达吾来提、郭文清：《巩乃斯河南岸出土珍贵文物》，《新疆艺术》1984年第1期，页73。
Bay dolat *et alii* (1984) Discovery of Rare Antiques in the south Bank of Künes River, *Xinjiang Yishu* (*Xinjiang Art*), 1, 73, Urumï.
2. 景骞（李滔）：《管窥伊犁巩乃斯河青铜器窖藏的功用与性质——观〈天山·古道·东西风〉有感》（2003年）参见 http://www.wangf.net/vbb2/showthread.php?postid=83870。
Jing Qian (Li Tao) (2003) A View of the Function and the Nature of the Bronze Ware Cache from Künes River,

Ili: Thoughts on the Exhibition of Mt. Tianshan・Ancient Roads・The Meeting of East and West. See: http://www.wangf.net/vbb2/showthread.php?postid=83870.

3. 李零：《入山与出塞》第三章《有翼神兽研究》，文物出版社（北京），2004年，页87—135，尤其页123—124的讨论。

Li Ling (2004) Research of the Wings Legend Beasts, *Rushan yu chusai* (*Entering the Mountains and Crossing the Borders*), ch. 3, Cultural Relics Publishing House, 87–135 (in particular 123–124), Beijing.

4. 林梅村：《丝绸之路考古十五讲》，北京大学出版社（北京），2006年，页85—91。

Lin Meicun (2006) *Sichouzhilu kaogu shiwujiang* (*Fifteen Lectures on Archaeology of the Silk Roads*), Peking University Press, 85–91, Beijing.

5. 穆舜英主编：《中国新疆古代艺术》，新疆美术摄影出版社（乌鲁木齐），1994年，页45、184，图版77。

Mu Shunying *et alii* (eds.) (1994) *Zhongguo Xinjiang gudai yishu* (*The Ancient Art in Xinjiang, China*), Xinjiang Art and Photography Press, 44, 184, fig.77, Urumqï.

6. 新疆博物馆文物队：《新源县七十一团一连鱼塘遗址》，原载《新疆文物》1987年第3期，亦收入新疆文物考古研究所编：《新疆文物考古新收获（1979—1989）》，新疆人民出版社（乌鲁木齐），1995年，页337—345。

Relics Working-Team of Xinjiang Museum (1987) The Ancient Site at Yuantang, Yilian, 71–tuan, Xinyuan County, *Xinjiang Wenwu* (*Cultural Relics of Xinjiang*), 3, Urumqï, also in Xinjiang Institute of Cultural Relics and Archaeology (ICRA) (1995) *Xinjiang wenwu kaogu xinshouhuo* (*New Achievement in Archaeological Research in Xinjiang during 1979–1989*), Xinjiang People's Publishing House, 337–345, Urumqï.

7. 史树青：《新疆文物调查随笔》，《文物》1960年第6期，页22—30。

Shi Shuqing (1960) Essay on Xinjiang Cultural Relics Survey, *Wenwu* (*Cultural Relics*), 6, 22–30, Beijing.

8. 新疆维吾尔自治区文物事业管理局等主编：《新疆文物古迹大观》，新疆美术摄影出版社（乌鲁木齐），1999年，页371，图版1055。

Xinjiang Uygur Autonomous Region Cultural Relics Administration, *et alii* (eds.) (1999) *Xinjiang wenwu guji daguan* (*A Grand View of Xinjiang's Cultural Relics and Historical Sites*), Xinjiang Fine Arts Photography Press, 371, fig.1055, Urumqï.

9. 张玉忠：《新疆伊犁地区发现的大型铜器》，《文博》1985年第6期，页79—80。

Zhang Yuzhong (1985) The Discovery of a Big Size Bronze Artifact in Ili, Xinjiang, *Wenbo* (*Relics and Museology*), 6, 79–80, Xi'an.

10. 张玉忠：《伊犁河谷土墩墓的发现和研究》，《新疆文物》1989年第3期，页11—22。

Zhang Yuzhong (1989) Ili Valley Mound Tomb Discovery and Research, *Xinjiang Wenwu* (*Cultural Relics of Xinjiang*), 3, 11–22, Urumqï.

11. 张玉忠、赵德荣：《伊犁河谷新发现的大型铜器及有关问题》，《新疆文物》1991年第2期，页42—48。

Zhang Yuzhong and Zhao Derong (1991) The large Copper-ware Newly Discovered in Ili Valley, *Xinijang Wenwu* (*Cultural Relics of Xinjiang*), 2, 42–48. Urumqï.

12. 赵丰主编：《丝绸之路美术考古概论》第一章《新疆史前美术考古》，文物出版社（北京），2007年，页31—36。

Zhao Feng *et alii* (eds.) (2007) *Sichouzhilu meishu kaogu gailun* (*Introduction to Silk Road Art Archaeology*), ch. 1, Cultural Relics Publishing House, 31–36, Beijing.

(*Bruno Genito*，耿朔 [*Geng Shuo*])

2. 青铜武士像

收藏单位：新疆维吾尔自治区博物馆。

出土信息：巩乃斯河流域出土（位于伊犁哈萨克自治州新源县境内）。1983年在一个窖藏里被发现。

器物概括描述：头戴高弯钩宽沿帽的武士形象。

材质、工艺及保存状况：青铜或铜，铸造。

尺寸：高40厘米。

器物详细描述：中空。

图像详细描述：人像面部丰腴，鼻子朝向前方，有高加索人种特征，腰部仅系短裙。双手原握有器物，可能是搏斗用的武器或弓箭，已失。武士呈蹲跪状，但两腿姿势不同，左腿蹲屈，右腿跪地，左脚的脚尖着地，看上去会随时跳起发动攻击。从塑像的头部侧面看，武士戴着很大的宽沿帽，帽的顶部呈鸡冠状。工匠铸造出高鼻和深目，武士目光凝视前方。上身赤裸，隐约可以看到胸部的肌肉。下身系短裙，无鞋。双手置于膝上，手的部分也是中空的。

风格分析：塑像的造型和服饰可能象征了游牧民族武士的风格，戴着塞人式的帽子。类似头戴尖帽呈跪坐状的人俑还见于北疆其他地区，如1999年巩留县曾出土一件很相似的铜武士。

地域、文化、年代属性及对比：景骞（李滔）（2003）推测武士像是希腊战神阿瑞斯，林梅村（2006）同意他的观点，进一步指出其与希腊古

2. Bronze Statue

Location: Xinjiang Uygur Autonomous Region Museum.

Context of Origin: Künes River basin (Xinyuan County, Ili Kasak Autonomous Prefecture); it was found in a cache in 1983.

Brief Description of the Object: the statue represents a warrior wearing a wide-brimmed hat with a high hook.

Material, Technique and Conservation: bronze/copper, casting.

Measurements: height 40cm.

Detailed Description of the Object: hollow.

Detailed Description of the Iconography: the human figure with a fleshy face with a Caucasian-like nose is looking forward and wears only a short skirt around his waist. The two hands should have kept some objects, may be wrestle weapons or archer wares, now lost. The warrior is in half-kneeling position, with the right leg kneels, and the left bends, whilst the left foot is little bit on tiptoe. It seems that the warrior is jumping up to attack anytime. From the side of the head, one can see that the figure presents big hat with the brim and cockscomb-shape top. The bronze smith molded a high bridge nose, as well as big deep eyes. It stares to the front brightly. There are no clothes on the upper body, so one can also see the chest muscle subtly. On the lower body, there is only a short kilt without any shoes. Both arms are put on legs; the inner parts of hands are also hollow.

Stylistic Analysis: the modeling of the figure and the costume possibly indicate a nomadic warrior-type with a characteristic Saka hat. Similar warriors squatting with such a pointed hat have been found in other areas of north Xinjiang, as for example, that found in 1999 in Tokkuztara County.

Comparing and Geographical, Cultural and Chronological Attribution: Jing Qian (Li Tao) (2003)

2. 青铜武士像 Bronze Statue

典艺术中某种阿瑞斯的造型一致，其头盔也与一种希腊式头盔非常相似。不过，至多可以认为这件武士像是远东地区最早的立体塑像，显示出斯基泰或塞人文化的因素。

suggests that the figure may represent a Greek god, Ares. Lin Meicun (2006) agreed with this opinion. At most, one can only say that the figure is the earliest 3-dimensional statue in the Far East, showing a Scythian or Sakā cultural element as well.

参考文献　References

1. 巴依达吾来提、郭文清：《巩乃斯河南岸出土珍贵文物》，《新疆艺术》1984年第1期，页73。
   Bay dolat *et alii* (1984) Discovery of Rare Antiques in the south bank of Künes River, *Xinjiang Yishu (Xinjiang Art)*, 1, 73, Urumqï.

2. 景骞（李滔）：《管窥伊犁巩乃斯河青铜器窖藏的功用与性质—观〈天山·古道·东西风〉有感》（2003年）参见http://www.wangf.net/vbb2/showthread.php?postid=83870
   Jing Qian (Li Tao) (2003) A View of the Function and the Nature of the Bronze Ware Cache from Künes River, Ili: Thoughts on the Exhibition of Mt. Tianshan · Ancient Roads · The Meeting of East and West. See: http://www.wangf.net/vbb2/showthread.php?postid=83870.

3. 林梅村：《丝绸之路考古十五讲》，北京大学出版社（北京），2006年，页85—91。
   Lin Meicun (2006) *Sichouzhilu kaogu shiwujiang (Fifteen Lectures on Archaeology of the Silk Roads)*, Peking University Press, 85–91, Beijing.

4. 穆舜英主编：《中国新疆古代艺术》，新疆美术摄影出版社（乌鲁木齐），1994年，页44、184，图版74。
   Mu Shunying *et alii* (eds.) (1994) *Zhongguo Xinjiang gudai yishu (The Ancient Art in Xinjiang, China)* Xinjiang Art and Photography Press, 44, 184. fig.74, Urumqï.

5. 新疆维吾尔自治区文物事业管理局等主编：《新疆文物古迹大观》，新疆美术摄影出版社（乌鲁木齐），1999年，页371，图版1054。
   Xinjiang Uygur Autonomous Region Cultural Relics Administration, *et alii* (eds.) (1999) *Xinjiang wenwu guji daguan (A Grand View of Xinjiang's Cultural Relics and Historical Sites)*, Xinjiang Fine Arts Photography Press, 371, fig.1054, Urumqï.

6. 赵丰主编：《丝绸之路美术考古概论》第一章，文物出版社（北京），2007年，页31—36。
   Zhao Feng *et alii* (eds.) (2007) *Sichouzhilu meishu kaogu gailun (Introduction to Silk Road Art Archaeology)*, ch. 1, Cultural Relics Publishing House, 31–36, Beijing.

（*Bruno Genito*，耿朔 [*Geng Shuo*]）

3. 铜盘

收藏单位及馆藏号： 新疆维吾尔自治区博物馆。

出土信息： 新疆托克逊县阿拉沟古墓群M30出土。

器物概括描述： 香炉。

材质、工艺及保存状况： 青铜，熔合，低温焊接。保存完好，普遍有铜锈。

尺寸： 高32厘米，盘边长29.6、侧边高3.2厘米。

器物详细描述： 这件器物由镂空的锥形高方座和宽平折沿长方盘组成。两者的焊接处没有被磨平。盘心中央并立双兽，朝向相同。

地域、文化、年代属性及对比： 塞人文化的遗物，公元前5至前3世纪。发现于阿拉沟古墓群M30的这件铜炉，与铜香炉、釜和大型方形祭台等构成的组合联系密切，它们在工艺、风格和造型上有很多相似之处，常被统称为"七河地区铜器"，这是根据哈萨克斯坦东南部的一个地区命名的，这里被普遍认为在公元前5至前3世纪是这些铜器的生产中心(Bernštam 1952, 40–50, figs.18–20; Moškova ed, 1992: pl. 27, 29–31, 34a–b, 36, 37; Bajpakov, Ismagil 1996: 41–51; Silvi Antonini, Bajpakov 1999, 37–38, 185–186 [nos. 350–352, 428])。相似的器物也在临近的中国境内有所发现（如新疆伊犁州新源县发现的一批铜器），完全与七河地区的塞人文化一致。

就外形而言，七河地区和新疆北部地区的

3. Bronze Tray

Location: Xinjiang Uygur Autonomous Region Museum.

Context of Origin: Ala Gully cemetery, tomb no 30 (Toksun County, Xinjiang Uygur Autonomous Region).

Brief Description of the Object: incense burner.

Material, Technique and Conservation: bronze; fusion; soldering; complete; widespread encrustations.

Measurements: height 32cm; side length (tray) 29.6cm; tray height 3.2cm.

Detailed Description of the Object: the object is composed of a pyramidal stand, with hollow sides, and a rectangular tray with upright border and large horizontal rim; the solder joints of the stand were not smoothed. In the middle of the tray, two winged felines in full relief, standing side by side, turned in the same direction.

Comparing and Geographical, Cultural and Chronological Attribution: "Saka" Archaeological Complex. 5th–3rd centuries BC. The burner can be related to a group of findings — incense burners, cauldrons and large rectangular altars — sharing a series of technical, stylistic and figurative elements and commonly known as "bronzes of Semireč'e", after the region in south-eastern Kazakhstan which is reputed to have been, in the 5th–3rd centuries, their main production centre (Bernštam 1952, 40–50, figs.18–20; Moškova [ed] 1992, pl. 27.29–31, 34a–b, 36, 37; Bajpakov, Ismagil 1996, 41–51; Silvi Antonini, Bajpakov 1999, 37–38, 185–186 [nos. 350–352, 428]). Similar findings are also known in the neighbouring Chinese territory, i.e. in the Xinyuan County (e.g. an incense burner from Narat, now in the Ili Kazak Autonomous Prefecture Museum, Yining), an area revealing a material record fully consistent with the "Saka" archaeological complex of Semireč'e. As far as the shape is concerned, the incense burners from Semireč'e and

3. 铜盘 Bronze Tray

铜炉存在着大量变体。它们通常有一个镂空的锥形座（时常风格化的展现一座山峰）。铜盘为长方形、方形或圆形，其上焊接小型动物塑像，常常是沿着盘子的边缘排成一圈，或者两两相对做搏斗状，少数标本还有一整圈人像。

　　这些器物带有宗教意义是无可争辩的。除了偶然的发现，大量标本发现在多少与游牧民族宗教专属区域直接有关的地方（例如七河地区的Chilpek），或者是被证实确实在他们的圣地（例如在七河地区Kirchin河谷的Semenovskoe发现的铜器窖藏，包括铜釜、香炉和祭坛）。尽管如此，这类器物的确切功能还没有定论。人像和装饰图案的象征意义也还没有得到充分的研究。概括地说，对于它们的宗教背景，我们依然知道得很少。

　　与阿拉沟铜炉最为接近的例子是在哈萨克斯坦境内偶然发现的一件，现藏于阿拉木图的中央政府博物馆(inv. KP 2281) (Bernštam 1952: fig.20; Silvi Antonini, Bajpakov 1999: no.351)。它的形制（锥形高方座，方形托盘）和尺寸（高27厘米，盘边沿长34.7厘米）与阿拉沟的那件都极为相似，在铜盘上焊接四件斜对的圆雕有翼神兽，都朝向盘心。每个动物的翅膀最后都是旋涡状的合并在一起，臀部有孔，可能是用来放置灯芯的。铜盘的边缘也有类似的小孔，盘的一边有一个直管。这件铜炉上的焊接处都经过了仔细的磨平处理。

　　阿拉沟古墓与七河地区塞人文化的关系也可以从两地发现的陶器上得到证明（后者如伊犁河谷发现的包括带把杯、碗、圆柱形和椭圆

northern Xinjiang are known in a number of variants. They often have an open-work decorated conical stand (sometimes evoking a stylized representation of a mountain); the tray is rectangular, square or round; animal figures are present in rows along the edge or in pairs engaged in combat; a few specimens include full round representations of human figures as well. The attribution of these findings to the ritual sphere is beyond question. Apart from chance finds, a number of specimens were found in more or less direct connection with nomadic ritual precincts (e.g. Čilpek, in Semireč'e) or in areas were such shrines are attested (e.g. the hoard of bronze cauldrons, incense burners and altars from Semenovskoe, in the Kirchin Valley, Semireč'e). Nonetheless the precise function they were meant for is not yet clarified; the symbolic meaning of their figural and ornamental elements is also to be fully investigated. More in general, the religious background to which they belong is still poorly understood. The closest parallel to the Ala Gully specimen is an incense burner from Kazakhstan (chance find), now in the Central Government Museum in Almaty (inv. KP 2281) (Bernštam 1952, fig.20; Silvi Antonin, Bajpakov 1999, no 351). It matches the Ala Gully specimen both in shape (pyramidal stand; square tray) and in size (height 27cm; tray side 34.7cm); on the tray, four winged felines in full relief are soldered, standing on the diagonal axes, turned toward the centre; each animal has the wings joined in one piece ending in a volute and a round hole on its croup, possibly meant to hold the wick; similar holes are along the tray edges. A vertical pipe is preserved on one of the tray sides. In this specimen, the solder joints of the stand were accurately smoothed. The close connection between the Ala Gully tomb and the Semireč'e "Saka" archaeological record is further indicated by the pottery finds, which can be compared to vases from *kurgans* of the Ili valley

形带把大口罐）（Moškova [ed] 1992: pl. 27.19, 27–34）。同样也反映在小件装饰品上，尤其是像哈萨克斯坦七河地区伊塞克湖流域古代墓葬中出土的带翼虎形金（？）牌饰那样风格化的造型（Silvi Antonini, Bajpakov 1999, nos. 273–274）。

(hand-made mugs with vertical round handle, bowls, cylindrical or pear-shaped vases with vertical round handle and large spout) (Moškova [ed] 1992, pl. 27.19, 27–34), as well as by ornamental items, in particular the stylized depictions of winged twisted felines on gold (?) plates which find close parallels in the Issyk kurgan (Silvi Antonini, Bajpakov 1999, nos 273–274).

参考文献   References

1. Bajpakov, K.M., Ismagil, R.B. (1996) Besagaškij klad bronzovoj posudy iz Semireč'ja, *Izvestija Nacional'noj Akademii nauk Respubliki Kazahstana*, 2, 41–51.

2. Bernštam, A.N. (1952) *Istoriko-arheologičeskie očerki Central'nogo Tjan-Šanja i Pamiro-Alaja* (*Materialy i Issledovanija po arheologii, 26*), Moskva.

3. 新疆社会科学院考古研究所：《新疆阿拉沟竖穴木椁墓发掘简报》，《文物》1981 年第 1 期，页 18—22，图版捌：6。
   Institute of Archaeology in Xinjiang (1981) Excavation of the Wooden-Chambered Tomb at Alagou in Xinjiang Uighur Autonomous Region, *Wenwu* (*Cultural Relics*), 1, 18–22, 6, Beijing.

4. Moškova, M.G. (ed.) (1992) *Stepnaja polosa Aziatskoj časti SSSR v skifo-sarmatskoe vremja*, Moskva.

5. Silvi Antonini, C., Bajpakov, K. (eds.) (1999) *Altyn Adam. L'Uomo d'Oro. La cultura delle steppe del Kazakhstan dall'età del Bronzo alle grandi migrazioni* (Catalogue of the exhibition, Naples 1999), Roma.

6. 新疆维吾尔自治区文物事业管理局等主编：《新疆文物古迹大观》，新疆美术摄影出版社（乌鲁木齐），1999 年，页 163，图版 0422。
   Xinjiang Uygur Autonomous Region Cultural Relics Administration, *et alii* (eds.) (1999) *Xinjiang wenwu guji daguan* (*A Grand View of Xinjiang's Cultural Relics and Historical Sites*), Xinjiang Fine Arts Photography Press, 163, fig.0422, Urumqï.

（*Ciro Lo Muzio*，耿朔 [*Geng Shuo*]）

4. 竖琴

收藏单位：新疆吐鲁番博物馆。

出土信息：新疆鄯善洋海1号墓地M90出土。

器物概括描述：角式竖琴。

材质、工艺和保存状况：木质琴身，羊肠弦（？）。

尺寸：全长61、宽9.8厘米。弦杆长22厘米。

器物详细描述：这件竖琴包括一个椭圆形的音箱，通过圆柱形的颈部连接一个方形底座，其上竖立弦杆。除了弦杆外，其余部分由整块木头（胡杨木）挖刻而成。中空的音箱被纵向掏开，凿刻了5个卯眼，被皮制共鸣板（羊皮）覆盖，其上穿有圆形音孔。琴弦的另外一头与弦杆相连，仅存一根羊肠（？）弦。

地域、文化、年代属性及对比：年代为约公元前500年。洋海墓地的竖琴是从近东（亚述）的竖琴演化而来的，也就是"角形竖琴"，与欧亚大陆发现的一组器物存在联系，它们分布在不同地区：如扎滚鲁克（Wang Bo 2003; Lawergren 2008, 264, fig.9c, d; Lawergren 2010, 122–123）、巴泽雷克（Altai, Russian Federation; 4th century; 2008, 264, fig.9a），黑海北岸的奥尔比亚（Olbia; Lawergren 2003, 89–90; 2008, 264, fig.9b）。与装配9根弦的亚述竖琴不同的是，这组竖琴只有5根弦。洋海的竖琴与后来从中亚传入中国的角形竖竖琴（"箜篌"）没有关系，后者是公元1世纪随着佛教传播而来。

4. Harp

Location: Turpan Museum.

Context of Origin: Yanghai cemetery (Shanshan County, Xinjiang Uygur Autonomous Region), tomb 90.

Brief Description of the Object: angular harp.

Material, Technique and Conservation: wood, gut.

Measurements: length 61cm; width 9,8; height (stringholder) 22cm.

Detailed Description of the Object: the harp consists of an elliptical sounding box with a cylindrical prolongation terminating with a square element from which rises a vertical rod. All these elements were carved in one piece of wood (except the vertical rod). The hollow sounding box is crossed by a longitudinal rip, presenting five string-holes, and covered by a leather sounding board pierced by circular sounding holes. The other end of the strings was tied to the vertical rod. Only one gut (?) string is preserved.

Comparing and Geographical, Cultural and Chronological Attribution: chronology, circa 500 BC. The Yanghai harp derives from a Near-Eastern (Assyrian) type, namely the horizontal angular harp, and can be linked to a group of specimens found in different parts of the Eurasian area: at Zaghunluq (Xinjiang) (Wang Bo 2003; Lawergren 2008, 264, fig.9c, d; Lawergren 2010, 122–123), at Pazyryk (Altai, Russian Federation; 4th century; Lawergren 2008, 264, fig.9a), and at Olbia, on the northern shore of the Black Sea (Lawergren 2003, 89–90; 2008, 264, fig.9b); unlike the Assyrian model, equipped with nine strings, the Eurasian examples have only 5 strings. The Yanghai harp has no relationship with the (vertical) angular harp (the *konghou*) which was later introduced into China from Central Asia, with the spread of Buddhism in the first centuries AD.

4. 竖琴 Harp

参考文献　References

1. 新疆吐鲁番学研究院、新疆文物考古研究所：《新疆鄯善洋海墓地发掘报告》，《考古学报》2011年第1期，页99—150。

Academia Turfanica, Xinjiang and Xinjiang Institute of Cultural Relics and Archaeology (2011) Excavation on the Yanghai Cemetery in Shanshan (Piqan) County, Xinjiang, *Kaoguxuebao (Acta Archaeologica Sinica)*, no. 1, 99–150, Beijing.

2. Lawergren, B. (2003) Western Influences on the Early Chinese Qin-zither, *Bulletin of the Museum of Far Eastern Antiquities*, 75, 79–109, Stockholm.

3. Lawergren, B. (2008) Angular Harps through the Ages; a Causal History, Both, A.A., Eichmann, R., Hickmann, E., Koch, L.-Ch. (eds.) *Studien zur Musik archäologie* VI, Orient-Archäologie 22, 261–281 (in part. fig. 9e), Rahden.

4. Lawergren, B. (2010) Harps on the Ancient Silk Road, in Agnew, N. (ed.) Conservation of Ancient Sites on the Silk Road. *Proceedings of the Second International Conference on the Conservation of Grotto Sites, Mogao Grottoes, Dunhuang, People's Republic of China*, June 28–July 3, 2004, 117–124.

5. 王博：《新疆扎滚鲁克箜篌》，《文物》2003年第2期，页56—62。

Wang Bo (2003) Harps from Zagunluk site, *Wenwu (Cultural Relics)*, 2, 56–62, Beijing.

（*Ciro Lo Muzio*，耿朔 [*Geng Shuo*]，范佳楠 [*Fang Jianan*]）

5. 釉陶杯

收藏单位：张家川回族自治县博物馆。

出土信息：甘肃张家川回族自治县马家塬墓地M1出土。

器物概括描述：直口、锥身、圆厚底、杯身施淡蓝色釉，足部以上有珠状装饰。

材质、工艺及保存状况：釉陶。器表有蓝色和紫色釉彩，化学成分尚未被检测。很可能是模制。表面光滑，可能经过仔细打磨。杯基本完整，保存很好。

尺寸：通高11.6厘米，口径6.6厘米，底径3.7厘米。

器物详细描述：杯身有珠状装饰，圆唇、斜壁、平底小而厚，杯身中下部七排圆突上施紫色釉。透明度低，很难看清杯内壁的材料情况。

风格分析：马家塬墓地反映了多重文化因素。包括西北戎人和秦文化因素。这件杯既有可能从西方传来，也有可能是本地产品。

地域、文化、年代属性及对比：该墓地属于战国时代晚期（474–221 BC），西戎文化。原报告（2008）指出该杯可能是玻璃杯，但未见检测报告。2010—2011年发掘的马家塬M19中也出土了一件类似的杯子，据报告为釉陶杯，因此我们推测2006年发掘的这件也是陶杯。王辉（2007）认为这件杯子的器形和风格反映其可能源自西方，但对圆突上所施紫色颜料的分析表明是人工合成的、只在中国使用的汉紫。另外李永平（2007）认为这件杯子是齐家

5. Glazed Pottery Cup

Location: Zhangjiachuan Hui Autonomous County Museum.

Context of Origin: Tomb M1 in Majiayuan cemetery, Zhangjiachuan County, Gansu Province.

Brief Description of the Object: this cup has a straight mouth, tapered body and a thicker, round base. The body presents a light blue glaze and a beaded decoration above the base.

Material, Technique and Conservation: pottery faience; well preserved, with the body blue and purple glazed; the chemical composition has not been tested. The cup was probably molded. Surface of the outer wall is smooth, may be carefully polished. The cup is complete except some wear of protuberances.

Measurements: height 11.6cm; rim diameter 6.6cm; bottom diameter 3.7cm.

Detailed Description of the Object: cup with beaded decoration. The cup has round lip, sloping wall, small, flat and thick base. The lower part whose surface is purple glazed is decorated with 7 rows of protuberances. The cup is almost opaque, and it is difficult to see the inner structure of the material.

Stylistic Analysis: the artefacts unearthed in the Majiayuan cemetery revealed diversified cultural elements, including those of the Northern Frontier Zone of China, those of Eurasian Steppes and of Qin Culture. The cup could be an import from the West, but most likely is a local artefact.

Comparing and Geographical, Cultural and Chronological Attribution: late Warring States Period (474–221 BC); Xi Rong culture. According to the original report the cup might be glass ware, but the archaeologists did not provide the report with chemical material tests. The excavation team discovered a similar cup in Tomb no.19 during their work of 2010 to 2011. According to the report, the newly find should be a pottery cup; so one can infer that also the cup from 2006's excavation is pottery. Wang Hui (2009) retains the shape and the style of the

文化的典型器形，因此为秦本土制作的可能性较大，而以圆突装饰器物的方法多见于寺洼、辛店及沙井文化中。李媛（2009）在她的硕士论文中提及了这件杯子，分析其风格并推测其很可能来自中亚。如果这件杯子不是中国生产，那它将是早期中西交往的证据，对研究中国早期玻璃技术和中西交流有着重要的学术意义。

cup is suggestive of western origin. Yet scientific tests indicate that the paint on the surface of pearl roundels is an artificially synthesized paint, called Chinese purple, which was used only in China. On the other hand Li Yongping (2007) retains that the glazed pottery has a shape typical of China Qijia Culture, thus being a local-made artifact of the area of Qin Culture. Objects decorated with protuberances could be found in Siwa Culture, Xindian Culture and Shajing Culture. Li Yuan (2009) mentions the glazed pottery cup in her master's thesis. She analyses the style of the glazed pottery cup and presumes that it could be an import from Central Asia. If the cup was not made in China, it could be an evidence of early exchanges between China and West. The object offers different ideas of study in glass-made technique and China-West communication.

5. 釉陶杯 Glazed Pottery Cup

参考文献   References

1. 早期秦文化联合考古队、张家川回族自治县博物馆:《张家川马家塬战国墓地2007—2008年发掘简报》,《文物》2009年第10期,页25—51。
Collaborative Archaeological Team of the Early Qin Culture, Museum of Zhangjiachuan Autonomous County (2009) 2007–2008 Excavation of Majiayuan Cemetery of Warring States Period in Zhangjiachuan, Gansu, Zhangjiachuan Hui, *Wenwu* (*Cultural Relics*), 10, 25–51, Beijing.

2. 早期秦文化联合考古队、张家川回族自治县博物馆:《张家川马家塬战国墓地2010—2011年发掘简报》,《文物》2012年第8期,页4—26。
Collaborative Archaeological Team of the Early Qin Culture, Museum of Zhangjiachuan Autonomous County (2012) Report of the 2010–2011 Excavation at the Majiayuan Cemetery Warring States Period in Zhangjiachuan Gansu, *Wenwu* (*Cultural Relics*), 8, 4–26. Beijing.

3. 甘肃省文物考古研究所、张家川回族自治县博物馆:《2006年度甘肃张家川回族自治县马家塬战国墓地发掘报告》,《文物》2008年第9期,页4—18。
Gansu Provincal Institute of Cultural Relics and Archaeology, Museum of Zhangjiachuan Autonomous County (2008) 2006 Excavation of the Majiayuan Cemetery of the Warring States Period in Zhangjiachuan Autonomous County of Hui Nationality, Autonomous County, Gansu, *Wenwu* (*Cultural Relics*), 9, 4–18, Beijing.

4. 李永平:《甘肃张家川马家塬战国墓地出土文物及相关问题探讨》,《文博》2007年第6期,页10—15。
Li Yongping (2007) Unearthed Relics from Majiayuan Cemetery of Warring States Period in Zhangjiachuan, Gansu and Discussions on Related Issues, *Wenbo* (*Relics and Museology*), 6, 10–15, Xi'an.

5. 李媛:《马家塬战国墓地文化性质及其与秦文化关系探讨》,西北大学硕士论文,2009年,页14。
Li Yuan (2009) *Research on the Cultural Characteristics of Majiayuan Cemetery and its Connections with Early Qin Culture*, Northwest University, master's thesis, 14, Xi'an.

6. 马清林:《战国与秦汉时期人工合成中国蓝和中国紫研究简介》,载干福熹主编《丝绸之路上的古代玻璃研究》,复旦大学出版社(上海),2007年,页77—80。
Ma Qinglin (2007) Brief Introduction on Research of the Synthetic Chinese Blue and Purple Pigments of the Warring States and the Qin-Han Dynasties, in Gan Fuxi (ed.) *Study on Ancient Glass along the Silk Road*, 77–80, Fudan University Press, Shanghai.

7. 王辉:《发现西戎——甘肃张家川马家塬墓地》,《中国文化遗产》2007年第6期,页77。
Wang Hui (2007) Xi Rong Finds: Majiayuan Cemetery in Zhangjiachuan County, *Chinese Cultural Heritage* (*Zhongguo wenhua yichan*), 6, 77, Beijing.

8. 王辉:《甘肃马家塬墓地相关问题初探》,《文物》2009年第10期,页70—77。
Wang Hui (2009) Related issues about Majiayuan Cemetery, *Wenwu* (*Cultural Relics*), 10, 70–77, Beijing.

(*Chiara Visconti*, 范佳楠 [*Fan Jianan*])

6. 银杯套

收藏单位：张家川回族自治县博物馆。

出土信息：甘肃张家川回族自治县马家塬墓地M1出土。

器物概括描述：圆筒形杯套，圆形环耳。

材质、工艺及保存状况：银、红铜，保存好。

尺寸：高8.4、口径6.6、底径6.2厘米，壁厚0.05厘米。

器物详细描述：这件银杯套由一张很薄的银片卷成。柄两侧各嵌一铜条饰用于杯套铆接，铜条与银条重叠的部分预先打孔，再用银丝仿皮囊缝制的方法将他们连接起来。耳用铆钉

6. Silver Cup-Sheath

Location: Zhangjiachuan Hui Autonomous County Museum.

Context of origin: Tomb M1 in Majiayuan cemetery, Zhangjiachuan County, Gansu Province.

Brief description of the object: cup cover with ring handle.

Material, technique and conservation: silver and copper; well preserved.

Measurements: height 8.4cm; rim diameter 6.6cm; bottom diameter 6.2cm; thickness of wall 0.05cm.

Detailed description of the object: this cover was obtained from a single silver-sheet rolled into shape and soldered by two copper strings. The object has no bottom and was probably intended to wrap a wooden cup.

6. 银杯套 Silver Cup-Sheath

铆接在杯身中部。保存状况良好。无底、单耳，素面无纹饰，耳呈环形，口部略宽于器底。它只是一件杯套，推测器内原应有木或竹制内胎。

风格分析：杯套的连接方式模仿了皮囊作风。

地域、文化、年代属性及对比：战国晚期，西戎文化。这件杯套的形制和制作风格反映了浓厚的欧亚草原游牧文化特征。

Stylistic analysis: the object imitates leather prototypes.

Comparing and geographical, cultural and chronological attribution: late Warring States Period (474–221 BC); Xi Rong culture. The simple execution of this object, with its body beaten from a single sheet of silver and the cut rim, is typical of the nomadic culture from Eurasia.

参考文献　References

1. 早期秦文化联合考古队、张家川回族自治县博物馆：《张家川马家塬战国墓地2007—2008年发掘简报》，《文物》2009年第10期，页25—51。
   Collaborative Archaeological Team of the Early Qin Culture, Museum of Zhangjiachuan Autonomous County (2009) 2007–2008 Excavation of the Majiayuan Cemetery of Warring States Period in Zhangjiachuan, Autonomous County, Gansu, *Wenwu (Cultural Relics)*, 10, 25–51, Beijing.

2. 甘肃省文物考古研究所、张家川回族自治县博物馆：《2006年度甘肃张家川回族自治县马家塬战国墓地发掘报告》，《文物》2008年第9期，页4—28。
   Gansu Provincal Institute of Cultural Relics and Archaeology, Museum of Zhangjiachuan Autonomous County (2008) Excavation of the Majiayuan Cemetery of the Warring States Period in 2006 in Zhangjiachuan Autonomous County of Hui Nationality, Autonomous County, Gansu, *Wenwu (Cultural Relics)*, 9, 4–28, Beijing.

3. 李永平：《甘肃张家川马家塬战国墓地出土文物及相关问题探讨》，《文博》2007年第6期，页10—15。
   Li Yongping (2007) Unearthed Relics from Majiayuan Cemetery of Warring States Period in Zhangjiachuan, Gansu, and Discussions on Related Issues, *Wenbo (Relics and Museology)*, 6, 10–15, Xi'an.

4. 李媛：《马家塬战国墓地文化性质及其与秦文化关系探讨》，西北大学硕士论文，2009年，页17。
   Li Yuan (2009) *Research on the Cultural Characteristics of Majiayuan Cemetery and its Connections with Early Qin Culture*, Northwest University, master's thesis, 17, Xi'an.

5. 王辉：《发现西戎——甘肃张家川马家塬墓地》，《中国文化遗产》，2007年第6期，页77。
   Wang Hui (2007) Discovering Xi Rong: Majiayuan Cemetery in Zhangjiachuan County, *Chinese Cultural Heritage (Zhongguo wenhua yichan)*, 6, 77, Beijing.

6. 王辉：《甘肃马家塬墓地相关问题初探》，《文物》2009年第10期，页70—77。
   Wang Hui (2009) Related issues about Majiayuan Cemetery, *Wenwu (Cultural Relics)*, 10, 70–77, Beijing

（*Chiara Visconti*，范佳楠 [*Fan Jianan*]）

7. 有柄铜镜

收藏单位：新疆维吾尔自治区博物馆。

出土信息：1965年新疆维吾尔自治区伊吾县盐池苇子峡墓地出土，具体信息不明。

器物概括描述：圆形镜面，上方焊接一只铸造而成的大角鹿。

材质、工艺及保存状况：青铜或铜，铸造。

尺寸：高16、直径7.7厘米。

风格分析：在东疆地区发现的早期铜器中，常见一种以动物题材为造型装饰艺术的实用器，主要表现在铜牌、铜镜、铜刀的柄部，运用浮雕、圆雕以及透雕的技术。新疆早期阶段即西汉及以前流行带柄镜和圆形镜两种类型，学者们已经在和静县、轮台县、乌鲁木齐市、伊犁州、吐鲁番地区等地发现了带柄镜，主要流行于公元前5至前1世纪，在中原则大概要到唐中期以后才出现。众所周知，带柄镜在埃及、希腊、罗马等文明中出现极早，而中国传统铜镜则是无柄的圆形镜。

地域、文化、年代属性及对比：这枚铜镜的年代可能在公元1世纪。《丝路传奇：新疆文物大展》（2005）一书认为从时间上来看这枚铜镜属于匈奴文化范畴。

7. Bronze Mirror

Location: Xinjiang Uygur Autonomous Region Museum.

Context of origin: the object was excavated from a tomb at Weizixia, in Yanchi, Yiwu County, Xinjiang Uygur Autonomous Region in 1965. Nobody knows about the specific situation of the find of this mirror.

Brief description of the object: round mirror surface, with waved horns stag-handle on the top.

Material, technique and conservation: bronze/copper, casting.

Measurements: height 16cm; diameter 7.7cm.

Stylistic analysis: objects with animal theme decoration are often found among the early bronze ware in eastern Xinjiang. Techniques vary from applied embossment, sculpture in the round and openwork carving mainly in the handles of bronze medals, mirrors and knifes. In Xinjiang, before and during the Western Han Dynasty, two types of mirrors, with handle and round, were quite popular. Scholars had found the ones with handles in areas like Hejing, Luntai counties, Urumqï, Ili and Turpan, which seems to be common from about the 5th to the 1st century BC. This type of mirror appears in central China not earlier than the Mid-Tang Dynasty. Mirrors with handle have a quite long history in Egypt, Greece and Rome, while China's traditional bronze mirror is round.

Comparing and geographical, cultural and chronological attribution: the mirror may be dated back to about the 1th century AD. According to a volume (2005) it should belong to the Xiongnu culture.

7. 有柄铜镜 Bronze Mirror

参考文献　References

1. 香港文化博物馆编：《丝路珍宝：新疆文物大展》，康乐及文化事务署（香港），2005年，页114—115，图版31。
Hong Kong Heritage Museum (ed.) (2005) *Silu zhenbao: Xinjiang wenwu dazhan* (*The Silk Road: Treasures from Xinjiang*), Exhibition Leisure and Cultural Services Department, 114–115, Plate 31, Hong Kong.

2. 刘学堂：《中国早期铜镜起源研究》，载中国社会科学院边疆考古研究中心编：《新疆的石器时代和青铜时代》，文物出版社（北京），2008年，页218—242。
Liu Xuetang (2008) Research on the origin of Early Bronze Mirror in China: Hypothesis of their Origin from Western Regions, The Institute of Archaeology of Chinese Academy of Social Sciences (ed.) *Xinjiang de shiqi shidai he qingtong shidai* (*Stone Age and Bronze Age in Xinjiang*), Cultural Relics Publishing House, 218–242, Beijing.

3. 穆舜英主编：《中国新疆古代艺术》，新疆美术摄影出版社（乌鲁木齐），1996年，页52、186，图版109。
Mu Shunying *et alii* (eds.) (1996) *Zhongguo xinjiang gudai yishu* (*The Ancient Chinese Art in Xinjiang*, China), Xinjiang Art and Photography Press, 52, 186, fig.109, Urumqï.

4. 历史博物馆编辑委员会编辑：《丝路传奇：新疆文物大展》，（台湾）历史博物馆（台北），2008年，页66—67。
"National" Museum of History editorial committee (ed.) (2008) *Silu chuanqi: Xinjiang wenwu dazhan* (*Legends of the Silk Road: Treasures from Xinjiang*), Exhibition Catalogue, "National" Museum of History, 66–67, Taipei.

（*Bruno Genito*，耿朔 [*Geng Shuo*]）

8. 金项饰

收藏单位：新疆文物考古研究所。

出土信息：这件金项圈出土于1996年发掘的交河沟西墓地M1，最初亦被称为金冠。该土坑墓中有两具遗骸，盗扰严重，但依然出有嵌绿松石金耳环、金戒指、星云镜等遗物，显示出墓主人在整个墓地中的地位非同一般。

器物概括描述：金冠或金项圈。

材质、工艺及保存状况：金制。

尺寸：直径14、宽1.9—4.1厘米，重77.7g。

器物详细描述：该器物主体由三条管状金片相叠而成，管状金片的上下各有一片带有动物纹装饰的金片，题材类似，但难以辨识。

图像详细描述：上下两条金片上的装饰主题很可能是两只蹲兽搏斗。可能是大型猫科动物正在捕杀有蹄类动物。下部的金片中心部位

8. Gold Torque

Location: Xinjiang Institute of Cultural Relics and Archaeology.

Context of Origin: Jiaohe Gouxi cemetery (Turfan), tomb 1 (excavated in 1996). The diadem, or torque, was found in a pit grave containing the remains of two skeletons. In spite of having been plundered, the tomb still preserved objects (a gold earring with turquoise inlay, a gold ring, a bronze mirror, etc.) which suggest that it must have been one of the richest in the whole cemetery.

Brief Description of the Object: gold diadem or torque.

Material, Technique and Conservation: gold.

Measurements: diameter 14cm; width 1.9–4.1cm.

Detailed Description of the Object: the object is made of three tubular plain gold plates, above and below which are two more plates with zoomorphic ornamentation based on one and the same subject, which, due to an apparently approximate workmanship, is not clearly intelligible.

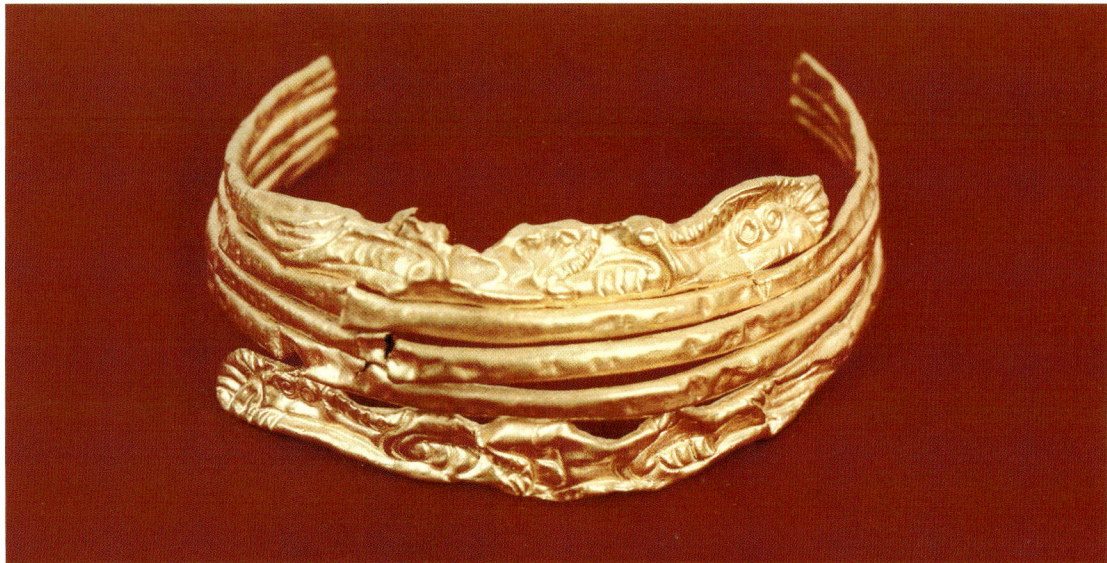

8. 金项饰 Gold Torque

可以看到一只猫科动物的爪中有一个绵羊或山羊头。

　　地域、文化、年代属性及对比：这件器物曾被认为是金冠，后又根据伊塞克金人墓（哈萨克斯坦东部的七河流域）中的类似发现定为金项饰，不过交河沟西的这件金饰直径较小，也很难确定一定是金项饰。时代被定为西汉（206 BC—23 AD）。

Detailed Description of the Iconography: the theme is probably a fight between two squatting animals; the aggressor is possibly a large feline, the prey is an ungulate; in the lower plate, in the centre, we can better discern the feline holding in its jaws the head of a mountain goat or ram.

Comparing and Geographical, Cultural and Chronological Attribution: previously interpreted as a diadem, this artefact has been later labelled as torque, on the ground of a comparison with a similar object unearthed in the Issyk kurgan (Semireč'e, Eastern Kazakhstan); the small diameter, however, makes this interpretation uncertain. Western Han period (206 BC–23 AD).

参考文献　References

1. Akišev, K.A. (1978) *Issyk Kurgan*, Moskva.

2. Janβen-Kim, M. (2007) Diadem oder Halsring mit Tierkopfenden, A. Wieczorek, A. und Lind, C. (hrsg.) (2007) *Ursprünge der Seidenstraße, Sensationelle Neufunde aus Xinjiang, China*, 273, Mannheim-Stuttgart.

3. 刘学堂：《论交河城的兴起、构筑特色、发展和废弃》，《边疆考古研究》，第3辑，科学出版社，2004年，页201—202。
Liu Xuetang (2004) The Origin. Structural Character, Development and Decline of Jiaohe city, *Research of China's Frontier Archaeology*, 3, 201–202. Science Press, Beijing.

4. 新疆文物考古研究所：《1996年新疆吐鲁番交河故城沟西墓地汉晋墓葬发掘简报》，《考古》1997年第9期，页46—54及图版柒、捌。
Xinjiang Institute of Cultural Relics and Archaeology (1997) Brief Report on the Excavation of Tombs in Han-Jin Dynasties at Gouxi Cemetery in Jiaohe city site, Xinjiang, 1996, *Kaogu (Archaeology)*, 9, 46–54, Plate 7,8, Beijing.

5. 新疆文物考古研究所：《交河沟西：1994—1996年度考古发掘报告》，新疆人民出版社，2001年，页4—9及彩版七、八。
Xinjiang Institute of Cultural Relics and Archaeology (2001) *Jiaohe Gouxi: 1994–1996 niandu kaogu fajue baogao (Jiaohe Gouxi: the Archaeological Excavating Report from 1994 to 1996)*, 4–9, Colorful Plate 7, 8, Xinjiang People's Publishing House, Urumqï.

（*Ciro Lo Muzio*, 李雨生 [*Li Yusheng*]）

9. 铅饼

收藏单位：甘肃灵台县博物馆。

出土信息：1976年10月25日，甘肃省灵台县中台公社社员在农田基本建设中发现这批外国铭文铅饼，县博物馆闻讯后立即进行了清理。出土地点在县城南2公里浦河川康家沟生产大队枣树台生产队的一个台地上，在紧靠西山的表土之下深约1米处的坑内发现一堆青石块，石块中间放置两块相互衔接的筒瓦，其上再用两块筒瓦盖合，在两端各挡有一块青石片。在筒瓦内放置四行铅饼，分上下两层整齐排列。出土地点四周采集到汉代瓦片，但没有发现其他遗物。铅饼出土后略有散失，但很快交回。

器物概括描述：铅饼上有西方铭文。这批铅饼共274枚，形制、图案、文字大致相同，外凸的一面铸造一个盘曲的异兽，长身躯，头部有角。内凹的一面中间印有两个方形的小戳记，戳记中有笔画简单的印文，外围是一周凸起的西方铭文。

材质、工艺及保存状况：其中两件标本经中国社会科学院考古研究所化验室化验，确定其成分以铅为主，1号重115.4克、2号116.5克，比重均为11，略低于纯铅（因为这些铅饼表面覆盖的灰色氧化层影响到了比重的测定）。

尺寸：直径5.5、最厚处1.2厘米，重110—118克，274枚铅饼总重量31.806千克。

地域、文化、年代属性及对比：这种西文铅饼在中国已有多枚出土，集中发现于陕西、甘

9. Lead Ingots

Location: Lingtai County Museum.

Context of Origin: these lead ingots with western character were found by peasants working in the fields in Lingtai County, Gansu Province in 1976. Lingtai County Museum cleaned up the ruins very quickly, after having heard the news. The find spot is located in a tableland near to Pu River belonging to Zaotaishu Village. A lot of lead ingots were buried regularly in the two layers in a pit about 1 meter deep. Pieces of tiles and rocks covered them, some of the tiles of Han Dynasty were collected around the spot, but no other artifacts. A little of ingots were once lost but handed in soon.

Brief Description of the Object: ingots with western characters. There are 274 lead ingots in all. Their shape, patterns and inscriptions are about the same. A coiled fantastic beast which might be dragon is on the bulge side, and two small stamps which have simple strokes and a circle of western character inscriptions are on the concave side of lead ingot.

Material, Technique and Conservation: two specimens were tested by the laboratory of Institute of Archaeology. Chinese Academy of Social Sciences; their main component is lead: no 1 weight 115.4g.; no 2 weight 116.5g., both specific gravity 11, slightly less than pure lead. It is because there was some grey oxide on the surface thus influenced on the analysis of specific gravity.

Measurements: diameter 5.5cm; thickness 1.2cm; weight from 110 to 118g. The total weight of 274 lead ingots is 31.806 kg.

Comparing and Geographical, Cultural and Chronological Attribution: this kind of lead ingots with western character has been found several times in China, mainly in Shannxi and Gansu Province. Thirteen lead ingots in a pottery jar were found in the ruins of Chang'an city of Han Dynasty, Xi'an, Shannxi Province, 1965. Two lead ingots were found

肃两省境内。如1965年陕西西安市汉代长安城址内发现13枚，放在一个罐子内；1973年陕西扶风姜塬发现2枚，与五铢钱同出于汉代文化层中，附近是汉鄠城故址，铅饼年代在西汉晚期至东汉晚期。此外，陕西西安市、长武县，甘肃礼县、西和县等地的文物机构中还各藏有少量的外文铅饼。安徽西部的六安市境内三次发现外文铅饼：1941年和1986年偶然发现，1988年在一座汉代木椁墓中又发现1枚。伯希和（1928）曾对一枚传世铅饼发表过简单意见，他未能释读出铭文，只是初步鉴定为希腊文字母拼写。密兴·黑尔芬（1952）认为这种铭文与晚期安息"德拉克麦"货币上的铭文最

in cultural layer of Han Dynasty (from later period of Western Han Dynasty to later period of Eastern Han Dynasty) with some bronze Wuzhu coins, near to the ruins of Tai County of Han Dynasty, in Fufeng County, Shaanxi Province, 1973. Moreover, some institutions of Xi'an City, Changwu County (in Shannxi Province), Li County and Xihe County (in Gansu Province) have collected a small quantity of lead ingots. Outside above areas, there are also finds three times of lead ingots in Lu'an City, Anhui Province. The third time is that one lead unearthed from a tomb of Han dynasty in Lu'an, 1988. Before that, it was reported that two unexpected finds in the same area respectively in 1941 and 1986. Pelliot (1928) gives his opinion simply about one lead ingot from China that the circle of inscriptions is the spelling of Greek alphabet. But he could not explain them. O. Maenchen — Helfen (1952) thinks this kind

9. 铅饼 Lead Ingots

为相似,货币上的铭文常采用缩写的办法,一个字中常省略掉几个字母,这些铭文可复原为能读得通的希腊字,因此是一种草体希腊文拼写的安息钱币铭文。他认为凸面龙形浮雕是中国风格,因此肯定是中国匠人所铸,铭文是中国人所仿抄而失真的希腊文。作铭(夏鼐)(1961)考察了中国历史博物馆和私人所藏的数枚外文铜饼(均不是科学发掘品,也未作成分测定,估计都是铅饼),认为它们来自西域某国,其上的铭文是传写失真的希腊文,仿抄公元1—2世纪的安息钱上的铭文,因此年代是东汉晚期或稍晚。林梅村(1988)不赞同密兴·黑尔芬的铭文转写,指出中亚的贵霜帝国也使用这种草体希腊文,这些铅饼可能是贵霜大月氏人在三辅及西邻地区频繁活动留下的遗物。党顺民(1994)认为铅饼可能是汉武帝元狩四年冬(前119)发行的"白金三品"之一的"龙币",另两种是"马币""龟币",恰好在安徽六安、陕西宝鸡发现了圆形外文铅饼、方形马币、椭圆形龟币同出的现象,铅饼上的外国铭文是武帝模仿安息货币的产物。Michael Alarm(2001)转述Joe Cribb的观点,认为同其他铜质或泥质仿制品一样,这种铅饼也是用于随葬的明器。他也指出这种被转写失真的希腊文不是来自帕提亚钱币,而是见于印度斯基泰或早期贵霜钱币上,曾在公元前1世纪至公元1世纪流通于巴克特里亚和印度西北部地区。无论如何,这些铅饼可以确定不是帕提亚或巴克特里亚的输入品,而是中国自己的产品。张骞通西域后,中国受到西域钱币的很大

of inscriptions on lead ingots are very similar to those present on drachms of later period of Parthia. Several abbreviated terms were adopted. He transcribed them to Greek, so the script style of Greek was used to spell inscriptions of Parthian coins but had some distorted information. He thought the dragon relief on the bulge side represented the style of China. These lead ingots came from Chinese artisans who were not good at copying Greek letter. Zuo Ming (Xia Nai) (1961) thinks these lead ingots with foreign character which handed down came from somewhere of the Western Regions and the inscriptions were distorted Greek. They imitated the inscription on Parthian coins belonging to the 1st and 2nd century AD. So the date may be the later period of Eastern Han Dynasty, or a little later. Lin Meicun (1988) disagrees with the idea of the transfer of the inscription form argued by Maenchen-Helfen. He pointed out that this script style of Greek also existed in Kushan Empire in Central Asia. These lead ingots maybe could, for this, belong to Kushans who once lived in the Guanzhong plain and its western area. Dang Shuming (1994) thinks that this kind of lead ingots was dragon-coin which belong to *Three Pieces of White Gold* minted in the five-year Yuanshou (119 BC). The inscription on lead ingots may come from an imitation of Parthian coins in Wudi' Period, Western Han Dynasty. Michael Alram (2001) retails Joe Cribb's opinion that these ingots, like other imitated ingots made of bronze or clay, are grave-goods. He has also convincingly pointed out that the barbarized Greek inscription could be copied not from Parthian coins but from the Indo-Scythian or early Kushan, circulating in Bactria and northwest India in the first centuries BC and AD. In any case, it is taken for sure that these ingots were not imported from Parthia or Bactria but manufactured in China. When the Han emperor Wudi sent Zhang Qian to Bactria in the 130s BC, the Chinese also came into contact with the coins they saw in the Western Regions; thus it is likely that some of these

影响，后者被带到中国来，可能就充当了这些铅饼的模型。周延龄（2004）认为白金三品是银质或银锡合金，而这种铅饼保留了白金三品的形制与纹饰，是民间盗铸品。

"exotic" coins were brought to China and served as a model for the lead ingots. Zhou Yanlin (2004) thought the texture of *Three Pieces of White Gold* was silver or silver-tin alloy, so these lead ingots should represent the folk imitations made in society.

参考文献　References

1. Alram, M. (2001) Lead Ingots with Barbarous Greek Inscription, *Monks and Merchants, Silk Road Treasures from Northwest China: Gansu and Ningxia, 4th–7th Century*, Asia Society, 37. Harry N. Abrams, Incorporated, New York.

2. 安志敏：《金版与金饼——楚、汉金币及其有关问题》，《考古学报》1973年第2期，页66—90。
   An Chin-min (1973) The chin Pan and Chin Ping coins- a study of the gold coins of the state of Ch'u and the Han Dynasty and some related problems, *Kaogu xuebao (Acta Archaeologica Sinica)*, 2, 66–90. Beijing.

3. 甘肃省文物局编：《甘肃文物菁华》，文物出版社（北京），2006年，页303，第318号器物。
   Cultural Relics Bureau of Gansu (ed.) (2006) *Gansu wenwu jinghua (Collection of Precious Cultural Relics in Gansu)*, Cultural Relics Publishing House, 303, no. 318, Beijing.

4. 党顺民：《外文铅饼新探》，《考古与文物》1994年5期，页84—89。
   Dang Shunmin (1994) Restudy on the Lead ingots with foreign inscriptions, *Kaogu yu wenwu (Archaeology and Cultural Relics)*, 5, 84–89, Xi'an.

5. 甘肃省博物馆编：《甘肃丝绸之路文明》，科学出版社（北京），2008年，页96、197，图版84。
   Gansu Museum (ed.) (2008) *Gansu sichouzhilu wenming (Civilization along the Silk Road within Gansu)*, Social Sciences Academic Press, 96, 197, fig.84, Beijing.

6. 中国社会科学院考古研究所资料室：《西安汉城故址出土一批带铭文的铅饼》，《考古》1977年第11期，亦收入中国社会科学院考古研究所汉长安城工作队、西安市汉长安城遗址保管所编：《汉长安城遗址研究》，科学出版社（北京），2006年，页28—29，及中国社会科学院考古研究所编：《夏鼐文集》（下册），社会科学文献出版社（北京），2000年，页10—11。
   Library of the Institute of Archaeology, Chinese Academy of Social Sciences (1977) Lead Discs with Inscriptions Unearthed from Ruined Han City at Xi'an, *Kaogu (Archaeology)*, 6, 428, Beijing, also in *Han Chang'an Excavation Team of the institute of Archaeology* CASS, *Preservation office of the Han Chang'an Site* (2006) *Han changancheng yizhi yanjiu (Research on Chang'an City Site in Han Dynasty)*, Science Publishing House, 28–29, Beijing, also in the Institute of Archaeology CASS (ed.) (2000) *Xia Nai wenji (A Collection of Xia Nai's Works)*, Volume Ⅲ, Social Sciences Academic Press, 10–11. Beijing.

7. 灵台县博物馆：《甘肃灵台发现外国铭文铅饼》，《考古》1977年第6期，页427，图一。
   Lingtai County Museum (1977) Lead Ingots with Foreign Inscriptions Discoveried in Lingtai, Gansu, *Kaogu (Archaeology)*, 6, 427, fig.1, Beijing.

8. 林梅村：《贵霜大月氏人流寓中国考》，《敦煌吐鲁番研究学论文集》，汉语大词典出版社（上海），1990年，页715—755，亦收入林氏：《西域文明：考古、民族、语言和宗教新论》，东方出版社（北京），1995年，页33—67。

Lin Meicun (1990) On the Great Yùeh-chih people's emigration from Kushān to China, *Dunhuang tulufan yanjiuxue lunwen ji* (*Collected Papers of Dunhuang and Turfan Studies*), Chinese Dictionary Press, 715–755, Shanghai. Also in his book (1995) *Xiyu wenming: kaogu, minzu, yuyan he zongjiao xinlun* (*The Serindian Civilization-New studies on Archaeology, Ethnology, Languages and Religions*), the Eastern Publishing Co. Lfd, 33–67, Beijing.

9. 罗西章:《扶风姜塬发现汉代外国铭文铅饼》,《考古》1976年第4期,页275—276。
   Luo Xizhang (1976) Lead Ingots with Foreign Inscriptions of Han Dynasty discoveried in Jiangyuan, Fufeng County, *Kaogu* (*Archaeology*), 4, 275–276, Beijing.

10. 李勇:《安徽六安汉墓出土铅饼》,《中国钱币》1996年第4期,页72。
    Li Yong (1996) Lead Ingot Unearthed from Han Dynasty Tombs in Lu'an, *Zhongguo qianbing* (*China Numismatics*), 4, 72, Beijing.

11. Maenchen-Helfen, O. (1952) A Chinese Bronzes Rest Money Inscription, *Asia Major*, 3, 1, London.

12. Pelliot, P. (1932) *T'oung Pao*, 194.

13. 王长启:《汉代希腊文铅饼一枚》,《陕西金融》1990年第10期。
    Wang Changqi (1990) The Han Dynasty Greek Lead Ingots, *Shaanxi jinrong* (*Shaanxi Finance*), 10, Xi'an.

14. 赵彩秀:《馆藏十枚希腊文铅饼》,《陕西金融》1990年第11期。
    Zhao Caixiu (1990) A Collection of Ten Greek Lead Ingots, *Shaanxi jinrong* (*Shaanxi Finance*), 11, Xi'an.

15. 周延龄:《西汉铅饼相关问题再探》,《西安金融》2004年第4期,页62—63。
    Zhou Yanling (2004) Rethinking at the Western Han Dynasty lead Ingots, *Xi'an jinrong* (*Xi'an Finance*), 4, 62–63, Xi'an.

16. 作铭:《外国字铭文的汉(？)代铜饼》,《考古》1961年第5期,页272—276,亦收入中国社会科学院考古研究所编:《夏鼐文集》(下册),社会科学文献出版社(北京),2000年,页3—9。
    Zuo Ming (Xia Nai) (1961) *Han* (*?*) Copper Discs with Inscription in Foreign Languages, *Kaogu* (*Archaeology*), 5, 272–276, Beijing. Also in *The Institute of Archaeology* CASS (ed.) (2000) *Xia Nai wenji* (*A Collection of Xia Nai's Works*),Volume Ⅲ, Social Sciences Academic Press, 3–9, Beijing.

(*Bruno Genito*, 耿朔 [*Geng Shuo*])

10. 印花棉布

收藏单位：新疆维吾尔自治区博物馆。

出土信息：1959年出土于新疆民丰尼雅遗址的M1。

器物概括描述：蜡染印花棉布残片。

材质、工艺及保存状况：蜡染棉布。

尺寸：长89、宽48厘米。

器物详细描述：这块棉布是该墓中出土的两块织物之一，两块棉布可以拼合成一幅更大的棉布的左下角。棉布表面装饰了呈方形和长方形的大小格子，之间以蓝色条纹隔开，每个方格内都有人像或装饰纹样，人像或者装饰纹样都是蓝地白花。左下角的方格内是一位半身女性形象，四分之三侧向右面，盘好的发髻映衬出椭圆形的脸，杏眼向右凝视、短柳叶眉、高鼻、小嘴；戴珍珠项链，耳环由两枚珍珠构成，戴臂环以及手镯等；袒胸露乳，有头光和背光，头光外还环绕一圈花瓣。手持丰饶角。半身女性之上的方格（也可能是长方形）中仅保存一只脚，右侧是一个满布棋盘格装饰的竖长方格，其下的横长格中描绘了一只野兽口吐波浪状的彩花带。横长格之上是一个更大的方格，仅保存了左下角，表现的是一只赤裸左足和狮爪狮尾。

图像详细描述：棉布左下角的女性形象可能表现的是一位女神，但很难确定是丰收女神（Tyche）或是东方地区类似的希腊神祇，例如在贵霜钱币和犍陀罗雕像中见到的丰收女神阿尔多克沙（Ardokhsho，参见 Bussagli 1984, 122–125）。正是基于以上判断，有一种观点便

10. Cotton Cloth

Location: Xinjiang Uygur Autonomous Region Museum.

Context of Origin: Niya cemetery (Minfeng, Xinjiang Uygur Autonomous Region), tomb 1 (excavated in 1959).

Brief Description of the Object: fragment of cotton cloth with stamped batik design.

Material, Technique and Conservation: wax-resist dyed cotton.

Measurements: length 89cm; width 48cm.

Detailed Description of the Object: this is one of two fragments preserving the lower left corner of the textile; it shows part of a network composed of square and rectangular compartments separated by blue stripes, each containing a figurative subject or ornamental pattern; all figures and patterns are white on a blue ground. On the left, within a square frame, the bust of a female figure in three quarter view to the right. She has oval face, framed by hair tufts regularly disposed, almond-shaped eyes gazing to the right, short arched eyebrows, large nose and small mouth; she wears a pearl necklace, earring made of two pearls, armlets (?), and bracelets; her bust is apparently naked. Her head is encircled by a halo composed of an inner dotted circle framed by an outer band with a row of petals. Her body is encircled by a "mandorla". She holds a *cornucopia*. Above, only the lower part of another (square?) compartment is preserved with a boot. To the right, a vertical rectangular compartment decorated with a checkered pattern and a horizontal rectangular compartment with a waving festoon pouring out from the fangs of a beast, at the extreme left. Above, there was a large compartment of which only the lower left corner is still extant, in which a left bare foot as well as the tail and a paw of a lion are visible.

Detailed Description of the Iconography: the female figure probably represents a goddess, although

10. 印花棉布 Cotton Cloth

认为这块棉布很可能产于犍陀罗地区或者中亚西部（Rhie 1999, 366）。另外考虑到棉布的主体部分表现的是人狮搏斗题材，所以这块织物已经基本排除了是佛教艺术品的可能性。

地域、文化、年代属性及对比：东汉。

it cannot be established whether she is to be identified with a Tyche or with an Oriental counterpart of the Greek deity, such as Ardokhsho the goddess, known from the Kushan coinage and the Gandharan sculpture (Bussagli 1984, 122–125); hence the hypothesis that the cloth might have been manufactured in the Gandhara area or in Western Central Asia (Rhie 1999, 366). Given the subject represented in the main field — a man fighting with a lion — it can be ruled out that the textile is a Buddhist artwork, as it has been sometimes considered.

***Comparing and Geographical, Cultural and Chronological Attribution*:** Eastern Han period (first two centuries AD).

参考文献   References

1. D'Arelli, F., Callieri, P.F. (eds.) (2011) *A Oriente. Città, Uomini, Dei sulle Vie dellaSeta*, 124, Roma.
2. Pirazzoli-t'Serstevens, M. (1994) Pour une archéologie des échanges. Apports étrangers en Chine - transmission, réception, assimilation, *Arts Asiatiques*, 49, 21–33 (in part. 21–22, fig. 2).
3. Rhie, M. M. (1999) *Early Buddhist Art of China and Central Asia, 1. Later Han, Three Kingdoms and Western Chin in China and Bactria to Shan-shan in Central Asia* (Handbuch der Orientalistik, IV Abteilung, 12 Band), 364–366. Leiden - Boston - Köln.
4. Watt, James C.Y. *et alii* (2004) *China: Dawn of a Golden Age, 200–750 AD*, Yale University Press (in part. 196–197, no. 103), New Haven and London.

（*Ciro Lo Muzio*，李雨生 [*Li Yusheng*]）

11. 裤子

收藏单位：新疆维吾尔自治区博物馆。

出土信息：出土于新疆洛浦县山普拉乡的戈壁墓地I区的M1。

器物概括描述：裤子残件，其上缀织马人和武士形象。

材质、工艺及保存状况：毛织物，染色。

尺寸：残长116、幅宽48厘米。

器物详细描述：原本为两条裤腿，后拼合在一起，最初很可能是一幅壁挂的一部分。下部表现的是一个四分之三面向右侧的男性形象，立于红色背景之中。身着长袖长袍，长袖由肩至腕装饰一道纵长条纹，上臂和腕部再各装饰一条横长条纹。长袍正面的直领上装饰菱格形四瓣花，腰部有腰带，方形带板，其上装饰三排圆圈纹。

图像详细描述：该男性梳黑长发，额前束白色发带，头盖骨很可能有后天的人工变形。面部表现极为成熟精确，晕染恰到好处，弯眉大眼，向右凝视；高鼻；嘴唇小而厚，下巴突出。手持长矛，矛尖穿过分隔带，一直延伸至上半块织物中。上半部的织物保存了一个更大的装饰主题的一部分：中心是一位马人（半人半马，马身红色）向左侧行进，前蹄飞起，正在吹奏某种管乐器（很可能是喇叭），领巾飞扬。马人被呈菱格形分布的彩黄色或粉红色的四瓣花围起；右上角还可以见到翅膀残段，可能属于一位小天使（*amorino*）；菱格形花瓣的外部下缘有更大造型的花朵。上半块织物

11. Trousers

Location: Xinjiang Uygur Autonomous Region Museum.

Context of Origin: cemetery I, grave 1, Sanpula, Hotan District, Xinjiang Uygur Autonomous Region.

Brief Description of the Object: trouser fragment with centaurs and warrior design.

Material, Technique and Conservation: wool; dye.

Measurements: length cm 116; width cm 48.

Detailed Description of the Object: left leg of a pair of trousers made of separate pieces once belonging to a wall tapestry. Two main fragments joined together by means of a band. The lower one shows a male figure standing in three quarter to the right on a red background. He wears a red long sleeved tunic; the sleeves are decorated by a longitudinal stripe (from the shoulder to the wrist) decorated by couples of lines, whereas two horizontal stripes, with a similar design, were sewn around the upper arm and the wrist. The front of the tunic shows a decoration of blue four-petal rosettes within a lozenge net. In the lower part of the tunic a band in relief is visible. The belt made of square plaques, decorated with three rows of circles.

Detailed Description of the Iconography: the man has long black hair tied with a white band on the sloping forehead, most probably due to artificial cranial deformation. The face shows a very skillful execution, with an accurate shadowing; arched eyebrows, large eyes looking towards to right, straight nose, small fleshy lips and prominent chin. The figure holds a long spear with a foliate blade, the tip of which overlaps the separating band and ends in the upper register. The upper register preserves part of a decorative composition. The centre is occupied by a centaur (red horse with human bust) walking to the left with front legs in a gallop, playing a long wind instrument, most probably a trumpet, and

11. 裤子 Trousers

的背景呈深蓝色，沿顶边还能见到两条横向分布的红色条纹。

地域、文化、年代属性及对比：时代约为汉代（206 BC—220 AD），织物上的植物装饰（四瓣花等）在公元前5世纪至公元3、4世纪广泛流行，很难提供精确的年代信息。下半部人物的表现方式，尤其是面部的表现在中亚地区的壁画中较为常见，其中眼睛、嘴唇以及明暗对比的手法在斯坦因发现的米兰佛寺壁画（M III和M V）中可以找到直接的例证，该佛寺位于新疆东部，时代为3—4世纪，壁画中也有天使形象（amorini，参见Stein 1912, I, 461–494; 1921, I, 492–533; Bussagli 1963, 18–29）。至于颅骨人工变形及头发上束发带等现象在乌兹别克斯坦贵霜时期的Khalčayan遗址（1世纪）中也有类似发现（Pugačenkova 1965）。

wearing a floating scarf. The figure is framed by a lozenge of four-petal rosettes, in different shades of cream and pink; in the upper right corner, a wing is visible, probably belonging to an *amorino*. Larger flowers are seen along the lower margin of the scene. The background is dark blue. Along the upper margin, part of a white band with two longitudinal red stripes is still preserved.

Comparing and Geographical, Cultural and Chronological Attribution: approximately Han period (206 BC–220 AD). Whereas the floral motifs (rosettes and other elements) do not provide a firm chronological indication, being attested during a very long time span (5th century BC – 3rd–4th century AD), the rendering of the human figure, especially his face, shows clear parallels with Central Asian painting; in particular, eyes, lips and *chiaroscuro* effects can be directly compared to several figures appearing in the murals unearthed by M.A. Stein in two Buddhist shrines (M III and M V) at Miran, in Eastern Xinjiang (3rd–4th centuries AD), where winged *amorini* are also attested (Stein 1912, I, 461–494; 1921, I, 492–533; Bussagli 1963, 18–29). For the cranial artificial deformation as well as the hair tied with a band, a parallel is provided by the clay frieze found in the early Kushan *pavilion* of Khalčayan (Uzbekistan, 1st century AD) (Pugačenkova 1965).

参考文献　References

1. Bussagli, M. (1963) *Central Asian Painting*, Geneva.
2. Jones, R.A. (2009) Centaurs on the Silk Road: Recent Discoveries of Hellenistic Textiles in Western China, *The Silk Road*, 6/2 (Winter-Spring), 23–32, Seattle.
3. Pugačenkova, G.A. (1965) La sculpture de Khaltchayan, *Iranica Antiqua*, 5, 116–127, Gent.
4. Rhie, M.M. (2000) *Early Buddhist Art of China and Central Asia*, Leiden - Boston - Köln, vol. 1, figs.4.12, 4.14a, 5.83c, Leiden - Boston - Köln.
5. Stein, A. (1912) *Ruins of Desert Cathay*, 2 vols, London.
6. Stein, A. (1921) *Serindia*, 5 vols, New York.
7. Wagner, M., Wang Bo, Tarasov, P., Westh-Hansen, S.M., Völling, E., Heller, J. (2009) The Ornamental

Trousers from Sampula (Xinjiang, China): Their Origins and Biography, *Antiquity*, 83, 322, 1065–1075, Durham.

8. Wieczorek, A. und Lind, C. (hrsg.) (2007) *Ursprünge der Seidenstraße, Sensationelle Neufunde aus Xinjiang, China*, Mannheim - Stuttgart.

（*Ciro Lo Muzio*, 李雨生 [*Li Yusheng*]）

12. 红地罽袍

收藏单位：新疆维吾尔自治区博物馆。

出土信息：新疆尉犁营盘墓地M15。

器物概括描述：红地对人兽树纹罽袍。

材质、工艺及保存状况：毛织品。

尺寸：最大宽185、长110厘米。

器物详细描述：这块长袍本是M15中的一位25岁左右男性的随身衣物，双层两面织成，其上的装饰包括以树木为中心的对人、对兽等。正反两面装饰相同，但颜色相反，正面为黄纹红地，背面为红纹黄地。

图像详细描述：织物上的纹样左右对称，每个装饰单元（80厘米长）包括了竖向分布的六组主题，即两对男性形象，一组对兽和一棵树。男性裸体，身着斗篷，自肩及背，头发卷曲，手执武器（或者是短矛，或者是短剑和盾），两两相对。对兽包括公牛和山羊两种。每棵树都分出左右两枝，另有少许枝杈及扁圆形叶子。

风格分析：织物装饰尤其是人物形象表现出自然主义风格，反映出来自古典世界或者罗马艺术的影响，所以有的观点认为这件长袍产于中亚希腊化地区或者犍陀罗。

地域、文化、年代属性及对比：东汉—晋（25–420 AD）。

12. Felt Caftan

Location: Institute of Cultural Relics and Archaeology of Xinjiang Uygur Autonomous Region.

Context of Origin: Yingpan cemetery (Xinjiang, Yuli District), tomb 15.

Brief Description of the Object: embroidered red caftan with paired humans, animals and tree design.

Material, Technique and Conservation: wool, silk.

Measurements: length 110cm; maximum width 185cm.

Detailed Description of the Object: the robe belonged to the mummy of a 25 year old male. It is made of a double weave with an ornamentation consisting of paired male human figures, isolated trees and paired animals. It was woven in two layers (surface and ground layer); both the obverse and the reverse display the same patterns, but with inverted colours (yellow patterns on a red ground on the obverse, red patterns on a yellow ground on the reverse).

Detailed Description of the Iconography: the patterns are arranged according to an accurately symmetrical scheme; each unit (80cm long) includes six rows with two couples of young male figures, a pair of animals and a tree, in vertical sequence. The male figures are naked but for a mantle falling from the shoulders on their back; they have curly hair, large eyes, and hold weapons in their hands (alternately a spear, and a short sword with a shield) with which they confront each other. The animal couples are addorsed rampant oxen and goats. Each tree consists of two main branches with few ramifications and oval pointed leaves.

Stylistic Analysis: the naturalistic style of execution suggests a Classical or Roman source of inspiration (particularly evident in the human figures); hence the hypothesis that the robe might have been manufactured in the Hellenised regions of Central Asia or in the Gandharan area.

Comparing and Geographical, Cultural and Chronological Attribution: Eastern Han — Jin dynasties (25–420 AD).

12. 红地罽袍 Felt Caftan

参考文献　References

1. Jäger, U. (2007a) Wer lebte an der Seidenstraße? Wieczorek, A. und Lind, Ch. (hrsg.) *Ursprünge der Seidenstraße, Sensationelle Neufunde aus Xinjiang, China*, 56–58, Mannheim - Stuttgart.

2. Jäger, U. (2007b) Ausstattung eines Verstorbenen, Wieczorek, A. und Lind, C. (hrsg.), *Ursprünge der Seidenstraße, Sensationelle Neufundeaus Xinjiang, China*, 260, Nr. 162, Mannheim-Stuttgart.

3. 李文瑛、周金玲:《营盘墓葬考古收获及相关问题》,载马承源、岳峰主编:《新疆维吾尔自治区丝路考古珍品》,上海译文出版社,1998年,页63—75。

   Li Wenying, Zhou Jinling (1998) *Yingpan muzang kaogu shouhuo ji xiangguan wenti (Archaeological Achievement and Discussion on the Yingpan Cemetery)*, in Ma Chengyuan and Yue Feng (eds.), *Xinjiang Weiwu'er zizhiqu silu kaogu zhenpin (Precious Archaeological Discoveries of Silk Road in Xinjiang Uygur Autonomous Region)*, 63–75, Shanghai.

4. Li Wenying (2006) Textiles of the 2nd to 5th Century Unearthed from Yingpan Cemetery, Schorta, R. (ed.), *Central Asian Textiles and Their Contexts in the early Middle Ages* (Riggisberger Berichte, 9), 243–264 (in part. 244–247, figs. 185–191), Abegg-Stiftung, Riggisberg.

5. Wieczorek, A. und Lind, C. (hrsg.) (2007) *Ursprünge der Seidenstraße, Sensationelle Neufunde aus Xinjiang, China*, 56–58, Mannheim-Stuttgart.

（*Ciro Lo Muzio*, 李雨生 [*Li Yusheng*]）

13. 玻璃杯

收藏单位：新疆文物考古研究所。

出土信息：出土于营盘墓地 M9，该墓地位于新疆维吾尔自治区尉犁县东南，1995年由新疆文物考古研究所发掘。遗址地处塔里木河下游大三角洲西北缘、孔雀河中游（南距孔雀河干河床约5公里），往东200公里即是楼兰古城，这里北通吐鲁番盆地，东接罗布泊地区，西抵库尔勒、库车地区。墓葬坐落于营盘古城西北，分布在库鲁克塔格山南麓的山前台地的东西长1公里、南北宽250米的范围内。整个遗址除墓地外，还包括古城、佛寺、烽燧等。

19世纪末20世纪初，科兹洛夫、斯文赫定、贝格曼、斯坦因等已对此地进行了考察，斯坦因还做过发掘，获得了一些遗物。近20年，营盘墓地进行了3次发掘清理，分别是1989、1995和1999年，新疆文物考古研究所等单位调查了遗址并发掘了大批墓葬。营盘墓地的时代跨度从公元前2世纪至公元4世纪，是目前罗布淖尔地区发掘的面积最大、发掘资料最为丰富的一处墓地。墓葬地表多以插立木棍标示，排列无甚规律，大多数墓葬成片分布，疏密有别，地层单一（不见打破和叠压关系）。墓葬形制和棺椁都有不同类型，以单人葬为主，也发现了双人合葬和多人合葬。

尸体多被纺织品包裹，因为气候干燥，保存很好。发现有木、漆、陶、铜、铁、玻璃、骨、石、金银、纺织品等质地的遗物，尤以木质器具最为丰富。根据文献记载，营盘位于汉代西域三十六

13. Glass Cup

Location: Institute of Cultural Relics and Archaeology of Xinjiang Uygur Autonomous Region.

Context of Origin: this object was excavated from Tomb no 9 in the cemetery of Yingpan, located in the south-eastern part of the Yuli County, during excavations carried out in 1995 by the Institute of Archaeology of Xinjiang. The site is located on the north-western edge of the Tarim River Delta's lower reaches, on the middle reaches of the Kongque River (5km south of its course), at about 200 km west of the ancient city of Loulan. Its area is bordered by the Turfan basin at north, by Lop Nor at east and by the cities of Korla and Kuqa at west. Beside the cemetery, (located at about 1km northeast of Yingpan, on an area of approximately 1km from east to west and 250m from north to south). The site includes other archaeological remains as traces of ancient settlements, Buddhist temples and beacon towers. Between the end of 19th century and the beginning of the 20th century AD, the site was surveyed by Pyotr Kuzmich Kozlov, Sven Anders Hedin, Folke Bergman and Marc Aurel Stein, who undertook some archaeological excavations bringing to the light various evidences. In the last 20 years three seasons of surveys and excavations were carried out at Yingpan. In 1989, 1995 and 1999, the Institute of Archaeology of Xinjiang and other organizations surveyed the site and excavated a large number of graves. The chronology of the Yingpan cemetery covers the span between the 2nd century BC and the 4th century AD. It is the largest and richest site in the Lop Nor area. The surface of the cemetery was marked by vertical poles set without any apparent regular pattern. Graves were distributed into several areas with different concentrations but always on a single layer (cases of overlapping are not attested). Of different types and with coffins of different forms, their most common finding is represented by a single funeral object, although double or multiple funeral objects were also found.

The bodies were covered with textiles, all well-

13. 玻璃杯 Glass Cup

国之一的山国（墨山国）境内。这些墓葬发现
的文物既有当地传统的文化因素，又有大量的
中国内地和西方成分（如部分纺织品、佉卢文
文书、黄铜饰、玻璃杯等），显示出该地在中西经
济文化交流中所起到的纽带作用。人骨研究的
结果表明，营盘墓地居民的体质特征属于欧洲
人种，但具有一些蒙古人种因素。

出土玻璃杯的M9，系1995年发掘，为竖穴
土坑墓，男女双人合葬在花卉纹箱式棺中，木棺
和衣服已朽，随葬品不多，有羊骨、铁箭镞、铜簪
等，玻璃杯放置于男墓主头端。

preserved thanks to the dry climate of the area. Among
funerary objects various items of different materials can
be listed as wood, lacquer, pottery, copper and iron ware,
glassware, bone and stone implements, gold and silver
objects, fabrics. Wood objects are especially numerous.
According to historical records, Yingpan belonged to the
Shanguo (Moshanguo) kingdom, one of the thirty six
political unities in the Western Regions during the Han
Dynasty. The cemetery presents cultural elements of a
local tradition mixed with other coming from China and
the West (especially textiles, documents in Kharosthi,
brass decorations and glassware) indicating intense East-
West contacts. Genetic researches on the human bones
indicate that people buried at Yingpan were Caucasian,

营盘墓地还发现了其他不少玻璃制品，以装饰品居多。

器物形制概述：有模吹制玻璃杯，外形为像截去顶部的圆锥形器皿，带有小凹面装饰。

材质、工艺及保存状况：基本无色（可能最初为白色泛黄的半透明玻璃器）。该器采用有模吹制技术，成型的同时也完成了外部装饰。利用带有图案的模子吹制玻璃的技术，不仅可以取得预想的器形，还可以同时塑造纹饰，这一技术出现在1至2世纪，之后向四方扩展，在罗马帝国晚期和拜占庭非常流行（Tatton-Brown 1991, 70; Whitehouse 1997, 1024）。其工艺流程是首先将一团熔融的玻璃吹进模子（木、陶或者金属质地），在吹出胚形后移出，再次加热，然后边吹边用工具加工，最后形成一个与模子在造型和装饰上粗略相似的产品。通过一些实例可知，使用同一个模子可以制作出多个不同的产品（Lledó 1997）。单模可以形成容器的器身，而一件完整的器物则需要由两个或三个部分组成的复合模。至于营盘玻璃杯上的圆形小凹面装饰，可能使用了轮制磨琢技术，虽然也不能完全排除模子压印的可能性。

器物在发现时已碎成几片，现已修复，口部有一部分缺失。内部和外部都被较厚的白色风化层覆盖，有虹彩现象。此外口部的断裂处清楚地表明玻璃内部不透明。

尺寸：高8.8、口径10.8、底径3.2厘米。

器物详细描述：有模吹制玻璃杯，外形为像截去顶部的圆锥形器皿。器物最初的颜色难以确定，因为表面已经发生了改变。玻璃内

with a few Mongolian traits.

Tomb no 9, an earthen pit grave, was excavated in 1995; two persons, a man and a woman, were buried together inside a decorated wooden coffin. Traces of their dresses were still preserved while some lamb bones, iron arrowheads, copper headpins and the cup at issue were put beside the head of the male skeleton as grave goods. Apart from this cup, other glass objects were found in the Yinpan cemetery, especially glass ornaments.

Brief Description of the Object: mould-blown glass cup with nearly cone-truncated profile and faceted decoration.

Material, Technique and Conservation: glass of hardly definable colour (probably translucent yellowish-white at the origin). This object was manufactured using the mould-blown technique. The technique of blowing glass into a patterned mould, in order to obtain not only the shape of the vessel but also its decoration at the same time, started spreading from the 1st and the 2nd centuries AD onwards and then became very common during the Late Roman and Byzantine Period (Tatton-Brown 1991, 70; Whitehouse 1997, 1024). With this technique, a gather of molten glass was first blown into a patterned mould (in wood, pottery or metal) and then, after the glass had assumed the shape of the mould internal wall, the so-called parison was removed to be further worked by re-heating, blowing and tooling. The final result was a vessel that could match the shape and the decoration of the original mould only very loosely; in some cases, in fact, a great variety of vessels with very different shapes and decorations could be produced starting from the same mould (Lledó 1997). A one-piece mould could be used to shape the body of a vessel or an entire vessel could be shaped in a complex mould consisting of two or more parts. In the case of the object at issue, however, the faceted decorative pattern was probably carried out by means of wheel-cutting techniques, even though an interpretation of the shallow concave elliptical and circular facets on the cup as a result of the impression of the mould itself could not be definitely excluded. The object is restored and made up by several fragments although a sizeable portion of its rim

部可能最初呈现淡淡的半透明的黄白色。尽管器物上半部有所缺失，但依然能看出口部较为平直并有些许外侈。器身上半部较为简洁，外壁的中部有一圈12个略微内凹的椭圆形装饰，其下方器身逐渐内收变成一个小平底，在下半部有另外一圈7个略微内凹的圆形装饰。尽管这件器物是有模吹制成型的，但椭圆形切面和圆形切面很可能是轮盘在器物表面磨琢而成的。

地域、文化、年代属性及对比：发掘者认为这批墓葬的年代上限到汉，下限到魏晋或略晚，因此玻璃杯的年代不会晚于4世纪上半叶。发掘者（周金玲1999，周金玲、李文瑛2002）认为这是一件典型的萨珊玻璃器皿。林梅村（2000）认为这件器物的年代要更早一些，可能属于帕提亚时代的产品。

斯坦因曾在营盘遗址编号为Ying.III.3的墓中发现过另一件带有切面装饰的玻璃器（Ying.III.3.06），"透明、白色、发绿的玻璃……，发现时保存很好，器底部分有一些液体的痕迹，表明可能是装酒或葡萄汁……，装饰一系列凹面斑点……，是……我考察生涯中发现的唯一完整的玻璃器皿"。(Stein 1928–II,756; 1928–III, Pl. CX)

在伊朗高原玻璃业的演变序列中，像营盘杯子这种带有的轮切圆形或椭圆形小凹面装饰常被视为萨珊文化的典型特征，通常装饰在杯、半球形碗或好像截去顶部的圆锥形器皿上（Fukai 1977, figs.14, 15, 20–35; Genito 1977, inv. no 876; Kordmahini 1994, 55, 150–151; Negro

is missing. Both the internal and the external surfaces are severely altered and covered by encrustations and a very thick whitish and somewhat iridescent patina; in addition, traces of leafed devitrification of the core are clearly detectable at the fractures on the rim.

Measurements: height 8.8cm; rim diameter 10.8cm; base diameter 3.2cm.

Detailed Description of the Object: mould-blown glass cup with nearly cone-truncated profile. The original colour of the glass is presently very difficult to be clearly discerned because of severe alterations on the surfaces, but it was probably of a somewhat translucent yellowish-white tinge. Although some of its upper portions are missing, the cup reveals a flat, very slightly outwards everted rim. While the upper part of the vessel body is plain, the central section of its wall is instead decorated by a row of twelve shallow concave elliptical facets. Beneath, at the point of the vessel where its profile appears to be slightly carinated narrowing towards the small flat base, another row of seven shallow concave circular facets decorates the wall. Both the elliptical and the circular facets, notwithstanding the object was mould-blown, seem to be cut into the outer surface of the vessel by means of a wheel.

Comparing and Geographical, Cultural and Chronological Attribution: according to the excavators, the cemetery of Yingpan dates back to a period between the Han and the Jin Dynasty or even later. By virtue of this date, the age of this glass cup cannot be later than the early 4th-5th century AD. Moreover, on the basis of its shape, the excavators hold (Zhou Jinling 1999; Zhou Jinling and Li Wenying 2002) that this cup is a typical Sasanian object. An earlier date is suggested by Lin Meicun (2000), who considers this cup as produced during the Parthian period. During his excavations at Yingpan, Marc Aurel Stein discovered another glass vessel with wheel-cut faceted decoration in the tomb numbered Ying.III.3; this cup (Ying.III.3.06) "... *in transparent greenish-white glass [...], found intact with traces at the bottom of some fluid which might have*

Ponzi 1968–69, nos 71–72; Negro Ponzi 1984, fig.4, nos 1 and 7; Pinder-Wilson and Scanlon 1987, no 15; Saldern 1963, fig.6）。

在形态上与营盘玻璃杯特别接近的是在伊朗里海沿岸Shimam发现的帕提亚晚期的杯子（1977, 29, 41, figs.14–15）。当然我们今天意识到，由于技术、风格和形态上的普遍性，将这些玻璃器（更普遍的存在于物质文化的每个方面）归入"萨珊"或"帕提亚"的把握还不够，我们已经很清楚一些技术不仅限于萨珊时期，也延续到伊斯兰时期，如小凹面装饰在伊斯兰早期的玻璃器上仍可见到，但磨琢得要浅一些，所装饰的器形也逐渐扩展到浅腹碗、大口杯、壶和瓶子上（Fukai 1977, 62–63; Kordmahini 1994, 65, 71, 99, 161; Kröger 1995, 123–128, nos 166–173; Kröger 1998, 135）。

除了磨琢技术外，类似的"蜂窝"装饰也存在于有模吹制技术制作的玻璃器中。根据Kröger（1998, 134–135）的研究，这种技术在萨珊晚期或伊斯兰早期被引入叙利亚地区。已经有许多例子（种类很多）被著录，其时空范围很大（Kordmahini 1994, 45–47, 91 93, 98, 106, 110, 118–120, 123, 126, 128, 135, 141, 144, 168, 176, 183; Kröger 1995, nos 118–130; Lamm 1931, Pl. LXXVI.7; Lledó 1997, figs.1–9; Negro Ponzi 1968–69, nos 38–43; Negro Ponzi 1970–71, nos 58, 62, 131, 135, 136–158, 162, 164, 166; Pinder-Wilson and Scanlon 1987, no.8）。

been wine or grape-juice [...] ornamented with bands of hollow-ground spots [...] is [...] the only complete piece of glass ware found by me in the course of my explorations" (Stein 1928–II,756; 1928–III, Pl. CX). In the evolution of glass production on the Iranian Plateau, wheel-cut circular or elliptical facets have often been considered as a typical example of decorative patterns related to a "Sasanian" cultural, political and/or chronological horizon. Often, the main medium on which this type of decoration was displayed were considered to be cups or bowls with hemispherical or cone-truncated profile (Fukai 1977, figs.14, 15, 20–35; Genito 1977, inv. no 876; Kordmahini 1994, 55, 150–151; Negro Ponzi 1968–69, nos 71–72; Negro Ponzi 1984, fig.4, nos 1 and 7; Pinder-Wilson and Scanlon 1987, no 15; Saldern 1963, fig.6). The cup from Tomb no 9 in the cemetery of Yingpan finds its closest morphological and decorative parallels with the glass cup from Shimam, in the Rudbar area, on the Iranian Caspian Sea coast, shown by Fukai (1977, 29, 41, figs.14–15) and dated to the late Parthian period. Anyway, today we are aware that loose and too general technical, stylistic or morphological criteria are not sufficient to label such examples of glass vessels (but more generally every manifestation of the material culture) as "Sasanian" or perhaps "Parthian". It is clear, for instance, that the taste for this kind of decoration was not limited to the "Sasanian" period; but survived the transition into the Islamic period. Facet-cutting of a different sort continued in the early Islamic centuries but the cutting was less deep, the facets were not only used in an all-over pattern and the vessel shapes gradually changed, with this type of decoration attested also on shallow bowls, flaring beakers, jugs or bottles (Fukai 1977, 62–63; Kordmahini 1994, 65, 71, 99, 161; Kröger 1995, 123–128, nos 166–173; Kröger 1998, 135). Apart from wheel-cut faceted glass, similar "honeycomb" patterns also existed in mould-blown examples. According to Kröger (1998, 134–135), this technique was introduced in Syria only in the latest phase of the Sasanian period or early in the Islamic period. Many examples (and with a lot of variants) are known in the scientific literature from this time-span (Kordmahini 1994, 45–47, 91–93, 98, 106, 110, 118–120, 123, 126, 128, 135, 141, 144, 168, 176, 183; Kröger 1995, nos 118–130; Lamm 1931, Pl. LXXVI.7; Lledó 1997, figs.1–9; Negro Ponzi 1968–69, nos 38–43; Negro Ponzi 1970–71, nos 58, 62, 131, 135, 136–158, 162, 164, 166; Pinder-Wilson and Scanlon 1987, no 8).

参考文献　References

1. Fukai, S. (1977) *Persian Glass*, New York - Tokyo.
2. Genito, B. (1977) *Vetri iranici. Schede del Museo Nazionale d'Arte Orientale* 10, Roma.
3. Kordmahini, H.A. (1994) *Glass from the Bazargan Collection*. Iranian Cultural Heritage Organization. Iran National Museum, Tehran.
4. Kröger, J. (1995) *Nishapur: Glass of the Early Islamic Period*. The Metropolitan Museum of Art, New York.
5. Kröger, J. (1998) From Ctesiphon to Nishapur: Studies in Sasanian and Islamic Glass, Curtis Sarkhosh, Vesta *et alii* (eds.) *The Art and Archaeology of Ancient Persia - New Light on the Parthian and Sasanian Empires*, 133–140, London.
6. Lamm, C.J.(1931) Les Verres trouvés à Suse. *Syria* 12, 358–67, Paris.
7. 林梅村:《古道西风——考古新发现所见中西文化交流》，生活·读书·新知三联书店（北京），2000年，页205—206。
   Lin Meicun (2000) *The Prevalence of Western Custom in Ancient and Medieval China*, Sanglian Publishing House, 205–206, Beijing.
8. Lledó, B. (1997) Mold Siblings in the 11th century Cullet from Serçe Limani, *Journal of Glass Studies*, 39, 43–55. The Corning Museum of Glass, Corning, New York.
9. Negro Ponzi, M. (1968–69) Sasanian Glassware from Tell Mahuz (North Mesopotamia), *Mesopotamia*, 3–4, 293–384, Torino.
10. Negro Ponzi, M. (1970–71) Islamic Glassware from Seleucia, *Mesopotamia*, 6–7, 67–104. Torino.
11. Negro Ponzi, M. (1984) Glassware from Choche (Central Mesopotamia), Boucharlat, R., Salles, J.F. (eds.) *Arabie Orientale, Mésopotamie et Iran Méridional, de L'âge du fer au Début de la Période Islamique*, Mémoire no 37. 33–40, Editions Recherche sur les Civilisations, Paris.
12. Pinder-Wilson, R.and Scanlon, G.T. (1987) Glass Finds from Fustat: 1972–1980, *Journal of Glass Studies*, 29, 60–71. The Corning Museum of Glass. Corning. New York.
13. Saldern, Von, A. (1963) Achaemenid and Sasanian Cut Glass, *Ars Orientalis*, 5, 7–16.
14. Stein, Marc Aurel (1928) *Innermost Asia*, vols. II–III, Oxford.
15. Tait, H. (ed) (1991) *Cinquemila anni di Vetro*. Milano. (Orig. Edit. *Five Thousand Years of Glass*. British

Museum Press, London. 1991).

16. Tatton-Brown, V. (1991) L'impero romano, Tait, H. (ed.) *Cinquemila anni di Vetro*, 62–97. Milano.

17. Whitehouse, D. (1997) s.v.Vetro, *Enciclopedia dell'Arte Antica*, 5 (secondo supplemento), 1022–1026. Istituto della Enciclopedia Italiana, Roma.

18. 新疆文物考古研究所：《新疆尉犁县营盘墓地1995年发掘简报》，《文物》2002年第6期，页4—45，图五九，图六六：7。
    Xinjiang Institute of Cultural Relics and Archaeology (2002) *Excavation of the Yingpan Cemetery in Yuli County, Xinjiang in 1995, Wenwu* (*Cultural Relics*), 6, 4–45, fig.59, 66: 7, Beijing.

19. 周金玲：《营盘墓地出土文物反映的中外交流》，《文博》1999年第10期，页59—64。
    Zhou Jinling (1999)*Exchange between China and abroad Reflected from Yinpan Cemetery, Wenbo* (*Relics and Museolgy*), 10, 59–64, Xi'an.

（*Giulio Maresca*, 耿朔 [*Geng Shuo*]）

14. 嵌宝石金戒指

收藏单位：新疆文物考古研究所。

出土信息：这枚戒指发现于新疆尼勒克喀什河河谷一棵树墓地B区，B区是一东西长约270、南北宽约80米的台地，台地外环绕很深的壕沟。戒指所出墓葬发现于台地西南部，地表有直径50米以上的封土，封土下有双墓室，A墓室长8、宽2—4、深5米以上，B墓室长7、宽2米，深同A墓室。墓室毁坏严重。地表环绕墓室有环状沟，环沟外径22米，沟宽5—6米，沟内有大量火烧灰，可能与丧葬祭祀活动有关，墓群年代推测相当于战国至汉晋时期（前5世纪至3世纪）。

14. Gold Ring

Location: Institute of Cultural Relics and Archaeology of Xinjiang Uygur Autonomous Region

Context of Origin: this ring was found in the largest tomb of Region B in Yikeshu cemetery (Catalogue of exhibition: Grab 11), in the Kashi river valley, Nilka, Xinjiang Uygur Autonomous Region. Region B of the cemetery was a large platform (270m long from East to West, 80m wide from North to South) with manmade deep ditches on the edges. The tomb in the southwest area of the platform, heavily damaged, was covered by a big mound (more than 50m in diameter), under which there were two chambers; chamber A, 8m long and 2–4m wide, 5m deep, and chamber B, 7m long, 2m wide, and having the same depth of chamber A. Surrounding the surface of the chambers was a ring like ditch (about 22m in diameter, 5–6m wide) filled with ashes, probably related to some kind of burial cult. The dating of the cemetery goes from the 5th century BC to the 3rd century AD.

Brief Description of the Object: finger-ring with engraved bezel representing a seated female figure holding a flower.

14. 金戒指 Gold Ring

器物概括描述：戒指，戒面刻出一位手持花朵的坐姿女性形象。

材质、工艺及保存状况：金制，嵌宝石，保存较好，某些地方略有损坏。

尺寸：高度不明，戒面尺寸不明，长4.8、宽2.8厘米。

器物详细描述：这枚戒指器形复杂，上半部主轴两端各有一个张口的鱼头形突起，眼部镶嵌凸圆形宝石；两鱼头之间的侧面部分装饰有五个金珠点焊而成的倒三角形；戒面的底座外装饰一圈联珠纹，恰好将两端的鱼头连接起来，戒面呈平整的椭圆形，截面呈窄矩形。

图像详细描述：戒面上雕刻一坐于椅上的女性形象，表现的是其四分之三右侧面，轻靠于椅背上，右手执一枝花，左手置于膝上。该女性身着一件有宽圆边缘的长袖长袍，腕部有一组平行线，或表示手镯或袖口；面部描绘非常精致，深目高鼻，线条洗练；额头上方的一条椭圆形发带束住头发，在脑后打结，并露出飘动的两端；手持长茎花，花下有两叶。身下的椅子仅露出呈一定角度的椅面和椅背，椅背顶端向后弯曲。

风格分析：这枚戒指刻工深浅适度，栩栩如生，极具自然主义风格。

地域、文化、年代属性及对比：刊载这枚戒指的德文图录（Parlasca & Crüsemann 2007）认为戒面上的女性形象并不是典型的希腊肖像，而更多的是带有希腊化因素，因此认为其来自希腊—巴克特里亚人的作坊，年代为汉代早

Material, Technique and Conservation: gold plate inlaid with ruby; whole; the ring is at places smashed.

Measurements: height 4.8cm; diameter 2.8cm.

Detailed Description of the Object: the ring has a complex shape, bearing at the upper extremities of the main axis two projections in the shape of a fish-head with open mouth, in which the eyes of the animals are underlined with a roundish cabochon ruby gem. The upper band of the ring, between the fish-heads, is decorated by a row of inverted triangles, five on each side, designed with small dots. The bezel is set in a mount with plain rim above an oval row of small pearls which connects the two fish-heads; it has an oval shape and a flat engraved surface, with shallow rectangular section.

Detailed Description of the Iconography: on the upper face of the bezel, a female figure, represented up until the hips, is seated in profile to right, body slightly three-quarters leaning against the back of a seat, holding a flower in her right hand, with the left leaning on the knee. The lady wears a tunic with long leaves and broad round hem underlined by a continuous line; at the wrist are two parallel lines which may represent bracelets (or the tunic hem). The facial features are represented in detail, with linear strokes underlining the nose, the mouth and the eye, which is open and large. The hair is confined by a row of oval segments which form a band round the forehead, beneath a plain diadem which is tied at the nape with floating streamers. The flower has the shape of a long budding stem with two small leaves at the bottom. Only the seat is schematically rendered with a line forming an angle between the horizontal side and the upright back, which ends with a volute.

Stylistic Analysis: the seal is in moderate relief and the engraving shows care over detail and finish. The treatment of the subject is very naturalistic.

Comparing and Geographical, Cultural and Chronological Attribution: the scholars who published the gem (Parlasca & Crüsemann 2007) underline its

期。不过来自大英博物馆马森收藏品（Masson Collection, Callieri 1997, 77, Cat 3.8）中的一枚印章提供了更多的可供对比的信息。这枚印章上表现的女性半身像与新疆的发现非常类似，尤其是头饰，不过脑后的飘带更加蜿蜒曲折；手中所持的花朵也类似，但手的位置不同，印章上刻有属于3—4世纪东马尔瓦（印度中部）的婆罗米文，这无疑透露出地域和年代信息。该印章铭文组成、面部的写实主义风格以及肖像上的萨珊文化特点都在暗示其很可能制作于南亚次大陆西北部的后犍陀罗时代，在公元1世纪的印度确实发现了类似的图像主题（Chanda 1928–29, 138, pl. LVI, 66–67; Fussman 1972, 46–47, no.33），亚洲古典晚期的这类图像主题亦见于萨珊金属器上，伊朗国家博物馆收藏的一件碗上的圆形装饰上，也表现出一位手持花朵的半身女性的形象，鼻前还有绶带（Harper 1981, 27, pl. 7），岩本笃志（A. Iwamoto, 2006）认为这位女性是安娜希塔，但证据还不够充分。整个墓地的年代为公元前5世纪到公元3世纪（德文图录给出的时间是汉晋之间，206 BC–420 AD），少量墓葬可能晚至唐代。

Hellenistic character and, while stressing the fact that it is not purely Greek, attribute it to a Graeco-Bactrian workshop, dating therefore the grave to the Early Han period. However in our opinion a seal which offers important comparative evidence pointing to another direction is in the British Museum, belonging to the Masson Collection (Callieri 1997, 77, Cat. 3.8). It represents a female bust very similar to ours; the diadem is similar even though the streamers are more winding than those of our seal; the flower also is similar, but the position of the hand is different. The interest of this piece of comparative evidence is given by the Brahmi inscription carefully engraved in the exergue, which belongs to 3rd–4th century eastern Malwa (Central India), thus allowing a geographical and chronological attribution. The inscription, closely incorporated in the composition, provides evidence for the origin of the seal, without which the naturalistic treatment of the face in particular, along with the Sasanian character of the iconography, might easily suggest an origin in the post-Gandharan North-West of the Indo-Pakistan subcontinent. And indeed the iconography finds other comparative evidence among Indian seals of the first centuries of our era (see Chanda 1928–29, 138, pl. LVI, 66–67; Fussman 1972, 46–47, no.33). The iconography in Late Antique Asia is also present on Sasanian metal ware, and a bowl in the National Museum of Iran, Tehran, has a central roundel representing a female bust holding a plant with circular flower bound with a ribbon before her nose (Harper 1981, 27, pl. 7). As for the identification of the female figure with the Iranian goddess Anahita, proposed by A. Iwamoto (2006), the hypothesis is not enough supported by actual evidence. About the dating of the whole cemetery, it goes from the 5th BC to the 3rd century AD (Catalogue of exhibition: Han-Jin Zeit: 206 BC–420 AD). Phase III (Han-Jin period, very few tombs date to the Tang Dynasty).

参考文献　**References**

1. 新疆维吾尔自治区文物局编：《新疆古墓葬》，科学出版社（北京），2011年，页319。
   Administration of Cultural Heritage of the Xinjiang Uygur Autonomous Region (2011) *Xinjiang gumuzang (Ancient Tombs of Xinjiang)*, Science Press, 319, Beijing.

2. Callieri, P. (1997) *Seals and Sealings from the North-West of the Indian Subcontinent and Afghanistan (4th century BC–11th century AD): Local, Indian, Sasanian, Graeco-Persian, Sogdian, Roman*. With contributions by E. Errington, R. Garbini, Ph. Gignoux, N. Sims-Williams, W. Zwalf (Istituto Universitario Orientale, Dissertationes I), Naples.

3. Chanda, R.B.R. (1928-29) Section IV. Museums. Indian Museum, Pearse Collection of Gems. *Archaeological Survey of India. Annual Report for the Years 1928–29*, 131–141, Calcutta.

4. Fussman, G. (1972) Intailles et empreintes indiennes du Cabinet de Médailles de Paris, *Revue Numismatique*, 14, 21–47.

5. Harper, P.O. (1981) *Silver Vessels of the Sasanian Period. Volume I: Royal Imagery*, New York.

6. Iwamoto, A. (2006) The Sogdians on Seals made of Precious Stone in Northern Dynasties and Sui, Tang Era, *East Asian Rim Research Center Annual Report*, 1, 16–27.

7. Parlasca, K. and Crüsemann, N. (2007) Goldener Fingerring, A. Wieczorek, A. und Lind, C. (hrsg.) (2007) *Ursprünge der Seidenstraße, Sensationelle Neufunde aus Xinjiang, China*, 295, no. 179, Stuttgart.

8. 祁小山、王博编著：《丝绸之路：新疆古代文化》，页258—261，新疆人民出版社（乌鲁木齐），2008年。
   Qi Xiaoshan, *et alii* (eds.) (2008) *The Silk Road: Xinjiang Ancient Culture*, 258-261. Xinjiang People's Publishing House, Urumqï.

（*Pierfrancesco Callieri*，李雨生 [*Li Yusheng*]）

15. 金饰件

收藏单位：新疆文物考古研究所。

出土信息：新疆尼勒克喀什河河谷的别特巴斯陶墓地。

器物概括描述：半月形耳饰。

材质、工艺及保存状况：保存完整，金制，镶嵌红宝石。

尺寸：高3.3、宽2.8厘米。

器物详细描述：镶嵌红宝石的凹槽之外点焊两圈金珠，外围装饰一周更大的小金球，金球顶端分别装饰小金珠。

地域、文化、年代属性及对比：汉晋时期。

15. Gold Ornament

Location: Institute of Cultural Relics and Archaeology of Xinjiang Uygur Autonomous Region.

Context of Origin: the gold ornament was found in Bietebasitao cemetery in the Kashi river valley, Nilka, Xinjiang Uygur Autonomous Region.

Brief Description of the Object: semilune-sh earrings.

Material, Technique and Conservation: gold and ruby; complete.

Measurements: height 3.3cm, width 2.8cm.

Detailed Description of the Object: the object has a fine grained decoration consisting of two circles of small spherical elements surrounding the stone and an outer ring of spherical larger elements, in turn surmounted by another fine grained decoration.

Comparing and Geographical, Cultural and Chronological Attribution: the tomb from which the gold ornament was found was dated from 3rd century BC to 3rd century AD (from Han Dynasty to Jin Dynasty).

15. 金饰件 Gold Ornament

参考文献　References

1. 新疆维吾尔自治区文物局编：《新疆古墓葬》，科学出版社（北京），2011年，页167—169。
Administration of Cultural Heritage of the Xinjiang Uygur Autonomous Region (2011) *Xinjiang gumuzang (Ancient tombs of Xinjiang)*, Science Press, 167–169, Beijing.

2. Iwamoto, A. (2006) The Sogdians on Seals made of Precious Stone in Northern Dynasties and Sui, T'ang Era, *East Asian Rim Research Center Annual Report*, 1, 16–27.

3. 刘学堂、托呼提、阿里甫：《新疆尼勒克县别特巴斯陶墓群大规模发掘》，《中国文物报》2004年1月16日1版。
Liu Xuetang *et alii* (2004) Introduction about the large-scale Excavation in Bietebasitao Cemetery, Nilka County, Xinjiang Uygur Autonomous Region, *China Cultural Relics News*, January 16, page 1, Beijing.

4. 刘学堂、托呼提、阿里甫：《新疆尼勒克县别特巴斯陶墓群全面发掘获重要成果》，《西域研究》2004年第1期，页108。
Liu Xuetang *et alii* (2004) New Foundings from the Full Scale Excavation in Bietebasitao Cemetery, Nilka County, Xinjiang Uygur Autonomous Region, *The Western Regions Studies*, 1, 108, Urumqï.

5. 历史博物馆编辑委员会编：《丝路传奇——新疆文物大展》，国立历史博物馆（台北），2008年，页63。
"National" Museum of History (2008) *Legends of the Silk Road: Treasures from Xinjiang*, 63, Taibei.

6. Parlasca, K. and Crüsemann, N. (2007) *Goldener Fingerring*, Alfried Wieczorek, A. und Lund, C. (hrsg.) *Ursprünge der Seidenstraße, Sensationelle Neufunde aus Xinjiang, China*, 295, Stuttgart.

（*Bruno Genito*，李雨生 [*Li Yusheng*]）

16. 玻璃杯

收藏单位：新疆维吾尔自治区博物馆。

出土信息：1996年新疆且末扎滚鲁克一号墓地M49出土，新疆维吾尔自治区博物馆等单位发掘。扎滚鲁克村绿洲及边缘区域内分布着大小不同的5处古墓葬群，一号墓地是面积最大的一处，自1985年以来已经过3次正式发掘，1996年新疆维吾尔自治区博物馆等单位清理了墓葬102座。这批墓葬以竖穴土坑墓为主，随葬器物有漆木器、陶器、铜铁器、纺织品、皮制品、牲畜、食物等，由于气候干燥，大多保存较好。发掘者将这批墓葬分为三期：第一期墓葬仅有1座，距今约有3000年；第二期墓葬较多，是本墓地文化的主体，时代约在春秋到西汉时期（持续约七八百年）；第三期墓葬有11座，大约相当于东汉至南北朝时期（1—6世纪）。

扎滚鲁克墓地被认为属于且末国，系汉代所谓西域三十六国之一，是地处沙漠南缘的丝绸之路南线上的一个绿洲国家。出土玻璃杯的M49系方形竖穴土坑棚架墓，通过墓中部分器物（玻璃杯、一具残木棺及木器、漆器等）与其他地区同类器物比较，判断该墓年代应在两晋，约公元3世纪中叶到5世纪以前（属于墓地年代分期的第三期）。

器物概括描述：有模吹制玻璃杯，有着差不多圆柱形的造型，逐渐下收至底部，有小凹面装饰。

材质、工艺及保存状况：透明，淡绿色，有

16. Glass Beaker

Location: Xinjiang Uygur Autonomous Region Museum.

Context of Origin: the object was brought to light from tomb no 49 in the Zagunluk cemetery, in Qiemo County, Xinjiang Uygur Autonomous Region, during the excavations carried out in 1996 by the Xinjiang Uygur Autonomous Region Museum. Five cemeteries were discovered between the oasis and the boundary at the village of Zagunluk. In cemetery no 1, the largest, three excavation campaigns has been undertaken since 1985. In 1996, the Xinjiang Uygur Autonomous Region Museum excavated 102 graves, mainly earthen pit tombs with funeral objects as lacquer and wood ware, pottery, copper and iron objects, textiles, leather, livestock bones, food, all generally well preserved because of the dry climate. From a chronological point of view, the archaeologists divided the cemetery no 1 into three phases: only one grave belongs to the first one, dating 3000 years ago, while the large number of graves of the second phase forms the main part of the whole cemetery (utilized for 700–800 years), dating from the Spring and Autumn Period to the West Han Dinasty; eleven later graves belong to the third phase, from the period of the Eastern Han to the Northern and Southern Dynasties (1st–6th century AD). The Zagunluk cemetery is believed to belong to the Qiemo kingdom, one of the thirty six political unities in the Western Region during the Han Dynasty, a country-oasis in the southern margin of the desert along the southern branch of the Silk Road. This glass beaker was excavated from tomb no 49, a square pit earthen grave dated between the second half of the 3rd and the 5th century AD (during the third phase of the cemetery) on the basis of comparisons between its funerary objects (the glass beaker a tissue, a quite damaged wooden coffin, some wood and lacquer ware) and similar examples from other contexts.

16. 玻璃杯 Glass Beaker

模吹制玻璃，已破成若干碎片，经修复，部分缺失。和No.13营盘发现的那件一样，外壁上的内凹小面可能是用轮制磨琢技术完成的，尽管也有人解释这种装饰可以由模子压印完成，但每一个球面锐利的边缘暗示更可能是采用了轮制磨琢，即在玻璃无模或有模吹制成型之后，用一种转动的砂磨工具进行加工，因此属于冷加工工艺（Kröger 1995, 120），这种工具用来在玻璃器皿的表面刻划纹饰，或者从壁面上磨去一部分而改变玻璃器的形态（Charleston 1964, 86–87）。所使用的棒钻是最普通的工具：一个锭子固定在轮盘（discs）上。这个钻子通过来回的运动对玻璃器进行切磨（Pinder-Wilson 1991, 119）。器物的内部和外部表面保存得都很好，口部有一些深色覆盖层，底部有虹彩现象。

尺寸：高6.8、口径6.8、底径1.6厘米。

器物详细描述：大口杯，有着差不多圆柱形的造型，有模吹制，淡绿色透明玻璃。口沿（部分缺失）局部有深色覆盖层。器身上半部简洁，外壁的中部有两圈各13个略内凹椭圆形装饰。在其下方，靠近底部，还有一圈7个略内凹椭圆形装饰。器身下半部逐渐内收形成底部。另有一个单独磨制的略内凹圆形装饰充当器底。就像所指出的那样，外壁这些内凹面装饰可能是通过轮盘在器物表面磨琢而形成的。

地域、文化、年代属性及对比：与No.13营盘出土的杯子有许多相似之处。王博、鲁礼鹏（2007）认为该器与罗马—萨珊传统系列的玻璃杯非常相似。林梅村（2006）认为这件器形高

Brief Description of the Object: mould-blown glass beaker with nearly sub-cylindrical profile narrowing towards the base and decorated with faceted pattern.

Material, Technique and Conservation: translucent mould-blown glass of very light green colour. As already pointed out for no 33, the faceted decorative pattern was probably carried out by means of wheel-cutting techniques, although an interpretation of the shallow concave facets as the result of the impression of the mould itself remains possible even if somewhat remote: the sharply marked edges around each facet (sharper than in no 33, but probably only by virtue of the worse conservation conditions of the latter cup) suggest with higher probabilities a wheel cutting technique. Wheel-cut glass was worked with a rotary, abrasive tool which was applied to the glass after it had been free-blown or mould-blown, and thus belongs to the category of cold-worked decorations (Kröger 1995, 120). The tool was used to engrave patterns into the glass surface or to grind down or cut away part of the glass surface to alter the shape of the original blown vessel (Charleston 1964, 86–87). The bow drill was the most common tool: it consisted of a fixed spindle to which the appropriate discs were attached; the drill was rotated by the backwards and forwards movement of the bow while the glass was held against the wheel (Pinder-Wilson 1991, 119). The object is restored and made up by several fragments (some of which missing). The internal and the external surfaces are quite well-preserved except from some dark encrustations around the rim and a thin iridescent patina detectable at the bottom.

Measurements: height 6.8cm; rim diameter 6.8cm; base diameter 1.6cm.

Detailed Description of the Object: beaker with nearly sub-cylindrical profile in mould-blown translucent very light green glass. Its rounded rim (some fragments of which are missing) is partially altered by spotted dark encrustations. While the upper part of the vessel body is plain, the central section of its wall is decorated by two

瘦的玻璃杯应该是帕提亚的产品。诚然目前发现了像No.13出土的采用这种装饰的器物，但在形态和尺寸方面可资比较的材料依然缺乏，将这件器物归属到帕提亚是非常牵强的。跟萨珊或伊斯兰时代磨琢小凹面装饰的半球形或切去顶部的圆锥形玻璃杯相比，在采用同样装饰的近圆柱形玻璃杯中，极少见到像扎滚鲁克玻璃杯这样口沿长度和器物高度成1：1的(Fukai 1977, figs.14, 15, 20–35; Genito 1977, inv. no 876; Kordmahini 1994, 55, 150–151; Kröger 1995, no 167; Negro Ponzi 1968–69, nos 71–72; Negro Ponzi 1984, fig.4, nos 1–2, 4–7; Pinder-Wilson and Scanlon 1987, no 15; Saldern 1963, fig.6)。基于这一点，扎滚鲁克玻璃杯和韩国天马冢(Laing 1991, 113, fig.10)出土的玻璃杯之间的相似性就很值得探讨。

superimposed rows, each consisting of thirteen shallow concave elliptical facets. Beneath, towards the bottom of the vessel, another decorative row of seven shallow concave elliptical facets marks the point where its profile appears to be slightly carinated and narrowing towards the base. A single shallow concave circular facet represents the decoration of the small flat base of the vessel. As already pointed out, the decorative facets seem to be cut into the external surface of the vessel by means of a wheel.

Comparing and Geographical, Cultural and Chronological Attribution: this glass beaker shows some features similar to the cup from the Yinpan cemetery already discussed (*infra*, no 33). Anyway, while Wang Bo and Lu Lipeng (2007) hold that the object is quite similar to well-known examples of wheel-cut faceted glass vessels of Roman-Sasanian tradition, Lin Meicun (2006) instead, pointing out the tall and thin character of this object, considered that it could be dated back to the Parthian period. Even if an attribution to the Parthian period seems to be quite debatable, it is however undeniable that this beaker, while finds a wide range of very close comparisons for its decorative pattern (*infra*, no 33), is, on the other way, poorly paralleled in terms of its morphological and dimensional features. Evidence for wheel-cut faceted glass beakers with a nearly sub-cylindrical profile and a 1:1 ratio between the measures of the height and the rim diameter is in fact quite scanty if compared with the richer evidence represented by similarly wheel-cut faceted glass vessels with hemispherical or cone-truncated profile dated to Sasanian or Islamic period (Fukai 1977, figs.14, 15, 20–35; Genito 1977, inv. no 876; Kordmahini 1994, 55, 150–151; Kröger 1995, no 167; Negro Ponzi 1968–69, nos 71–72; Negro Ponzi 1984, fig.4, nos 1–2, 4–7; Pinder-Wilson and Scanlon 1987, no 15; Saldern 1963, fig.6). For this reason a certain similitude between our object and the glass beaker from the so-called "Heavenly Horse Tomb" in Korea (Laing 1991, 113, fig.10) could be considered as particularly intriguing.

参考文献　References

1. Charleston, R.J. (1964) Wheel-Engraving and Cutting: Some Early Equipments, *Journal of Glass Studies*, 6, 83−100, The Corning Museum of Glass, Corning, New York.

2. 成倩、王博、郭金龙：《新疆且末扎滚鲁克墓地出土玻璃杯研究》，《文物》2011年第7期，页88—92。
   Cheng Qian, Wang Bo and Guo Jinlong (2011) Research on the Glass Cup found at Zagunluk Cemetery, Qiemo County, Xinjiang, *Wenwu (Cultural Relics)*, 7, 88−92, Beijing.

3. Fukai, S. (1977) *Persian Glass*, New York - Tokyo.

4. Genito, B. (1977) *Vetri iranici. Schede del Museo Nazionale d'Arte Orientale* 10, Roma.

5. Kordmahini, H.A. (1994) *Glass from the Bazargan Collection*. Iranian Cultural Heritage Organization. Iran National Museum, Tehran.

6. Kröger, J. (1995) *Nishapur: Glass of the Early Islamic Period*, The Metropolitan Museum of Art, New York.

7. Laing, E.J. (1991) A Report on Western Asian Glassware in the Far East, *Bulletin of the Asia Institute*, 5 (n.s.), 109−121, Bloomfield.

8. 林梅村：《丝绸之路考古十五讲》，北京大学出版社（北京），2006年，页124—125。
   Lin Meicun (2006) *Sichouzhilu kaogu shiwujiang (Fifteen Lectures on Archaeology of the Silk Roads)*, Peking University Press, 124−125, Beijing.

9. Negro Ponzi, M. (1968−69) Sasanian Glassware from Tell Mahuz (North Mesopotamia), *Mesopotamia*, 3−4, 293−384, Torino.

10. Negro Ponzi, M. (1984) Glassware from Choche (Central Mesopotamia). Boucharlat, R., Salles, J.F. (eds.) *Arabie Orientale, Mésopotamie et Iran méridional, de L'âge du fer au Début de la Période Islamique*, Mémoire no 37. 33−40, Editions Recherche sur les Civilisations, Paris.

11. Pinder-Wilson, R. (1991) I Paesi Islamici e la Cina, Tait, H. (ed.) *Cinquemila anni di Vetro*, 112−138, Milano.

12. Pinder-Wilson, R. and Scanlon, G.T. (1987) Glass Finds from Fustat: 1972−1980, *Journal of Glass Studies*, 29, 60−71. The Corning Museum of Glass, New York.

13. Saldern, Von, A. (1963) Achaemenid and Sasanian Cut Glass, *Ars Orientalis* 5, 7−16.

14. Tait, H. (ed.) (1991) *Cinquemila anni di Vetro*. Milano. (Orig. Edit. *Five Thousand Years of Glass*. British Museum Press, London.

15. 王博、鲁礼鹏：《扎滚鲁克和山普拉古墓出土古代玻璃概述》，载干福熹主编《丝绸之路上的古代玻璃研究》，复旦大学出版社（上海），2007年，页126—138。
   Wang Bo and Lu Lipeng (2007) General Description of the Early Glasses Unearthed from the Tombs in Shan-pu-la and Zha-gun-lu-ke, in Gan Fuxi (ed.) *Sichouzhilu shang de gudai boli yanjiu (Study on Ancient Glass along the Silk Road)*, Fudan University Press, 126−138, Shanghai.

16. 新疆维吾尔自治区博物馆等：《新疆且末扎滚鲁克一号墓地发掘报告》，《考古学报》2003年第1期，页89—136，图38.2，图版拾陆4。
   Xinjiang Uygur Autonomous Region Museum *et alii* (2003) Excavation of Graveyard no. 1 at Zagunluk in Charchan, Xinjiang, *Kaoguxuebao (Acta Archaeologica Sinica)*, 1, 89−136, fig.38:2, XVI: 4, Beijing.

（*Giulio Maresca*, 耿朔 [*Geng Shuo*]）

17. 玻璃高足杯

收藏单位：新疆维吾尔自治区博物馆。

出土信息：1989年新疆库车著名的森木塞姆石窟附近发现，具体情况不明。森木塞姆石窟位于新疆库车东北约40公里处的库鲁科塔格山，是古代西域重要国家——龟兹王国境内的一座重要石窟，时间跨度从4至9世纪。该石窟目前有编号石窟52个，分布范围直径约800米，按其位置可分成东、南、西、北、中五个区，在中区还发现有地面寺院遗址。在11世纪以后，伊斯兰文化进入新疆，这些洞窟逐渐被废弃。

器物概括描述：无模自由吹制的高足玻璃杯，带有贴花装饰。

材质、工艺及保存状况：半透明绿色玻璃。这件器物由无模自由吹制技术制成。这项技术可能在公元前1世纪后半叶在东地中海沿岸某地出现（Tatton-Brown 1991；Whitehouse 1997），这个地区当时在罗马帝国的统治之下。罗马人发现可以将熔融的玻璃液挑在一个中空吹管的一头，就像吹泡泡那样吹出器物形状来，再用简单的工具进行修整。玻璃吹制技术在朱里亚·克劳狄（Julio-Claudian）王朝时期得到了迅速传播，取代了传统的铸造和卷芯法制作玻璃的技术，从而导致了玻璃的大批量生产，玻璃也变成普通而廉价的产品。

这件杯子发现时已破碎为几片，经修复仍有部分缺失。器物的内部和外部表面（尤其是底部），如同贴敷的纹饰一样，都有厚厚的淡黄

17. Glass Goblet

Location: Xinjiang Uygur Autonomous Region Museum.

Context of Origin: this object was found near the famous Simsim caves complex in the Kuqa County, Xinjiang Uygur Autonomous Region, in 1989, although unfortunately no detailed information has been given about its context of finding. This important archaeological complex is located about 40km northeast of the city of Kuqa, close to the Kuruk Tag Mountain Range. It represents one of the largest Buddhist cave-sites of the Qiuci Kingdom, an important kingdom in the Western Regions. The grottoes can be dated to a time span ranging from the 4th to the 9th century AD. The complex is quite large, with 52 numbered caves distributed over an area with a diameter of about 800m, and can be divided into five districts, the central one characterized by the presence of a temple. After the 11th century AD, Islamic culture entered Xinjiang and the grottoes were gradually abandoned.

Brief Description of the Object: free-blown glass goblet with applied decorations.

Material, Technique and Conservation: translucent green glass. The object was manufactured with the free-blown technique. This technique was probably introduced during the second half of the 1st century BC somewhere on the Eastern Mediterrancan coast (Tatton-Brown 1991; Whitehouse 1997), a region at that time under the control of the Roman Empire. Romans discovered that an object could be formed by gathering molten glass on the end of a hollow blowing pipe, inflating it like a bubble and then shaping and refining it with simple tools. Glass blowing spread particularly under the Julio-Claudian dynasty, taking the place of the ancient casting and core-forming techniques and paving the way towards a mass-production of common and quite inexpensive glass vessels. This goblet is restored and made up by several fragments (some of which missing). Both the internal and the external

17. 玻璃高足杯 Glass Goblet

白色覆盖层。颜色较暗的高足是趁着杯身仍处于熔融状态的时候连接上去的，表面泛着黄白色的光泽。

尺寸： 高 9.7、口径 12.1 厘米。

器物详细描述： 器物的口部微外侈，半球形杯身，外壁有两圈贴敷上去的圆形饰，每圈有 6 个，每个扁平的圆形饰大小相似，相错排列。一个暗绿色的柄被接到与其等高的器物的平底上，它轮廓上的特点是中心部位有一个算珠状凸起和一个平坦的喇叭形足部。

surface of the vessel (especially at the bottom) as well as the surface of the flat circular appliqués are altered by a quite thick white-yellowish layer of encrustation; the stem, darker in colour, applied at the bottom of the vessel when the glass was still at a high temperature and quite molten, reveals a surface covered by a white-yellowish patina.

Measurements: height 9.7cm; rim diameter 12.1cm.

Detailed Description of the Object: the vessel, with a slightly outwards everted rim on a body with rounded profile, is decorated by two superimposed rows each with six circular and quite flat appliqués of similar dimensions alternately arranged. A stem of a darker green tinge and with almost the same height of the vessel is applied at the

地域、文化、年代属性及对比：这件器物在2004年美国大都会艺术博物馆《走向盛唐》展览的图录中有著录。安家瑶（2004）指出这件玻璃器的一些形态特征也见于伊朗银器，时代在6—7世纪，认为它是隋代通过贸易的方式从伊朗来到中国内地的诸多商品中的一件。在此前数年（Various Authors 1999），已有若干学者指出这件杯子是萨珊制品。在伊朗高原的玻璃生产史上，圆形磨琢小凹面装饰（单重或双重，也被称作圆盘）常被视为萨珊文化的典型装饰特点（Von Saldern 1963; Fukai 1977; 亦参见No.33相关讨论），这种工艺传统持续到萨珊末期并延续至伊斯兰时期，这可以从内沙普尔发现的一些9至10世纪的带有类似磨琢小凹面装饰的玻璃器得到证实（Kröger 1995: 129-135 and nos 174-184）。而像森木塞姆这件玻璃杯贴敷圆形饰的做法，在一定程度上会让人想起前述的磨琢小凹面装饰，是萨珊晚期或伊斯兰时代第一个世纪出现的新时尚，类似的例子如在伊朗的苏萨遗址发现的一些玻璃器，发掘者将其年代定为5至7世纪（Lamm 1931, Pl. LXXVI, 1-3 and 5-6），再如伊朗国家博物馆收藏的一件小罐（Kordmahini 1994, 69, 159），还有众所周知的法门寺发现的一件玻璃瓶（即No.46），时代不晚于874年（安家瑶1991, 123, fig.2），可能与这种初始形态的圆形小磨琢面或具有浮雕效果的圆形饰有关。另外一些例子则在器身贴敷简单的圆环形装饰。东亚地区有三件类似的发现，即中国西安唐代何家村窖藏的凸纹玻璃杯（8世

flat base of the latter; its profile is marked by a rounded central bulge and by a flattened trumpet base.

Comparing and Geographical, Cultural and Chronological Attribution: in the catalogue of an exhibition at the Metropolitan Museum of Art in New York, An Jiayao (2004 a, b) pointed out the similarity of some features of this goblet with examples of Iranian silverware, dating it to the 6th or the 7th century AD and considering it as an object of Iranian origin testifying to the trades between East and West during the Sui period in the Central Plain of China. Also some years before (Various Authors 1999) this goblet was already considered as an example of Sasanian production. In the evolution of glass production on the Iranian Plateau, wheel-cut circular (single or double) facets (otherwise called discs) in relief have always been considered a typical example of decorative patterns related to Sasanian cultural and/or chronological horizon (Von Saldern 1963; Fukai 1977; see also *infra* the discussion for object no 33). A particular taste for this decorative tradition continued towards the end of the Sasanian period and entered the Islamic period as well. This is testified, for instance, by the permanence of a similar wheel-cut decoration in examples from the glass assemblage at Nishapur, dated to the 9th-10th century AD (Kröger 1995: 129-135 and nos 174-184). Moreover, applied circular discs as on the goblet at issue, always in some way reminiscent of the wheel-cut facets/discs decorative pattern, were "fashionable in the late Sasanian period" (Kröger 1998, 136) and can be seen on some published glass object (all of them restricted vessels) dating from the Late Sasanian period to the first centuries of the Islamic period. Examples were in fact brought to light at Susa (Lamm 1931, Pl. LXXVI,1-3 and 5-6) and dated by the excavator to the 5th-7th century AD; a small jar of the early Islamic period is in the Iran National Museum at Teheran (Kordmahini 1994, 69, 159), with the well-known bottle of the Famen Temple (see no 46) offers a *terminus ante*

纪)、韩国庆尚北道漆谷郡松林寺的凸纹玻璃杯 (7 世纪) 和藏于日本奈良东大寺正仓院的凸纹蓝色高足玻璃杯，它们被认为起源于伊朗 (Laing 1991, figs.9, 19, 20)。

quem of AD 874 (An 1991, 123, fig.2). Probably related to the original decorative concept of circular facets/discs in relief, are also others examples of circular motifs consisting in very simple rings of glass applied to the vessel. Three well-known specimens are found on objects coming from China (a glass cup from a 8th century treasure cache at Xi'an), Korea (a glass cup from the Songyim-sa temple near Teagu) and Japan (a glass goblet from the Shoso-in storehouse in the Todai-ji temple at Nara), and are sometimes considered to be of Iranian origins (Laing 1991, figs.9, 19, 20).

参考文献　References

1. 新疆维吾尔自治区文物事业管理局等主编：《中国新疆文物古迹大观》，新疆美术摄影出版社 (乌鲁木齐)，1999 年，页 206，图版 0547。
   Administration of Cultural Heritage of the Xinjiang Uygur Autonomous Region *et alii* (eds.) (1999) *Xinjiang wenwu guji daguan (A Grand View of Xinjiang's Cultural Relics and Historic Sites)*, 206, fig.0547, Urumqï.

2. An Jiayao (1991) Dated Islamic Glass in China. *Bulletin of the Asia Institute* 5 (n.s.), 123–38, Bloomfield.

3. An Jiayao (2004a) The Art of Glass along the Silk Road, Watt, James C.Y. *et alii* (eds.) *China: Dawn of a Golden Age, 200–750 AD,* 57–66. The Metropolitan Museum of Art, New York, Yale University Press, New Haven and London.

4. An Jiayao (2004b) Goblet with applied decoration. Cat. no. 96. Watt, James C.Y. *et alii* (ed.) *China: Dawn of a Golden Age, 200–750 AD,* 189. The Metropolitan Museum of Art, New York.Yale University Press, New Haven and London.

5. Fukai, S. (1977) *Persian Glass,* New York - Tokyo.

6. Kordmahini, H.A. (1994) *Glass from the Bazargan Collection.* Iranian Cultural Heritage Organization. Iran National Museum, Tehran.

7. Kröger, J. (1995) Nishapur: Glass of the Early Islamic Period. The Metropolitan Museum of Art, New York.

8. Kröger, J. (1998) From Ctesiphon to Nishapur: Studies in Sasanian and Islamic Glass Curtis Sarkhosh, Vesta *et alii*, (eds.) *The Art and Archaeology of Ancient Persia - New Light on the Parthian and Sasanian Empires,* 133–140, London.

9. Laing, E.J. (1991) A report on Western Asian Glassware in the Far East, *Bulletin of the Asia Institute*, 5 (n.s.), 109–121. Bloomfield.

10. Lamm, C.J. (1931) Les Verres trouvés à Suse, *Syria*, 12, 358–67, Paris.

11. Saldern, Von, A. (1963) Achaemenid and Sasanian Cut Glass, *Ars Orientalis* 5, 7–16.

12. Tait, H. (ed.) (1991) *Cinquemila anni di Vetro.* Milano. (Orig. Edit. *Five Thousand Years of Glass.* British Museum Press, London. 1991).

13. Tatton-Brown, V. (1991) L'impero romano, in Tait, H. (ed.) *Cinquemila anni di Vetro*, 62–97. Milano.

14. Whitehouse, D. (1997) s.v.Vetro. *Enciclopedia dell'Arte Antica*, 5 (secondo supplemento), 1022–1026. Istituto dell' Enciclopedia Italiana, Roma.

（*Giulio Maresca*，耿朔 [*Geng Shuo*]）

18. 印章

收藏单位：新疆维吾尔自治区博物馆。

出土信息：1959年新疆巴楚县脱库孜萨来遗址出土。

器物概括描述：印章，带有椭圆形的雕刻平面上刻有一个有翼男子形象。

材质、工艺及保存状况：灰黄色玉髓，保存完整。

尺寸：高2.2、长2.5、宽1.5厘米。

器物详细描述：印章正面为椭圆形雕刻面，背面有一个用于悬挂的小孔。

图像详细描述：雕刻面上有一个侧面向右呈行进状的带翼的男子形象，两个胳膊外张，握着一个带有三角形缎带的圆形王冠。男子看上去裸体，腹部鼓起。环绕头部一道斜线可能代表了头发（或是一顶头盔）。面部细节得到了体现，然而非常的程式化。

风格分析：印章使用了浅浮雕技术，器物成型和细节塑造都有相当的写生风格，这种处理方式是概括式的，一些要素没有被细致地结合在一起。

地域、文化、年代属性及对比：印章的图像主题非常接近白沙瓦博物馆的一件藏品（Callieri 1997, Cat. 2.5），也类似于法国国家图书馆收藏的一件（Gyselen 1993, 144, no 40. A.9），不过三角形缎带看上去像挂在手中所持的三个棍子上。带翼的裸体小天使形象也出现在萨珊雕刻上，例如属于沙普尔一世时期的比沙普尔第二和第三崖刻，其姿态和罗马胜利女

18. Seal

Location: Xinjiang Uygur Autonomous Region Museum.

Context of Origin: the seal was found in Tokozsarai, Bachu County, Xinjiang Uygur Autonomous Region in 1959.

Brief Description of the Object: independent seal with oval flat engraved surface with a winged male figure.

Material, Technique and Conservation: grey-yellow chalcedony; whole.

Measurements: height 2.2cm; length 2.5cm; width 1.5cm.

Detailed Description of the Object: the independent seal has a circular suspension hole parallel to the flat oval engraved surface.

Detailed Description of the Iconography: on the engraved face is a walking winged male figure in profile to right, arms outstretched, holding a circular crown bound with a triangular ribbon. The figure seems nude and has a round belly. An oblique line encircling the head may be the hair (or a helmet). The facial traits are rendered in detail, though very schematically.

Stylistic Analysis: the seal is in low relief and the execution of both finish and details rather sketchy. The treatment is schematic and the elements of the engraving are not carefully joined.

Comparing and Geographical, Cultural and Chronological Attribution: the iconographic scheme of the seal is extremely similar to the one on a seal in the Peshawar Museum (Callieri 1997, Cat. 2.5), as well as to the one on a seal in the Bibliothèque Nationale, Paris (Gyselen 1993, 144, no 40. A.9), where however the triangular ribbon seems to hang from three sticks held in the hand; a winged putto appears also in Sasanian sculpture, as for example also on the Bishapur II and III rock reliefs of king Shapur I, in a position corresponding to that of a Roman Victoria (Herrmann

18. 印章 Seal

神维多利亚相一致（Herrman 1980–1983），萨珊印章上出现的有翼男性形象已被解释为转变为男性的维多利亚形象（Bivar 1969, 60; Brunner 1978, 66）。这件印章因此可以归为萨珊波斯的产品，但因萨珊雕刻年代研究的不确定性，无法对此印章的年代背景进行更多的讨论。

1980–1983). And indeed the winged male figures on Sasanian seals have been explained as Victoriae, transformed into masculine figures (Bivar 1969, 60; Brunner 1978, 66).

Our seal can therefore be attributed to the seal production of Iran of the Sasanian period, without being able to a more detailed chronological setting, given the uncertainty of chronology in Sasanian glyptics.

参考文献　References

1. 新疆维吾尔自治区文物事业管理局等主编：《中国新疆文物古迹大观》，新疆美术摄影出版社（乌鲁木齐），1999年，页266，图版0725。

   Administration of Cultural Heritage of the Xinjiang Uygur Autonomous Region *et alii* (eds.) (1999) *Xinjiang wenwu guji daguan* (*A Grand View of Xinjiang's Cultural Relics and Historic Sites*), 266, fig.0725, Urumqï.

2. Bivar, A.D.H. (1969) *Catalogue of the Western Asiatic Seals in the British Museum. Stamp Seals, II. The Sassanian Dynasty*, London.

3. Brunner, C.J. (1978) *Sasanian Stamp Seals in the Metropolitan Museum of Art*, New York.

4. Callieri, P. (1997) *Seals and Sealings from the North-West of the Indian Subcontinent and Afghanistan* (*4th century* BC–*11th century* AD): *Local, Indian, Sasanian, Graeco-Persian, Sogdian, Roman*. With contributions by E. Errington, R. Garbini, Ph. Gignoux, N. Sims-Williams, W. Zwalf (Istituto Universitario Orientale, Dissertationes I), Naples.

5. Gyselen, R. (1993) *Catalogue des Sceaux, Camées et Bulles Sassanides. I. Collection Générale*, Paris.

6. Herrmann, G. (1980–83) *The Sasanian Rock Reliefs at Bishapur*, 3 vols. (Iranische Denkmäler, Lfg. 9–11. Reihe 2, Iranisches Felsreliefs E–G), Berlin.

7. 穆舜英主编：《中国新疆古代艺术》，新疆美术摄影出版社（乌鲁木齐），1994年，页161、206，图版414。

   Mu Shunying *et alii* (eds.) (1994) *Zhongguo xinjiang gudai yishu* (*The Ancient Art in Xinjiang, China*), Xinjiang Art and Photography Press, 161, 206, fig.414, Urumqï.

（*Pierfrancesco Callieri*，耿朔 [*Geng Shuo*]）

19. 印章

收藏单位：新疆吐鲁番博物馆。

出土信息：新疆维吾尔自治区吐鲁番高昌故城采集，具体情况不明。该城位于吐鲁番市东南30公里处，始于汉代戍军的"高昌壁"，晋代高昌郡治所在，公元5世纪为北凉都城，唐代被称为西州，9世纪后的回鹘王朝定都于此，该城至元、明时废弃。现存遗迹规模形成于唐代。城市面积1.58平方公里，由外城、内城、宫城三部分组成，城墙夯筑而成。保存有宫殿、寺院、佛塔和一些居住址，都为土结构。在高昌城北郊的阿斯塔那和哈拉和卓村分布有大量晋唐时代的墓葬，约10平方公里，1959年以来已多次发掘，以唐代墓葬最引人注目，出土了大量珍贵文物。

器物概括描述：在斜切的环形边缘内雕刻有一个站立的男子形象。

材质、工艺及保存状况：橘红色玛瑙，雕刻面的右侧边缘似有缺损(?)。

尺寸：高2厘米。

器物详细描述：宝石呈椭圆形，雕刻面平整，外侧是梯形状斜切面。

图像详细描述：宝石朝上的一面雕刻出一个男性的正面身体和四肢，身体扭向左边。右手置于腰部，握住一个直抵胸部的长权杖，左臂上举，手指张开朝向鼻子。须发皆长，头发由平行斜线构成，露出带有似耳环装饰的耳朵。面部特征刻画得很细致，高鼻。他身着朴素的齐膝长袖衣服，底边向中线弯折。腰部系有腰带，

19. Seal

Location: Turfan Museum.

Context of Origin: it was collected at Gaochang ruins, Turfan county-level city, Xinjiang Uygur Autonomous Region. The context of the excavation is unclear. The ruins are located 30km south-east of Turfan. It became Gaochang military post when a border defense garrison was established during the Western Han Dynasty. During the Jin Dynasty it was the Gaochang County, and then in succession it became the capital of the Northern Liang Dynasty in the 5th century, in the Tang Dynasty was called Xizhou and after the 9th century became the capital of the Uygur-Gaochang Kingdom. The city was abandoned in the Yuan and Ming Dynasties. The present site reflects a Tang Dynasty layout. The City, with an area of 1.58 sq. km, can be divided into three parts: the outer city, the inner city, and the imperial city; palace temple, pagoda and some residential area are preserved; their structure is made of packed earth. A large number of tombs, dating to the Jin and Tang Dynasties, were found in the village of Astana and Harahojo. The cemetery covers an area of 10 sq. km. Since 1959, many tombs have been excavated; most date to the Tang Dynasty and many precious cultural relics have been unearthed.

Brief Description of the Object: engraved ring bezel showing a standing male figure.

Material, Technique and Conservation: orange color agate; chipped on the right rim on the engraved face (?).

Measurements: height of seal 2cm.

Detailed Description of the Object: the gem has an oval shape and a flat engraved surface with chamfered edge, with shallow trapezoidal section.

Detailed Description of the Iconography: on the upper face of the gem is represented a male figure standing with frontal body and legs and head turned in profile to left, with right hand kept at his waist

领部无翻领，呈 V 型，脚着高靴。衣物边际刻画平整，中间及领部皆为单线条，底边及侧边皆为双线条。

风格分析：这枚印章风格适度，细部刻画十分到位，人物呈静态，较为传统，连头部刻画也呈自然风格。

地域、文化、年代属性及对比：尽管岩本笃志（2006）认为这枚印章的时代属于萨珊时期，但相当多不同材质的可作比较的例子起源于中亚西部匈人的领地，从第尔伯金发现的壁画到银质容器——尤其是圣彼得堡艾尔米塔什博物馆收藏的所谓"斯特洛加诺夫"碗（Callieri 2002, 124–127）。特别要提到，虽然因单层领缺

on the body of a long mace reaching his breast, and left forward to side with bent forearm and open hand facing his nose. He is bearded and has long hair rendered with oblique parallel strokes which leave visible the ears with earrings (?); his facial traits are rendered in detail, with large nose. He wears a plain knee-length caftan with lower edges rising to the centre, fastened at the waist and leaving the neck exposed in a V-shaped décolletage with no folded lapel, and high boots; the caftan has smooth raised border, single in the centre and at the neck and double along the lower and sideedges.

Stylistic Analysis: the seal is in moderate relief, carefully engraved in considerable detail, and the subject rather static and conventional, even though the head is not without naturalism.

19. 印章 Seal

失而有所不同，这枚印章上的衣物刻画还是让人想起私人收藏的一枚印章上刻画的匈人统治者Khiṅgila，后者时代属于公元5世纪上半叶或晚到5世纪中叶（Callieri 2002）。因此这枚印章可以看作是公元5世纪前后，活动在中亚西部区域的当地匈人统治者的肖像作品。

Comparing and Geographical, Cultural and Chronological Attribution: Although Iwamoto (2006) thinks this seal stone is datable from Sasanian time, it rather finds comparative evidence in various media stemming from the Hunnish environment of Western Central Asia, from the wall paintings at Dilberjin to the silver vessels, among which particularly the so-called "Stroganov" bowl in the Hermitage Museum of St. Petersburg (Callieri 2002, 124–127). In particular, although differing for the absence of the single lapel, the caftan recalls the one worn by the Hunnish ruler Khiṅgila on a seal in private collection, dated to the first half of the 5th century AD or to mid–5th century AD (Callieri 2002). Our gem therefore can be interpreted as a portrait of a Hunnish local ruler of an area in Western Central Asia of a time centered around the 5th century AD.

参考文献　References

1. 新疆维吾尔自治区文物事业管理局等主编：《新疆文物古迹大观》，新疆美术摄影出版社（乌鲁木齐），1999年，页133，图版0325。
Administration of Cultural Heritage of the Xinjiang Uygur Autonomous Region *et alii* (eds.) (1999) *Xinjiang wenwu guji daguan* (*A Grand View of Xinjiang's Cultural Relics and Historic Sites*), 133, fig.0325, Urumqï.

2. Callieri, P. (2002) The Bactrian Seal of Khingila, *Silk Road Art and Archaeology*, 8, 121–141, Kamakura.

3. Iwamoto, A. (2005) The function of stone seals in North Dynasties and Tang Dynasty, *The history and culture of East Asia*, East Asian Studies of Niigata University, no 14.

4. 穆舜英主编：《中国新疆古代艺术》，新疆美术摄影出版社（乌鲁木齐），1994年，页161、206，图版413。
Mu Shunying *et alii* (eds.) (1994) *Zhongguo xinjiang gudai yishu* (*The Ancient Art in Xinjiang, China*), 161, 206, fig.413, Xinjiang Art and Photography Press, Urumqï.

5. The first Tokyo Department of the Cultural Planning Bureau Asahi Shimbun (ed.) (1992) *Forever Beauty of Loulan, an Exhibition to commemorate the 20th anniversary of the Establishment of Diplomatic Relations between China and Japan*, 128.

6. Tokyo National Museum (2000) *The Brocade and Gold from the Silk Road*, Exhibition Catalogue, 148, Tokyo.

7. 薛宗正：《魏晋南北朝时期塔里木绿洲城邦诸国的社会生活》，《新疆文物》1996年第2期，页64。
Xue Zongzheng (1996) Social Life of the kingdoms in Tarim Basin during Wei Jin Southern and Northern Dynasties, *Xinjiang Wenwu* (*Cultural Relics of Xinjiang*), 2, 64, Urumqï.

（*Pierfrancesco Callieri*，耿朔 [*Geng Shuo*]）

20. 金面具

收藏单位：新疆伊犁哈萨克自治州博物馆。

出土信息：在新疆伊犁哈萨克自治州昭苏县境内，西距中哈边境约2公里处，有3座沿东南—西北方向一线分布的大土墩墓，间距近30米，高0.7—1.5米，直径为20—30米。1997年10月，当地居民在基本建设取土过程中，在中间一座土墩墓范围内（坐标位置为80°15′11.4″E，42°41′30.4″N）挖掘出数量可观的珍贵文物，包括镶嵌红宝石的金器、武器、织物，还有人骨和殉葬马骨等。发现文物后随即遭哄抢和肆意挖掘，墓葬的形制结构及相关信息已破坏殆尽。经现场勘查，文物出土处距现地表约3.5米。另外两座土墩墓也遭到不同程度的破坏。警方收缴的出土品包括两部分，一部分材料见于1999年简报，后来昭苏垦区公安局介入调查，又从社会上收缴回部分文物，包括镶嵌红宝石的圆柄金杯、金指套、金护臂、金丝编织带、金片等共十几件，这些材料连同之前发表的器物图片一同收入2008年出版的《丝绸之路：新疆古代文化》中。

除去上述简报和图录之外，作为这批材料的经手人，安英新先生曾在《东南文化》撰写通俗性文字予以介绍，并在这批材料面世约10年后，在《伊犁日报》上回忆昭苏波马宝藏的发现、收缴全过程。值得注意的是，安英新先生在这篇回忆性文章中提到，在收缴过程中，不同群众均证实见到但是在最终交接过程中却始终未见的两件文物，一件为"像短拐杖一样、手柄处

20. Gold Mask

Location: Ili Kasak Autonomous Prefecture Museum.

Context of Origin: Boma Gold Treasure (Ili, Xinjiang Uygur Autonomous Region). About 2km from the frontier between China and Kazakhstan, at Zhaosu, Ili, three big earth-mounds are arranged on the same axis. The distance among each other is about 30m; each mound is 0.7–1.5m high, 20–30m in diameter. In October 1997, while digging some soil from the central mound (longitude 80°15′11.4″ E, latitude 42°41′30.4″ N) local inhabitants discovered a large number of precious objects, such as gold and silver ware, fragments of fabric, weapons, along with horse bones and human skeletons. The tomb was completely destroyed during the digging and its objects rashly snatched away: it is impossible to reconstruct the structure of the tomb. An investigation by experts after the finding showed that all the relics were unearthed at about 3.5m below the earth's surface. The other two mounds met a similar fate. Two sets of objects were rescued by the police; the first (consisting of 8 objects) was published in the 1999 report, whereas the second, including a gold cup, a gold wire woven band, a gold finger and an arm guard, was rescued later; the photographs of the second lot can be seen in an exhibition catalogue (Qi Xiao shan *et alii* ed, 2008). In 2000, the officer in charge at Yingxin wrote an article to present this important archaeological discovery. In a further article published in the *Ili Daily* in 2007, he recalled the process of discovering and the recovery of these objects; he also referred to two items seen by locals, but later lost. One was "a short crutch with the shaft inlaid gems", the other a porcelain bowl (diameter approximately 20cm); he speculated that the "short crutch" might have been a scepter.

Brief Description of the Object: funeral mask, almost complete; left eyebrow missing; deformations in the lower part.

20. 金面具 Gold Mask

镶嵌有宝石的器物",安先生推测这应该是一件权杖;另一件为"直径约20厘米的瓷器"。

器物概括描述:该面具为丧仪所需,几乎保存完好,左眉遗失,下半部变形。

材质、工艺及保存状况:金镶红宝石;熔化焊接工艺。

尺寸:宽17、高16.5厘米,重245.5克。

器物详细描述:该面具表现的是一张男性的脸,由左右两部分拼接,面部中间清晰可见一道竖向垂线,笔直穿过鼻子和嘴唇。

图像详细描述:眉毛(左眉遗失)和髭须均先单独制成,然后焊铆接于面具之上,眉毛和胡须被分为小方格以镶嵌宝石(眉毛中嵌贵榴石,胡须上的镶嵌物已经遗失),髭须由长条金饰焊铆于两腮,金饰条上镶嵌肾形的红贵榴石,贵榴石边廓点焊一周细工金珠;眼眶呈轮廓分明的杏仁状,中间镶嵌贵榴石作为瞳孔;双颊饱满,双唇线条分明,在眉心和左右眉梢及下颌部各焊有三个小挂钩。

风格分析:髭须上的肾形镶嵌工艺,在欧洲匈人遗存中可以见到类似工艺,不过该面具在外貌上(眉毛、鼻梁、髭须、面部器官比例等)表现的是早期突厥人的形象,与6—8世纪欧亚草原东部广泛分布的石人的相貌十分相似(Šer 1966; Pletneva ed, 1981, 29 ff.; Stark 2008, 128–137)。

地域、文化、年代属性及对比:由于墓葬已被完全破坏,目前围绕这批材料所展开的研究皆从出土遗物入手,通过对器物的种类组合、工艺技术、装饰风格进行分析,来考察该宝藏的年代、族属、等级、文化因素及渊源等问题。这其

Material, Technique and Conservation: gold inlaid with ruby, fusion; welding.

Measurements: height, cm 16.5; width, 17; weight, 245.5 gr.

Detailed Description of the Object: the mask, representing a male face, consists of two golden sheets joined in the middle; a vertical joint, crossing the nose and the lips, is clearly visible.

Detailed Description of the Iconography: the eyebrow (the left one is missing), the moustache and the beard were worked separately and applied. Eyebrow and moustache are subdivided into square settings for incrustations (almandine in the eyebrow, completely lost in the moustache). The beard is indicated by a long and narrow golden stripe with red almandine kidney-shaped incrustations, each bordered by a granulated ornament. The almond-shaped eyes, with an outline in sharp relief, contain large pupils with almandine incrustation. The face shows full cheeks and well-defined lips with edges slightly downward. On the forehead, above the eyebrows, there are two small circular loops.

Stylistic Analysis: Although the kidney-shaped incrustations decorating the beard band have parallels in the European Hunnic materials, the general treatment of the physiognomy (eyebrows, nose, moustache, proportions) recalls early Turkic iconography, as evidenced by the funeral steles widespread over Eastern Eurasia between the 6th and the 8th centuries (Šer 1966; Pletneva ed, 1981, 29 ff.; Stark 2008, 128–137).

Comparing and Geographical, Cultural and Chronological Attribution: the study of the treasure is limited to the objects, since the state of preservation of the tomb does not allow any reconstruction. Dating them is crucial. The ornamental design on the fabrics; the shape, decoration and technology of the gold and silver articrafts; the weapons (arrowheads) are all elements capable of providing evidence for dating. Different dates have been suggested; the main

中，断代研究是一切研究得以深入的前提。出土遗物中的箭镞、织物、金银器的器形、工艺及装饰技法都具有不同程度的时代属性。原简报（2002）比较谨慎地将这批东西的年代下限定在6—7世纪，并认为是突厥人的宝藏。林英（2001）在此基础上考察了虎柄金杯的拜占庭文化因素；王炳华（Wang Binghua 2003）通过对土墩墓的分布、突厥葬俗、金银器和丝织品风格的综合分析认为，这批金银器与突厥人无关，其时代最迟也在6世纪突厥进入此地区之前（4—5世纪），比较有可能属于悦般；林梅村（2005）据共出的织物将年代定在公元5—6世纪，这批宝藏应是乌孙王生前的财宝；俄罗斯学者阿尔金（C.B. Arguin 2002）通过对出土的箭镞、织物、墓葬规模及面具的简略分析后认为这批财宝的年代要更早一些（2—4世纪），应该属于匈奴—萨尔马特时代的遗物。另外，在吉尔吉斯斯坦的沙姆西墓地（Shamsi，5—7世纪）的一座女性墓中曾出土过一件金面具，不过其表现手法更为模式化（Pletneva ed, 1981, 114, fig.10.16）。

viewpoints can be summarized as follows: the report (An Yingxin 1999) dated the latest item in the treasure between the 6th and the 7th century AD; Lin Meicun had already pointed out that the Tekes river valley was the place where the Western Turks established their royal court; An Yingxin suggested that this treasure was further evidence supporting Lin's view. Based on the view that the hoard belonged to a Western Turkic aristocrat; LinYing highlighted a Byzantine cultural element in the gold cup with a handle in the shape of a tiger. Considering the Turks' cremation burial custom and other elements, after further analysis of the objects, Wang Binghua (2003) thought the date of the treasure should be not later than the 6th century AD, when the Turks entered the Tekes river valley, most probably the 4th–5th century AD. The master of the grave should be a noble of Yue Ban. According to the possible structure of the grave, Lin Meicun dated the treasure to 5th to 6th century AD and attributed it to the king of the Wu Sun. Argin (2002) argued that the tomb should be dated much earlier, 2nd to 4th century AD, and that the treasure was related to the Hun-Sarmatian culture. A golden funeral mask was unearthed in a female grave of the Shamsi cemetery (Kirghizstan, 5th–7th centuries) (Pletneva ed, 1981, 114, fig.10.16); in this case, however, the face shows a much more schematized treatment.

参考文献　References

1. 安英新：《新疆伊犁昭苏县古墓葬出土金银器等珍贵文物》，《文物》1999年第9期，页4—15及彩版壹～肆、封面。

   An Yingxin (1999) Discovery of Gold and Silverware Unearthed from an Ancient Tomb at Zhaosu Country, Yili, Xinjiang, *Wenwu* (*Cultural Relics*), 9, 4–15, Color version no. 1–4 and the front cover, Beijing.
2. C·B·阿尔金著，安英新译，托乎提校（2002）：《关于北天山古代匈奴—萨尔马特时代的划分问题》，《新疆文物》2002年第3、4期，页149—150。

   Argin, S.V. (2002) Study about the Ancient Huns-Sarmatian Era in Northern Tjan' Šan Mountain, *Xinjiang Wenwu* (*Cultural Relics of Xinijang*), translated by An Yingxin, revised by Tohti, 3, 4, 149–50, Urumqï.

3. 林梅村:《毗伽可汗宝藏与中世纪草原艺术》,《上海文博论丛》2005年第1期,页74,后收入林氏所著:《松漠之间：考古发现所见中外文化交流》,生活・读书・新知三联书店（北京）,2007年,页231。

Lin Meicun (2005) Treasure of Bilge Khagan and the Steppe Art of Middle Ages, *Shanghai Wenbo* (*Forum of Relics and Museology in Shanghai*), 1, 74; revised edition could be found in the book: Lin Meicun (2007) *Between Song and Mo: Cultural Exchange between China and Foreign Countries Reflected on the New Archaeological Findings*, 231. SDX Joint Publishing Company, Beijing.

4. 林英:《新疆波马出土的虎柄金杯中的拜占庭因素》,《艺术史研究》第3辑,中山大学出版社,2001年;后收入林氏所著:《唐代拂菻丛说》,中华书局,2006年,页157—168。

Lin Ying (2008) The Byzantine Element in the Turkic Gold Cup with the Tiger Handle excavated at Boma, Xinjiang, *The Silk Road*, 5, 2, 20–26, (in part. p. 20) (description figs. 2, 3), Seattle.

5. Pletneva, S.A. (ed.) (1981) *Stepi Evrazii v epohu srednevekov'ja*. Moskva.

6. 祁小山、王博编著:《丝绸之路：新疆古代文化》,新疆人民出版社（乌鲁木齐）,2008年,页258—261。

Qi Xiaoshan *et alii* (eds.) (2008) *The Silk Road: Xinjiang Ancient Culture*, Xinjiang People's Publishing House, 258–261, Urumqï.

7. Šer, Ja. A. (1966) *Kamennye izvajanija Semireč'ja*, Moskva-Leningrad.

8. Stark, S. (2008) *Die Alttürkenzeit in Mittel-und Zentralasien. Archäologische und Historische Studien* (Nomaden und Sesshafte, Bd. 6), Wiesbaden.

9. Wang Binghua (2003) Gold and Silver Discovered in Boma, Xinjiang, Li Jiang (ed.) *The Glory of the Silk Road: Art from Ancient China*, 56–64, fig. 8, Dayton.

10. Wieczorek, A. und Lind, C. (hrsg.) (2007) *Ursprünge der Seidenstraße, Sensationelle Neufunde aus Xinjiang, China*, 302–303. Mannheim-Stuttgart.

11. 于志勇:《新疆昭苏西突厥黄金宝藏》,《文物天地》2000年第2期,页27—30;

Yu Zhiyong (2000) The Western Turks Gold Treasures from Zhaosu Xinjiang, *Wenwu Tiandi* (*Cultural Relics World*), 2, 27–30, Beijing.

(*Ciro Lo Muzio*, 李雨生 [*Li Yusheng*])

21. 带盖金罐

收藏单位：新疆伊犁哈萨克自治州博物馆。

出土信息：属于新疆伊犁发现的波马金银器，具体情况如前述。

器物概括描述：带盖罐。

材质、工艺及保存状况：金镶红宝石。

21. Gold Covered Jar

Location: Ili Kasak Autonomous Prefecture Museum.
Context of Origin: Boma Gold Treasure (Ili, Xinjiang Uygur Autonomous Region).
Brief Description of the Object: covered jar.
Material, Technique and Conservation: gold inlaid with ruby.
Measurements: height 14cm; opening diameter 7cm.

21. 带盖金罐 Gold Covered Jar

尺寸：高14、口径7厘米，重489克。

器物详细描述：球腹、矮圈足，圈足单独制成，器盖半球形，以铆钉固定的盖把丢失，仅留有四个铆接点。

图像详细描述：金壶肩部焊接一周锁绣状装饰（编织纹）金线，其下镶嵌一周30颗圆形红宝石，再往下是一周14组镶嵌红宝石的三叶状装饰，器足装饰一周金珠。

风格分析：器盖可能属于另一个完全不同的器物，器盖表面的莨苕纹装饰常见于萨珊晚期的建筑装饰之中。

地域、文化、年代属性及对比：5—7世纪。

weight 489g.

Detailed Description of the Object: jar with globular body on a low, separately worked base, covered with a hemispheric lid. It originally had a ring handle riveted to the body, as shown by the presence of four holes.

Detailed Description of the Iconography: on the shoulder, there is a decoration consisting of an intertwined gold wire from which gold circular sockets containing rubies hang; below there is a repetition of a three-foiled motif (almond-shaped leaves joined together). The edge of the base is decorated by a band of tiny gold beads.

Stylistic Analysis: the lid was probably crafted to complete a different vase, as its decoration suggests: a schematised acanthus calyx, which can be found in the late Sasanian architectural decoration.

Comparing and Geographical, Cultural and Chronological Attribution: 5th–7th centuries AD.

参考文献　References

1. 安英新：《新疆伊犁昭苏县古墓葬出土金银器等珍贵文物》，《文物》1999年第9期，页4—15及彩版壹~肆、封面。
   An Yingxin (1999) Discovery of Gold and Silverware Unearthed from an Ancient Tomb at Zhaosu Country, Yili, Xinjiang, *Wenwu* (*Cultural Relics*), 9, 4–15, Color version no. 1–4 and the front cover, Beijing.
2. Marshak, B.I. (2004) Covered Jar (no. 94), Watt, James C.Y. *et alii* (eds.) *China: Dawn of a Golden Age, 200–750 AD*, 188, no 94. Yale University Press, New Haven and London.
3. Wang Binghua (2003) Gold and Silver Discovered in Boma, Xinjiang, Li Jiang (ed.) *The Glory of the Silk Road: Art from Ancient China*, 56–64, fig. 8, Dayton.

（*Ciro Lo Muzio*，李雨生 [*Li Yusheng*]）

22. 金杯

收藏单位：新疆伊犁哈萨克自治州博物馆。

出土信息：属于新疆伊犁发现的波马金银器，具体情况如前述。

器物概括描述：虎柄金杯，镶嵌红玛瑙。

材质、工艺及保存状况：器物变形，腹部和口沿外的镶嵌物有遗失。

尺寸：高16、宽8.8厘米，重70克。

器物详细描述：卵形腹，口沿外翻，动物形柄。

图像详细描述：金杯腹部模压出双线菱格形，每个菱格中嵌一枚椭圆形红玛瑙，沿外口沿有一周长方形凹槽，所嵌宝石已遗失；口沿下有一周点状装饰。

风格分析：杯把呈立虎状，立虎身形瘦长，通体錾刻条纹，圆耳张口，口爪焊铆于杯子的颈、肩和腹部。

地域、文化、年代属性及对比：5—7世纪。该金杯属于1997年在伊犁发现的波马金银器，墓葬破坏严重，其年代也有不同，有4—5世纪（王炳华2003）、早期突厥时代（6—7世纪，安英新1999）、5—7世纪（Marshak 2004）三种不同观点，其中马尔沙克（Marshak 2004）认为该器物体现了欧亚草原上的游牧风格，但也不排除是萨珊工匠制作的可能；林英（Lin Ying 2008）认为这件突厥金杯中的虎柄反映的是来自拜占庭（基本可以认为是罗马文化）的影响，最初可能与酒神崇拜有关。

22. Gold Cup

Location: Ili Kasak Autonomous Prefecture Museum.

Context of Origin: Boma Gold Treasure (Ili, Xinjiang Uygur Autonomous Region).

Brief Description of the Object: gold cup with tiger-shaped handle with red agate inlays.

Material, Technique and Conservation: deformed, incrustations missing on the body and on the rim.

Measurements: height, 16cm; width 8.8cm; weight 70g.

Detailed Description of the Object: gold vase with ovoid body, everted rim and zoomorphic handle.

Detailed Description of the Iconography: the whole surface is decorated by a mould-pressed lozenge pattern, defined by a double line; in each lozenge an oval red agate is inlaid. Along the rim, a row of rectangular hollows, once containing precious stones; beneath the rim, a row of small circles in relief.

Stylistic Analysis: The handle is shaped as a standing tiger, with elongated body, marked by undulated stripes, rounded ears and jaws opened; the muzzle and the paws are soldered to the neck, shoulder and body of the vase.

Comparing and Geographical, Cultural and Chronological Attribution: 5th–7th centuries AD. The vase belongs to the Boma (Ili County) hoard found in 1997 in a mound; the tomb suffered serious damage, as well as the other two mounds. On the chronology of the graveyard different hypothesis have been advanced; it has been assigned to the 4th–5th centuries (Wang Binghua 2003) or to the early Turkic period (6th–7th centuries) (An Yingxin 1999); Marshak (2004) postulates a little longer time span ranging between the 5th and the 7th centuries, considering the vase as a product of Eurasian nomadic style, although he does not rule out a Sasanian craftsmanship. According to Lin Ying (2008, 25) the vase is a Turkic work revealing a Byzantine (and ultimately Roman) influence in the presence of a tiger handle, originally alluding to the Dionysiac cult.

22. 金杯 Gold Cup

参考文献　References

1. 安英新：《新疆伊犁昭苏县古墓葬出土金银器等珍贵文物》,《文物》1999年第9期，页4—15及彩版壹～肆、封面。

An Yingxin (1999) Discovery of Gold and Silverware Unearthed from an Ancient Tomb at Zhaosu County, Ili, Xinjiang, *Wenwu* (*Cultural Relics*), 9, 4–15, Color version no. 1–4 and the front cover, Beijing.

2. Lin Ying (2008) The Byzantine Element in the Turkic Gold Cup with the Tiger Handle Excavated at Boma, Xinjiang, *The Silk Road*, 5, 2, 20–26, (in part. 20) (description figs. 2, 3).

3. Marshak, B.I. (2004) Covered Jar (no. 94), Watt, James C.Y. *et alii* (eds.) *China: Dawn of a Golden Age, 200–750 AD*, 188, no. 94. Yale University Press, New Haven and London.

4. Wang Binghua (2003) Gold and Silver Discovered in Boma, Xinjiang, in Li Jiang (ed.) *The Glory of the Silk Road: Art from Ancient China*, 56–64, fig. 9, Dayton.

（*Ciro Lo Muzio*，李雨生 [*Li Yusheng*]）

23. 金剑鞘

收藏单位：新疆伊犁哈萨克自治州博物馆。

出土信息：属于新疆伊犁发现的波马金银器，具体情况如前述。

器物概括描述：剑鞘。

工艺、技术及保存状况：金片、镶嵌红宝石。

尺寸：长21.7、宽5.6厘米。

图像详细描述：剑鞘上镶嵌了三排红宝石，中间一排的红宝石呈半圆形或半椭圆形，上下两排的红宝石呈心形或者盛开的花朵形，镶嵌宝石之外的剩余空间由细金珠点焊拼成三角形、菱形等图案，宝石所嵌的凹槽外也点焊金珠。鞘身边缘以金珠点焊成两道装饰线。

风格分析：剑鞘上的装饰基本可以视作所谓的"多彩风格"（polychrome style），被认为是早期游牧艺术最后阶段（约3世纪之前）的代表性装饰，也是萨尔马提亚（Sarmatian）考古学文化的代表性特征，不过这种装饰技术在萨尔马提亚文化结束之后还继续在欧亚草原和东欧地区使用和传播。

地域、文化、年代属性及对比：5—7世纪。欧亚大陆的中西部地区发现有许多类似的珠宝装饰，不过人们对其流行年代的认识也互相矛盾。一方面，在乌克兰的Melitopol'（Pletneva ed, 1981, fig.7.6）发现的一件头饰，以及Čjuripin'sk（ibidem, fig.7.21）发现的垂饰，哈萨克斯坦的Kara Agač（ibidem, fig.7.11）发现的一件项圈都被认定属于6—7世纪；另一方面，在哈萨克斯坦中部的Kanattas墓地（2—4世纪, Silvi Antonini, Bajpakov,

23. Gold Sword Scabbard

Location: Ili Kasak Autonomous Prefecture Museum.

Context of Origin: Boma Gold Treasure, Ili, Xinjiang Uygur Autonomous Region.

Brief Description of the Object: sword scabbard.

Material, Technique and Conservation: gold sheet inlaid with ruby.

Measurements: length, 21.7cm; width, 5.6cm.

Detailed Description of the Iconography: the decoration consists of three rows of ruby inlays of semi-circular or semi-elliptical shape, in the central row, and heart and blossom shape, in the side rows. The residual space is filled with triangular and rhomboid patterns in granulation; a granulation outline frames each stone. Along the borders of the central decorated space runs a double line in granulation.

Stylistic Analysis: for the ornamentation (technique and material), the scabbard can be loosely related to the so-called "polychrome style", which represents the final stage of the art of early nomads (from the 3rd century BC *circa* onwards) and is considered peculiar to the Sarmatian archaeological culture. The use and spread of this technique, however, continued well beyond the end of the Sarmatian culture, both in the Asian steppes and in the Eastern Europe.

Comparing and Geographical, Cultural and Chronological Attribution: 5th–7th centuries AD. A number of parallels are provided by western and central Eurasian jewellery, although the chronological hypothesis advanced for them appear conflicting: on one hand, in particular a diadem from Melitopol' (Pletneva ed, 1981, fig.7.6), a pendant from Čjuripin'sk (Ukraine) (*ibidem*, fig.7.21), both in Ukraine, and a torques termination from Kara Agač (Kazakhstan) (*ibidem*, fig.7.11), are all assigned to the 6th–7th centuries, on the other hand, an earlier date is suggested for a diadem from the Kanattas cemetery

23. 金剑鞘 Gold Sword Scabbard

eds, 1999, 227, no 498）发现的一件头饰，七河地区 Aktasty 和 Kzyl Kajnar Tobe 墓地发现的三件垂饰（东哈萨克斯坦，3—4世纪，*ibidem*, 236, nos 518–520）的年代又早得多。类似的装饰工艺在哈萨克斯坦的 Borovoe 湖地区的一些偶然发现中也可以见到（Akišev ed, 1983, 196–201）。

(Central Kazakhstan; 2nd–4th centuries) (Silvi Antonini, Bajpakov eds, 1999, 227, no 498) and three pendants from the Aktasty and Kzyl Kajnar Tobe cemetery (Semireč'e, Eastern Kazakhstan; 3rd–4th centuries) (*ibidem*, 236, nos 518–520). A similar technique and ornamentation is found in some chance finds from the Borovoe Lake area (Kazakhstan) (Akišev ed, 1983, 196–201).

参考文献　　References

1. Akišcv, K. (cd.) (1983) *The Ancient Gold of Kazakhstan*. Alma-Ata.

2. Pletneva, S.A. (ed.) (1981) *Stepi Evrazii v epohu srednevekov'ja*. Moskva.

3. Silvi Antonini, C., Bajpakov, K. (eds.) (1999) *Altyn Adam. L'Uomo d'Oro*. Roma.

4. Wang Binghua (2003) Gold and Silver Discovered in Boma, Xinjiang, in Li Jiang (ed.) *The Glory of the Silk Road: Art from Ancient China*, 56–64, fig. 6, Dayton.

（*Ciro Lo Muzio*, 李雨生 [*Li Yusheng*]）

24. 银瓶

收藏单位：新疆伊犁哈萨克自治州博物馆。

出土信息：属于新疆伊犁发现的波马金银器，具体情况如前述。

器物概括描述：束颈、卵形腹、平底、口沿微外侈。

材质、工艺及保存状况：银制、锤揲制成、颈部鎏金。

尺寸：高17、口径7.3厘米。

风格分析：兼具游牧和萨珊文化因素，颈部的简化莨苕纹常见于伊朗5-7世纪的萨珊晚期典型建筑装饰之中。

地理、文化、年代属性及对比：马尔沙克（Marshak 2004）将波马金银器的时间定在5—7世纪，并认为波马的这批宝藏可以确定是为游牧人而做，体现出游牧人的趣味，但也不排除萨珊工匠制作的可能。

24. Silver Vase

Location: Ili Kasak Autonomous Prefecture Museum.

Context of Origin: Boma Gold Treasure (Ili, Xinjiang Uygur Autonomous Region).

Brief Description of the Object: low necked ovoid jar, flat base, with slightly folded rim.

Material, Technique and Conservation: silver, made by hammering skill, inlaid with gold.

Measurements: height, 17cm; opening diameter, 7.3cm.

Stylistic Analysis: both nomadic and sasanian character; the simplified acanthus calyx on the lip seems to be typical of the late Sasanian architectural decoration in Iran from the 5th to the 7th century.

Comparing and Geographical, Cultural and Chronological Attribution: Marshak analyzed the jar and the cup with a handle, which he dated between the 5th and 7th century AD. The Boma vessels were certainly made for nomads and reflect nomadic character, but one cannot rule out the possibility that they were produced by Sasanian craftsmen. The lid was perhaps made for a different vessel, since its design exhibits a decoration different from the one of the jar.

参考文献　References

1. 安英新：《新疆伊犁昭苏县古墓葬出土金银器等珍贵文物》，《文物》1999年第9期，页4—15及彩版壹～肆、封面。
   An Yingxin (1999) Discovery of Gold and Silverware Unearthed from an Ancient Tomb at Zhaosu County, Ili, Xinjiang, *Wenwu (Cultural Relics)*, 9, 4–15, Color version no. 1–4 and the front cover, Beijing.

2. Marshak, B.I. (2004) Covered Jar (no. 94) and Cup with a Handle in the Shape of a Tiger (no. 95), Watt, James C.Y. *et alii* (eds.) *China: Dawn of a Golden Age, 200–750 AD*, 188–189. Yale University Press, New Haven and London.

3. 祁小山、王博编著：《丝绸之路：新疆古代文化》，新疆人民出版社（乌鲁木齐），2008年，页260。
   Qi Xiaoshan *et alii* (eds.) (2008) *The Silk Road: Xinjiang Ancient Culture*, Xinjiang People's Publishing House, 260, Urumqï.

4. Wang Binghua (2003) Gold and Silver Discovered in Boma, Xinjiang, Li Jiang (ed.) *The Glory of the Silk Road: Art from Ancient China*, 56–64, Dayton.

（*Bruno Genito*，李雨生 [*Li Yusheng*]）

24. 银瓶 Silver Vase

25. 金饰件

收藏单位：新疆伊犁哈萨克自治州博物馆。

出土信息：属于新疆伊犁发现的波马金银器，具体情况如前述。

器物概括描述：垂饰。

材质、工艺及保存状况：以金片制成。

尺寸：长5.5、6.6厘米，宽3.5、5.3厘米。

器物详细描述：这两件金片制成的垂饰形状相似但大小不一，上半部的内外两缘有双线装饰，下半部仅外缘突起，水滴状装饰的尖端各有一条突起的短线。

图像详细描述：上半部顶端为悬挂用的小圆环，然后是两个相对的肾形装饰，末端弯曲；下部与之相连的是三个彼此焊接在一起的水滴状装饰，两侧水滴直接与上半部装饰相

25. Gold Plaques

Location: Ili Kasak Autonomous Prefecture Museum.

Context of Origin: Boma Gold Treasure (Ili, Xinjiang Uygur Autonomous Region).

Brief Description of the Object: two pendants.

Material, Technique and Conservation: plated gold.

Measurements: length, 5.5 and 6.6cm; width, 3.5 and 5.3cm.

Detailed Description of the Object: two gold-foil pendants of identical shape and different size. From each of them hangs, by means of a double loop, a small circular plain disc. But for the lower discs, all elements have borders in relief; the teardrop patterns show a short line in relief near the tip.

Detailed Description of the Iconography: the upper part is made of two kidney-shaped patterns with inward curved ends and a small loop at the top. The lower part is made of three teardrop-shaped elements, soldered

25. 金饰件 Gold Plaques

连，中间的水滴状装饰则通过一短金片与上部相连。

风格分析：该金饰上的卷曲装饰以及其他元素多发现在7世纪的遗物中。

地理、文化、年代属性及对比：5—7世纪。

together and to the upper motif (the central one by means of a short "bridge").

Stylistic Analysis: the simple and essential character of the elements together with the use of a curve decoration suggests a date in 7th century.

Comparing and Geographical, Cultural and Chronological Attribution: 5th–7th centuries.

参考文献　References

1. 安英新:《新疆伊犁昭苏县古墓葬出土金银器等珍贵文物》,《文物》1999年第9期,页4—15及彩版壹～肆、封面。

   An Yingxin (1999) Discovery of Gold and Silverware Unearthed from an Ancient Tomb at Zhaosu County, Ili, Xinjiang, Wenwu (*Cultural Relics*), 9, 4–15, Color version no. 1–4 and the front cover, Beijing.

2. Wang Binghua (2003) Gold and Silver Discovered in Boma, Xinjiang, Li Jiang (ed.) *The Glory of the Silk Road: Art from Ancient China*, 56–64 (in part. 60, fig. 10), Dayton.

（*Ciro Lo Muzio*，李雨生 [*Li Yusheng*]）

26. 编织金带

收藏单位：新疆伊犁哈萨克自治州博物馆。

出土信息：属于新疆伊犁发现的波马金银器，具体情况如前述。

器物概括描述：编织金带。

材质、工艺及保存状况：金丝细工。

尺寸：分别长9、5.7厘米，宽2厘米。

图像详细描述：两块金带由金线编织而成，背面中间及上下边缘的金线突出。

地理、文化、年代属性及对比：5—7世纪。

26. Gold Woven Band

Location: Ili Kasak Autonomous Prefecture Museum.

Context of Origin: Boma Gold Treasure (Ili, Xinjiang Uygur Autonomous Region).

Brief Description of the Object: band woven with golden wires.

Material, Technique and Conservation: gold, filigree.

Measurements: length 9 and 5.7cm; width 2cm.

Detailed Description of the Iconography: two segments of a band made of intertwined golden wires. On the reverse, there are a couple of intertwined wires in relief on both edges and in the middle.

Comparing and Geographical, Cultural and Chronological Attribution: 5th–7th centuries.

26. 编织金带 Gold Woven Band

参考文献　References

1. 安英新：《新疆伊犁昭苏县古墓葬出土金银器等珍贵文物》，《文物》1999年第9期，页4—15及彩版壹～肆封面。
   An Yingxin (1999) Discovery of Gold and Silverware Unearthed from an Ancient Tomb at Zhaosu County, Ili, Xinjiang, *Wenwu* (*Cultural Relics*), 9, 4–15, Color version no. 1–4 and the front cover, Beijing.
2. 祁小山、王博编著：《丝绸之路：新疆古代文化》，新疆人民出版社（乌鲁木齐），2008年，页258—261。
   Qi Xiaoshan *et alii* (eds.) (2008) *The Silk Road: Xinjiang Ancient Culture*, Xinjiang People's Publishing House, 258–261, Urumqï.

（*Ciro Lo Muzio*，李雨生[*Li Yusheng*]）

27. 金杯

收藏单位：新疆伊犁哈萨克自治州博物馆。

出土信息：属于新疆伊犁发现的波马金银器，具体情况如前述。

器物概括描述：金杯，镶嵌宝石。

材质、工艺及保存状况：金制。

尺寸：高5、口径8.5厘米。

器物详细描述：杯体圆柱形，侈口，圆环状杯柄，带指垫；口沿下以及接近杯底处各有锁

27. Gold Cup

Location: Ili Kasak Autonomous Prefecture Museum.

Context of Origin: Boma Gold Treasure, Ili, Xinjiang Uygur Autonomous Province.

Brief Description of the Object: gold cup inlaid with gem stones.

Material, Technique and Conservation: gold.

Measurements: height 5cm; opening diameter 8.5cm.

Detailed Description of the Object: gold cup with cylindrical body, everted rim, ring handle with thumb

27. 金杯 Gold Cup

绣状金线环杯一周。

图像详细描述：杯身的装饰带可以分为上、中、下三部分,中间的圆槽内曾镶嵌宝石,圆槽之间的剩余空间依然有暗色的宝石,上下部分的装饰带稍窄,内有忍冬纹,枝叶间镶嵌暗色宝石；杯柄截面半圆形,外侧居中镶嵌一枚圆形宝石,指垫上镶嵌一排4枚红色圆形宝石,指垫边缘也装饰锁绣纹。

rest. Beneath the rim and on the lower edge of the body, there is a gold intertwined wire.

***Detailed Description of the Iconography*:** the body is covered with an ornamentation subdivided into three sectors: a larger central band containing a scroll of circular insets, once filled with stones; dark stones still fill the residual spaces among the circles; two narrower bands, above and below, containing a vine scroll which partially preserves the same stone as in the central band. The ring handle, with semi-circular section, is decorated with a circular stone inlay. The thumb rest is decorated with a row of four circular stone inlays and, along the edge, with a gold intertwined wire.

参考文献　References

1. 安英新:《新疆伊犁昭苏县古墓葬出土金银器等珍贵文物》,《文物》1999年第9期,页4—15及彩版壹～肆、封面。
An Yingxin (1999) Discovery of Gold and Silverware Unearthed from an Ancient Tomb at Zhaosu County, Ili, Xinjiang, *Wenwu* (*Cultural Relics*), 9, 4–15. Colorversion no. 1–4 and the front cover.
2. Wang Binghua (2003) Gold and Silver Discovered in Boma, Xinjiang, Li Jiang (ed.) *The Glory of the Silk Road: Art from Ancient China*, 56–64 (in part. 60, fig.10), Dayton.

(*Ciro Lo Muzio*,李雨生 [*Li Yusheng*])

28. 金指套和护臂

收藏单位：新疆伊犁哈萨克自治州博物馆。

出土信息：属于新疆伊犁发现的波马金银器，具体情况如前述。

器物概括描述：护臂，指套。

材质、工艺及保存状况：金器。

尺寸：护臂长48、宽20厘米，指套长7.2、宽2.6厘米。

器物详细描述：是金护臂及指套的残件，共计5件，包括了2件金护臂残件以及3件金指套，金片上布满褶皱。

地域、文化、年代属性及对比：5—7世纪。

28. Gold Finger and Arm Guard

Location: Ili Kasak Autonomous Prefecture Museum.

Context of Origin: Boma Gold Treasure, Ili, Xinjiang Uygur Autonomous Region.

Brief Description of the Object: arm and finger covers.

Material, Technique and Conservation: gold plate.

Measurements: arm piece, length 48cm; width 20cm; finger pieces, max. Length 7.2cm; max. Width 2.6cm.

Detailed Description of the Object: fragments of arm and finger covers in gold plate (five fragments). Two separate fragments of the arm covers and three finger covers are preserved. The gold plate appears wrinkled throughout.

Comparing and Geographical, Cultural and Chronological Attribution: 5th–7th centuries.

28. 金指套和护臂 Gold Finger and Arm Guard

参考文献　References

1. 安英新:《新疆伊犁昭苏县古墓葬出土金银器等珍贵文物》,《文物》1999年第9期,页4—15及彩版壹～肆、
封面。

An Yingxin (1999) Discovery of Gold and Silverware Unearthed from an Ancient Tomb at Zhaosu County, Ili,
Xinjiang, *Wenwu (Cultural Relics)*, 9, 4–15, Color version no. 1–4 and the front cover, Beijing.

2. 安英新:《伊犁出土的金银器》,《东南文化》2000年第4期,页9—13。

An Yingxin (2000) Unearthed Gold and Silver from Ili, *Southeast Culture*, 4, 9–13, Nanjing.

3. 安英新:《昭苏波马镶嵌红宝石金面具等珍贵文物出土记》,《伊犁日报》2007年4月23日,据中国新疆网新
闻转引,网址为:http://www.chinaxinjiang.cn/news/tpxw/t20070423_229646.htm。

An Yingxin (2007) Story about How Inlaid Ruby Gold Masks and Other Precious Relics Unearthed in Boma,
Zhaosu, *Ili Daily*, April 23, quoted from http://www.chinaxinjiang.cn/news/tpxw/t20070423_229646.htm

4. 祁小山、王博编著:《丝绸之路：新疆古代文化》,新疆人民出版社(乌鲁木齐),2008年,页258—261。

Qi Xiaoshan *et alii* (eds.) (2008) *The Silk Road: Xinjiang Ancient Culture*, Xinjiang People's Publishing House,
258–261, Urumqï.

(*Ciro Lo Muzio*,李雨生 [*Li Yusheng*])

29. 陶来通

收藏单位：新疆维吾尔自治区博物馆。

出土信息：1976年在新疆维吾尔自治区和田县约特干偶然被发现。同时被发现的还有1件残陶罐和另一件人首残陶来通杯。约特干遗址在今和田县10公里巴格其乡约特干村，可能是古代于阗国的都城，也可能是古代墓地或其他废弃遗址。

器物概括描述：人首牛头形陶质来通。

材质、工艺及保存状况：细泥黄陶质，很可能是模制的。它不施釉，可与帕提亚晚期的来通（late-Parthian rhytons）进行比较，如尼普尔（Nippur）遗址出土的残品。尽管后者很可能参照了中亚的萨珊样品制作，正如阿夫拉西阿卜（Afrasiab）和赫拉清真寺（Kohna Masdjid）遗址的出土品。这件来通保存完好，仅在口沿处小有缺失。

尺寸：长19.5厘米。

器物详细叙述：这件来通杯以人首作为伸长且轻微卷曲的器身的上半部；器身下部变窄，以小牛头为底，牛嘴部穿孔以作流。人首之上是外敞的唇部。

图像学描述：人像广额隆眉，高鼻，长翘美髯须髭，眼目传神，形神毕肖，为典型的域外人物形象，而与伊朗人相比更像粟特人。前额有深纹两道，头戴缠绕的软布，像是头巾。相似的形象见于新疆库木吐剌、舒尔楚克、图木舒克、伯孜克里克等地壁画和雕像中的婆罗门形象。人像雕刻精致，但牛头的形象简约，仅粗略雕出

29. Rhyton

Location: Xinjiang Uygur Autonomous Region Museum.

Context of Origin: the rython was found by chance in 1976 in Yotkan by a local officer, together with a broken jar and another rhyton of the same shape, though fragmentary. Yotkan is an archaeological site 10km away from Bageqi, in the Hetian County, deemed to be the capital of the ancient Khotan kingdom.

Brief Description of the Object: pottery human-headed rhyton with ox-head spout.

Material, Technique and Conservation: the rhyton is made of terracotta, possibly moulded; it is not glazed, in contrast with late-Parthian rhytons — such as the fragmentary specimen from Nippur — though in conformity with Sasanian specimens from Central Asian — such as the Afrasiab and Kohna Masdjid ones. The vessel is perfectly preserved, though a little fragment of the rim is missing.

Measurements: length 19.5cm.

Detailed Description of the Object: the rhyton is shaped in the form of a male head constituting the upper part of an elongated and slightly curved vessel, whose lower part gets narrower and ends in a small ox-head, pierced in order to provide a spout for libations. Above the human head, the neck of the vessel abruptly widens out into an everted rim.

Detailed Description of the Iconography: the male head is distinguished by a massive nose, pointed beard and tortile moustaches, phisionomical traits that mark him as a foreigner, very likely a Sogdian rather than an Iranian. Above the forehead, furrowed with two deep wrinkles, the man wears a headdress seemingly made up of twisted soft tissue, likely a turban. Similar features remind of some portraits of Brahmins in paintings and sculptures from Eastern Turkestan (namely from Kumtura, Tumschuq, Shorchuk and Bezeklik), thus suggesting that a Brahmin may be depicted here too.

29. 陶来通 Rhyton

双眼和短的弯牛角。

　　风格分析：人头面部特征和表情的塑造透露出来自印度的影响，尤其是眼睛部分，眼珠和眼睑在同样类型的其他来通上通常是缺失的。然而，牛头的形象与约特干以及和田地区发现的其他红陶制品却有着精确的吻合度。

　　地域、文化、年代属性及对比：目前我们至少知道6件此类型的来通，有保留了整个或部分人面的例子，还发现了三件牛首流口，看上去是此类型来通的一部分。据说所有的此类型来通都出土于约特干。这些约特干来通是同类器物，它们表现出相近似的图像特征。人首形来通在萨珊时期曾广为流行，器例见于赫拉清真寺（Kohna Masdjid）遗址、阿夫拉西阿卜遗址

While the human features are attentively rendered, the ox-head is highly schematical, with simply engraved eyes and eyebrows and short curved horns.

Stylistic Analysis: the rendering of physiognomical traits of the human head betrays an Indian influence — especially as regards the eyes, eyebrows and lips — that is absent in the other rhytons of the same type. On the contrary, the ox-head exactly matches the stylistic patterns of other terracottas found in Yotkan and in the Khotan region.

Comparing and Geographical, Cultural and Chronological Attribution: at least other six rhytons of this type are known, retaining parts of or the whole human face, while three ox-head spouts likely belonging to such vessels are known too; all the specimens allegedly come from Yotkan. These rhytons make up a strongly homogeneous group of vessels, sharing common iconographical features after a

（Afrasiab）和阿卡塔佩遗址（Aktepe）的出土品，以及著名的克利夫兰博物馆收藏的银来通。这些约特干来通的相貌及表情的表现法不能和目前发现的任何一件作品划等号。因此，我们设想对它们的制造来说最为简便的做法，比如产自约特干，而人物形象表现得像婆罗门风格。我们在德里博物馆保存的红陶像上也能观察到来通在约特干的使用场面。一人坐着从来通中倒液取饮，尽管此来通与约特干来通的形状并不一样。这种来通和相似品的年代，能被模糊地断在4至7世纪之间，可能是一件本地制品。

widely spread model of Sasanian age human-headed rhytons, known through the samples of Kohna Masdjid, Afrasiab, Aktepe and the magnificent silver rhyton in the Cleveland Museum. The phisionomical traits of these rhytons, however, are not matched by any other specimen known so far, thus leading to suppose a common place of manufacture for them, likely Yotkan itself, and a common identity for the man represented, likely a Brahmin. The use of rhytons in Yotkan is also witnessed by terracotta preserved at the Delhi Museum, depicting a sitting man pouring from a rhyton, albeit of a different shape. The rhyton and its analogues as well, can be dated vaguely between the 4th and the 7th century, and be ascribed to local craftsmanship.

参考文献　References

1. 新疆维吾尔自治区文物事业管理局等主编：《新疆文物古迹大观》，新疆美术摄影出版社（乌鲁木齐），1999年，页97。
   Administration of Cultural Heritage of the Xinjiang Uygur Autonomous Region *et alii* (eds.) (1999) *A Grand View of Xinjiang's Cultural Relics and Historic Sites*, 97, Xinjiang Fine Arts, Photography Press, Urumqï.

2. Djakonova, N.V., Sorokin, S.S. (1960) *Hotanskie drevnosti. Katalog terrakota i shtuk*, pl. 26, Leningrad.

3. 香港文化博物馆编：《丝路珍宝：新疆文物大展》，香港康乐及文化事务署（香港），2005年，页74—75。
   Hong Kong Heritage Museum (ed.) (2005) *The Silk Road: Treasures from Xinjiang*, Exhibition Leisure and Cultural Services Department, 2005, 74–75, Hong Kong.

4. Jäger, U. (2006) Rhyta im präislamische Zentralasien (4.–8. Jh. n. Chr.), Form und Verwendung. Einfache Trinkgefässe oder Libationsgefässe in synkretystischen Religions systemen? *Iranica Antiqua*, XLI, 187–220, figs. 27–29.

5. Mair, V. (2010) *Secrets of the Silk Road: An Exhibition of Discoveries from the Xinjiang Uyghur Autonomous Region, China*, 154, no. 43, Santa Ana.

6. Manassero, N. (2008) *Rhyta e corni potori dall'Età del Ferro all'epoca sasanide. Libagioni pure e misticismo tra la Grecia e il mondo iranico*, 224, no. 24, pl. LXIX, Oxford.

7. Marshak, B.I. (2004) Rython in the Shape of Human Head, Watt, James C.Y. *et alii* (eds.) (2004) *China: Dawn of a Golden Age, 200–750 AD*, 191. The Metropolitan Museum of Art, New York, Yale University Press, New Haven and London.

8. Stein, A. (1907) *Ancient Khotan*, vol. 2, pl. XLIV, Oxford.

9. Stein, A. (1921) *Serindia. Detailed Report of Explorations in Central Asia and Westernmost China*, vol. 4, pl. II, Oxford.

10. 孙机：《论西安何家村出土的玛瑙兽首杯》，《文物》1991年第6期，84—93页。
    Sun Ji (1991) Note on the Animal-Headed Cup of Agate Unearthed at Hejiacun, Xi'an, *Wenwu (Cultural relics)*, 6, 84–93, Beijing.

(*Niccolò Manassero*，耿朔 [*Geng Shuo*]，范佳楠 [*Fan Jianan*]）

30. 梳妆托盘

收藏单位：新疆维吾尔自治区博物馆。

出土信息：巴基斯坦，有可能来自开伯尔—普赫图赫瓦省（Khyber Pukhtunkhwa Province）的斯瓦特（Swat）（前西北边界省）。

器物概况描述：饮酒纹饰的六边形托盘（或为盒盖？），公元5或6世纪。

材质、工艺及保存状况：灰绿色片岩或滑石；浮雕；断为两片，已修复。向左侧断裂。

尺寸：长19.6、宽10.4、厚0.6厘米。

器物详细描述：这块饰板呈不规则的六边形，纵轴瘦长，两端制成不规则的台阶形。表面被一些由两条细线夹的联珠纹带划分为不同的装饰区域。单看器物的形状，主要部分是中部的四边形区域，内有人像，两端的三角形区域则填满植物纹。

图像详细描述：主体图案在四边形区域的上部，描绘了四个男子的饮酒场面。主人身体朝向前方，侧面的头部轮廓经过变形处理，偏向右侧，倚坐在一个大垫子上，右臂内弯，左臂外伸。身着浓密褶皱的长袖紧身外衣和长裤，带着大耳环和较短的珍珠项链（也可能是衣服领口）。精巧雕琢的胸部暗示着身着一层薄纱，也许这种非正式的场合允许穿着舒适的衣服并呈现放松的姿态。主人头部无冠、短发、轻微卷曲，面部特征显著。右手持叶片纹装饰的大碗，一个朝向左方的侍者正从一个壶往碗里倾倒液体。右侧有另一个手持掸子的侍者

30. Toilet Tray

Location: Xinjiang Uygur Autonomous Region Museum.

Context of Origin: Pakistan. Possibly from Swat, Khyber Pukhtunkhwa Province (former NWFP).

Brief Description of the Object: hexagonal-shaped tray (or box lid?) with drinking scene. 5th/6th century AD.

Material, Technique and Conservation: gray-green schist or steatite. Relief. Recomposed from two fragments; broken to left.

Measurements: height 19.6cm; width 10.4cm; thickness 0.6cm.

Detailed Description of the Object: the plaque is in the shape of an irregular hexagon, with elongated longitudinal axis and opposite vertices with stepped profile. The surface is subdivided in different figured and decorated fields by rows of pearls between fillets. Playing along with the object's shape, the main subdivision is between the central rectangle, which bears the figured scenes, and the two opposite triangles, which are fully occupied by vegetal motives.

Detailed Description of the Iconography and stylistic analysis: the main figured scene, on the upper register of the rectangular field, depicts a drinking scene with four male characters. The protagonist, who is represented frontally with head in profile to left, is sitting on a big cushion, with right leg folded and left extended outwards. He wears densely pleated long sleeved tunic and trousers, large ear-rings and maybe a short pearl necklace (or neckline?). The neatly sketched chest forms suggest a tiny tissue and, probably, the informal context of the scene, which allows comfortable clothes and, as in this case, relaxed postures. The character shows bare head, short straight hair with slightly curly tips, and pronounced facial features. He holds in the right hand a large lobed bowl where a servant, standing

30. 梳妆托盘 Toilet Tray

在服侍主人。像主人一样，这两个侍者的侧面头像也经过了变形处理。他们短发，戴着同样的纽扣型耳环和项链（或为衣服领口），身着不同的衣服：左边的侍者可见部分身体，穿着和主人一样的起褶紧身外衣；至于右边的侍者，身着腰布（dhoti）、长项链和手镯，虽然手镯图像也不能否定是平纹外衣的袖口。第四个人物侧面朝左，面向主人做跪拜状。除了腰饰外，服装上并无其他因素显示出他的身份。同样他脖子和腰部的浮雕图案，可能是项链，也可能是衣服的边缘。除了姿势以外，他的发型也和别人不一样，呈波浪形且更长。一个令人好奇的问题是，这些差别是否显示了主人（以及他的私人侍者）和这个顺从的人在种族文化

to left, pours a liquid from a jug. To right, another standing servant fans him with a fly whisk. Like their master, both the servants are shown frontally with head in profile. They have short hair and wear button-like ear-rings, necklace (or neckline?) and different clothes: the one to left, only partially visible, wears the same pleated tunic as the master; as for the other to right one cannot exclude a short *dhoti*, a long necklace and bracelets, although these latter could be also interpreted as the edges of a plain tunic. A furth character is represented in profile to left, in the act of bowing down before the master. Apart from a waist there are no elements for the identification of his dress. Also in his case, the embossed elements at neck and wrist could be either ornaments or the edges of a garment. Besides his posture, a further element of differentiation is represented by his hair, wavy and longer than the other characters; one wonders whether such differences

上的差异？[1]主人的比例略大而且遮挡了旁边的人，这进一步突出了他的主体地位。这片区域的上角装饰着植物纹样，两片侧面的叶子拥簇果实或花朵，和器物两端三角形区域的图案一致，后者更大，细部也更清楚。尽管抽象的描绘导致植物的种属不确定，但无论哪种植物，肯定与整个场景具有象征性的联系。一些印度地区的植物会有这样的形态——例如东印度团花（kadamba）和菠萝蜜，其排毒、止痛、解乏的功用被传统医学所熟知。不过，三片叶子形状的植物可能是藤蔓，或者第二种可能：蛇麻草（Humulus lupulus）。后者被一些科学家列在酿造苏玛酒（soma）的植物类别之下（Sharma, Sirwani and Shastry 1972, 42; Padhy and Kumar Dash 2004,19）。主体图案的另外部分被进一步分为两块：上面由三块连续的矩形区域组成，两边各有一只完全相同的四足兽（作行走状）朝向右边，鼻口部瘦长，小耳，庞大的身躯（可能是野猪或犬科动物），中间的矩形区域浅内凹（也许有某种用途），并有一块抵到底部边缘的半圆形的凸出部分，后者被叠压的两条纹饰带所装饰：下面是一条直线型的纹饰，上面则由多条平行线构成的反向三角形组成。

地域、文化、年代属性及对比：这件器物的价值仅仅从艺术的角度看不足为奇，但其重要意义在于和那个我们对其文化和社会历史

imply any ethno-cultural distinction between the master (and his personal attendants) and this obsequious character[1]. The prominence of the seated character is further enhanced by his slightly bigger proportions, and his overlapping — although only barely — the figures at his sides. The upper corners of the field are occupied by a vegetal element, a cluster fruit or flower between two leaves in profile. The same plant is depicted also on the triangular fields, this time much bigger and with more details, although the schematic rendering makes uncertain the identification of the species. Whatever the specific botanical identification, this plant must have had a symbolic link with the scene. Several plants from Indian flora could match its shape — for instance the *kadamba* and the jackfruit whose detoxifying, analgesic and invigorating properties are well known in traditional medicine. Nevertheless, the three-lobed shape of the leaves points towards the vine or, as a second option, the hop (*Humulus lupulus*) — this latter listed by some authors among the specific plant species from which the *soma* might have been produced (Sharma, Seerwani and Shastry 1972, 42; Padhy and Kumar Dash 2004, 19). The remaining space below the main scene is further divided in two registers, the upper one composed by a row of three rectangles. The lateral rectangles are occupied by two identical quadrupeds (walking?) in profile to right and characterized by elongated muzzles, small ears and heavy body (wild boars? Canids?). The central rectangle appears as a shallow empty cavity (to serve some purpose?), with a semi-circular projection that reaches the lower edge of the object and interrupts the lower register, this latter decorated by two superimposed motifs separated by a fillet: a rectilinear festoon (below) and a row of opposite triangles filled with parallel lines (above).

---

[1] 这里的族属划分很宽泛，参见De La Vaissière, É. 在2003年对此问题的再反思。
The reference to ethnicity is to be intended here in very broad terms (see De La Vaissière 2003 for a reassessment of the question with specific relevance to this topic).

知之甚少的时代间的关系，也就是笼统上说的匈人（Hūṇa）。这个断代的理由来自肖像、风格和工艺等方面。硬朗的脸部特征、短发、符合匈人生活环境的衣服（Callieri 1997, 267; Grenet and Riboud 2003, 138; Filigenzi 2010, 169）。在图像学上对应了犍陀罗、萨珊和笈多王朝的传统，还与今巴基斯坦克什米尔地区后犍陀罗时代宗教作品中的世俗内容有强烈的形式上的一致性（Paul 1986, figs.47–53, 58–59, 69, 71）。更确切地说，与这件器物最接近的类比材料是一小批盒盖，它们均不是考古发掘品，但据报道都发现于巴基斯坦，有的来自斯瓦特（Ghose 2003）。这些器物的题材包括超现实的事物、动物搏斗、人类英雄擒杀野兽、皇室狩猎和奏乐场面，描绘了上层贵族的奢华风气以及在特定场合下的品味和习惯。无疑这些器物构成了一个性质类似的群体，正如它们中的一些所展示的那样，即便不是来自同一作坊，也可以将其划分成某种特定的艺术风格（Lerner and Kossak 1991, 92）。这件器物的造型与一件饰板残片非常相似，后者台阶纹三角形尖端上带有狩猎图案（Bopearachchi et alii 2003, 355, cat. no 316），骑马者的服装也非常接近于这件饰板上主人的穿着，很容易使人想起Alkhan Huns（白匈奴）钱币上的衣着特征。植物纹样也很典型，但在一些盒盖上有细微的不同（Ghose 2003: figs.5, 7, 10, 13）。这类物品在新疆的发现（亦可参考 *The State Hermitage Museum et alii 2008*: nos 47–48, 94–95）证明其在相当广泛的区域中都被视作

Comparing and Geographical, Cultural and Chronological Attribution: the value of this object, quite modest from a mere artistic point of view, rather lies in its significance with relation to the cultural and social history of a period still little-known that can generically be defined as Hūṇa. This period is hinted at by the whole of iconographic, stylistic and technical elements. The strong and heavy facial features, the short hair, and the costumes by and large comply with models known from the Hūṇa environment (Callieri 1997, 267; Grenet and Riboud 2003, 138; Filigenzi 2010, 169). The iconographic lexicon echoes Gandharan, Sasanian and Gupta traditions, while bearing at the same time a strong formal unity that seems to represent the secular counterpart of post-Gandharan works of religious subject known from the Pakistani-Kashmiri areas (Paul 1986, figs.47–53, 58–59, 69, 71). More specifically, this object finds its closest comparisons with a small number of box lids, all of them from non-archaeological contexts but reportedly from Pakistan and more precisely, in some cases, from Swat (Ghose 2003, with references). The range of subjects, which include fantastic beings, animals in combat or human heroes killing a beast, royal hunting, and musical entertainment, conveys an image of refined luxury in an intimate atmosphere and captures the taste and habits of the upper classes in a specific time and environment. No doubt, these objects constitute a homogeneous group whose production can be safely attributed to a well defined artistic milieu, if not to a single atelier, as already suggested for some of them (Lerner and Kossak 1991, 92). In particular, the shape is most probably the same as a fragment of plaque preserving a stepped triangular vertex occupied by a hunting scene (Bopearachchi et alii 2003, 355, cat. no 316), where the horseman wears a costume very similar to the main character of our piece, and closely recalls the conventional portrait of the Alkhan Huns as we know

奢侈品，同时也反映出丝绸之路沿线的物品流通和文化交流状况。

it from their coins[1]. The vegetal motif also appears quite identical, notwithstanding marginal differences, in some of these box lids (Ghose 2003, figs.5, 7, 10, 13). The specimens found in Xinjiang (cf. also *The State Hermitage Museum et alii* 2008: nos. 47–48, 94–95) attest to these artifacts being appreciated as luxury objects over a broad area, at the same time providing a glimpse into the international mobility and cultural exchanges across the Silk Road.

参考文献　References

1. Alram, M. and Pfisterer, M. (2010) Alkhan and Hephthalite Coinage. Alram, M., Klimburg-Salter, D., Inaba, M. and Pfisterer, M. (eds.) *Coins, Art and Chronology II. The First Millennium C.E. in the Indo-Iranian Borderlands*, Wien.

2. Bopearachchi, O., Landes, C., and Sachs, C. (2003) *De l'Indus à l'Oxus: Archéologie de l'Asie Centrale*, Lattes.

3. Callieri, P. (1997) *Seals and Sealings from the North-West of the Indian Subcontinent and Afghanistan* (4th century BC–11th century AD): *Local, Indian, Sasanian, Graeco-Persian, Sogdian, Roman*. With contributions by E. Errington, R. Garbini, Ph. Gignoux, N. Sims-Williams, W. Zwalf (Istituto Universitario Orientale, Dissertationes I), Naples.

4. De La Vaissière, É. (2003) Is there a "Nationality of the Hephtalites"? *Bulletin of the Asia Institute*, 17, 119–132, Bloomfield Hills.

5. Filigenzi, A. (2010) Post-Gandharan/non-Gandharan: An Archaeological Inquiry into a Still Nameless Period, Alram, M., Klimburg-Salter, D., Inaba, M. and Pfisterer, M. (eds.) *Coins, Art and Chronology II. The First Millennium C.E. in the Indo-Iranian Borderlands*, 381–406, Wien.

6. Ghose, M. (2003) The Impact of the Hun Invasion: a Nomadic Interlude in Indian Art, *Bulletin of the Asia Institute* 17, 145–158, Bloomfield Hills.

7. Grenet, F. and Riboud, P. (2003) A Reflection on the Hephtalite Empire: The Biographical Narrative in the Reliefs of the Tomb of the Sabao Wirkak (494–579), *Bulletin of the Asia Institute*, 17, 133–143, Bloomfield Hills.

8. Lerner, M., Kossak, S. (1991) *The Lotus Transcendent: Indian and Southeast Asian Art from the Samuel Eilenberg Collection*, New York.

9. Padhy, S. and Kumar Dash, S. (2004) The *Soma* Drinker of Ancient India: an Ethno-Botanical Retrospection, *Journal of Human Ecology* 15/1, 19–26, Gurgaon.

10. Paul, P.G. (1986) *Early Sculpture of Kashmir (Before the Middle of the 8th Century AD). An Approach to Art History and Epigraphy of the Jhelum Valley and Its Peripheral Regions*, Leiden.

[1] For a reassessment of the relevant evidence see now Vondrovec 2008; Alram and Pfisterer 2010.

11. 祁小山、王博编著:《丝绸之路：新疆古代文化》，新疆人民出版社（乌鲁木齐），2008年，页181。
Qi Xiaoshan *et alii* (eds.) (2008) *The Ancient Culture in Xinjiang along the Silk Road*, 181, Xinjiang People's Publishing House, Urumqï.

12. Sharma, A.L., Sheerwany, A.B. and Shastry, V.R. (1972) Botany in the Vedas (Part I). *Indian Journal of History of Science*, 7, 38–43, New Delhi.

13. The State Hermitage Museum *et alii* (2008) *The Caves of One Thousand Buddhas: Russian Expeditions on the Silk Route on the Occasion of 190 Years of the Asiatic Museum* (exhibition catalogue), Saint Petersburg.

14. Vondrovec, K. (2008) Numismatic Evidence of the Alchon Huns Reconsidered. *Beiträge zur Ur- und Frühgeschichte Mitteleuropas* (*BUFM*) 50, 25–56.

15. Watt, James C.Y. *et alii* (eds.) (2004) *China: Dawn of a Golden Age, 200–750* AD, no. 99, 192–193. Yale University Press, New Heaven and London.

(*Anna Filigenzi*, 耿朔 [*Geng Shuo*], 范佳楠 [*Fan Jianan*])

31. 三耳陶罐

收藏单位： 新疆维吾尔自治区喀什博物馆。

出土信息： 该陶罐1992—1993年间出土于新疆喀什市疏附县亚吾鲁克遗址。亚吾鲁克遗址位于新疆喀什市北12公里的疏附县浩罕乡亚吾鲁克村西，伯什克然木河南面的黄土台地上。遗址面积较大，南北长900米左右，东西宽450米，被严重破坏。1984和1988年，喀什地区文物管理所曾进行两次调查，采集了一些文物，主要是陶器及残片。1989年新疆博物馆也调查了这一遗址，并发掘了290平方米。1992—1993年清理佛教寺院1座，即在这座唐代佛寺中发现了这件陶罐以及贝叶经和钱币等遗物。根据典型陶器特征判断，亚吾鲁克遗址的持续时间较长，约在3—9世纪之间。

器物概括描述： 三耳罐，红陶制作，器物经复原。

材质、工艺及保存状况： 红陶、器身模制，出土时残破，后经修复。

尺寸： 高57、口径28.5、底径19厘米。

器物详细描述： 三耳，长颈，圆唇，腹部有模制的联珠纹装饰。联珠纹徽章内有菩萨或国王形象，左手持水瓶，右手持碗形器。把手的上部装饰男性头像，头戴三轮新月装饰的王冠。

图像详细描述： 马尔沙克（Marshak 2004，190–191）认为柄上部的人物头像，似乎在模仿希腊神祇—潘。他们与同一遗址发现的胡人形象很接近（霍旭初、祁小山 2006，17）。马尔沙克（Marshak）也认为带着新月形冠冕的国王形

31. Pottery Jar

Location: Kashgar Museum.

Context of Origin: Unearthed at Yawuluk, Shufu County, Kashgar City, Xinjiang Uygur Autonomous Region in 1992–1993. The archaeological site of Yawuluk, measuring 900m × 450m, is located on a loess platform 12 kilometers north of Kashgar. Two surveys on the site were launched by the Kashgar Administration of Cultural Relics in 1984 and 1988, and some objects were collected, mostly earthen ware and shards. The Xinjiang Museum also investigated the site in 1989, and excavated 290m². A Buddhist temple was brought to light between 1992 and 1993. This pottery jar was found together with palm leaf Buddhist scripture, coins, etc., which date back to the Tang Dynasty. This site had a long period of utilization; the investigation of 1989 revealed a pottery sequence from the 3rd to the 9th century AD.

Brief Description of the Object: jar with three handles, made of red clay; this jar is restored.

Material, Technique and Conservation: red earthenware; patterns were pressed or moulded around the belly of the jar.

Measurements: height 57cm; mouth diameter 28.5cm, bottom diameter 19cm.

Detailed Description of the Object: this jar has three handles, long neck, round mouth and shows a moulded decoration on the belly. The beaded medallions encircle, alternately, the head of a celestial being or a king and the figure of a celestial being holding a water vase in the left hand and a bowl-shaped vessel in the right hand. The upper part of the handles is decorated with a male head.

Detailed Description of the Iconography: Marshak (2004, 190–191) retains that the heads on the handles imitate the image of the Greek god Pan. They are, however, similar to a head of a Hu man found in the same site (Huo Xuchu and Qi Xiaoshan 2006, 17). Marshak also suggests that the celestial being or the king wearing a crescent-shaped coronet in the medallions of the present jar may be identified with Kubera.

31. 三耳陶罐 Pottery Jar

象浮雕表现的是俱毗罗（Kubera）。

风格分析：马尔沙克（Marshak 2004, 190–191）认为这种三耳罐的形制源于希腊罗马式的安弗拉罐（amphora），但在帕提亚和大夏晚期已发生了一些改变。同样的三耳罐在图木舒克、库车、和田等地的唐代遗址中比较常见。

地域、文化、年代属性及对比：马尔沙克（Marshak 2004, 190–191）指出这种三耳陶罐的年代不会晚于6世纪，霍旭初、祁小山（2006）把它断为7—8世纪。殷福兰等（2002）认为这件陶罐有典型的唐代特征。陶罐腹部徽章中表现的俱毗罗应该也是和田地区的保护神。这件陶罐体现了新疆西部（陶罐的制作地）、大夏和兴都库什山南部地区之间的文化联系。

Stylistic Analysis: Marshak (2004, 190–191) thinks that the form of the jar derives from Greco-Roman amphoras by way of Parthians and late Bactrian variants. Three-handle jars, however, have been found also in the areas of Tumshuq, Kucha and Khotan and are quite common during Tang dynasty (618–907).

Comparing and Geographical, Cultural and Chronological Attribution: Marshak (2004, 190–191) suggests that this jar has to be dated no later than the 6th century, while Huo Xuchu and Qi Xiaoshan (2006, 17) date it to the 7th–8th century. As pointed out by Yin Fulan (2002), the shape of the jar is typical of Tang dynasty. Kubera, who is depicted in the medaillons on the belly, was also the divine protector of Khotan. This jar is, thus, to be considered a fine example of the interaction between the cultures of Western Xinjiang — producing area of the jar — the Bactrian region, and the lands to the south of the Hindu Kush.

参考文献　References

1. 霍旭初、祁小山：《丝绸之路：新疆佛教艺术》，新疆大学出版社（乌鲁木齐），2006年，页14—17。
   Huo Xuchu, Qi Xiaoshan (eds.) (2006) *The Buddhist Art in Xinjiang along the Silk Road*, Xinjiang University Press, 14–17, Urumqï.

2. 殷福兰、阿不都热依木江：《亚吾鲁克遗址出土的三耳陶罐》，《吐鲁番学研究》2002年第2期（总第6期），页128—129。
   Yin Fulan *et alii* (2002) Jar with Three Handles Found from Yawuluk Site, *Tulunfanxue yanji (Journal of Turfan Studies)*, 2, 128–129, Turfan.

3. Marshak, B.I. (2004) Covered Jar (no 94), Watt, James C.Y. *et alii* (eds.) *China: Dawn of a Golden Age, 200–750 AD*, 190–191, The Metropolitan Museum of Art, New York, Yale University Press, New Haven and London.

4. 新疆文物考古研究所、喀什地区文管所：《亚吾鲁克遗址发掘简报》，《新疆文物》1997年第3期，页52—58。
   Xinjiang Institute of Cultural Relics and Archaeology, Administration of Cultural Relics of Kashgar (1997) Excavation of Yawuluk site, *Xinjiang wenwu (Cultural Relics of Xinjiang)*, 3, 52–58, Urumqï.

（*Chiara Visconti*，耿朔 [*Geng Shuo*]）

32. 金戒指

收藏单位：宁夏固原博物馆。

出土信息：宁夏固原市南郊深沟村北周李贤与夫人吴辉合葬墓发现，1983年宁夏博物馆、固原博物馆发掘。在墓葬封土之下有长斜坡墓道、三个天井、三个过洞、甬道和墓室。根据出土的两方墓志可知，墓主为合葬于569年的李贤（字贤和，鲜卑拓跋氏后裔）和夫人吴辉。李贤是北周时期（557—581）的一位外交官、高级将领以及河西地区边防长官。墓葬所在地固原（古称原州），是北朝时期的重镇，西魏北周更是派出亲信大臣为都督镇守此地。墓中出土的鎏金银壶、镶蓝宝石的金戒指、玻璃碗、中亚式环首刀等文物，是从西方传入我国的精美手工艺产品，年代上与李贤曾出任河西边防长官的特殊经历相符。墓道、甬道、墓室等处都绘有壁画，墓室平面近似方形，东西长4、南北长3.85米。这种墓葬是北朝至唐代中国北方高等级墓葬的标准形制。该墓曾被盗掘，但仍发现大量器物，共计300余件，多集中放置在甬道、墓室门口及墓室东南、西南角，以250余件各类陶俑为大宗。此外还有陶制模型明器、实用器、金银器、铜器、铁器、玉石器等，大多数器物的工艺水平都很高。鎏金银壶和玻璃碗都发现于墓室西壁下部，彼此相邻。金戒指放置于女棺内中部左侧。环首铁刀发现于李贤棺椁之间的右侧空隙。

器物概括描述：造型简洁的戒指，带有一个斜切面。一块蓝灰色硬石镶嵌在金戒指上。

32. Gold Ring

Location: Guyuan Museum.

Context of Origin: tomb of Li Xian and his wife Wu Hui at Shengou village of Nanjiao countryside, Yuanzhou district of Guyuan city, Ningxia Hui Autonomous Region, excavations in 1983 by the Ningxia Museum and Guyuan Museum. The Grave-mound presents a long sloping passage, three shafts, three compartments, a covered corridor and a chamber; on the basis of two inscribed epitaphs there found, the tombs has been constructed for Li Xian (also known as Xian He, a descendant of the Toba Clan of Xianbei Nationality), buried in 569 AD, and his wife Wu Hui. Li Xian was a diplomat, senior general, duke of the Hexi region during the rule of the Northern Zhou Dynasty (557 to 581 AD). The tomb is located in Guyuan (called Yuanzhou in ancient times), a strategically important townduring the Northern Dynasties, so much that the authorities of Western Wei and Northern Zhou Dynastiesuse to appoint their most trustworthy functionaries as military governors to guard this town. Superb remains were found in this tomb, such as a gilt silver ewer, a gold ring with a carved stone seal, glass bowl, iron sword with ring pommel etc., all objects of Western origin, chronologically close to the period when Li Xian took his position as senior officer in Hexi for the defense of the frontier. Mural paintings were found in the corridor, in the entrance and in the tomb chamber. The tomb chamber, almost square in plan, 4m from East to West × 3.85m from South to North, is a regular upper class type of tomb in northern China from the Northern Zhou to the Tang Dynasties. Amongst the 300 funerary artifacts most were found in the corridor, in the entrance leading to the main hall, and in the south-eastern and south-western corners of the chamber. More than 250 of them were pottery figurines; the others were terracotta funerary objects made with a mold, items of daily use, gold, silver, bronze and iron ware, jade, etc.; in most cases the workmanship was excellent. Both the gilt silver

32. 金戒指 Gold Ring

材质、工艺及保存状况：金、蓝灰色硬石，保存完整。

尺寸：最大外径2.4厘米，内径1.75厘米；宝石（印章）直径0.8厘米；重10克。

器物详细描述：这件戒指有着简洁而扁平的戒身，顶部逐渐扩大成带有宽唇的圆形斜切面。圆形宝石，表面平坦带雕刻，边缘斜收。

图像详细描述：宝石的表面有一个裸体女性形象，身体的四分之三朝向右侧，双手握住一个长条形围巾上举，在其上方形成拱形，围巾的两端各垂一个囊状物。

风格分析：尽管尺寸很小，这件雕刻品却

ewer and the glass bowl were found close to the west wall of the burial chamber, next to each other. The golden ring was found at the center of the female coffin, slightly to the left. The iron sword was found between the right gap of Li Xian' coffin and outer coffin.

Brief Description of the Object: plain ring with an engraved bezel. Blue-grey hard stone bezel set in a plain golden ring.

Material, Technique and Conservation: gold and blue-grey hard stone; whole.

Measurements: ring, greatest outer diameter of hoop 2.4cm; inner diameter 1.75cm; diameter of nicolo (onyx) seal 0.8cm; weight: 10g.

Detailed Description of the Object: the finger-ring has a plain flattened body which widens gradually in order to englobe the circular bezel with a wide smooth band all around. The gem has a circular shape and a flat

有着出色的浮雕效果，人物呈现非常自然的舞蹈形态。

地域、文化、年代属性及对比：其形状与河南洛阳北魏吕达墓（524）、山西太原北齐徐显秀夫妇墓（571）以及河北赞皇东魏至北齐李希宗夫妇墓（576）[1]出土的金戒指基本相同。罗丰（1999）认为李贤墓戒指的原产地是萨珊或中亚某地。根据金戒指放置于女棺内中部左侧的位置，可知为李贤妻子吴辉所佩戴。从图像学角度说，有一些可以类比的材料，如在一枚私人收藏的萨珊风格的椭圆体玛瑙器上，雕刻着类似的图案，因为尺寸更大，所以可以了解到更多细节：女性似乎身着贴身服饰，脚踝和脖子部分有浮雕状的边缘（Gignoux and Gyselen 1982, 37, no.10.6, pl. III; 亦可参见 Bivar 1969, nos. CB 3, 4）。还可以参考一件萨珊银盘上的装饰图案，系一个手持在头顶形成拱形的长围巾的舞蹈状裸体女性，大概5.7厘米高（Trever and Lukonin 1987, 119, no 44, fig.118, S–286）：那些装饰在印章上由于太小无法被准确辨别出来（更不用说尾部还有囊状物）的部分，在这件器物上清楚显示是一条围巾。着衣的女性舞者，手持在头顶形成拱形的长围巾的形象，同样出现在一件嚈哒时代的粟特银碗上（Marshak 1986, figs.11–13）。我们也很容易想到，一个女性站在拱形物下的形象，也频繁出现在萨珊

engraved surface with chamfered edge.

Detailed Description of the Iconography: on the upper surface of the gem, a naked (?) female figure is represented dancing three-quarters to right, holding with both hands raised to the sides a long and narrow scarf forming an arch above her figure and ending with wide flaps at both ends.

Stylistic Analysis: despite the small dimensions, the engraving has a good relief and the posture of the figure is quite naturalistic in her dancing.

Comparing and Geographical, Cultural and Chronological Attribution: for the shape, the ring resembles the rings unearthed from Lüda's tomb of Northern Wei Dynasty at Luoyang, Henan province, dated to 524 AD, Xu Xianxiu and his wife's tomb of Northern Qi Dynasty at Taiyuan, Shanxi province, date to 571 AD, Li Xizong and his wife's tomb of Eastern Wei to Northern Qi Dynasties at Zanhuang, Hebei province, dated to 576 AD[1]. Luo Feng (1999) suggests the ring was made in Sasanian Central Asia. On the basis of its position at the discovery, at the centre of the female coffin, the ring can be attributed to Wu Hui, wife of the owner of the tomb, Li Xian. An appropriate comparative evidence for the gem is represented by a Sasanian agate ellipsoid in a private collection with the same iconography rendered in a larger scale and therefore bearing more details: in this seal the female figure seems to be dressed with a close-fitting dress with relief rims at ankles and neck (Gignoux and Gyselen 1982, 37, no 10.6, pl. III; see also Bivar 1969, nos CB 3, 4). An interesting comparative evidence for our gem is a small (h. 5.7cm) silver relief decoration from a plate representing a naked female dancer who holds a long scarf with widening end, forming an arch

[1] 这枚戒指属于李希宗妻子崔幼妃，根据墓志记载，她卒于575年，于576年下葬。
One gold ring excavated from this tomb belongs to Li Xizong's wife, Cui Youfei. According to the inscription of her epigraph, Cui Youfei died in 575 A.D. and was buried in next year.

印章上，其拱形部分通常由两根墙柱及其支撑的穹顶构成（Gyselen 1993, 77–78, nos 10. A.11–17, pl. II）。这都反映出李贤墓的这枚印章可能是萨珊波斯的产品。

above her head (Trever and Lukonin 1987, 119, no 44, fig.118, S–286): on this item the identity of the object forming the arch, which on the seals is too small for being identified apart from the end flaps, is clearly a scarf. A clothed female dancer with a scarf above her head is also appearing on a Sogdian silver bowl of the Hephthalite period (Marshak 1986, figs.11–13) We must also recall that the compositional scheme with a female figure under an arch is quite common on Sasanian seals, where the arch-shaped element consists in an architectural "canopy" with two side pillars (Gyselen 1993, 77–78, nos 10. A.11–17, pl. II). The examination of the comparative evidence suggests an attribution to the Sasanian seal production.

参考文献　References

1. 石家庄地区革委会文化局文物发掘组：《河北赞皇东魏李希宗墓》，《考古》1977年第6期，页382—390，图版陆：5。
Archaeological Team of the Bureau of Cultural Revolutionary Committee of the Shijiazhuang Prefecture (1977) Excavation of Tomb of Li Xizong of Eastern Wei Dynasty in Tsan-huang County, Hebei province, *Kaogu* (*Archaeology*), 6, 382–390, VI, 6: 5, Beijing.

2. Bivar, A.D.H. (1969) *Catalogue of the Western Asiatic Seals in the British Museum. Stamp Seals, II. The Sassanian Dynasty*, London.

3. Gignoux, P. and Gyselen, R. (1982) *Sceaux Sasanides de Diverses Collections Privées* (*Cahiers de Studia Iranica*, 1), Paris.

4. 固原博物馆：《固原历史文物》，科学出版社（北京），2004年，页129，第80号器物。
Guyuan Museum (2004) Guyuan lishi wenwu (*Historical and Cultural Relics from Guyuan*), Science publishing House, 129, no.80, Beijing.

5. Gyselen, R. (1993) *Catalogue des Sceaux, Camées et Bulles Sasanides. I. Collection Générale*, Paris.

6. 山西省考古研究所、太原市文物考古研究所：《太原北齐徐显秀墓发掘简报》，《文物》2003年第10期，页4–40，图十九：1，图八八。
Institute of Archaeology of Shanxi, Institute of Archaeology of Taiyuan (2003) Excavation of the Xu Xianxiu's Tomb of the Northern Qi in Taiyuan, *Wenwu* (*Cultural Relics*), 10, 4–40, fig.19:1, 88, Beijing.

7. Juliano, A.L. and Lerner, J.A. (2001) *Monks and Merchants: Silk Road Treasures from Northwest China, Gansu and Ningxia, 4th–7th century*, 101, no 32. Catalogue of the Exhibition, Asia Society Museum, New York.

8. 洛阳市文物工作队：《河南洛阳市吉利区两座北魏墓的发掘》，《考古》2011年第9期，页44—57，图版拾叁：3。
Luoyang Municipal Archaeological Team (2011) The Excavation of Two Northern Wei Tombs in Jili District,

Luoyang City, Henan, *Kaogu (Archaeology)*, 9, 44–57, XII: 3, Beijing.

9. Marshak, B.I. (1986) *Silberschätze des Orients*, Leipzig.

10. 宁夏博物馆、宁夏固原博物馆发掘组:《宁夏固原北周李贤夫妇墓发掘简报》,《文物》1985第11期,页1—20,图二五,图版叁: 2。

Ningxia Museum, Guyuan Museum (1985) Excavation of Northern Zhou Dynasty Tomb of Li Xian and His Wife at Guyuan, Ningxia, *Wenwu (Cultural Relics)*,11, 1–20, fig. 25, Ⅲ : 2, Beijing.

11. Trever, K.V. and Lukonin, V.G. (1987) *Sasanidskoe serebro. Sobranie Gosudastvennogo Ermitaža. Hudožestvennaja kul'tura Irana III–VIII vekov*, Moskva.

(*Pierfrancesco Callieri*,耿朔 [*Geng Shuo*])

33. 玻璃碗

收藏单位：宁夏固原博物馆。

出土信息：1983年发现于固原的一座墓葬中。玻璃碗和鎏金银壶都发现于墓室西壁下部，彼此相邻。该墓发现的玻璃制品还有深青色玻璃珠118粒、深绿色玻璃珠119粒。

器物概括描述：半球形的雕花装饰玻璃碗，通体呈碧绿色，透明，内含均匀分布的气泡。

材质、工艺及保存状况：玻璃碗的内壁光洁平滑，外壁有风化层。经X荧光法无损检测，不含铅钡，因此非常有可能是钠钙玻璃。来自罗马和波斯的钠钙玻璃与中国传统的铅钡玻璃非常不同。这件碗系有模吹制，又经过了磨琢雕花处理，后一点是来自对外壁、底部和口部的圆形凸饰的认识。大多数学者依靠成分测定和考古学研究，认为这类玻璃器属于萨珊王朝制品。目前所公认的许多萨珊玻璃器，事实上属于一种钾和镁含量很高的钠钙玻璃。另一方面，罗马和帕提亚的玻璃原料采用矿物盐（天然碱）做助熔剂（Freestone 2006; Mirti *et alii* 2009）。因此，不同配方没有明显的先后关系，没有一个完整的年代序列。另外，萨珊玻璃和其他以草木灰为助熔剂的钠玻璃也有不同。Freestone（2006）测定表明叙利亚—巴勒斯坦的玻璃器的镁含量要低于萨珊制品。Brill（2005，75）研究发现萨珊玻璃与之后的伊斯兰玻璃两者之间存在重合，但又不完全吻合；以及前者

33. Glass Bowl

Location: Guyuan Museum.

Context of Origin: the object was found in a grave in Guyuan in 1983. Both this glass bowl and the gilt silver ewer were found close to the west wall of the burial chamber, next to each other. Other glassware was also found in the tomb: 118 dark blue glass beads and 119 dark green glass beads.

Brief Description of the Object: hemispherical cut-work relief bowl in transparent green glass with bubbles evenly distributed.

Material, Technique and Conservation: the inner surface is clean and smooth; the outer presents weathered surface.An X-ray fluorescence non-destructive examination, indicating the absence of lead barium, suggests that the bowl most probably was made of soda-lime glass. Soda-lime glasses from Rome and Persia are quite different from the lead barium glass of China. The manufacture of the bowl includes glass mold-blowing and carving technique, the latter for the realization of the medallions disk-shaped on the outer face, foot and mouth rip. Most of the scholars, in order to identify and attribute the glasses, in time attributed to the Sasanian dynastic period, utilized very much technical and archaeometric analyses. Most of the recognized Sasanian glasses present, in fact, a silica-soda-lime composition with high levels of K and Mg. The Roman and the Parthian material, on the other hand, employed mineral salts for this purpose (Freestone 2006; Mirti *et alii* 2009). Consequently, there is no chronological continuation of the utilized formula. Moreover, Sasanian glasses also show differences when compared with other plant-ash soda glasses. Freestone analysis has revealed that the Syro-Palestinian productions were lower in Mg than the Sasanian, and Brill (2005, 75) concluded that there is a general overlapping but no close relationship between the Sasanian and the later Islamic glass and that the former do not bear a close enough chemical resemblance to any of the particular groups of

33. 玻璃碗 Glass Bowl

不存在一种和后者中的任何一组充分接近的化学成分。三种不同的化学成分组成在萨珊玻璃制造业里已经被辨识出来（Mirti et al. 2008）：第一种是广泛出现在3世纪帝国早期的钠钙玻璃。第二种被进一步分为两组，都使用草木灰，但选择的植物原料不同，其中一组在帝国开始阶段就已出现，而另一组则在4世纪以后被制造出来，它们之间最关键的区别在于第二组产品采用了纯度更高的硅石。第三种用来制造更为透明的玻璃，生产出另外两种成分更为精美的器物（Mirti *et alii* 2009）。这已被解释为萨珊时期为了制造质量不同的玻璃而存在多种配方。同样重要的是，为了追求符合萨珊品味的透明效果，高纯度的硅石也偶尔被用在第一种配方中。

尺寸：高8、口径9.5、腹深6.8、下腹最大径9.8厘米，重245.6克。

器物详细描述：这件玻璃碗系绿色透明玻璃有模吹制而成，腹部贴有两层凸状圆饰，上层8个，下层6个，下部也贴有一个圆饰，充作圈足底。每个圆饰都将棱角磨去，从碗内部看就像一个个圆形光环。圆饰凸出碗壁数毫米，碗的口部厚数毫米。这种采用冷加工磨琢工艺的完整玻璃碗在中国首次发现，加深了对已发现的采用同样工艺的其他玻璃产品的理解。

地域、文化、年代属性及对比：安家瑶（1986，178–181）认为这件玻璃碗是产自伊朗高原地区的萨珊玻璃器，它曾现身2004年纽约大都会艺术博物馆"走向盛唐"展（An Jiayao

Islamic glasses. Three different chemical compositions have been identified for the Sasanian glassmaking (Mirti *et alii* 2008): the first is a silica-soda-lime glass mainly appearing in the earliest phases of the empire in the 3rd century; the second is sub-divided into two groups, both using sodic ash, but exploiting different plants. One of them is present from the beginning of the Dynasty and the other from the 4th century onwards. Crucial difference between them is that the second group always utilized a purer source of silica. The third group has produced more transparent glass, mainly in more sophisticated objects than the ones worked with the other compositions (Mirti *et alii* 2009); this has been interpreted as an argument for the existence of diverse recipes in order to satisfy the demand of different qualities of glass. It is significant that, in the quest for the transparency meeting the taste of the Sasanian context, purer silica was also occasionally utilized in the first subgroup.

Measurements: height 8cm; rim diameter 9.5cm; depth 6.8cm; diameter of lower belly 9.8cm; weight 245.6g.

Detailed Description of the Object: the bowl was mold-blown from greenish translucent glass, decorated with cut-work relief patterns, by an upper row of 8 and a lower of 6 protruding circular medallions. A single circular medallion larger than those on the body forms the bowl's base in place of a foot. Each of the circles on the body presents its corners planed off and from the interior of the bowl each one shows as a round circle of light. The protruding medallions come out few mm from the wall of the cup. The straight mouth of the bowl is few mm thick. The discovery of this first complete and intact glassware with cold working and polishing technique excavated in China has, largely developed the understanding and comprehension of the glassware production with the same technique.

Comparing and Geographical, Cultural and Chronological Attribution: An Jiayao (1986, 178–181) believes that the glass bowl is a Sasanian artifact made

2004, 61, and 258, no 158），类似的残片有中国新疆巴楚脱库孜萨来遗址的佛寺中采集到的两片（4至5世纪）（Laing 1991,111, fig.8）。但遗憾的是在伊朗高原迄今还没有科学发掘过如此完整的玻璃碗，使得这些伊朗前伊斯兰时期的产品以及这件器物的年代和文化归属蒙上了一层不确定的阴影。极为类似的碗很可能在伊朗法尔斯（Fars）的Qasr-i Abu Nasr有发现，也见于意大利罗马东方艺术馆（Rome, inv. no 2705）、日本京都Miho美术馆（2001年展览）、美国新泽西康宁玻璃博物馆的藏品。该种风格的玻璃碎片已在日本的冲之岛（Okinoshima Island）发现（Fukai 1977, 44–45; Laing 1991, 118, fig.29），亦见于奈良东大寺正仓院和京都上贺茂。所谓的"波斯"玻璃分布广泛，绝大多数发现于与帝王关系密切的高级贵族墓中（Whitehouse 2005）。它历尽艰辛被从西方运输到中国，同样被中国的上层社会当作至宝。迄今为止中国出土的早期玻璃器，多出土于高级官吏和贵族阶层墓葬，以及寺院塔基。像李贤墓这件玻璃碗上的装饰，也见于5—8世纪的玻璃杯，Saldern（1963）已经指出它们的年代不早于6世纪，并为出土玻璃器的墓葬本身的年代所证实。

那个在文献里被描述成拥有无数财富，例如带有皇家图案的鎏金银盘、装饰着歌舞者形象的容器、珍贵的玻璃器皿、丝绸和高级羊毛织物、奢侈的武器、带雕刻的宝石、印章、青铜盘、马赛克的萨珊宫殿，对其准确的定位和复原，目前还缺乏足够的考古学背景的支

in the Iranian plateau. The bowl was published in the exhibition at New York in 2004 (An Jiayao2004, 61, and 258, no 158). Another similar item has been uncovered at Barchuk in Xinijang (Laing 1991,111, fig.8). Unfortunately there are very few entire and complete glass bowls coming from a secure archaeological context in the Iranian Plateau and this yields a great shadow to the chronological and cultural attribution on the Iranian pre-Islamic production for this item as well. Very similar bowls are anyway documented at Qasr-i Abu Nasr (Fars) (Whitcomb 1985, 156, fig.58k), in the Oriental Art Museum (Rome, inv. no.2705) (Genito 1977, 16, fig.in the cover), Miho Museum (Kyoto,Exhibition 2001) and Corning Museum (Corning, Inv.72.1.21) (Sassanides 2006, 149, fig.93). Fragments of this type have been discovered also in the sanctuary of Munakata on the Okinoshima Island of Japan (Fukai 1977, 44–45; Laing 1991, 118, fig.29), and are present at Shoshoin treasure and at Kamigamo; this indicates the very wide range of distribution of the so called "Persian" glass mostly appeared in the tombs of high-status nobility related to the Emperor (Whitehouse 2005). The difficulty in obtaining glassware from the West made it precious in China and for that it was treasured by the upper classes of people. Ancient glassware unearthed in China so far, is usually found in the tombs of high-ranking officials and nobles, as well as in the underground palaces of Buddhist temples. For this kind of decoration, present also in bottles belonging to 5th–8th centuries, Saldern (1963) has proposed a chronology not earlier than 6th century AD, which would be certainly confirmed by the dating of the tomb where the bowl is coming from.The so-called presumed extraordinary luxury of the Sasanian court represented by gilded silver plates with royal imagery, vessels decorated with dancers and musicians, precious glass wares, silk and fine wool textiles, luxurious arms, carved gems, seals, bronze plates, stucco panels, and mosaics, is still lacking of any secure archaeological context into which to locate them. The extension of the Sasanian culture widespread far beyond the empire's

撑。萨珊文化的影响已超出帝国的疆域，远达西欧、非洲、中国和印度。萨珊和罗马—拜占庭文化之间的联系还没有被充分认识，但是它们的相互作用对早期伊斯兰和欧洲中世纪的生活产生了重大影响，这体现在许多方面，包括王权观念、宫廷生活仪轨、建筑、文学等艺术领域的发展等。通过向东对中亚地区的渗透以及某些时期对丝绸之路部分路段的控制，波斯的创作和设计思想还影响到了东亚艺术。

territorial borders, as far as western Europe, Africa, China, and India. The relationship between the Sasanian and Roman-Byzantine cultures has not yet been widely investigated, although the interactions between them had a significant influence on the character of early Islamic and medieval European culture and life. These aspects are visible in many grounds, including the concept of majesty, the structure and procedures of court life, and the development of the arts, including architecture and writing. The political and military penetrations of the Sasanians eastward into Central Asia and their control for a time of parts of the great Silk Road go back ultimately to the influence of Iranian forms and designs on the art of East Asia.

参考文献　References

1. 安家瑶：《北周李贤墓出土的玻璃碗——萨珊玻璃器的发现与研究》,《考古》1986年第2期,页173—181。
An Jiayao (1986) A Glass Bowl from Li Xian's Tomb of the Northern Zhou Dynasty: Discovery and Research of the Sasanian Glassware, *Kaogu (Archaeology)*, 2, 173–181, Beijing.

2. An Jiayao (2004) Bowl, in Watt, James C.Y. *et alii* (eds.) *China: Dawn of a Golden Age, 200–750 AD*, The Metropolitan Museum of Art, New York, Yale University Press, no. 158, 258, New Haven and London.

3. Brill, R.H. (2005) Chemical Analyses of Some Sasanian Glasses from Iraq, in Whitehouse, D., *Sasanian and Post Sasanian Glass in the Corning Museum of Glass*, 65–88. Corning, NY: Corning Museum of Glass.

4. Demange, F (2007) *Glass, Gilding and Grand Design, Art of Sasanian Iran (224–642)*. New York: Asian Society.

5. Freestone, I.C (2006) Glass Production in Late Antiquity and the Early Islamic Period: a Geochemical Perspective, Maggeti, M. and Messiga, B. (eds.) *Geo-materials in Cultural Heritage*, Special publications 257, 201–216, Geological Society, London.

6. Fukai, S. (1977) *Persian Glass*, Kyoto.

7. Genito, B. (1977) *Vetri Iranici, Schede n. 10, Museo Nazionale d'Arte Orientale*, Roma.

8. Goldstein, S.M. (1980) Pre-Persian and Persian Glass: Some Observations on Objects in the Corning Museum of Glass, Schmandt-Besserat D. (ed.) *Ancient Persia: The Art of an Empire*, Malibu. Undena.

9. Goldstein, S.M (2005) *Glass from Sasanian Antecedents to European Imitations*. The Nour Foundation in association with Asimuth editions, London.

10. Goldstein, S.M., Rakow, L.S. and Rakow, J.K. (1982) *Cameo Glass: Masterpieces from 2000 Years of Glassmaking*. The Corning Museum of Glass, Corning, New York.

11. 固原博物馆：《固原历史文物》,科学出版社(北京),2004年,页127,第78号器物。
Guyuan Museum (2004) Guyuan lishi wenwu (*Historical and Cultural Relics from Guyuan*), Science Publishing

House, 127, no.78, Beijing.

12. Gyselen, Rika (2007) *The Sasanian World. Glass, Gilding and Grand Design: Art of Sasanian Iran (224–642)* by Demange, F., 13–20, New York.

13. Laing, E.J. (1991) A Report on Western Asian Glassware in the Far East, *Bulletin of the Asia Institute*, n.s., 5, 109–121, Bloomfield Hills.

14. Maeda Akiyo (ed.) (2001) Ancient Glass: Catalogue of the Exhibition Held by the Miho Museum, Kyoto.

15. Meyer, C. (1996) Sasanian and Islamic Glass from Nippur, Iraq, *Annales du 13° Congrès de l'Association International pour l'histoire du Verre. Pays Bas / 28 août-1 septembre 1995*, 247–255.

16. Mirti, P. *et alii* (2008) ICP-MS Analysis of Glass Fragments of Parthian and Sasanian Epoch from Seleucia and Veh Ardasir (Central Iraq), *Archaeometry* 50 (3), 429–450, Goodwood.

17. Mirti, P. *et alii* (2009) Sasanian Glass from Veh Ardasir: New Evidences by ICP-MS Analysis, *Journal of Archaeological Science* 36, 1061–1069, Amsterdam.

18. Negro Ponzi, M (1968–69) Sasanian Glassware from Tell Mahuz (North Mesopotamia), *Mesopotamia* 3–4, 293–384, Torino.

19. Negro Ponzi, M. (1969) A Group of Mesopotamian Glass Vessels of Sasanian Date, Charleston, J.R, Evans, W. and Werner, A.E. (eds.) *Studies in Glass History and Design, VIIIth International Congress on Glass. London 1st–6th July 1968.* Old Woking, Surrey: Gresham Press.

20. Negro Ponzi, M (1972) Glassware from Abu Skhair (Central Iraq), *Mesopotamia*, 7, 214–233, Torino.

21. Negro Ponzi, M. (1984) Glassware from Choche (Central Mesopotamia), Boucharlat, R. and Salles, J.F (eds.) *Arabie Orientale, Mésopotamie et Iran Méridionale de Láge du fer au Début de la Période Islamique*, Mémoire no 37. 33–40, Editions Recherche sur les Civilisations, Paris.

22. Negro Ponzi, M. (1987) Late Sasanian Glassware from Tell Baruda, *Mesopotamia*, 22, 265–275, Torino.

23. Negro Ponzi, M (2002) The Glassware from Seleucia (Central Iraq), *Parthica* 4, 63–156.

24. Newman, H. (1977) *An Illustrated Dictionary of Glass*, Thames and Hudson, London.

25. 宁夏博物馆、宁夏固原博物馆发掘组：《宁夏固原北周李贤夫妇墓发掘简报》，《文物》1985第11期，页1—20，图26，图版叁：1。
    Ningxia Museum, Guyuan Museum (1985) Excavation of Northern Zhou Dynasty Tomb of Li Xian and His Wife at Guyuan, Ningxia, *Wenwu* (*Cultural Relics*),11, 1–20, fig.25, Ⅲ : 1, Beijing.

26. Saldern, Von, A. (1963) Achaemenid and Sasanian Cut Glass, *Ars Orientalis*, 5, 7–16.

27. Saldern, Von, A. (1966) Ancient Glass, *Boston Museum Bulletin*, 64 (335), 4–17.

28. Simpson, St. John (2000) Mesopotamia in the Sasanian Period. Settlement Patterns, Arts and Crafts, Curtis J. (ed.) *Mesopotamia and Iran in the Parthian and Sasanian Periods, Rejection and Revival c.238 BC–642 AD*, British Museum Press, 57–66, London.

29. Sassanides (2006) *Les Perses Sassanides, Fastes d'un Empire Oublié (224–642)*, Musée Cernuschi, Musée de l'Asie de la Ville de Paris, 15 septembre-30 décembre, Paris.

30. Watt, James C.Y. *et alii* (eds.) (2004) *China. Dawn of a Golden Age, 200–750 AD, Exhibition Catalogue*, The Metropolitan Museum of Art, New York, no. 158, 258–259, Yale University Press, New Haven and London.

31. Whitcomb, D.S. (1985) *Before the Roses and the Nightngales, Excavations at Qasr-i Abu Nasr, Old Shiraz*, New York.

32. Whitehouse, D. (2005) *Sasanian and post Sasanian Glass in the Corning Museum of Glass*. Corning, New York.

33. Whitehouse, D. (2006) *La Verrerie Sassanide. Les Perses Sassanides. Fastes d'un Empire Oublié* (224–642), 138–154, Editions Findankly, Paris.

34. Whitehouse, D. (2007) *Sasanian Glassware. Glass, Gilding and Grand Design: Art of Sasanian Iran* (224–642), Demange, F., 29–33, Asian Society, New York.

（*Bruno Genito*, 耿朔 [*Geng Shuo*]）

34. 对羊对鸟灯树纹锦

收藏单位：新疆维吾尔自治区博物馆。

出土信息：1972年发掘的新疆吐鲁番阿斯塔那墓地M186。

器物概括描述：绿地对羊对鸟灯树纹锦。

尺寸：长24.1、宽21厘米。

图像详细描述：织锦上的装饰左右对称，恰好是织机的宽度。绿地。下部是两只屈膝相对的红色山羊，各有一只前蹄飞起。双目圆

34. Brocade

Location: Xinjiang Uygur Autonomous Region Museum.

Context of Origin: Astana cemetery (Turfan, Xinjiang Uygur Autonomous Region), tomb 186 (excavated in 1972).

Brief Description of the Object: textile with confronting mountains goats, birds and tree design against green background.

Measurements: length 24.1cm; width 21cm.

Detailed Description of the Iconography: the textile shows a symmetrical design which occupies one complete loom width. On a green ground, two

34. 对羊对鸟灯树纹锦 Brocade

睁，瞳孔深色，项后有红色飘带，鬃毛中有呈三角形的米黄色斑。对羊之上是一棵风格化的树（灯树），树干像有凹槽的柱子，树顶红色，其余为黄色。整个树冠由6个呈花瓣状的部分组合而成，每一部分中都有一盏叶形灯，树冠的底部呈螺旋状。灯树上部两边有两组对鸟，鸟头红色，鸟身米黄色并夹杂着其他颜色（上部两只有红色斑点，下部两只有米黄色斑点），顶端的两只鸟共含一支倒置的花朵（百合？）。顶部相背的两只鸟间以葡萄状灯树。蓝绿色地，外轮廓白色。

地域、文化、年代属性及对比：4—10世纪。

kneeling red mountain goats facing each other, with one of the front legs lifted. They have wide opened eyes with dark pupil, a collar from which an *infula* floats backwards; the mane has triangular beige patches. Above the goats, a stylised tree ("lamp tree") with a trunk shaped like a fluted column. The foliage — yellow except for the top, which is red — is subdivided into six lobes, each containing a leaf-shaped lamp; the lower ends are shaped like volutes. Two couples of confronted birds are represented on both sides of the upper part of the tree; their head is red, their body is beige with patches of different colours (red in the upper couple, yellow in the lower one); the two on the top hold in their beaks the stalks of an upturned flower (lily?). A small tree with grape-shaped lamps separated the upper couples of birds. The ground is blue and green, the outline white.

Comparing and Geographical, Cultural and Chronological Attribution: 4th–10th centuries AD.

参考文献   References

1. 新疆维吾尔自治区博物馆编：《新疆维吾尔自治区博物馆》，文物出版社，1991年。
   Xinjiang Weiwuer zizhiqu bowuguan (1991) *Xinjiang Weiwuer zizhiqu bowuguan (Xinjiang Uygur Autonomous Region Museum)*, Cultural Relics Publishing House, Beijing.
2. Watt, James C.Y. *et alii* (eds.) (2004) *China: Dawn of a Golden Age, 200–750 AD*, Yale University Press (in part. 336, no. 235), New Haven and London.

（*Ciro Lo Muzio*，李雨生 [*Li Yusheng*]）

35. 覆面

收藏单位：新疆维吾尔自治区博物馆。

出土信息：1960年发掘的新疆吐鲁番阿斯塔那墓地M325。

器物概括描述：织锦残片，被制成覆面，织锦上有联珠纹，联珠圈内有一野猪头。

材质、工艺及保存状况：丝织品。

尺寸：长17.8、宽23.5厘米。

器物详细描述：该覆面是一块长方形的织锦残片，上饰联珠纹，保存基本完好，联珠纹中有一野猪头，联珠纹外右侧还保存了与之相连的另一圈联珠纹的一部分。联珠呈八边形，珠圈的顶端和底端的联珠呈方形。两联珠圈之间以一个稍小的联珠圈相连，小珠圈中有花卉纹。野猪头侧向右面，表现相当概括和模式化：黑毛，鬃毛被描绘成中间填横线的新月形，白耳，长菱形眼，长方形鼻子，上獠牙向内卷曲，下獠牙外伸，猪舌以长条纹表现，颈部有两个三角形的白色斑块。

地域、文化、年代属性及对比：约公元663年左右。墓中发现的萨珊银币（以及文书）可以提供该合葬墓的年代上限。联珠纹中织有徽章式的兽头（野猪、狼）或者鸟衔绶带，或者更为罕见的人侧脸等主题起源于萨珊（起源于6世纪晚期，参见cf. Marshak 2001, 244），随后广泛流行于中亚西部及新疆地区。20世纪初，斯坦因在阿斯塔那墓地的另一座墓中曾发现相同装饰的织锦覆面，这件遗物目前收藏在新德里的印度国家博物馆之中（inv. Ast.

35. Brocade

Location: Xinjiang Uygur Autonomous Region Museum.

Context of Origin: Astana cemetery (Turfan, Xinjiang Uygur Autonomous Region Museum), tomb 325 (excavated in 1960);

Brief Description of the Object: fragment of textile reused as a face cover, with a boar's head in rounded pearls circular frame.

Material, Technique and Conservation: silk.
Measurements: length 17.8cm; width 23.5cm.

Detailed Description of the Object: face cover made of a rectangular fragment of a silk textile decorated with pearl roundels. In the fragment an almost complete roundel, containing a boar's head, and part of the adjoining roundel to the right are preserved. The pearls are of octagonal shape; at the top and bottom of the roundel, instead of a pearl a square gem is inserted. A small pearl roundel containing a floral motif interlocks the two adjoining roundels. The boar head, in profile to the right is rendered in a stylized and rather sketchy manner: black hair, neck fur described as a crescent filled with horizontal lines, white ear, rhomboidal eye, rectangular snout, upright upper tusk curved inward, lower tusk curved outward, tongue indicated by a rectangular stripe, two triangular white spots on the neck.

Comparing and Geographical, Cultural and Chronological Attribution: circa third quarter of the 7th century AD. The chronology of the grave, containing two inhumations, is based on the presence of late Sasanian silver coins, which provide a *terminus post quem*. The motif of the pearl roundel containing a heraldic animal head (boar, wolf), or a bird holding two ribbons in its beak or, more seldom, a human head in profile stems from the Sasanian tradition (late 6th century, cf. Marshak 2001, 244); it soon spread throughout Western Central Asia and the Xinjiang. A silk face cover with the same subject was found in

35. 覆面 Brocade

i.5.03; cf. Stein 1928, vol.2,682–683, pl. LXXVI; Ghirshman 1962,230, fig.282; Meister 1970, 264, fig.3）。阿斯塔那墓地中发现的这些织锦残片很可能产于中亚，而非萨珊，在巴米扬（Cave D; Klimburg-Salter 1989, pl. LIII, fig.68）和阿夫拉西阿卜（Otavsky 1996, fig.94）的壁画中可以找到类似的装饰。

another tomb of the Astana cemetery by Sir A. Stein, in the early 20th century, now in the National Museum of New Delhi (inv. Ast. i.5.03; cf. Stein 1928, vol.2, 682–683, pl. LXXVI; Ghirshman 1962, 230, fig.282; Meister 1970, 264, fig.30). Rather than Sasanian, the cloths to which the Astana fragments belonged were most likely of Central Asian workmanship. They find close parallels in the mural paintings of Bamiyan (Cave D; Klimburg-Salter 1989, pl. LIII, fig.68) and Afrasiab, Samarkand (Otavsky 1996, fig.94).

参考文献 References

1. Ghirshman, R. (1962) *Arte persiana. Parti e Sassanidi*, Milano.
2. Klimburg-Salter, D. (1989) *The Kingdom of Bāmiyān. Buddhist Art and Culture of the Hindu Kush*, Naples-Rome.
3. Marshak, B. (2001) La Thématique Sogdienne dans L'art de la Chine de la Seconde Moitié du VIe Siècle, *Comptes-rendus des Séances de l'Académie des Inscriptions et Belles-Lettres*, 145, 1, 227–264.
4. Meister, M. (1970) The Pearl Roundel in Chinese Textile Design, *Ars Orientalis*, 8, 255–267 (in part. fig.30).
5. Otavsky, K., (1998) Zur Kunsthistorischen Einordung der Stoffe,Otavsky, K. (hrsg.)*Entlang der Seidenstraße: Frühmittelalterliche Kunst Zwischen Persien und China in der Abegg-Stiftung*, 119–214, Riggisberg.
6. Stein, A. (1928) *Innermost Asia: Detailed Report of Explorations in Central Asia, Kan-su and Eastern Īrān*, Oxford.

（*Ciro Lo Muzio*，李雨生 [*Li Yusheng*]）

36. 联珠鹿纹锦

收藏单位：新疆维吾尔自治区博物馆。

出土信息：1960年出土于新疆吐鲁番阿斯塔那墓地M332。

器物概括描述：织锦残片，上有联珠鹿纹装饰，被制成覆面。

材质、工艺及保存状况：丝织品。

尺寸：残长20、宽21厘米。

器物详细描述：这件覆面是一块长方形的织锦残片，其上装饰联珠纹，联珠纹基本保持完好，珠圈内织有一只侧面向左行进的鹿。联珠圈之间彼此以更小的联珠圈相连，更小联珠圈中有方块形装饰（宝石？），织工较为写意，联珠呈八边形。珠圈中的鹿正在向左行进，鹿角呈水平状，小头，长菱形眼，黑皮上装饰有白色几何纹斑点，鹿身中间是一排三个圆圈形装饰，圆圈中有蓝色斑点，圆圈上部有新月形装饰，颈部系绶带，绶带由一排小三角形组成，飘向身后。

地域、文化、年代属性及对比：不早于665年。联珠纹中织有徽章式的兽头（野猪、狼）或者鸟衔绶带，或者更为罕见的人侧脸等主题起源于萨珊（6世纪晚期，参见Marshak 2001, 244），随后广泛流行于中亚西部及新疆地区。阿斯塔那墓地的M322中曾出土类似的织锦覆面，共出的萨珊银币（库思老二世）表明这座墓的年代与M332大体接近，珠圈中的鹿较模式化，但织工更为粗劣。

36. Brocade

Location: Xinjiang Uygur Autonomous Region Museum.

Context of Origin: Astana cemetery (Turfan, Xinjiang Uygur Autonomous Region Museum), tomb 332 (excavated in 1960).

Brief Description of the Object: fragment of textile with deer design in a pearl roundel circular frame, reused as a face cover.

Material, Technique and Conservation: silk.

Measurements: length 20cm; width 21cm.

Detailed Description of the Object: face cover made of a rectangular fragment of a silk textile decorated with pearl roundels. The fragment preserves an almost complete roundel containing the representation of a stag in profile to the left. The cloth was decorated with a network of similar roundels interlocked by small pearl roundels containing a square dot (gem?). The workmanship is sketchy; rather than round, the pearls show an octagonal shape; the stag is shown as walking towards the left, with elongated antlers disposed horizontally, small head, rhomboidal eyes, black coat with white geometrical spots and a central row of three circles containing a blue dot and a crescent shaped. A ribbon consisting of a row of triangular elements, tied to the animal's neck, floats backwards.

Comparing and Geographical, Cultural and Chronological Attribution: circa third quarter of the 7th century AD. The motif of the pearl roundel containing a heraldic animal head (boar, wolf), or a bird holding two ribbons in its beak or, more seldom, a human head in profile stems from the Sasanian tradition (late 6th century, cf. Marshak 2001, 244); it soon spread throughout Western Central Asia and the Xinjiang. A silk face cover with the same subject was found in the Astana cemetery (tomb 322), which, based on numismatic evidence (coins of the Sasanian king Khusrau II), can be dated to the same period (third quarter of the 7th century AD); the stag shows the same stylization but a coarser workmanship (Meister 1970, fig.33).

36. 联珠鹿纹锦 Brocade

参考文献　References

1. Marshak, B. (2001) La Thématique Sogdienne dans l'art de la Chine de la Seconde Moitié du VIe Siècle, *Comptes-rendus des Séances de l'Académie des Inscriptions et Belles-Lettres*, 145, 1, 227–264.
2. Meister, M. (1970) The Pearl Roundel in Chinese Textile Design, *Ars Orientalis*, 8, 255–267 (in part. fig. 30)

（*Ciro Lo Muzio*，李雨生 [*Li Yusheng*]）

37. 金壶

收藏单位：肃南裕固族自治县民族博物馆。

出土信息：这件金壶于1979年8月14日由当地村民发现于甘肃省肃南裕固族自治县的一座墓中，考古工作者抵达现场时，该墓葬已经被严重破坏，随葬品也被哄抢，尽管如此，还是征集和清理出各类器物143件，这件金壶即为其中之一，一同出土的还有鎏金菱花形三折叠银高足盘（见编号No.38）、鎏金六龙银杯、鎏金银洗、金马具、鎏金铜壶、鎏金铜龙头、鎏金铜盏托、鎏金马具、菱花形二龙戏珠锡盘、铁甲、铁剑、木版画等。这座墓是前后双室土洞墓，甬道口封门墙外有两匹马的尸骨，前室横置木床，后室正中放置木棺，后室后壁用松木板镶制，其上绘制十二生肖图，后室以木条铺放拱顶，上盖一层黄色丝绸帐幔。墓主是一名男性，头南脚北，头戴银丝网盔帽，内用黄色织物缝制，头上有20厘米长的两条发辫，上用黄色织物缠绕。上身着衣16层，下身内外12层，外层织物以金线织成，内层丝绸有黄黑两色菱花图案，脚穿高腰牛皮马靴。

器物概括描述：带盖罐，有环形把手。

材质、工艺及保存状况：金制，镶嵌绿松石。

尺寸：高17.5、口径6.5、底径6.5厘米，重709克。

器物详细描述：小口、直颈、球腹、圈足。器盖上有芽状突起的钮，壶把上部有尖状指垫，指垫上镶嵌绿松石，器表磨光，无装饰。

37. Gold Pot

Location: Sunan Ethnographical Museum.

Context of Origin: Sunan Yugur Autonomous County Gansu province. This pot was unearthed from a tomb that was discovered by local inhabitants in 14 April 1979 in Sunan Yugur Autonomous County, Gansu. When the archaeologists arrived on the site, the tomb had already been looted and damaged. Nonetheless it was possible to collect 143 funerary items, this gold pot being one of them. Together with the pot, there were other important unearthed items such as a gilded silver plate with three folding foots (see n. 38), a gilded silver cup with six dragons motif, a gilded copper pot, a gilded copper dragon head, a gilded copper cup stand, gold and gilded horse gears, a tin plate decorated with two dragons playing with the pearl, a ferric armor, a ferric sword, paintings on board, and so on. The tomb had two earthed chambers; two horse-skeletons were discovered out of the door in the corridor. There was a transverse wooden bed in the front chamber, and a few wooden coffin in the back chamber. The rear wall of the back chamber was found inlayed with deal board, on which was painted twelve Chinese zodiac signs, and there was a layer of yellow silk on the top of the wooden roof of the back chamber. The tomb's owner was a man; his head was on the south, and was covered by reticular silver helmet which was sewed on a yellow fabric. The man wore 16 layers of clothes, and 12 layers of trousers decorated with yellow or black ornaments in rhombus shape. His feet wore long riding boots.

Brief Description of the Object: covered jar with ring handle.

Material, Technique and Conservation: gold inlaid with turquoise.

Measurements: height 17.5cm; diameter of the mouth 6.5cm; diameter of the foot 6.5cm; weight 709g.

Detailed Description of the Object: this lidded jar

37. 金壶 Gold Pot

地域、文化、年代属性及对比：造型类似的把手在粟特东部彼尔姆（Perm）地区发现的银壶和银杯上可以见到，这批器物目前收藏在圣彼得堡的埃米尔塔什博物馆中（Dumoulin 2000, nos 39–41），它们的装饰更精致，圈足更明显，其年代被确定在公元8世纪，在埃米尔塔什博物馆还可以见到一些装饰要朴素得多的银壶（Smirnov, ed, 1909, nos 170, 181）。肃南的金壶是目前这类器物中少数的几件金制品之一。这件金壶（很可能是在甘肃制作）与其他共出的器物共同反映出甘肃吐蕃与粟特地区之间的文化交流。

has a narrow mouth, straight neck, bulging body and a ring base. The knob on the lid is shaped like a small bud. The ring handle with upper cusped panel is inlaid with turquoise. The body is polished and undecorated.

Comparing and Geographical, Cultural and Chronological Attribution: some similar silver jugs or cups with the same type of handle were found in the district of Perm in Eastern Sogdiana and are now in the Hermitage Museum in St. Petersburg (Dumoulin 2000, nos 39–41). More elaborate than the present example and with a more pronounced foot, they are dated to the 8th century. Always in the collection of the Hermitage Museum, some silver, undecorated examples can also be seen (Smirnov ed, 1909, nos 170, 181). The present jug is one of the rare examples made out of gold. The finding spot, together with the other objects from the tomb, suggest that it may be an import or an example of the interaction between the Tubo (ancient Tibet) culture in Gansu — where it was perhaps made — and the Sogdian region.

参考文献　References

1. Dumoulin, B. (2000) *L'Asie des steppes d'Alexandre le Grand à Gengis Khan*. Paris.
2. Smirnov, Ja.I. (ed.) (1909) *Vostočnoe serebro. Atlas drevnej serebrjanoj i zolotoj posudy vostočnogo proishoždenija, naidennoj preimuščestvenno v predelah Rossiiskoj imperii. Izdanie Imperatorskoj Arheologičeskoj Kommissii ko dniu piatidesjatiletija eia dejatel'nosti*, Saint Petersburg.

（*Chiara Visconti*，李雨生 [*Li Yusheng*]）

38. 鎏金铜盘

收藏单位：肃南裕固族自治县民族博物馆。

出土信息：出土于甘肃肃南西水大长岭唐墓，具体情况参见No.37。

器物概括描述：三足盘。

材质、工艺及保存状况：铜鎏金，有锈迹。

尺寸：高19.5、盘径29.5厘米，重2191克。

器物详细描述：菱花形浅盘，三足可折叠，上有折线纹饰。

38. Gilded Bronze Tray

Location: Sunan Ethnographical Museum.

Context of Origin: from a tomb in Sunan Yugur Autonomous County of Gansu province (see n. 37).

Brief Description of the Object: tripod tray.

Material, Technique and Conservation: gilded bronze; oxidized.

Measurements: height 19.5cm; diameter of the plate 29.5cm; weight 2191g.

Detailed Description of the Object: poly-lobed round tray or dish with flared mouth and rim and three folding legs decorated with zigzag lines.

38. 鎏金铜盘 Gilded Bronze Tray

风格分析：根据银盘的造型以及墓中共出的其他发现，这件银盘应该属于甘肃境内的吐蕃文化。

地域、文化及年代属性与对比：菱花形盘在唐代非常流行，在何家村窖藏（Michaelson 1999, no 66, 69）、法门寺地宫（Michaelson 1999, 110）和河北宽城（Wyatt 2004, no 215）都有发现，另外在伏尔加河流域的萨马拉（Samara）也曾发现过类似的三足银盘，时代被确定为公元8世纪。这件肃南发现的银盘可能产于本地。

Stylistic Analysis: lobed dish; judging also from the other items found in the tomb, the tray should belong to the Tibetan culture in Gansu.

Comparing and Geographical, Cultural and Chronological Attribution: lobed dishes were very popular during Tang Dynasty and have been found in the Hejiacun hoard (Michaelson 1999, no 66, 69) in the Famen si crypt (Michaelson 1999, 110) and elsewhere (see for example the tripod platter with deer excavated at Dayejiyu, Hebei province, cf. Wyatt 2004, no 215). Even if a tripod silver dish similar in shape and datable to the 8th century has been found as far as Samara province (Darkevich 1976, no 12, pl. 11/3, 13–14), the tray from Sunan is probably a local product.

参考文献　References

1. Darkevič, V.P. (1976) *Hudožestvennyi metall Vostoka VIII–XIII vv. Proizvedenija vostočnoj torevtiki na territorii evropeiskoj časti SSSR i Zaural'ia*, Moskva.
2. Michaelson, C (1999) *Gilded Dragons*, London.
3. Watt, James C.Y. *et alii* (eds.) (2004) *China. Dawn of a Golden Age, 200–750 AD*, The Metropolitan Museum of Art, New York, Yale University Press, New Haven and London.

（*Chiara Visconti*，李雨生 [*Li Yusheng*]）

39. 印章

收藏单位：宁夏固原博物馆。

出土信息：印章出土于宁夏固原南郊乡羊坊村的唐代史诃耽夫妇墓中，该墓1986年由固原博物馆发掘。固原南郊隋唐墓地东西长4.6公里，已经发现了10余座墓葬，大体呈一字形排列，每座墓葬基本上都有封土。1982—1995年对其中的9座墓葬进行了发掘，其中6座属于史氏家族，他们是流寓中国的中亚粟特地区的史国人，自北朝晚期移居原州。这些墓在墓葬形制上与关中地区的隋唐墓基本一致，为长斜坡墓道、多天井的方形土洞或砖室墓。有的墓内装饰壁画。出土物虽然不多，但来源丰富，既有中国本土的器物出土，还有一些外来物品被发现。例如，几乎每座墓中都有一枚外国金币出土，有的墓内发现的金银货币是萨珊银币或东罗马金币的仿制品。金银币或含或握在墓主人口中、手中。史道德墓出土的金覆面，上饰一轮半月托住一个圆球，被认为与摩尼教或拜火教有关。

史诃耽夫妇墓由封土、墓道、过洞、天井、甬道、墓室六部分组成。封土现存高度6米，底径东西20、南北22米，在墓群中最为高大。长斜坡土洞墓道长9.75米，共有5个过洞、5个天井；甬道为砖砌，分为前后两端，有石墓门和砖墓门，后甬道中间放置墓志。墓室砖砌，长宽都在3.5—4米之间，穹隆顶，高5米。内有石棺床。墓葬被洗劫一空，仅在淤土中发现零星小件物品，散落于墓室各处，唯有棺床边的东罗马

39. Seal

Location: Guyuan Museum.

Context of Origin: the gem was excavated from a tomb at Xiaomazhuang Village, Nanjiao Town, Guyuan, Ningxia Hui Autonomous Region by the archaeological team of Guyuan Museum in 1986. The tomb occupant was Shi Hedan, buried with his wife. The Sui-Tang cemetery of Guyan is located in Yangfang Village, Nanjiao Town, a large cemetery developing from East to West for 4.6km. More than ten tombs have been found, each with its own mound. Between 1982 and 1995 nine tombs were excavated; among them six belonged to the Shi family, a Central Asian family from Kesh in Sogdiana, which lived in China, settling in Yuanzhou in the late Northern Dynasties. All the tombs had been robbed. The tomb type is similar to the Sui-Tang tombs of the Guanzhong area: a long sloping passage with vertical shafts, a doorway and a brick chamber. The walls of the tomb revealed a number of valuable paintings. Funerary objects are few, among them, mainly are Chinese objects and a few are Western in origin. For instance, gold coins were found in almost every tomb, in some tombs there were also silver Sasanian coins or imitation of Eastern Roman gold coins; the coins were found in the tomb occupant's hand or mouth. In Shi Daode's tomb was unearthed a gold vizard, with a half moon lifting up a ball, which was thought to be related to the Manichaean or Zoroastrian religion. The Shi Hedan tomb is composed of 6 parts: mound, sloping passage, compartments, vertical shafts, entrance, and tomb chamber. Presently the mound is 6m high, with a diameter of 20m from East to West and 22m from North to South, the largest in this cemetery. The long, sloping tomb passage is 9.75m long. It has five compartments and shafts, brick corridor, which divided into front and back end, with two sets of tomb doors, one made of stone, the

39. 印章 Seal

金币仿制品，可能在原位。墓主尸骨已朽成粉末状。该墓出土器物不多，大部分为铜器，少部分为玻璃器。蓝色圆形宝石印章发现于石棺床上。从墓志和《唐会要》的记载可知，墓主史诃耽，是生活在中国的粟特人，在唐王朝曾历游击将军、虢州刺史，还曾以语言优势任职中书省朝会翻译，深受朝廷器重，他于总章二年（669）九月二十三日卒于原州，次年下葬。

在蓝色宝石上雕刻图案的做法，在传入中国的其他西方文物上也有发现，大多用于镶嵌戒面，如河北赞皇东魏李希宗墓的金戒指的戒面宝石上就刻有一鹿，边饰一周联珠纹。这种装饰作风还见于内蒙古土默特右旗毕克齐镇发

other made of bricks. The memorial tablet (epitaph) was placed in the middle of the entrance. The tomb chamber was made of bricks; its length and width are 3.5 and 4m; the height at the top of the dome is 5m. In it there is a stone-made coffin platform. The tomb was thoroughly ransacked and only a few small items were found in the soil, scattered around; only the imitations of Eastern Roman coins next to coffin platform could be in the original position. Most bones of the occupant had decayed into powder. The few unearthed artifacts were mainly copper ware, and some glass ware. The gem seal was found on the coffin platform. From the epitaph we know the occupant of the tomb was Shi Hedan, who came from Sogdiana and lived in China. He had been a Youji general, the fifth term of officeand the prefectural governor of Guozhou, translator of the Central Secretariat due to his language skills. Highly

现的金戒指、李贤墓发现的金戒指以及西安隋代李静训墓发现的项链上。

器物概况描述：戒面上雕刻一只斜倚在植物纹样之前的狮子，周缘刻有中古波斯文。

材质、工艺及保存状况：该印章经地质矿产部陕西省中心实验室的测试分析，证实材质为石英单晶体，二氧化硅的含量高达99.51%。石英印章的雕刻面上有天蓝色表层，经X衍射分析似乎是一种"非晶态物质"，是用颜料涂抹上去的。保存完整。

尺寸：直径1.6、厚0.6厘米。

器物详细描述：宝石有着圆形轮廓、平的雕刻面和凸起边缘，底部或凸起。

图像详细描述：雕刻面上为一卧狮，狮身侧向右方，头朝前，爪子向前伸展。身后立三棵树状物，顶似花蕾。上有一周波斯文铭文。中部的波斯文被林梅村（1997）释读为"自由、繁荣、幸福"，被P.O. Skjaervø 释读为"generosity, generosity, generosity"（Juliano and Lerner 2001, 260, fn.6）。

风格分析：这枚印章使用的是高浮雕技法，整体和局部的处理都很细致。图案的表现方式是概括性的。狮子的身体被三个球状花瓣所装饰，颈部的鬃毛垂直，和右前爪的处理一样。

比较分析以及地域、文化、年代学讨论：与这种肖像式构图可以比较的材料有法国国家图书馆收藏的两枚印章，尽管后者还有一些差别，比如在狮子身体的下方可以看见树的底部，叶子也不同（Gyselen 1993: 112–13, nos. 30. E.45

regarded by the imperial court, he was recorded in The System of Etiquette and Rituals about Tang; he died in 669 in Yuanzhou. The engraved patterns on the blue gem have also been noticed in other western artifacts introduced into China, mostly in stone ring bezels. For example, in Li Xizong's tomb of the Eastern Wei Dynasty, excavated at Zanhuang County, Hebei province, a gold ring had a bezel engraved with a deer surroundedby a pearl roundel pattern. Similar gold rings were discovered in Bikeqi Town, Tumote Right Banner, Inner Mongolia and in Li Xian's tomb, Northern Zhou. Blue gemstones were found on a necklace discovered in Li Jingxun's tomb of the Sui Dynasty in Xi'an.

Brief Description of the Object: engraved ring bezel (?) showing a reclining lion in front of a vegetal element, with a Middle Persian inscription around the edge.

Material, Technique and Conservation: "Nicolo (Onyx)" single crystal quartz with silica content as high as 99.51% (analysis by the Central Laboratory of Shanxi Province of department of Geology and Mineral Resource); light blue thin surface over black layer. Complete.

Measurements: diameter 1.6cm; thickness 0.6cm.

Detailed Description of the Object: The gem has circular shape and flat engraved surface with chamfered edge; protruding bottom (?).

Detailed Description of the Iconography: on the engraved face is a reclining lion, body in profile to right, head frontal, paws stretching forwards; behind him, three straight branches bearing a tulip flower or pomegranate fruit each, stemming from a central branch. All round the edge, Middle Persian engraved inscription starting from 3 o'clock, read by Lin Meicun as "freedom, prosperity, happiness" (Lin 1997, 171) and by P.O. Skjærvø as "generosity, generosity, generosity" (Juliano and Lerner 2001, 260, no 6).

Stylistic Analysis: the seal is in fairly high relief and

---

and 30. E.52, pl. XX）。同样的图样也被压印在了一块泥土上（Gyselen 1993: 224, no.30. B.1, fig.224）。

　　狮子的形象可以与法国国家图书馆收藏的一些印章相比较，特别是与一枚印章有着爪子伸展、鬃毛和右前爪垂直的共同特征（Gyselen 1993: 112, 30. E.35, pl. XIX），这也见于巴基斯坦白沙瓦博物馆的一枚印章（Callieri 1997: 66, no.Cat 2.27），大英博物馆被认为是4到6世纪的两枚印章（Bivar 1969: 69, nos. 119772 and 119756, DA 5 and DA 6, pl. 9），以及私人收藏的一枚印章（Gignoux & Gyselen 1982: 89, pl. XIII, no.30.10）。总体上看，蹲伏的狮子形象在印章上很常见（Gyselen 1993: 224）。类似的在展开的枝干上带有石榴花果的图像，也见于这些印章上（Gyselen 1993: 154, nos. 50. A.15–50. A.20, pl. XLI），被解释为一种三瓣花。狮子形象是高级官员和贵族的常用纹样（Gyselen 2007: 65–66）。关于萨珊艺术中狮子形象的概况，可参考Brunner 1978: 94–96。因此该印章很可能制作于伊朗萨珊时期，但不同于大多数萨珊印章的形制，可能产于伊朗王朝的最东省份。

the execution of both finish and details quite careful. The treatment is schematic; the body is rendered with three deep globular segments, the mane with a vertical hatching, as is the right front paw.

Comparing and Geographical, Cultural and Chronological Attribution: the iconographic scheme can be compared with that on two Sasanian seals in the Bibliothèque Nationale, Paris, where however the base of the tree is visible below the lion's body, and where the tree has different leaves (Gyselen 1993, 112–13, nos 30. E.45 and 30. E.52, pl. XX); also on a clay sealing from the same collection, an impression with the same motif is present (Gyselen 1993, 224, no 30. B.1, fig.224). The lion image can be compared with those on several Sasanian seals in the Bibliothèque Nationale, Paris, particularly with one sharing the stretched paws and the hatching of the mane and right front paw (Gyselen 1993, 112, 30. E.35, pl. XIX); with one seal in the Peshawar Museum (Callieri 1997, 66, no Cat. 2. 27), with two seals in the British Museum dated to the 6th and 4th centuries respectively (Bivar 1969, 69, nos 119772 and 119756, DA 5 and DA 6, pl. 9), and with one in a private collection (Gignoux and Gyselen 1982, 89, pl. XIII, no 30.10). Crouching lion is on the whole quite frequently seen on clay sealings (Gyselen 1993, 224). Similar vegetal motifs of a pomegranate flower or fruit, above open wings, are present on several seals (Gyselen 1993, 154, nos 50. A.15–50. A.20, pl. XLI): here they are interpreted as three-petalled flowers. The lion motif appears as one of the motifs used by high-rank state officials and dignitaries (Gyselen 2007, 65–66). For the lion motif in general in Sasanian art, see Brunner 1978, 94–96. On these bases, the seal could be attributed to the seal production of Sasanian Iran. Its shape, however, is different from the most common shapes of Sasanian seals, and could point to a provincial origin in the easternmost provinces of the Sasanian Empire.

参考文献　References

1. Brunner, C.J. (1978) *Sasanian Stamp Seals in the Metropolitan Museum of Art*, New York.

2. Callieri, P. (1997) *Seals and Sealings from the North-West of the Indian Subcontinent and Afghanistan (4th century BC–11th century AD)*: *Local, Indian, Sasanian, Graeco-Persian, Sogdian, Roman*. With contributions by E. Errington, R. Garbini, Ph. Gignoux, N. Sims-Williams, W. Zwalf (Istituto Universitario Orientale, Dissertationes I), Naples.

3. Gignoux, Ph. and Gyselen, R. (1982) *Sceaux Sassanides de Diverses Collections Privées* (Cahiers de *Studia iranica*, 1), Paris.

4. 固原博物馆、原州中日联合考古队：《固原古墓集成》，文物出版社（北京），1999年，图版122。
Guyuan Museum, Yuanzhou Archaeological Joint Group (China-Japan) (1999) *Collection of the Ancient Tombs in Yuanzhou*, Cultural Relics Publishing House, no. 122, Beijing.

5. Gyselen, R. (1993) *Catalogue des Sceaux, Camées et Bulles Sasanides. I. Collection Générale*, Paris.

6. Gyselen, R. (2007) *Sasanian Seals and Sealings in the A. Saeedi Collection* (Acta Iranica, 44), Lovanii.

7. Juliano, A.L. and Lerner, J.A. (2001) *Monks and Merchants. Silk Road Treasures from Northwest China. Gansu and Ningxia, 4th–7th Century*, Catalogue of the Exhibition, Asia Society Museum, (in part. 260, no 86), New York.

8. 林梅村：《固原粟特墓所出中古波斯文印章及其相关问题》，《考古与文物》1997年第1期，页48—52。
Lin Meicun (1997) A Middle Persian Seal from the Sogdian Tomb in Guyuan, Ningxia and the Related Problems, *Kaogu yu Wenwu (Archaeology and Cultural Relics)*, 1, 48–52, Xi'an.

9. 罗丰编著：《固原南郊隋唐墓地》，文物出版社（北京），1996年，页240—247。
Luo Feng (1996) *Graveyard of Sui and Tang Dynasties in the South Suburbs of Guyuan*, Cultural Relics Publishing House, 240–247, Beijing.

（*Pierfrancesco Callieri*，耿朔 [*Geng Shuo*]，范佳楠 [*Fan Jianan*]）

40. 鎏金铜覆面

收藏单位：宁夏固原博物馆。

出土信息：这套覆面出土于史道德墓中，史道德墓是固原南郊墓地发现的八座墓葬之一，其概况见上文（No.39），据发掘者研究，史氏家族在原州势力强大，多为中级官员。该墓发掘于1982年，是一座长斜坡墓道带七天井的单室土洞墓。墓葬被严重盗掘，随葬品多已不在原位，在近墓门处发现墓主头骨，口含一枚金币，面部原有鎏金铜覆面一具，连缀覆面的丝织物已经腐朽，因后世扰乱，多不在原位。根据共出的墓志记载，墓主史道德生前是一位主管马政的低级官员（牧监监正），葬于公元678年（仪凤三年）。

器物概括描述：鎏金铜覆面共包括11部分。

材质、工艺及保存状况：以鎏金铜片制成。

尺寸：

护额饰一件，圆形直径1.9、半月形直径3、长条残长5、宽1.2厘米。

护眉饰两件，其中一件长5.9、宽1厘米，另一件长4.5、宽0.9厘米。

护眼饰两件，其中一件长4.3、宽2、孔径1厘米，另一件长3.9、宽1.9、孔径1厘米。

护鼻饰一件，残长6.3、中宽1.6、下宽2.5、高1.5厘米。

护唇两件，其中一件长4.4、宽1.2厘米，另一件长4、宽1.1厘米。

护颌饰一件，两侧长17.3、宽1.4厘米。长8.4、宽4.5厘米。

40. Gilt Bronze Mask

Location: Guyuan Museum.

Context of Origin: this whole suit of gilt bronze mask was excavated from Shi Daode's tomb, one of the eight tombs in the Sui-Tang cemetery of Guyuan Southern Suburbs, which has already been surveyed in the aftermentioned object (no 39 Blue ground gem seal). Based on epigraphs and further research, the family of Shi enjoyed powerful status in Yuanzhou (Guyuan, Ningxia province) with lots of family members serving as mid-level officials. Based on the studies of epigraphs of all the members of Family Shi, Luo feng and other scholars believe this family immigrated into northwest China from Shahrisabz in the end of 5th century AD. Excavated in 1982, the tomb was a single-chamber earth-made one jointing a long sloping tomb path with 7 vertical airshafts. Unfortunately it has been badly robbed and most of its burial objects were not in their original positions. The skull of the deceased was found near the entrance of the tomb chamber with a gold coin in his mouth. The face part was covered with a suit of gilt bronze mask which was supposed to be fastened together by silk fabrics. However due to the decay process and robbery, most parts of the mask were not in place. As mentioned in his epigraph found in the level corridor, Shi Daode was a low-ranking official in charge of horsing administration before his death and was buried in 678 AD.

Brief Description of the Object: gilt bronze mask consisting of 11 parts.

Material, Technique and Conservation: Gilt bronze foils.

Measurements:

Forehead cover: length 5cm, width 1.2cm; upper part diameter 3cm; rounded raise diameter 1.9.

Eyebrows covers: 2 pieces: A: length 5.9cm, width 1cm;

B: length 4.5cm, width 0.9cm.

Eyes covers: 2 pieces; A: length 4.3cm; width 2cm,

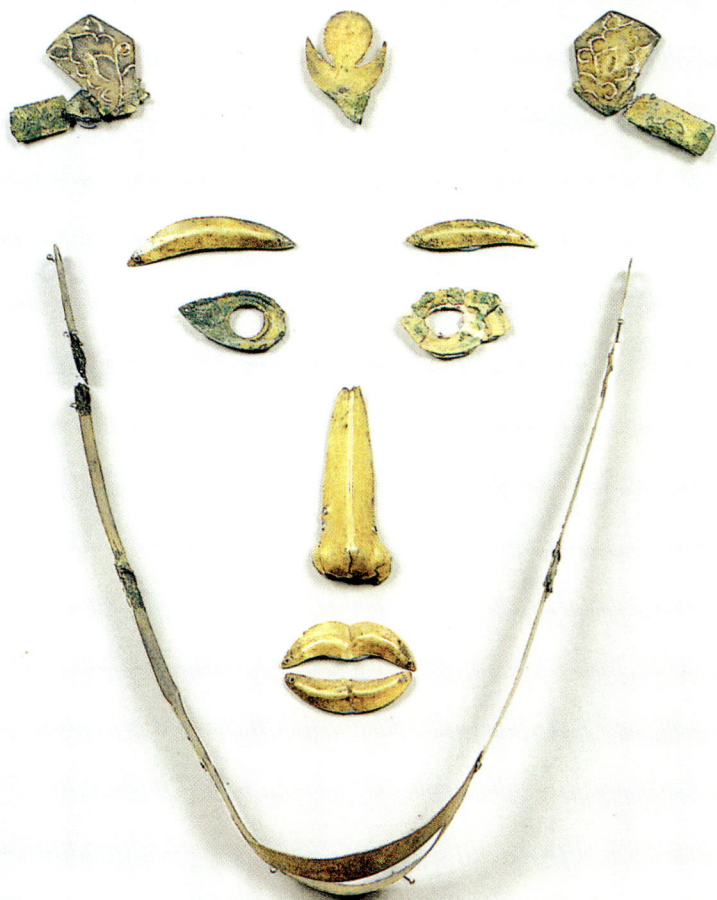

40. 鎏金铜覆面 Gilt Bronze Mask

护鬓饰两件，一件残长5.1、宽3.8厘米，另一件残长4.8、宽4厘米。

器物详细描述：

护额饰一件，下部为一长条形薄片，两端均残，右侧缺。其上为一半月形，半月间托一圆形。下端有一穿孔。

护眉饰两件，形似柳叶，上凸下凹，两端尖

Circular hole diameter 1cm; B: length 3.9cm; width 1.9cm; Circular hole diameter 1cm.

Nose cover: 1 piece, length. 6.3cm, middle part width 1.6cm, bottom width 2.5cm, height 1.5cm.

Lips covers: 2 pieces, A: length 4.4cm, width 1.2cm; B: length 4cm, width 1.1cm.

Jaw cover: 1 piece, each side there is an elongated flank, length 17.3cm; width 1.4cm; the middle has a length of 8.4cm, and a width of 4.5cm.

弯，各有一穿孔。

护眼饰两件，均为鎏金铜片打制，已有锈蚀，左眼稍残。上有圆孔，孔边及边缘均起凸棱。端部有一穿孔。

护鼻饰一件，形似鼻状，上端稍残，有一圆孔。中部起脊，较平直，背面凹下，下端有两孔，两侧有斜对三穿孔。

护唇两件，合起之后形似上下嘴唇，表面稍鼓，背凹，两端稍尖，端有两孔。

护颌饰一件，两侧为长条形，上端呈圆形，有一穿孔。每侧由三节铆接而成，上两节有四叶状铆片，四叶间各有一枚铆钉，下端则由两铆钉直接铆制。中部形似枣核。

护鬓饰两件，形制相同，均稍有残缺。下有一长条形扁片，上焊接一长方形片饰，一角削去，上锤揲突起叶纹。

风格分析： 赵超认为覆面中由日、月图形组成的额饰，可能是摩尼教徒的信仰标志。以罗丰为代表的发掘者认为覆面表现出某些中亚、西亚的风格，而其中的额饰应当与中亚、西亚人崇拜日月的习俗相关。具体说来，应是祆教信仰的产物。

Sidebums covers: 2 pieces, A: length 5.1cm; width 3.8cm; B: length 4.8cm, width 4cm.

Detailed Description of the Object:

Forehead cover: 1 piece, the lower part is an elongated foil which remains fragmentary. The upper part is made into a half-moon-shape with a roundel raised in the middle and a small punch in the bottom.

Eyebrows covers: they share similarity in form with arched willow leaves, and each have a raised top and a concave bottom with two punched ends.

Eyes covers: they are eye-shaped with convex ribs on the edge and punches at the end. Both are made of gilt copper which have been rusted by now, especially the left eye one. On each of them there is a circular hole with convex ribs on the edge.

Nose cover: nose shape with the upper end damaged a little and remaining a little circular hole. The flat middle part is ridged and its back concaved. The lower part has two holes at bottom and three punches on both sides.

Lips covers: two pieces form a lip shape with slightly convex surface and concave back and two punches at the end.

Jaw Cover: its upper end is circular with a punch. Each flank is riveted together by three smaller ones and the upper two have four-foiled riveting slice with a rivet in the middle. The lower one is directly jointed together by two rivets. The middle part resembles jujube pit in shape.

Sidebums covers: both pieces are incomplete but share similarities in shape and structure. The lower part is an elongated flank with an irregular pentagon welded on it. The pentagon is decorated with hammering convex leaf pattern.

Stylistic Analysis: Zhao Chao believed that the pattern of the forehead cover represents the sun and the moon, which were probably Manichean symbols. As the leader of excavators, Luo Feng suggested that the gold mask shows some Central and West Asian style factors and the forehead cover should have something to do with the worship of sun and moon in Central and West Asia. Specifically speaking, it was the product of Zoroastrian belief.

地域、文化、年代属性及对比：类似的例子见于参考文献3的图录及相关书目；亦见于吉尔吉斯斯坦匈人时期的发现（PKK 1983; Genito a cura di, 2002），伊朗西部卢里斯坦（Luristan）的Kalmakareh也有类似发现，但时代偏早，属于公元前1千纪中叶。

Comparing and Geographical, Cultural and Chronological Attribution: similar example are the one in this catalogue (*infra* no 3 and the related bibliography), two examples from Kirghisistan (PKK 1983; Genito, a cura di, 2002) of Hun period, and also in Iran (Catalogue of the Selective Exhibition 2005) from Kalmakareh, Luristan, mostly probably more earlier dating back to the middle of the 1st millennium BC.

参考文献　References

1. Catalogue of the Selective (2005) *Catalogue of the Selective Exhibition of the Golden and Silver Objects in the National Museum of Iran*, 35, Teheran.

2. Genito, B. (a cura di) (2002) *Pastori erranti dell'Asia, popoli storia e archeologia nelle steppe dei Kirghisi*, Museo Nazionale Archeologico (3 maggio-31-agosto) 109–110, fig.41, 116–118, fig.62. Napoli.

3. Juliano, A.L. and Lerner, J.A. (2001) *Monks and Merchants: Silk Road Treasures from Northwest China. Gansu and Ningxia, 4th–7th Century*, 101, Catalogue of the Exhibition, Asia Society Museum, New York.

4. 罗丰：《也谈史道德族属及相关问题》，《文物》1988年第8期，页92—94。
   Luo Feng (1988) New studies about Shi Daode's nationality and other questions, *Wenwu (Cultural Relics)*, 8, 92–94, Beijing.

5. 罗丰编著：《固原南郊隋唐墓地》，文物出版社（北京），1996年，页87—96。
   Luo Feng (1996) *Graveyard of Sui and Tang Dynasties in the South Suburbs of Guyuan*, Cultural Relics Publishing House, 87–96, Beijing.

6. PKK (1983) *Pamjatniki Kul'tury i iskustva Kirgizii*. Katalog Vystavky, no 141, 46.

7. 赵超：《对史道德墓志及其族属的一点看法》，《文物》1986年第12期，页87—89。
   Zhao Chao (1986) My Perspective toward Shi Daode's Epigraph and his Nationality, *Wenwu (Cultural Relics)*, 12, 87–89, Beijing.

（*Bruno Genito*，李雨生 [*Li Yusheng*]，童歆 [*Tong Xin*]）

41. 铜壶

收藏单位：陕西临潼博物馆。

出土信息：出土于陕西省临潼庆山寺舍利塔基地宫。

器物概括描述：铜壶，腹部装饰外国人脸。

材质、工艺及保存状况：青铜，出土时，器、足分离，壶底有修理痕迹。

尺寸：高29.5、最大腹径14、口径4—6、圈足直径8厘米。

器物详细描述：铜壶细长的颈部有三道凸弦纹，壶口呈凤首形，龙柄，高圈足外侈，器身被模铸成6个高浮雕人头，这些人头均大眼，弯眉，高直鼻，小嘴。中分的发型彼此相接，将6个人头连起来，两两之间垂下三节状的发辫，这些特征似都在表现印度人的面部形象。卡尔·迈克尔森（1999, cat. 103）认为铜壶上的人脸与巴基斯坦信德（Sind）省Brahminabad发现的属于8世纪的象牙雕像类似（参见British Museum藏品，馆藏号1857.11–18.1,4,6）；铜壶的形状是唐代中亚地区广泛流行的凤首壶（在中国和其他国家的博物馆中有许多例子），弯曲优雅的把手则反映出萨珊和早期伊斯兰造型的影响（例如埃米尔塔什博物馆中被定为6—7世纪的Perm地区银壶以及维多利亚和阿尔伯特博物馆中收集自呼罗珊地区的铜壶（馆藏号434–1906），还有大英博物馆中被定为8—9世纪的铜壶（馆藏号1959.10–23.1）），类似的发现在马尔沙克发表的粟特容器中也可以见到（1971, T7–T8; T22）。

41. Bronze Ewer

Location: Lintong Museum.

Context of origin: from the crypt at the base of the pagoda in the Qingshan Monastery, Xinfeng town, Lintong county, Shaanxi province.

Brief description of the object: ewer decorated with human foreign faces.

Material, technique and conservation: bronze; When it was excavated, the foot ring and the body of the ewer had become separated and the bottom of the ewer had several repair marks.

Measurements: 29.5 × 14cm; diameter of the mouth 4–6cm; diameter of the foot 8cm.

Detailed description of the object: this ewer has a long slender neck with three raised rings halfway up. The mouth is shaped like a phoenix head and there is an elegant coiled 'dragon' handle on one side. The ewer has a spreading foot and the body is composed of six human heads in high relief. Their faces are round, with large eyes and curved eyebrows that lead into long, straight, high-bridged noses protruding over small mouths. The loops of the centrally parted hairstyles link the heads, with small buns in between each. All features are strongly suggestive of Indian faces. Carol Michaelson (1999, cat. 103) has suggested that the faces are similar to those on ivory figures from Brahminabad, Sind which are datable to the 8th century (British Museum, inv. 1857.11–18.1, 4, 6). The shape of the object is reminiscent of the phoenix-headed ewers from Central Asia that were so popular during the Tang dynasty (examples of which can be found in many museums in China and elsewhere) while the sinuous handle recalls Sasanian and Early Islamic models (see, for example, the silver ewer from Perm dating to the 6th-early 7th century now in the Hermitage Museum or the bronze ewer from Khorasan province in the Victoria and Albert Museum, (inv. 434–1906); see also the bronze ewer dating to the 8th–9th century in the British

41. 铜壶 Bronze Ewer

风格分析： 铜壶的形状及腹部所表现的人脸都暗示出这是一件来自西方，很可能是中亚、伊朗或者印度的外来物品。结合铜壶出于庆山寺地宫以及铜壶腹部所表现的典型的印度人的面部特征可以推测，这件铜壶很可能是由印度入华的佛教朝圣者或旅行者带回。

地域、文化、年代属性及对比： 伊朗或北印度；7世纪末（据舍利塔记在741年之前），类似的发现可以在大英博物馆、维多利亚和阿尔伯特博物馆以及埃米尔塔什博物馆中见到，具体情况已如前述。

Museum, inv. 1959.10–23.1). Other affinities can be found with the Sogdian vessels published by Marshak (1971, T7–T8; T22).

Stylistic analysis: the non-Chinese shape of the jug, together with the human heads depicted on it, suggest that it was an import from the West, possibly from Central Asia, Iran or India. The finding spot, the crypt of the Qingshan Monastery, together with the *Indian look* of the ewer suggest that it could be brought from India by a Buddhist pilgrim or traveler.

Comparing and geographical, cultural and chronological attribution: Iran or Northern India; end of the 7th century (ante 741 AD). Comparable objects from Iran and Central Asia can be found in the collections of the British Museum, of the Victoria and Albert Museum, of the Hermitage Museum as in the following texts.

参考文献　References

1. Barrett, D. (1955) A Group of Medieval Indian Ivories, *Oriental Art*, 1, 2, London.

2. 葛承雍：《唐长安印度人之研究》，《唐韵胡音与外来文明》，中华书局，2006年，112—129页。
   Ge Chengyong (2006) The Tang Chang'an Indians, *Tangyun huyin yu wailai wenming* (*Tang Yun Hu Tone with Alien Civilization*), Zhonghua Book Company, 112–129, Beijing.

3. Kuhn, D. (ed.) (1993) *Chinas Goldenes Zeitalter: Die Tang Dynastie (618–907 n.Chr.) und das kulturelle Erbe der Seidenstraße*, Nr. 93, Heidelberg.

4. 临潼县博物馆：《临潼唐庆山寺舍利塔基精室清理记》，《文博》1985年第5期，页12—37及图版叁、肆、彩版。
   Lintong County Museum (1985) Brief Report of the Excavation of Sarira Crypt of Qingshan Buddhist Temple, Lintong, *Wenbo* (*Relics and Museolgy*), 5, 12–37 and Plate Triple IV color version, Xi'an.

5. Maršak, B.I. (1971) *Sogdiiskoe serebro. Očerki po vostočnoj torevtike* (Moskva: Izd-vo "Nauka" : Gl. red. vostočn. lit-ry).

6. Melikian-Chirvani, A.S. (1982) *Islamic Metalwork from the Iranian World*, London.

7. Michaelson, C. (1999) *Gilded Dragons*, no. 103, London.

8. Rastelli, S. (2008) *Cina: alla Corte degli Imperatori. Capolavori mai visti*, dalla tradizione Han all'eleganza Tang (25–907), no. 47, Milano.

9. Smirnov, Ja.I. (ed.) (1909) *Vostočnoe serebro. Atlas drevnej serebrjanoj i zolotoj posudy vostočnogo proishoždenija, naidennoj preimuščestvenno v predelah Rossiiskoj imperii. Izdanie Imperatorskoj Arheologičeskoj Kommissii ko dniu piatidesiatiletija eja dejatel'nosti*, Saint Petersburg.

10. Tokyo National Museum (1998) *The Glory of the Court: Tang Dynasty Empress Wu and Her Times*, no. 42,

Tokyo.

11. Ward, R. (1993) *Islamic Metalwork*, London.

12. Whitfield, R. (1999) Bronze Ewer, Xiaoneng Yang (ed.) *The Golden Age of Chinese Archaeology: Celebrated Discoveries from the People's Republic of China*, no 169, 486–487. Yale University Press, New Haven.

13. Whitfield, R. (2008) Brocca con facce esotiche, Rastelli, S. (a cura di) *Il Celeste Impero dall'Esercito di Terracotta alla via della Seta*, n. 76, 184–185, 285. Skira, Milano, Italy.

14. Yang Xiaoneng (ed.) (1999) *The Golden Age of Chinese Archaeology: Celebrated Discoveries from the People's Republic of China*, no 169. New Haven.

15. 徐苹芳:《考古学上所见中国境内的丝绸之路》,《十世纪前的丝绸之路和东西文化交流》, 新世界出版社 (北京), 1996年, 页244。

Xu Pingfang (1996) An Archaeological View of the Silk Road in China, *Land Routes of the Silk Roads and the Cultural Exchanges between East and West before the 10th Century*, New World Press, 244, Beijing.

(*Chiara Visconti*, 李雨生 [*Li Yusheng*])

42. 玻璃瓶

收藏单位：陕西临潼博物馆。

出土信息：出土于陕西省临潼庆山寺舍利塔地宫。

器物概括描述：球腹束颈小瓶。

材质、工艺及保存状况：半透明状黑褐色吹制玻璃瓶，瓶身装饰出圆环及之字形玻璃条纹。

尺寸：口径3.9、底径3、高7厘米。

42. Glass Bottle

Location: Lintong Museum.

Context of Origin: from the crypt at the base of the pagoda in the Qingshan Monastery, Xinfeng town, Lintong county, Shaanxi province.

Brief Description of the Object: small globular necked bottle.

Material, Technique and Conservation: translucent brownish colored blown glass with applied decoration constituted by circular and zig-zag lines.

Measurements: opening diameter 3.9cm; bottom diameter 3cm; height 7cm.

42. 玻璃瓶 Glass Bottle

地域、文化、年代属性及对比：齐东方（2006）认为这件玻璃瓶是西亚输入的萨珊器物。同时地宫中出土的2件带铜质莲花座的绿色玻璃瓶和玻璃球应该属于中国本土制造。阿卜杜拉·马文宽（2006）指出在伦敦的维多利亚和阿尔伯特博物馆中有一件类似藏品，以前认为这种玻璃瓶属于罗马晚期，但庆山寺塔基封闭年代为741年，据此可知这种风格的玻璃器应延续到伊斯兰时期。这件玻璃瓶是中国发现最早的伊斯兰玻璃。这种器形和装饰的瓶子广泛发现于伊朗和伊斯兰世界，包括主要的玻璃产地如伊朗、叙利亚、埃及等。

Comparing and Geographical, Cultural and Chronological Attribution: Qi Dongfang believed this glass bottle, which had a Sasanian style, was imported from the western Asia, but the other glass objects unearthed from the underground palace should be made in China. Abdullah Ma Wenkuan pointed out that there is a glass bottle, which is collected in the Victoria and Albert Museum similar to this one. In the past, glass bottles like this kind were dated to later period of Roman Empire, but the underground palace of Qingshan Temple wassealed at 741 AD which means glass bottles like this style were stillpopular in Islamic period. He thought the bottle has been the earliest Islamic glass in China so far. The morphology and the typology and the decoration as well is widespread over the Iranian and Islamic world, including the areas of the main glass production centers, Iran, Syria, Egypt etc.

参考文献　References

1. 齐东方：《唐代玻璃及其西来东传》，《西域文史》第一辑，科学出版社（北京），2006年，页27—47。
   Qi Dongfang (2006) Tang Glass and its West to East Biography, *Western Literature and History*, first series, 27–47, Science Press, Beijing.

2. 阿卜杜拉·马文宽：《伊斯兰世界文物在中国的发现与研究》，宗教文化出版社（北京），2006年，页3—4。
   Ma Wenkuan, Abdullah (2006) *Discoveries and Studies of Islamic Cultural Relics in China*, Religion and Culture Publishing House, 3–4, Beijing.

3. Lane, A. (1937) Medieval finds at Al Mina in North Syria, *Archaeologia*, 87, 19–78, pl. 28, 3.

(*Bruno Genito*，李雨生 [*Li Yusheng*])

43. 银带把杯

收藏单位：陕西历史博物馆。

出土信息：何家村唐代窖藏出土。1970年10月在西安市南郊何家村一个基建工地发现了两个陶瓮和一件银提梁罐，位于唐代长安城的兴化坊。该窖藏出土了1000多件各种文物，包括各种金银器、玉器、铜器，中外钱币，还有银锭、银饼、银板以及其他珍贵的宝石和药材。69件器物上带有墨书文字，表明存放物品的名称以及器物自身或器物的重量。钱币有39种466枚。这个窖藏的文物数量极大、品种极多、工艺极精，反映了唐代高超的工艺技术和社会经济文化标准。一些器物被认为来自萨珊波斯、东罗马、粟特和日本等地，如粟特输入的罐形带把银杯，西亚的兽首玛瑙杯、凸纹玻璃杯，罗马风格的狩猎纹高足银杯，萨珊银币、拜占庭金币，日本和同开珎。带有粟特风格的人物忍冬纹八棱金带把杯、伎乐纹银杯、鎏金伎乐纹八棱金杯，其厚重的器体和工艺上的一些做法又不同于粟特本土的制品，很可能是生活在唐朝境内的粟特工匠所作。还有一些器物，则可能是中国工匠对异域文化的吸收、改造和创新，如仿照萨珊多曲长杯制作的白玉忍冬纹八曲长杯、水晶八曲长杯，保留粟特带把杯遗风的鎏金仕女狩猎纹八瓣银杯等。

器物概括描述：带把杯。

材质、工艺及保存状况：银质。

尺寸：高9.9、口径9、足径7.1厘米，重395克。

器物详细描述：银杯有着简洁的球形杯

43. Silver Cup

Location: Shaanxi History Museum.

Context of Origin: Hejiacun hoard; in October 1970, two pottery urns and a silver handled pot were unearthed during an infrastructure construction at Hejiacun Village, in the southern suburbs of Xi'an, where the Xinghua place of Changan during the Tang Dynasty had been located. The hoard consisted of two pottery urns and a silver jug containing more than 1000 silver and gold ware, as well as jade and copper items, ancient Chinese and foreign coins, silver ingots and lumps, plates and other precious stones and medicine; inscriptions were found in 69 items, indicating their name and their weight. The 466 coins belong to 39 different types. Number, variety and workmanship are impressive, a reflection of the high technical and artistic skills of the Tang Dynasty and of the economic and cultural social standards. Some of these artifacts are thought to be imports from Sasanian Persia, the Byzantine Empire, Sogdiana and Japan; for instance, a silver cup with handle comes from Sogdiana, an agate rhyton and glass cup come from western Asia; there are a Roman-style silver stem cup with hunting patterns, Sasanian silver coins, the Byzantine gold coins and a Japanese Wado Kaichin silver coin. Compared with the original Sogdian models, the artifacts with Sogdian features in this hoard — such as the gilt silver cup with handle, the gold cup with handle and musician patterns, and the gilded cup with handle and musician patterns — reveal differences in manufacturing techniques and in their heavier bodies, suggesting that these artifacts might have been made by a Sogdian craftsman living in Tang China; or else, they may have been made by a Chinese craftsman who inherited and developed techniques from foreign lands — as in the case of the white jade lobed elliptical bowl with honeysuckle pattern, and the crystal lobed ellipticalbowl after a Sasanian model; or the gilt silver cup with handle

43. 银带把杯 Silver Cup

身，束颈、侈口、圜底、圈足，肩部下方焊接环形
把手，手指要靠把上的尖叶状的指垫和下方的
指扳才能握住银杯。器物内壁有旋纹。圈足内
部有直行墨书题记，可能标明器物重量。

地域、文化、年代属性及对比：可以将这
件杯子与粟特及伊斯兰早期的一种银容器（7
至9世纪）在形制和装饰方面作比较（Maršak
1971, figs.22, 23, 25），不过很难断定它是粟特
地区的产品，还是中国工匠的仿制品，时代在7
至9世纪。

which continues the Sogdian tradition of vessels with a handle.

Brief Description of the Object: cup with handle.
Material, Technique and Conservation: silver.
Measurements: height, 9.9cm; mouth diameter, 9cm. base diameter 7.1cm; weight, 395g.

Detailed Description of the Object: silver cup with plain globular body, reduced neck, flaring rim, round base, ring foot, ring handle welded below the shoulder, with fingersrest in the shape of a cusped leaf and finger spanner. The inner face is decorated with a spiral pattern; on the foot, a columnar inscription probably indicating the weight.

何家村遗宝是中国考古史上最重要的发现之一，但这批财宝的主人及埋藏原因仍然有待于进一步探索。通过该窖藏出土的一些器物上的雕刻，金银器上的波状图案以及中外钱币，发掘者（1972）认为何家村遗宝的时代不晚于"盛唐"晚期（约8世纪末期）；根据发现文物的地点，参照唐长安城布局的有关研究，发掘者（1972）判断在兴化坊内，初步认定是在《两京新记》所记载的邠王府内。通过对何家村出土金银器装饰纹样的研究，段鹏琦（1980）认为其年代下限为德宗时期（779–805），并认为何家村遗宝的埋葬地点不在邠王府内。韩伟（1985）认为何家村窖藏的金银器年代不晚于安史之乱爆发伊始（756），这也代表了他对何家村窖藏年代的判断。齐东方（2003）认为何家村遗宝应属于唐代尚书租庸使刘震，窖藏埋藏年代应为泾原兵变时（783）。韩建武（2007）指出何家村窖藏中的金银器包括外国器物、地方官府贡奉品、中央和地方官营作坊生产的产品，窖藏中还存在未完成品和金银器部件，认为何家村窖藏可能是皇家窖藏。

Comparing and Geographical, Cultural and Chronological Attribution: the cup can be compared to silver vessels, both plain and decorated, well attested in the Sogdian pre-Islamic and early Islamic production (7th–9th centuries) (Maršak 1971, figs.22, 23, 25). Nevertheless it is difficult to establish whether this specimen is a Sogdian work or a Chinese copy inspired to Sogdian models. 7th–9th centuries.

The treasure of Hejiacun is one of the major finds in the history of the Chinese Archaeology. Nevertheless, the definite conclusion about who was the owner of the workshop about the reason for which the hoard was buried remains unclear, and needs for further exploration. Judging from the carvings on some of the objects, wavy patterns on the gold and silver wares, and Chinese and foreign coins discovered at the site, the excavators (1972) believes that the Hejiacun treasures date back to no later than 8th century AD. Based on research about about the layout of Chang'an, these artifacts are preliminarily considered to belong to Fenwang Palace in Xinhua. Based on the research of the decorative patterns of Hejiacun's gold and silver wares, Duan Pengqi (1980) thinks of the one that was latest prevalent in the period of De Zong (779–805 AD). According to his opinion, these artifacts were not buried within Fenwang Palace. Han Wei (1985) suggests Hejiacun's gold and silver wares date back to no later than the An-Shi Rebellion (756 AD). The same conclusion stands for to the time when the Hejiacuntreasures were buried. Qi Dongfang (2003) argues that this treasure belongs to Liu Zhen, the FinanceMinister of Tang Dynasty, buried during the Jing Yuan Mutiny time in 783 AD. Han Jianwu (2007) points out that Hejiacun's gold and silver wares include imports, tributes from local offices, products made in some workshops of both local and central government. Some unfinished products and parts of gold and silver wares were also found. The Hejiacun treasures could possibly be a royal hoard.

参考文献　References

1. 程旭:《朝贡・贸易・战争・礼物——何家村唐代金银器再解读》,《文博》2011年第1期,页42—48。
   Cheng Xu (2011) Envoy, Trade, Warfare, Gift. A Reinterpretation of the Tang Dynasty Gold and Silver Wares from the Hejiacun Hoard, *Wenbo (Relics and Museology)*, 1, 42–48, Xi'an.

2. 段鹏琦:《西安南郊何家村唐代金银器小议》,《考古》(北京),1980年第6期,页636—541。
   Duan Pengqi (1980) Research on Gold-Silver Ware in Tang Dynasty from Hejiacun, Xi'an, *Kaogu (Archaeology)*, 6, 536–541, Beijing.

3. 韩建武:《西安何家村唐代窖藏几个问题的再探讨》,《收藏家》2007年第7期,页39—44。
   Han Jianwu (2007) Further Discussion on the Tang Dynasty Hoard Discovered in Xi'an, *Shoucangjia (Collectors)*, 7, 39–44, Beijing.

4. 韩伟、陆九皋:《唐代金银器概述》,载镇江市博物馆、陕西省博物馆主编:《唐代金银器》,文物出版社(北京),1985年,页1—19。
   Han Wei, Lu Jiugao (1985) Overview on Gold and Silver Ware in Tang Dynasty,Zhenjiang Museum and Shaanxi Museum (eds.) *Tangdai jinyinqi(Gold and Silver in Tang Dynasty)*, Cultural Relics Publishing House, 1–19, Beijing.

5. Li Jian (ed.) (2003) *The Glory of the Silk Road. Art from Ancient China*, 193, no 103, Plain City (OH).

6. Maršak, B. (1971) *Sogdijskoe serebro*, Moskva.

7. 齐东方:《何家村遗宝的埋藏地点和年代》,《考古与文物》2003年第2期,页70—74。
   Qi Dongfang (2003) The Burial Location and Dating of the Hejia Village Treasures, *Kaogu yu wenwu (Archaeology and Cultural Relics)*, 2, 70–74, Xi'an.

8. 陕西省博物馆革委会写作小组等:《西安南郊何家村发现唐代窖藏文物》,《文物》1972年第1期,页30—42。
   Shaanxi History Museum *et alii* (1972) Excavation of a Hoard at Hejiacun in the Southern Suburbs of Xi'an, *Wenwu (Cultural Relics)*, 1, 30–42, Beijing.

9. 沈睿文:《素面罐形带把杯》,载《花舞大唐春:何家村遗宝精粹》,文物出版社(北京),2003年,页86—88,第6号器物。
   Shen Ruiwen (2003) Silver Cup with Handle, in Shaanxi History Museum *et alii* (eds.) *Huawu datangchun: Hejiacun yibao jingcui (Selected Treasures from Hejiacun Tang Hoard)*, Cultural Relics Publishing House, 86–88, no. 6, Beijing.

(*Ciro Lo Muzio*,耿朔 [*Geng Shuo*])

44. 玻璃杯

收藏单位：陕西历史博物馆。

出土信息：何家村窖藏。

器物概括概述：稍泛黄绿色，透明度较高。杯子有着圆形口沿，斜直内收的器身以及平底。口沿外翻成圆唇，其下方装饰一周凸弦纹，器身外壁有八组上下相连的凸起圆环纹。

材质、工艺及保存状况：玻璃质，透明。

44. Glass Cup

Location: Shaanxi History Museum.

Context of Origin: Hejiacun hoard.

Brief Description of the Object: light yellowish green glass, presenting a high degree of transparency. The cup has rounded mouth rim, straight sloping body, and flat base. The mouth rim projects as to form a circular decoration, under which is applied a string decoration circling the cup. The middle of the body is decorated with eight groups of applied ring decoration.

Material, Technique and Conservation: glass, transparency.

44. 玻璃杯 Glass Cup

尺寸：高9.7、口径14.3、底径10.3厘米。

地域、文化、年代属性及对比：安家瑶（1984）认为这件玻璃杯吹制成型，在器壁上用热玻璃条缠出环纹做为装饰，这种技术在罗马时代出现，萨珊玻璃工匠继承和发展了这一技术。可能来自伊朗高原，年代约在7世纪初。齐东方（2003）认为该杯是一件萨珊玻璃器。何家村窖藏的埋藏年代在8世纪后半，这件凸纹玻璃杯的制作时间应更早，可能是7世纪。

Measurements: height 9.7cm; mouth diameter 14.3 cm; bottom diameter 10.3cm.

Comparing and geographical, cultural and chronological attribution: An Jiayao (1984) thinks that this glass cup was blown into a shape with the decorations constituted by applied glass-strip, a hot-working decoration, a technique dating back to the Roman glass. Sasanian glass workers inherited and developed this technique, therefore, this cup came from the Plateau of Iran. The date of cup is about early 7th century AD. Qi Dongfang (2003) suggests that the glass cup is a Sasanian product. Hejiacun hoard was buried in the late 8th century AD, but the glass cup is considered to belong to an earlier time, which might be 7th century AD.

参考文献　References

1. 安家瑶：《中国的早期玻璃器皿》，《考古学报》1984年第4期，页413—447。
   An Jiayao (1984) Early Glass Vessels of China, *Kaoguxuebao (Acta Archaeologica Sinica)*, 4, 420–421, Beijing.
2. Hansen, V. (2003) The Hejia Village Hoard: A Snapshot of the China Silk Road Trade, *Orientations*, 34, 2, 14–19, Hong Kong.
3. 齐东方：《凸纹玻璃杯》，载《花舞大唐春：何家村遗宝精粹》，文物出版社（北京），2003年，页101，第12号器物。
   Qi Dongfang (2003), Glass cup, in Shaanxi History Museum *et alii* (eds.) *Huawu datangchun: Hejiacun yibao jingcui (Selected Treasures from Hejiacun Tang Hoard)*, Cultural Relics Publishing House, 101, no 12, Beijing.
4. 陕西省博物馆革委会写作小组等：《西安南郊何家村发现唐代窖藏文物》，《文物》1972年第1期，页30—42，图十三。
   Shaanxi History Museum *et alii* (1972) Excavation of a Hoard at Hejiacun in the Southern Suburbs of Xi'an, *Wenwu (Cultural Relics)*, 1, 30–42, fig.13, Beijing.

（*Bruno Genito*，耿朔 [*Geng Shuo*]）

45. 兽首玛瑙杯

收藏单位：陕西历史博物馆。

出土信息：1970年陕西西安何家村一件银罐中发现，地点在唐代都城长安的兴化坊，这是靠近长安宫城的数个精英社区之一。该窖藏在两个陶瓷和一件银罐中发现了1000多件各种文物。它们可能是在公元8世纪的某个动荡时刻被匆忙埋下的，可能是一个粟特商人或古董商所为，也可能是在公元783年泾原兵变中所埋，主人是租庸使刘震（据齐东方2003）。

器物概括描述：玛瑙质来通，羚羊形首，金质塞子。

材质、工艺及保存状况：这件来通由一块红黑相间的玛瑙雕成的杯身和一个装在兽首口部的金质塞子组成。杯身部分使用了凿边、钻孔和抛光技术，金塞子使用了铸造和穿孔技术。

尺寸：高6.5、长15.6、口径5.6厘米。

器物详细描述：这件来通由一块红黑相间的玛瑙制成，在中国，从史前时代起，玛瑙便备受青睐，不过这种类型的玛瑙应该是从国外进口的。这件杯子有圆形大口，口沿外刻划两圈凸弦纹。杯身略微弯曲，直径逐渐缩小，与另一端的羚羊首连接在一起，双眼呈圆形，两角曲长，与杯身相连，可以作为杯柄使用。金塞子嵌在玛瑙杯上，塞在兽嘴里，塞子在雕刻上准确表现出了羚羊的唇部和胡须特征。玛瑙本身多彩和半透明的特点，为器物增添了动感，它表面上有一些鲜亮的白色条纹。

图像详细描述：从羚羊角的造型看像是一

45. Rhyton

Location: Shaanxi History Museum.

Context of Origin: found in a silver urn in the Hejiacun hoard, discovered in 1970 in Xinghua place, one of the most élite neighborhoods near the Palace City of Chang'an, capital of the Tang Empire. The hoard, composed of more than 1000 items contained in two clay jars and the mentioned silver urn, was hidden during turmoil sometime in the 8th century, possibly by a Sogdian merchant or antique dealers, or during the *Jingyuan Mutiny* (783) by the tax-officer Liu Zhen (Qi Donfgang 2003).

Brief Description of the Object: agate rhyton with antelope's head and golden cork.

Material, Technique and Conservation: the rhyton is composed of a cup carved from a block of red and white agate, and a cork made of gold, fitting the open muzzle of the animal; manufacturing entailed chiseling, drilling and polishing as regards the agate cup, casting and punching as regards the golden cork.

Measurements: height, 6.5cm; length, 15.6cm; diameter of the mouth 5.6cm.

Detailed Description of the Object: the rhyton is made from a block of red and white agate, a material favored in China since prehistoric times, though this variety is deemed to be foreign to China. The cup has a wide, round, upper opening, whose rim is underlined by two parallel carved lines; the cup is slightly curved, its diameter progressively narrows and blends with a finely modeled antelope's head, with round eyes and tortile, elongated horns, whose ends merge with the cup's walls and could eventually be used as handles. A golden cork is joined to the vessel, fitting the spout in the animal's muzzle; the cork bears linear and punctual carvings describing the antelope's lips and whiskers. The polychrome and translucence of the agate add a dynamic value to the object, its sides being crossed by white, bright veins.

Detailed Description of the Iconography: the

种雄性瞪羚（拉丁语学名：*gazella subgutturosa subgutturosa*），曾经广泛分布在从土耳其至内蒙古的整个中亚。众所周知，羚羊首造型的来通和杯子，从前阿契美尼德（如在伊朗 Ziwiye 发现的标本）到萨珊时代（如 Khonjakowo hoard）都有发现（Manassero 2008）。然而，从材质、技术和风格上，它们和何家村的这件并不完全相似。

风格分析：这件来通采用了写实主义的表现方式，羚羊首的外观被塑造得很精细，面颊和眉毛从头部柔和地浮现出来。这种写实主义倾向是其根本特征，暗示出希腊化时代的特点。这和萨珊时代的风格不同，如华盛顿赛克勒美术馆藏的一件萨珊银制来通（Gunter, Jett 1992, 205–210, cat. 38），也不同于片治肯特的粟特壁画上的形象（Belenitzky 1980, pl. 56）。此外，没有清楚的证据

antelope's horns witness that a male of the Persian or guttered gazelle (*gazella subgutturosa subgutturosa*), once widespread in the whole Central Asia from Turkey to Inner Mongolia, is depicted. Antelopes' head rhytons and cups are well known, since the pre-Achaemenid samples from Ziwiye to the Sasanian ones from the Khonjakowo hoard (Manassero 2008); however, the material, technique and stylistic features never match those of the Hejiacun antelope.

Stylistic Analysis: the rhyton is executed in a pretty naturalistic way, the surface of the antelope's head being sensitively modeled. The surface of the antelope's head is very finely modeled, the cheeks and eyebrows emerge softly from the volume of the head: naturalism is a decisive feature of this vessel's design, pointing to a plastic sensitivity typical for the Hellenistic age. Its stylistic features have nothing to share with specimens attributed to Sasanian Iran, as the Sackler rhyton (Gunter, Jett 1992, 205–210, cat. 38), nor with those depicted

45. 兽首玛瑙杯 Rhyton

显示唐代还存在其他动物首造型的来通（Louis 2007, 232 ff.）。何家村的这件来通显示了希腊化时代雕刻羚羊首的造型特征，它的形状让人想起在巴比伦发现的希腊化时代的陶器。

地域、文化、年代属性及对比：从材质和生产技术方面说，只有埃及的科普托斯（Coptos）发现的一件来通与何家村的这件完全相似（Adriani 1938/1939, fig.9; Fattah 1998, 93–94, fig.III:1），然而，从风格特征上看，何家村来通在优雅程度和写实主义倾向上比在科普托斯发现的要明显得多，说明了此前所谓的这种器物源于托勒密王朝的观点并不可靠，应该还有别的发源地。希腊化时期的巴克特里亚看来是来通的最重要的生产地区，这是凭借了在希腊化时期西方工艺传统发展中的领导角色，特别是在玉石器生产方面（希腊化时期中亚的玉石器标本可参看 Al-Sabah Collection, Kuwait, Keene 2004 and 2007）。

in Sogdian paintings at Pendžikent (Belenitzky 1980, pl. 56); moreover, there is no clear evidence for the existence of other animal's head rhytons dated to the Tang period (Louis 2007, 232 ff.). The Hejiacun rhyton rather shows features of Hellenistic carving as regards the modeling of the antelope's head, and its shape recalls that of Hellenistic pottery samples found in Babylon.

Comparing and geographical, cultural and chronological attribution: the rhyton finds just one proper match in a rhyton coming from Coptos, Egypt (Adriani 1938/1939, fig.9; Fattah 1998, 93–94, fig.III: 1), as regards its material — agate — and manufacturing technique. However, the stylistical features of the Hejiacun rhyton are much more refined and naturalistic than those of the Coptos' vessel, making a Ptolemaic origin unreliable and indicating a different provenance for the item. Hellenistic Bactria seems to be the most plausible place where the rhyton may have been produced, by virtue of its leading role in the development of Western artistic traditions during Hellenistic age, and specifically for its production of jade artifacts (for some samples of Hellenistic Bactrian jades in the Al-Sabah Collection, Kuwait, see Keene 2004 and 2007).

参考文献　References

1. Adriani, A. (1938/1939) Rytha, *Bulletin de la Societé d'Archéologie d'Alexandrie*, 10, 350–362.
2. Allchin, B. (1975) The Agate and Carnelian Industry of Western India and Pakistan, *South Asian Archaeology*, 91–105.
3. Belenitzky, A. (1980) *Mittelasien. Kunst der Sogden*, Leipzig.
4. Bühler, H.P. (1966) *Antike Gefässe aus Chalcedonen*, Stuttgart.
5. Fattah, A. *et alii* (eds.) (1998) *La Gloire d'Alexandrie: 7 mai–26 juillet 1998*, Musée du Petit Palais, Paris.
6. Gunter, A., Jett P. (1992) *Ancient Iranian Metalwork in the Arthur Sackler Gallery and the Freer Gallery of Art*, Washington.
7. Hansen, V. (2003) The Hejia Village Hoard: A Snapshot of China's Silk Road Trade, *Orientations*, 34, 2 (February), 14–19.
8. Keene, M. (2004) Old World Jades Outside China, from Ancient Times to the 15th Century, Section One, *Essays in Honour of J.M. Rogers, Muqarnas*, 21, 193–214.

9. Keene, M. (2007) Jade, *Encyclopaedia Iranica*, online Edition, 15 December, available at www.iranicaonline. org/articles/jade-index.

10. Louis, F. (2007) The Hejiacun Rython and the Chinese Wine Horn (Gong), Intoxicating Rarities and their Antiquarian History, *Artibus Asiae*, 67, 2, 201–242, Zurich.

11. Melikian-Chirvani, A.S. (1997) Precious and Semi-Precious Stones in Iranian Culture. Chapter I. Early Iranian Jade, *Bulletin of the Asia Institute*, 11, 123–173, Bloomfield Hills.

12. Parlasca, K. (1975) Ein hellenistisches Achat-Rython in China, *Artibus Asiae*, 37, 280–286, Zurich.

13. 齐东方:《何家村遗宝的埋藏地点和年代》,《考古与文物》2003年第2期,页70—74。
   Qi Dongfang (2003) The Burial Location and Dating of the Hejia Village Treasures, *Kaogu yu wenwu (Archaeology and Cultural Relics)*, 2, 70–74, Xi'an.

14. 陕西省博物馆革委会写作小组等:《西安南郊何家村发现唐代窖藏文物》,《文物》1972年第1期,页30—42,图三五。
   Shaanxi History Museum *et alii* (1972) Excavation of a Hoard at Hejiacun in the Southern Suburbs of Xi'an, *Wenwu (Cultural Relics)*, 1, 30–42, fig.35, Beijing.

15. 杨亮:《镶金兽首玛瑙杯》,载《花舞大唐春:何家村遗宝精粹》,文物出版社(北京),2003年,页91—93,第8号器物。
   Yang Liang (2003) Agate horn rhyton, in Shaanxi History Museum *et alii* (eds.) *Huawu datangchun: Hejiacun yibao jingcui (Selected Treasures from Hejiacun Tang Hoard)*, Cultural Relics Publishing House, 91–93, No.8. Beijing.

(*Niccolò Manassero*, 耿朔 [*Geng Shuo*])

46. 玻璃瓶

收藏单位：陕西法门寺博物馆。

出土信息：1987年法门寺地宫出土。

器物概括概述：窄颈瓶，有成组的五角星形、圆形和水滴形装饰。

材质、工艺及保存状况：透明无色玻璃；无模自由吹制；使用工具进行修饰；铁棒加工[1]；贴花装饰；钳子加工痕迹；保存完好；有零散的小气泡；瓶内曾放置一张带有两行墨书的纸笺，损坏甚为严重，仅可辨识"莲""真"二字。

尺寸：高21.3、口径4.7、壁厚0.4—0.45、底径3.6、底厚0.1—1.0厘米。重405克。

器物详细描述：底部有一个低圈足，器身椭圆形，颈部较窄，上接杯形的口部。装饰分布于器身，即在颈腹相连处的一周凸棱下方。第一层为8个深蓝色同心圆装饰，每个的中间有压印出的脐形，第二层为6个无色的不规则五角星饰，第三层为交替排列的6个深蓝色的水滴形饰和6个无色的圆形饰，后者每一个的内部都包括风格相对固定的七瓣莲芯纹饰，由中间一个圆点和周围七个显著代表花瓣的圆点组成。

地域、文化、年代属性及对比：这件玻璃瓶借鉴了萨珊金属器的造型，风格上可能源于罗马。该瓶展现出的技术特征，在分布上并不广泛，但有一定数量的遗物被著录（Carboni 2001,

46. Glass Bottle

Location: Famen Temple Museum.

Context of Origin: temple excavations (1987).

Brief Description of the Object: narrow-necked bottle with squad five-pointed stars, circles and drops.

Material, Technique and Conservation: translucent colorless glass; free blown; tooled; worked on the pontil[1]; applied; impressed with a tong; complete; the glass includes scattered small bubbles. A piece of paper with two Chinese inscribed lines was placed in the bottle, damaged beyond recognition, and only two characters could be identified *Lian* and *Zhen*.

Measurements: height 21.3cm; opening diameter 4.7cm; body thickness, 0.4–0.5cm; base diameter 3.6cm; belly depth 20cm; base thickness, 0.1–1cm; weight: 405g.

Detailed Description of the Object: the base of the bottle consists of a low ring-foot, the body is oval, and the bi-conic narrow neck ends in a cup-shaped rim. The decoration runs around the body, under an applied colorless string circling the shoulder. Immediately below, the same applied pattern in dark blue is repeated eight times, namely an applied circular medallion with a central impressed *omphalos*; the second decorative row consists of six colorless applied motifs in the shape of squad five-pointed stars; lastly, six applied drops in dark blue alternate six applied colorless circular medallions, each including an impressed and stylized seven-petal rosette formed by a central dot and seven dots in relief representing the petals.

Comparing and Geographical, Cultural and Chronological Attribution: the shape is a modification of a Sasanian metalwork form, probably deriving

---

[1] 玻璃器在制作过程中使用铁棒，在吹制出基本器形后，趁热将吹管取下，同时用一根金属杆顶在器物的底部做进一步加工。铁棒加工的技术在早期伊斯兰时代变得非常普遍（Carboni 2001, 414）。

"Also called punty, a solid metal rod applied to the base of a vessel to hold it during manipulation after the blowpipe is cut off at the opposite end. The use of the pontil became widespread in the early Islamic period" (Carboni 2001, 414).

46. 玻璃瓶 Glass Bottle

cat. no 69b: Kuwait, Dar al-Athar al-Islamiyya, inv. no LNS 32 KG; and cat. no.3.51: Kuwait, Dar al-Athar al-Islamiyya, inv. no LNS 11 KG）。

　　然而, 法门寺这件瓶子在装饰工艺上呈现出的混合性让人惊讶。一方面, 通常一件玻璃器上不会同时使用多种装饰技术; 另一方面, 这种形状不太常见的瓶子上却混合了这些装饰。至于装饰图案本身, 粘贴圆形饰和星形饰被频繁使用, 亦存在于叙利亚地区的伊斯兰玻璃器上（7至8世纪）, 后者同样也采用两种不同的颜色（Carboni 2001, cat. no.5a-b: Kuwait, Dar al-Athar al-Islamiyya, inv. nos LNS 39 KG and 47 KG; and cat. no 1.4a-b: Kuwait, Dar al-Athar al-Islamiyya, inv. nos LNS 29 KG and 63 KG）。水滴形装饰非常少见, 通常在叙利亚地区生产的玻璃吊灯的挂耳尾部使用这种装饰。环绕一个突起的圆点和花心的圆形饰也十分少见。（参见一件拥有类似装饰的破碎的长颈瓶, 可能发现于东地中海地区, 8至10世纪, 藏于希腊雅典的贝纳基博物馆, inv. no 3214 [Clairmont 1977, cat. no 231]）。

　　此外, 伊朗和美索不达米亚很流行带中心圆点的装饰和这种形状的瓶子。这件器物的归属地可以考虑在美索不达米亚地区, 时间为8至9世纪。

from a Roman type. The contextual use of applied and impressed techniques is not so widespread, but a certain number of related objects is mentionable (Carboni 2001, cat. no 69b: Kuwait, Dar al-Athar al-Islamiyya, inv. no LNS 32 KG; and cat. no.3.51: Kuwait, Dar al-Athar al-Islamiyya, inv. no LNS 11 KG). However, the very puzzling mixture regards, on the one hand, the presence of many decorative patterns generally not present all together and, on the other hand, the unusual shape of the bottle, combined with this decoration. With regard to the patterns, while applied motifs in shape of circular medallions and squad star-elements are very frequent — also both present — on Islamic glasses coming from the Syrian region (7th–8th century), as well showing two different colors (Carboni 2001, cat. no.5a-b: Kuwait, Dar al-Athar al-Islamiyya, inv. nos LNS 39 KG and 47 KG; and cat. no 1.4a-b: Kuwait, Dar al-Athar al-Islamiyya, inv. nos LNS 29 KG and 63 KG), it is very rare the presence of "drops", generally used as ending parts of suspension loops of hanging lamps coming from the Syrian region (8th–9th century; see Carboni 2001, cat. no 3.18: Kuwait, Dar al-Athar al-Islamiyya, inv. no LNS 43 KG). The presence of circular medallions enclosing *omphalos* pattern and of circular medallions enclosing stylized rosettes is also very rare [(see a fragmentary flask with impressed decoration, maybe from Eastern Mediterranean, 8th–10th century, at the Benaki Museum, Athens, inv. no 3214 (Clairmont 1977, cat. no 231)]. Furthermore, the *omphalos* pattern is typically Iranian and Mesopotamian. Iranian or Mesopotamian is also the shape of this bottle. The suggested attribution is Mesopotamian region, 8th–9th century.

参考文献　References

1. 安家瑶:《试探中国近年出土的伊斯兰早期玻璃器》,《考古》1990年第12期, 页1116—1126。
　　An Jiayao (1990) Study of the Early Islamic Glasses Discovered in China in Recent Years, *Wenwu (Cultural*

Relics), 12, 1116−1126, Beijing.

2. An Jiayao (1991) Dated Islamic Glass in China, *Bulletin of the Asia Institute* (N.S.), 5, 123−138, fig. 2 Bloomfield Hills.

3. Carboni, S. (2001) *Glass from Islamic Lands, The al-Sabah Collection-Kuwait National Museum*, New York.

4. Clairmont, C.W. (1977) *Catalogue of Ancient and Islamic Glass*. Based on the notes of C.J. Lamm, Athens.

5. Koch, A. (1995) Der Goldschatzfund des Famensi. Prunk und Pietät in chinesischen Buddhismus der Tang-Zeit, *Jahrbuch des Römisch-Germanischen Zentralmuseums Mainz*, 42/2, 403−542, fig. 42.3 Mainz.

6. 陕西省考古研究院等编著：《法门寺考古发掘报告》，文物出版社（北京），2007年，页212—213，图一四一：2，彩版一八三。

Shaanxi Provincial Institute of Archaeology *et alii* (2007) Famensi kaogu fajue baogao (*Report of Archaeological Excavation at Famen Temple*), Cultural Relics Publishing House, 212−213, fig.141:2, CLXXXIII, Beijing.

（*Maria Vittoria Fontana*, 耿朔 [*Geng Shuo*]）

47. 黄玻璃盘

收藏单位：陕西法门寺博物馆。

出土信息：1987年法门寺地宫出土。

器物概括概述：盘，敞口，器壁弯曲，平底，盘心微微隆起[1]。

材质、工艺及保存状况：半透明黄绿色玻璃；无模自由吹制；使用工具进行修饰；铁棒加工；彩绘。保存完好；玻璃中有零散的小气泡；着色（或光泽）彩绘罂粟科花卉图案。

尺寸：高2.5—2.8、口径14、壁厚0.3、腹深2.3—2.6、底厚0.5厘米。重84克。

器物详细描述：装饰不透明的橙灰色以及一种更深颜色的彩绘[2]，包括在盘心绘制的一株罂粟花科图案，被盘口边沿十一个相连的弧形面围绕。

地域、文化、年代属性及对比：这件玻璃盘的风格和配色，都与伊朗Takht-i Sulayman遗址出土的残破绿彩玻璃容器存在着联系（Berlin, Museum für Islamische Kunst, inv. Nr. I. 19/69; Kröger 1998, 8–9, und Nr. 7），亚美尼亚的Dvin遗址也曾发现类似的玻璃碎片。

着色玻璃最早出现在罗马时期的埃及（大约3世纪），使用了银和铜，将其附加到玻璃表面之前先在炉中加热。对以银为基本成分的颜料进行加热处理，大概是埃及科普特玻璃工匠在6

47. Glass Dish

Location: Famen Temple Museum.

Context of Origin: Famen Temple excavations (1987).

Brief Description of the Object: dish with curved profile, an everted rim and a flat base raised at the center[1].

Material, Technique and Conservation: translucent yellowgreen glass; free blown; tooled; worked on the pontil; stained-painted. Complete; the glass includes scattered small bubbles. Stain (or luster)-painted with poppy design.

Measurements: height 2.5–2.8cm; opening diameter 14cm; body thickness 0.3cm; belly depth 2.3–2.6cm; base thickness 0.5cm; weight 84g.

Detailed Description of the Object: the decoration is an opaque orangey-grey and a darker colored stain[2] and consists of a poppy design at its center, surrounded by eleven semi-circular splotches along the dish's rim.

Comparing and Geographical, Cultural and Chronological Attribution: the style and the color scheme of this dish links it both to a fragmentary vessel of greenish stained-painted glass coming from the excavations of Takht-i Sulayman (Berlin, Museum für Islamische Kunst, inv. Nr. I. 19/69; Kröger 1998, 8–9, und note 7), and to a similar fragment excavated in Dvin in Armenia (Kröger 1998, 9, and no 8); the origin of glass staining dates back to the Roman period (about 3rd century) in Egypt, using silver and copper, before they were applied to a surface using heat in a furnace. The heating of silver-based pigments was in all probability "invented" by Coptic glassmakers in Egypt,

---

[1] 底部凸起是由于外侧有铁棒加工的缘故。
　　The central protrusion is caused by the kick of the pontil.
[2] Brill（1993, 64）认为这两种颜色都是光泽装饰的变体。
　　Brill (1993, 64) believes that both the colors are variants of a luster stain.

47. 黄玻璃盘 Glass Dish

至7世纪发明的（Carboni 2001, 51）。在伊斯兰早期，埃及和叙利亚地区生产着色玻璃。法门寺的这件盘子可能是8世纪叙利亚地区的产品。

6th–7th century (Carboni 2001, 51). In the early Islamic epoch the stained-glass was produced in Egypt and in Syria. Probably Syrian region, 8th century.

参考文献　References

1. 安家瑶：《试探中国近年出土的伊斯兰早期玻璃器》，《考古》1990年第12期，页1116—1126。
An Jiayao (1990) Study of the Early Islamic Glasses Discovered in China in Recent Years, *Wenwu* (*Cultural Relics*), 12, 1116–1126, Beijing.

2. An Jiayao (1991) Dated Islamic Glass in China, *Bulletin of the Asia Institute* (N.S.), 5, 123–138 (in part. 13, fig. 10), Bloomfield Hills.

3. Brill, R.H. (1993) Glass and Glassmaking in Ancient China, and Some Other Things from Other Places, *Glass Art Society Journal: The Toledo Conference*, 56–69 (in part. 64).

4. Carboni, S. (2001) *Glass from Islamic Lands, The al-Sabah Collection-Kuwait National Museum*, New York.

5. Koch, A. (1995) Der Goldschatzfund des Famensi. Prunk und Pietät in chinesischen Buddhismus derTang-Zeit, *Jahrbuch des Römisch-Germanischen Zentralmuseums Mainz*, 42/2, 403–542 (in part. 499, fig.42.1), Mainz.

6. Kröger, J. (1998) Painting on Glass before the Mamluk Period, Ward, R. (ed.) *Gilded and Enamelled Glass from the Middle East*, 8–11 (in part. 8), London.

7. Moore, O. (1998) Islamic Glass at Buddhist Sites in Medieval China, Ward, R. (ed.) *Gilded and Enamelled Glass from the Middle East*, 78–84 (in part. fig. 19.1), London.

8. 陕西省考古研究院等编著：《法门寺考古发掘报告》，文物出版社（北京），2007年，页213，图一四二：1，彩版一八四：1、2。
Shaanxi Provincial Institute of Archaeology *et alii* (2007) Famensi kaogu fajue baogao (*Report of Archaeological Excavation at Famen Temple*), Cultural Relics Publishing House, 213, fig. 142:1, CLXXXIV, Beijing.

（*Maria Vittoria Fontana*，耿朔 [*Geng Shuo*]）

48. 蓝玻璃盘

收藏单位：陕西法门寺博物馆。

出土信息：1987年法门寺地宫出土。

器物概括描述：盘，带有几何形图案。

材质、工艺及保存状况：深蓝透明玻璃；无模自由吹制；使用工具进行修饰；铁棒加工；刻花工艺；可能最初有涂金；保存完整；玻璃中有零散的小气泡。

尺寸：高2、口径18、深1.6、壁厚0.2、底厚0.5厘米。重150克。

器物详细描述：器身较浅，平底，盘心有凸起。唇部较厚，外翻。盘内装饰由二重结构组成，内部刻划了一个圆形图案，以十字划分为四等分，每等分中都有花瓣形图案；外部分布着锯齿形纹饰，由一系列三角纹构成，每一个角都包括叶尖形纹饰。盘内最初可能涂金（An 1991, 135, and, specifically, Kröger 1998, 10）。

地域、文化、年代属性及对比：法门寺地宫还发现了另外5件使用相同技术的蓝色玻璃盘（安家瑶 1991,123–124, figs 3–8; Koch 1995, 499–502, figs 41.2–4）。尽管只有两件有金彩填涂的痕迹，但Kröger（1998, 10）断定这件曾经也有涂金装饰。伊斯兰早期的这种着色刻纹玻璃器有各种各样的形状，其中最常见的装饰图案是锯齿纹。1939年美国大都会艺术博物馆的考古学家曾在伊朗东北部的内沙普尔（Tepe Madraseh）发现过一件破碎的蓝色玻璃盘（参见New York, The Metropolitan Museum of Art, inv. no.40.170.131; Kröger 1995,117–119, no and fig.164; Kröger 提供了

48. Glass Dish

Location: Famen Temple Museum.

Context of Origin: Famen Temple excavations (1987).

Brief Description of the Object: dish with geometrical motifs.

Material, Technique and Conservation: translucent dark blue glass; free blown; tooled; worked on the pontil. Incised; probably originally gold painted. Complete; the glass includes scattered small bubbles.

Measurements: height, 2cm; opening diameter, 18cm; depth 1.6cm; body thickness, 0.2cm; base thickness, 0.5cm; weight, 150g.

Detailed Description of the Object: the body is shallow, with a flat base raised at the center, the thickened rim turns up. The decoration consists of two parts. The inner part is inscribed into a circular medallion, filled with a cross motif including a floral pattern in each of the four contour panels; the outer part shows a "sawtooth" motif, formed by a row of triangles, each containing a vegetal pattern. Originally, the entire inner surface was covered by gold paint (An 1991, 135, and, specifically, Kröger 1998, 10).

Comparing and Geographical, Cultural and Chronological Attribution: other five intact dishes of dark blue glass and decorated in the same technique came from the site (An 1991, 123–124, figs 3–8; Koch 1995, 499–502, figs 41.2–4). Although only two dishes show traces of gold paint, Kröger (1998, 10) affirms that it might once have been enhanced with gold. The production of this early Islamic glass, characterized by a graffito technique on a surface frequently colored, includes a variety of shapes, furthermore, one of the most common decorative element is the *sawtooth* motif. A fragmentary dark blue plate was also excavated at Nishapur (Tepe Madraseh), in Northeastern Iran, by the Metropolitan Museum archaeologists in 1939 (New York, The Metropolitan Museum of Art, inv. no 40.170.131; Kröger

48. 蓝玻璃盘 Glass Dish

其他地点发现的这类玻璃的一个列表和相关文献,亦可参见 Carboni 2001, 136, no 23)。

尽管目前还不能辨认出这组伊斯兰刻纹玻璃器的精确产地,Stefano Carboni 认为可能产自叙利亚或美索不达米亚地区,而内沙普尔处于连接中国和伊斯兰世界的交通要道上,只是重要的商贸中心。法门寺地宫封闭于874年(Carboni 2001, 76–81),因此这件玻璃盘可能是9世纪叙利亚或美索不达米亚地区的产品。

1995, 117–119, no and fig. 164; Kröger provided us with a list of similar items coming from other excavations, and includes the related bibliography, but see also Carboni 2001, 136, no 23). Although the origin of this group of Islamic incised glass cannot be precisely identified, Stefano Carboni suggests that the region of manufacture was probably Syria or Mesopotamia, while Nishapur has been only an important commercial center along the caravans way from both Chinese and Islamic lands; a date *ante quem* is provided right by the Famen Temple finds, 874 AD (Carboni 2001, 76–81). Syrian or Mesopotamian region, 9th century.

参考文献　References

1. 安家瑶:《试探中国近年出土的伊斯兰早期玻璃器》,《考古》1990年第12期,页1116—1126。
   An Jiayao (1990) Study of the Early Islamic Glasses Discovered in China in Recent Years, *Wenwu (Cultural Relics)*, 12, 1116–1126, Beijing.
2. An Jiayao (1991) Dated Islamic Glass in China, *Bulletin of the Asia Institute* (N.S.), 5, 123–138 (in part. fig.5), Bloomfield Hills.
3. Carboni, S. (2001) *Glass from Islamic Lands, The al-Sabah Collection-Kuwait National Museum*, New York.
4. Koch, A. (1995) Der Goldschatzfund des Famensi. Prunk und Pietät in chinesischen Buddhismus der Tang-Zeit, *Jahrbuch des Römisch-Germanischen Zentralmuseums Mainz*, 42/2, 403–542 (in part. 499), Mainz.
5. Kröger, J. (1995) *Nishapur. Glass of the Early Islamic Period*, The Metropolitan Museum of Art, New York.
6. Kröger, J. (1998) Painting on Glass before the Mamluk Period, Ward, R. (ed.) *Gilded and Enamelled Glass from the Middle East*, 8–11, London.
7. 陕西省考古研究院等编著:《法门寺考古发掘报告》,文物出版社(北京),2007年,页215,图一四四:2,彩版一八八:1。
   Shaanxi Provincial Institute of Archaeology *et alii* (2007) Famensi kaogu fajue baogao (*Report of Archaeological Excavation at Famen Temple*), Cultural Relics Publishing House, 215, fig.144:2, CLXXXVIII: 1, Beijing.

(*Maria Vittoria Fontana*,耿朔 [*Geng Shuo*])

49. 玻璃杯

收藏单位：陕西法门寺博物馆。

出土信息：1987年法门寺地宫出土。

器物概括描述：圆柱形杯,有菱形花纹装饰。

材质、工艺及保存状况：淡黄色透明玻璃；吹制,在玻璃从炉中取出后使用工具（钳子等夹具）进行装饰；使用工具进行修饰；铁棒加工；保存完好；底部表面部分风化；玻璃中有零散的小气泡。

尺寸：高8.5、口径7.8、深8.1、壁厚0.2—0.5、底厚0.3—0.6厘米。重130克。

器物详细描述：杯底平坦,口部微敛。器壁有四组装饰,似以矩形钳子制成,纹饰的侧面留下了边棱的痕迹,变成了一部分装饰：短小的压痕组成两条平行的垂直线。每个区域的中间为内饰菱形纹的小圆圈,在其上下各饰一组3个小圆环纹。

地域、文化、年代属性及对比：带有相似压印装饰的玻璃残片（即菱形纹和成组的由三个圆圈组成的纹饰）曾在叙利亚西部城市哈马（现藏大英博物馆, inv. no.I.-N.998; Lamm 1928, no.165, fig.32）和伊拉克城市萨马拉（Samarra, 现藏丹麦哥本哈根国家博物馆, inv. no.K7/1934; Riis & Poulsen 1957, figs 132, 133）出土,时代为9到10世纪。此外,还有两件有着相同尺寸和装饰的杯子,被收藏在奥地利维也纳（自然史博物馆, inv. no.83. 790; Lamm 1929–30, pl. 18:7）和德国汉堡（艺术与手工业博物馆, inv. no.1964. 20; von Saldern 1968, pl. 17）,它们分别来自高加索地区的Kobanj和伊朗北部玛兰达兰省。

49. Glass Cup

Location: Famen Temple Museum.

Context of Origin: Famen Temple excavations (1987).

Brief Description of the Object: cylindrical cup with lozenges.

Material, Technique and Conservation: yellowish translucent glass; blown and impressed with tongs after the object was taken off the kiln; tooled; worked on the pontil. Complete; surface partially weathered at the bottom; the glass includes scattered small bubbles.

Measurements: height 8.5cm; mouth diameter 7.8cm; depth 8.1cm; body thickness 0.2–0.5cm; base thickness 0.3–0.6cm; weight 130g.

Detailed Description of the Object: the base of the cup is flat, the wall curves slightly inward at the opening. The decoration consists of four panels obtained with a rectangular tong whose lateral edges appear as marks, becoming part of the decoration: two vertical and parallel lines of short indentations. Each panel shows a lozenge including in the center a small circle, and provided with two clusters of three small circles above and below.

Comparing and Geographical, Cultural and Chronological Attribution: glass fragments bearing a similar impressed decoration (with lozenges and groups of three circles) have been found at Hama, in Syria (London, The British Museum, inv. no I.-N.998; Lamm 1928, no 165, fig.32) and Samarra, in Iraq (Copenhagen, National Museum, inv. no K7/1934; Riis and Poulsen 1957, figs 132, 133), dated to 9th–10th century. Furthermore, two cups showing the same dimensions and decoration housed in Wien (Naturhistorisches Museum, inv. no 83. 790; Lamm 1929–30, pl. 18:7) and Hamburg (Museum für Kunst und Gewerbe, inv. no 1964. 20; Saldern 1968, pl. 17) namely come from Kobanj (Caucasus area) and

有关这种玻璃容器的产地有一个很有趣的讨论，见于Carboni（2001, 261–262, 269）对科威特国家博物馆藏 Dar al-Athar al-Islamiyya（inv. no.LNS 116 G）发现的一件与法门寺玻璃杯非常相似的杯子的研究 (Carboni 2001, cat. no.71a)。这件杯子产于伊斯兰世界的中心区域，很可能是美索不达米亚地区。法门寺发现的这件杯子可能是9至10世纪美索不达米亚或伊朗北部的产品。

Mazandaran (Iran), respectively. A very interesting discussion related to the geographical attribution of this kind of glass vessels can be found in Carboni (2001, 261–262, 269), in reference to a cup very similar to that of Famen Temple, in the Dar al-Athar al-Islamiyya, Kuwait National Museum, inv. no LNS 116 G (Carboni 2001, cat. no 71a). The central Islamic lands, possibly the Mesopotamian region are suggested. Mesopotamia or northern Iran, 9th–10th century.

49. 玻璃杯 Glass Cup

参考文献　References

1. 安家瑶：《试探中国近年出土的伊斯兰早期玻璃器》，《考古》1990年第12期，页1116—1126。

An Jiayao (1990) Study of the Early Islamic Glasses Discovered in China in Recent Years, *Wenwu* (*Cultural Relics*), 12, 1116–1126, Beijing.

2. An Jiayao (1991) Dated Islamic Glass in China, *Bulletin of the Asia Institute* (N.S.), 5, 123–138 (in particular 124, 129, fig. 9), Bloomfield Hills.

3. Carboni, S. (2001) *Glass from Islamic Lands, The al-Sabah Collection-Kuwait National Museum*, New York.

4. Koch, A. (1995) Der Goldschatzfund des Famensi. Prunk und Pietät in chinesischen Buddhismus der Tang-Zeit, *Jahrbuch des Römisch-Germanischen Zentralmuseums Mainz*, 42/2, 403–542 (in part. 499, fig. 42.2) Mainz.

5. Lamm, C.J. (1928) *Das Glas von Samarra*, Berlin.

6. Lamm, C.J. (1929–30) *Mittelalterliche Gläser und Steinschnittarbeiten aus dem Nahen Osten*, 2 vols., Berlin.

7. Riis, P.J., Poulsen, V. (1957) *Hama: fouilles et recherches de la fondation Carlsberg, 1931–1938*, IV.2, *Les verreries et poteries médiévales*, Copenhagen.

8. Saldern, Von, A. (1968) Sassanidische und islamische Gläser in Düsseldorf und Hamburg, *Sonderdruck aus dem Jahrbuch der Hamburger Kunstsammlungen*, 13, 33.

9. 陕西省考古研究院等编著：《法门寺考古发掘报告》，文物出版社（北京），2007年，页220，图一四六：2，彩版一九〇。

Shaanxi Provincial Institute of Archaeology *et alii* (2007) *Famensi kaogu fajue baogao* (*Report of Archaeological Excavation at Famen Temple*), Cultural Relics Publishing House, p. 220, fig.146:2, CXC, Beijing.

（*Maria Vittoria Fontana*，耿朔 [*Geng Shuo*]）

结　语
Conclusions

葛嵓、齐东方 撰，童歆 译

Bruno Genito, Qi Dongfang, trans. by Tong Xin

本书是北京大学考古文博学院的中国学者与来自意大利多所大学、意大利亚非研究院（IsIAO，现已重组为意大利地中海与东方学国际研究协会［ISMEO］）以及那不勒斯东方大学亚洲、非洲和地中海系的学者们多年合作的结晶，旨在为共同挑选的49件器物提供一套文献及出土背景的诠释框架，以此引起学界和读者的关注。

书中呈现的器物种类多样，包括了青铜器、金银器、陶器、玻璃器、纺织品、木制品以及石制品，主要发现于中国西部及北部的墓葬中。依据其出土背景或工艺、风格及装饰纹样，它们在文化上可能都有"外来"渊源，主要包括塞人或斯基泰，伊朗或中亚，祆教、佛教和伊斯兰教等方面。除个别断代上的例外，大部分器物的年代范围在公元前500年到公元500年之间，而其中一些器物早已是学界讨论的焦点，也曾出现在众多中西展览图录的介绍与研究之中。

The volume on which Chinese scholars of the Department of Archaeology and Museology of Peking University and Italian scholars, belonging to different universities, and referring to IsIAO (now New ISMEO) and to the Dipartimento Asia, Africa e Mediterraneo of the Università di Napoli "L'Orientale"[1] have been working for several years, had as its main purpose to provide a documentary and original interpretative framework related to 49 objects jointly selected and proposed to the attention of the scholars and readers.

The objects presented, mainly found in tombs in western and northern China, and possibly referring, on the basis of context of the discovery and or of technical, stylistic and decorative patterns, to a cultural "foreign" ground, especially Saka/Scythian, Iranian/Central Asian, Zoroastrian, Buddhist and Islamic, represent a very interesting and significant collection of items in bronze, silver, gold, ceramic, glass, tissue, wood, stone. Most of them are dating from the middle of the 1st millennium BC to the middle of the 1st Millennium AD, with a few chronological exceptions, and some are already well known in the scientific debate, and have been also the subject of descriptive and interpretative notes in some catalogues of exhibitions in China and West.

---

[1] 意大利的研究机构与北京大学签署了多份考古合作协议，包括2007年开始跟亚非研究院、2011年开始跟那不勒斯东方大学的合作。
Italian Institutions signed with Peking University different agreement of archaeological cooperation since 2007 with IsIAO and since 2011 with UNO.

众所周知，由于不同原因和方法，"外来者"以及他们在中国的文化影响向来是中西方传统研究中的主要课题之一。中国与西方的文化交往可以追溯至非常久远的年代，包括历史时期的帝国时代，即编年官修史料记载中国与西域之间的种种差异。也必须要指出的是，尽管内在的阐释体系与范式不尽相同，此类与外来文化的关联贯穿于所有伟大的古代文明之中。我们可以举出比如美索不达米亚、伊朗或地中海诸文明的例子，不过这些文明往往有着较强的以自我为中心的认知，而其中的多样性及外来者只扮演了次要角色。

近年来在中国，相关墓葬及棺床的发现又增加了这一课题研究及阐释的复杂性。也正因如此，读者很容易联想到本书的缘起、合作方式和背景：发端于2007至2010年间，中意双方经过共同分析与研究，尝试整合双方不同的研究方法，并最终出版本书——《异宝西来：考古发现的丝绸之路舶来品研究》。

本书包含编者们的撰稿以及图录两部分。相较于迄至当下绝大多数学者遵从的器物类型学研究，我们的方法论取自不同的阐释方向，并不仅限于在纯粹风格与图像学的基础上对器物进行特征描述。这一认识已经在很多场合之下，被不同学派以不同的方式提及并强调。在我们看来，本书采用的研究方向更进一步提出了一个与考古背景更加相关的阐释层次，而以往研究已经表明了纯粹图像学方法的局限性，该方法即便没有遗漏，也经常忽略考古学信息。

As is well known the scientific issue of "the foreigners" and their cultural impact in China has been a major concern exploited, on the basis of different reasons and methodological approach, by the Chinese and western tradition of study as well. The cultural relations between China and the West can be traced back to the very ancient times, including the historical imperial age, when the annalistic official sources describe the differences between China and the western regions. There must also be said that this kind of relationships with the otherness, went a bit through all the great ancient civilizations, albeit using inherently different interpretative systems and paradigms. We can mention e.g. the case of Mesopotamian, Iranian or the Mediterranean civilizations, whereas they have always had a rather self-centred perception of themselves, within which the diversity, the others played a distinctly minor role.

The discoveries of tombs and the related funerary beds in China with their panels have recently dramatically expanded, contributing very much also to major interpretative complications of the issue. Precisely because of this, you can easily imagine, then, how and in what context this volume and the idea of putting together two very different schools of study, such as the Chinese and Italian, was originated between 2007 and 2010, finalizing the studies and the analyses jointly done, to a publication that now sees the light, under the title *West and East: archaeological objects along the Silk Roads*.

The volume contains, a part from the contributions of the editors, also a catalogue, which, methodologically, arises, in a different interpretative direction with respect to the one up to now followed by most of the scholars dealing with such typology of objects, and that does not want to be only descriptive in character in a purely stylistic and iconographic ground. This, however, as it has been said, in many cases, has been already addressed in a differentiated manner from different schools of studies. The direction adopted, in our opinion, proposes, furthermore, an interpretative

很难说我们做出的努力是否达到了原先设定的目标。但毫无疑问，纯粹的图像学研究已经带来了很多详细分析，而考古学视角却仍然在几个世纪以来形成的风格学和图像学传统的遮盖之下艰难前行，后者并不总是能对发现的器物做出有效且合理的解释。

当中意双方同仁决意共同开展工作之时，正是我们想要应对的真正挑战。相对于在中亚、丝绸之路以及与中国西部文化关系研究传统中长时间占主导的视觉与图像阐释，我们更希望从器物出土的背景出发开展研究。另一方面，中国学者的研究之外，在西方严格的汉学研究背景之下，还有其他学术传统使用着比意大利学者更加细致的分析方法，研究着上述课题。

还应该指出的是，西方与中国的文化交往，无论是年代跨度上还是地理分布上，都异常丰富。我们只能将学者和读者的注意力，一方面集中到青铜时代和铁器时代文化的相关方面（例如玉石之路、塞人—斯基泰人等等），而另一方面则集中到公元4至7世纪中古早期的粟特人。

被中国和西方文献记载所印证的不同游牧民族，比如一开始的塞人、匈奴人、乌孙人、月氏人，以及后来的粟特人，标识出了这一文化上的二分法，而这样的二分法不可避免地塑造了本书所探讨问题的研究史。所有这些都以一种非常不同的方式，展现出可能比我们想象的要更加相似的文化动力与面貌。与此同时，也需要强调的一点是，如果说通过种族—

level, more relating to the archaeological ground. The history of studies has shown the limits of a purely iconographic methodological approach, which has been often overlooked, if not neglected, the archaeological data.

It is hard to say if the efforts made by the working team, have or not reached the originally aim. Certainly there is no doubt that the dimension of pure iconographic studies has proposed extensive and detailed levels of analyses, whilst the archaeological dimension still struggles to get ahead, obscured by a stylistic and iconological centuries-old tradition that does not always find an effective response within the classes of objects found.

This is, nonetheless, the real challenge that the Chinese and the Italian colleagues wanted to undertake when it was decided to jointly start to work; to propose an interpretative reading of the selected items more on the background of their contexts of provenance than on the basis of the interpretations of the visual and iconographic aspects, which have always played a large part in the tradition of studies related to Central Asia, Silk Roads and the cultural relations with the Western China. On the other hand, there are in the West, next to the school of studies in China, other traditions that have addressed the issues at hand in a more detailed and analytical way than the Italian, always in the context of a strictly sinological reference.

We should also point out that the cultural western relationships with China have been both chronologically and geographically much ample. We cannot but draw the attention of scholars and readers to the difficult combination of cultural aspects correlated to the Bronze and Iron Age cultures on one hand (Routes of the Jade, Saka-Scythian people, etc.), and of the others, instead, more properly defined as Sogdian, belonging, to the early medieval period from the 4th century AD to the 7th century AD, on the other.

This cultural dichotomy marked by the presence of nomadic often different populations, attested by the Chinese and Western sources such as Saka (Sai/Se),

遗传手段识别第一个历史阶段的那些人群是困难且复杂的，那么对于更纯粹的考古学背景来说，把这些器物归于特定的几个或单个人群也越来越困难。

外来人群出现在中国的可能性，一直都被这里所呈现的一些器物以及中国西部和北部发现的一些墓葬所证明。这些墓葬的年代基本都属于公元6世纪后半叶。出土的石棺床和石棺都有大量的浮雕石板装饰，描绘的场景和主题显然不属于中国传统。迄今为止发现的这些图像学材料已成为众多研究和分析的对象，并且也有了多样的认识与解读，不过这些解读并不总是具有充分的说服力。尽管所描绘的场景在很大程度上归属于一个非中国的文化根源，但由于风格、工艺和主题的来源不同，予以明确识别仍然非常困难。中亚和伊朗的考古学全景中缺乏其他可比较的元素，这在一开始就被大多数学者在研究时提出，使得这个问题更加复杂化。

通过中国西部所进行的中西文化交流，始终与丝绸之路历史上繁琐的文化背景、粟特聚落的存在以及祆教、佛教、景教和伊斯兰教等非中国宗教思想的传播点缀在一起。 对于丝绸之路来说，最新的研究方向提供了一个解读，并在地理上和时间上对其背后的文化问题进行了非常广泛的诠释，而对于粟特聚落和中国外部宗教思想体系的存在问题，则依旧不可避免地固定于一个更精确的地理和时间框架内，基本在公元1至4世纪到8世纪之间。在这些不同宗教的基础上，我们可

Hsiung-nu, Wusun, Yueh-Chih first, and then Sogdians, inevitably has characterized the history of the studies on the issues raised in this book. All this has effectively represented, in a very different way, cultural dynamics and aspects, perhaps, instead, more similar than we can imagine. At the same time it should also be emphasized that if the ethno-genetic processes characterizing the first historical stages of those populations is often difficult and complex to be analysed and identified, to attribute classes of objects to certain groups or individual populations is more and more difficult as well, even to the more purely archaeological background.

The possible presence of foreign populations in China has been always both evidenced by some of the objects presented here, and some funerary contexts in the western and northern China; these last ones all dating to the second half of the 6th century. The beds and funerary *sarcophagi* richly decorated with relief panels, depict scenes and themes certainly not traditionally Chinese. The iconographic material found so far, has been the subject of numerous studies and analyses, and the various related advanced proposals interpretations, not always appeared fully convincing. Although there is no doubt that the scenes depicted are attributable, in large part, to a non-Chinese cultural *substratum*, clear identifications are still very difficult because of different stylistic, technical and thematic origin. The lack of other elements of comparison within the archaeological *panorama* of central Asia and Iran, which, in the first instance, has always addressed by the majority of scholars for its interpretations, gives further complication to the matter.

The western relationship with China through its western part has been always dotted with the historically cumbersome cultural background of the *Silk Roads*, the presence of the Sogdian community and the spread of non-Chinese religious ideologies, such as Zoroastrism, Buddhism, Nestorian Christianism and Islam. Whether for the *Silk Roads* the latest methodological study

以说书中器物与它们的关联很小，相反与它们开始传播的原初区域有更多的联系，将器物或其某一方面和主题归属于宗教思想则更加困难。

同样，我们认为印章、银制杯碟以及一些玻璃器属于萨珊时代的伊朗，这一点远比其祆教属性更加可靠。本书选取的器物中没有能够明确归属于景教的，只有一组玻璃盘可以算作伊斯兰器物，佛教器物也仅有少量的几件。

本书选定的器物展现出一些独特的特征，从前三件（nos 1-3）开始，我们将以非常细致的

orientations offers a reading and an geographically and chronologically very wide interpretation of the cultural issues underlying them, for the question of the presence of Sogdian community and of the religious ideologies external to China, inevitably they remain anchored to a much more precise geographical and chronological framework which can be considered extended between the 1th-4th and 8th centuries A.D. On the basis of those different religions we can say that the objects presented here have very scarce relationships with them and show more links, instead, to the original area of their diffusion. It is more difficult to attribute objects or their single aspects and motifs to religious ideologies.

As far as Zoroastrism[1] is concerned we can say that the seals, the silver cup and dishes, and some glasses are reliable to the Sasanian Iran more than to

---

[1] 祆教是一神论的宗教，其宗教经典以《阿维斯塔》为代表。根据学者的观点，只有偈颂（宗教歌曲）可以直接与先知查拉图斯特拉相联系。对《阿维斯塔》的批判性分析以及对历史和考古资料的分析表明，该宗教的发展经历了一开始的一神论教义，单一主神到二神并最终又回归一神论。《阿维斯塔》作为一个整体，为这个单一主神的宗教（而非"宗教系统"）提供了框架，这是基于更为古老的多神基础，并经过二神概念的修饰和调整。阿契美尼德铭文提供了一神教发展的趋势图，其特点是明确的道德二元论和随后仍然由阿胡拉·马兹达主导的多神论。从6世纪开始，祆教在中国北方扩展，并在一些政权中取得了官方地位。祆教寺庙至少到公元1130年左右还在开封和镇江地区有迹可循，而从13世纪开始，逐渐在中国的宗教背景中失去了其重要性。在公元7世纪，萨珊王朝被阿拉伯穆斯林推翻，祆教徒们被第二任奥马尔哈里发称作"有经者"（阿拉伯语称为 Ahl al-Kitab），不过《阿维斯塔》和古代波斯语言被禁止使用。伊斯兰征服者认为琐罗亚斯德的教义属于多神教。作为曾经一度在从安那托利亚到波斯湾和中亚的区域占据统治地位的宗教，祆教没有像基督教之于拜占庭帝国那样形成外国军事力量同盟，因此慢慢失去了影响。

Zoroastrianism was a monotheistic religion, whose sacred text are represented by Avesta. Only the Gatha (religious songs) would be, according to scholars, directly attributable to the Zarathustra prophet. The critical analysis of the Avesta, and the analysis of historical and archaeological data shows that this religion has developed through doctrinal readings monotheistic in origin, henotheist, dualist and finally again monotheistic. Avesta, as a whole, provides the framework for a religion (rather than a "religious system") of henoteistic type, which underlies a fundamental more archaic polytheism, modified and conditioned by the dualistic conception. The Achaemenid inscriptions offer a picture of a trend in monotheism, characterized by a clear ethical dualism, and a subsequent polytheism, still dominated by Ahura Mazda. Starting from the 6th century Zoroastrism expanded in northern China achieving an official status in some Chinese States. Zoroastrian temples remained until at least about 1130 in the regions of Kaifeng and Zhenjiang, and from the 13th century, gradually lost its importance in the Chinese religious background. In the 7th century, Sasanian dynasty was overthrown by the Arab Muslims and Zoroastrians obtained the status of *"People of the Book"* (Arabic Ahl al-Kitab) by the second Caliph Omar. However, the use of the Avesta and ancient Persian language was forbidden. The Islamic conquerors considered the teachings of Zoroaster as a polytheistic religion. Zoroastrism, which had once been a dominant religion in a region extending from Anatolia to the Persian Gulf and Central Asia, was not a foreign military power as an ally, as the Byzantine Empire to Christianity was, and slowly lost its influence.

观察和深思熟虑的分析进行强调。这三件器物明显属于斯基泰、乌孙和塞人文化，或者从它们的考古学背景来看，年代可追溯到公元前5世纪至前3世纪，肯定在汉代以前。第7号铜镜几

the underlying religious aspects. To the Nestorianism[1] no object selected can, reasonably, be attributed, and clearly referred, whereas to Islam[2] only a group of few glass dishes, and to the Buddhism[3] few objects as well.

The selected objects for this volumes present some

---

[1] 景教的起源可以追溯到叙利亚主教聂斯脱利和基督教教会关于其宗教人物的基督教教义。景教教义拒绝对基督其人的神圣解读，而是谈论基督的两个本性，即人与神的完全分离，否认位格合一。景教的这种教义在431年被以弗所议会谴责。该教得名由来于君士坦丁堡（约381—451）的主教聂斯脱利。根据其教义，在耶稣基督中存在两个截然不同的格，人与神共存，玛丽只是耶稣人格的母亲。

This ideological thought goes back to the Christological doctrine advocated by the Syrian bishop Nestorius (381-451) and the Christian Church pertaining to its religious figure. Nestorianism, rejecting the divine interpretation of the figure of Christ, talks about the total separation of the two natures of Christ, human and divine, denying the hypostatic union. The Nestorian doctrines were condemned by the Council of Ephesus in 431. The doctrine takes its name from Nestorius, patriarch of Constantinople (ca. 381-451). According to the doctrine, in Jesus Christ two distinct persons, the Man and God lived together; Mary was the mother only of the human person of Jesus.

[2] 伊斯兰教在中国已有1400年之久，这期间与中国社会持续互动。伊斯兰教进入中国可以追溯到该教的萌芽时期，当先知穆罕默德的叔父萨德·伊本·阿比·沃卡斯在651年，也就是第三任乌斯曼哈里发统治期间，受到唐朝高宗的欢迎。若干年后，还可以追溯到在广州修建的中国第一座清真寺，阿拉伯和波斯商人将伊斯兰教带入中国。根据中国穆斯林的传说记载，伊斯兰教在公元616年至618年由先知穆罕默德的伴侣（Sahaba）萨德·伊本·阿比·沃卡斯、萨义德、瓦哈卜·伊本·阿布·卡布察等人首次传入中国。瓦哈卜·伊本·阿布·卡布察（即瓦哈卜·阿比·卡布察）可能是艾卜哈斯·伊本·阿卜杜勒·欧萨（又称阿布·卡布察）的儿子。有些记载则将伊斯兰教的首次传入定在了公元650年，即在乌斯曼哈里发治下，萨德·伊本·阿比·沃卡斯以官方使节的身份谒见唐高宗，这也是他第三次外教出使任务。萨德·伊本·阿比·沃卡斯的早期出访在阿拉伯史料中有记录，这一时期正是宗教狂热和战争相混杂的时代。

Islam in China existed through 1,400 years of continuous interaction with Chinese society. The Islamic reality in China date back to the dawn of Islam, when the uncle of the prophet Muhammad, Saad ibn Abi Waqqas, was welcomed by Emperor Gaozong of the Tang Dynasty, during the reign of the third Caliph Uthman in 651. A few years later you also can date back the building of China's first mosque at Canton and the introduction of Islam to the work of Arab and Persian merchants, entered the country. According to Chinese Muslims' traditional legendary accounts, Islam was first introduced to China in 616–18 AD by Sahaba (companions) of Prophet Muhammad: Sa'd ibn Abi Waqqas, Sayid, Wahab ibn Abu Kabcha and another Sahaba. Wahab ibn abu Kabcha (Wahb abi Kabcha) may have been be a son of al-Harth ibn Abdul Uzza (also known as Abu Kabsha). Some sources date the introduction of Islam in China to 650 AD, the third sojourn of Saad ibn abi Waqqas, when he was sent as an official envoy to Emperor Gaozong during Caliph Uthman reign. Earlier visits of Saad ibn abi Waqqas were noted in Arab accounts since it was a period of nascent Islam mixed with events of many hectic preaching and warfare.

[3] 佛教传入中国通常被追溯至公元1世纪中叶的东汉时期，当时汉朝的势力已经覆盖到中亚部分地区。除传说外，这一事件并没有明确的记载。其中最著名的流传说法就是东汉明帝（刘庄，57-75）夜梦金人。此梦令人难忘，他的大臣提出这可能是一个外国的神佛。明帝于是派人出使西方，并带回两名印度僧侣迦叶摩腾（Kasyapa Matanga）和竺法兰（Gobharana），由白马驮经。僧侣们带来了部派佛经文本，其中包括四十章经文，于公元67年在洛阳白马寺翻译。而事实上，明帝的弟弟刘英也保护了一些刚刚兴起的佛教社团。有赖于中国佛寺的编年史，到公元2世纪有了更多记载。大约在公元150年左右，佛教徒安息王子安世高作为人质来到中国，翻译了数篇部派佛经（编年史记载为35篇）。公元181年波斯商人安玄成为安世高的弟子，翻译了其他派的佛经并积极讲法。在这之后，公元2世纪来自贵霜的僧人支娄迦谶（Lokaksema）才翻译并将大乘佛教传入中国。

The introduction of Buddhism in China is commonly dating back to the mid-1st century A.D. during the Eastern Han Dynasty, which had extended its protectorate over part of Central Asia. There is no definite information on this event

乎可以肯定是属于公元1世纪的匈奴文化。第
4号木琴的年代被认为是公元1世纪佛教传播
的早期阶段，当然这还有待商榷。刻有西方铭
文的第9号铅饼可能属于汉代，基本可以追溯
到西汉后期至东汉后期，不过目前对铭文的解
读还存在各种困难。

　　作为特定的研究类别，多数玻璃器在形制
和工艺上都与伊朗的萨珊文化有着密切关联，
不过它们还是有着非常丰富的年代和文化跨度
的。第13号玻璃杯时代在公元4世纪到5世纪
的汉晋之间，16号玻璃杯在罗马—萨珊时期的
轮刻磨花传统中有许多相似品，在公元6世纪
的朝鲜半岛也有类似发现。16号高足杯的时代
为萨珊晚期至伊斯兰早期，根据相关考古发现，
其年代下限不会晚于公元874年。第33号玻璃
碗清晰地展现了透过罗马—拜占庭世界而来的
萨珊文化影响，年代在公元5到8世纪之间；第
42号玻璃瓶则明显属于萨珊晚期到伊斯兰时代
早期，而第44号玻璃杯则很可能来自公元7世
纪的伊朗。

　　第45号来通能在埃及和希腊化时期的巴

peculiar characteristics and we are very pleased to emphasize them to the light of very careful and well thought analyses starting from the first 3 (nos 1-3) objects clearly referring to the Scythian, Wu Sun, Saka cultural world or to their archaeological complex, and dating back to the 5th and 3rd century BC, certainly before the Han dynasty. Bronze mirror no 7 almost certainly belongs, nevertheless, to the 1st century, and to the Hun culture actually. Different considerations should be, instead, made for the wooden harp no 4 which has been considered dating back to the first centuries AD, at the time of the early diffusion of the Buddhism. Lead ingots with western inscription no 9, probably belong, instead, to the Han dynasty period and basically can be dating back from the later period of the Western Han Dynasty to the later period of the Eastern Han Dynasty, though with all the difficult interpretative issues of the western letters used.

A particular category of object examined are the glasses which present a very ample chronological and cultural span time as well, even whether most of them present typological and technical affinities with the Iranian Sasanian world. Glass cup no 13 is dating between the Han and Jin dynasty in 4th-5th century AD; meanwhile glass beaker no 16 finds numerous parallels with the Roman-Sasanian wheel-cut faceted glass tradition and with Korea of the 6th century AD. Glass goblet no 17, attributable to the late Sasanian early Islamic time, on

but only legends, the largest of which would like the Emperor Ming (also known as Liú Zhuang, A.D. 57-75) dreamed of a golden man. Particularly impressed from happening, his advisor suggested it might be a foreign god Buddha's name. Míng sent some ambassadors to the West, who returned along with two Indian monks, Kasyapa Matanga (also known by the Chinese name: She Moteng) and Gobharaṇ (Chinese: Zhu Fǎlán), conducted on a white horse. The monks brought with them texts of Buddhist schools of Nikāya, including the Sutra in forty chapters, who translated in 67 A.D. in Luòyáng where they founded the White Horse Monastery (Báimǎ-yes). It turns out, however, that even the brother of Emperor Ming, Liú Ying, protect some nascent Buddhist communities. We have some more news from the second century. thanks to the Chinese monastic chronicles. Around 150 A.D. as a hostage, An Shigao, a Buddhist Persian prince who would have translated several sutras, arrived in China, (the chronicles speak of 35 texts) of the Buddhist schools of Nikāya. In 181 came the Persian An Xuán, a merchant who became a disciple of An Shigao, translated texts always other schools of Buddhism of Nikāya and actively preached the Buddhist doctrine. Then, still in the second century, it was the turn of Lokaksema (Chinese: Zhi Lóujiāchèn) a real missionary Mahāyāna coming from Kushan empire who translated many texts but of schools of Mahayana Buddhism.

克特里亚找到相似品，而第46号玻璃瓶则与公元8到9世纪美索不达米亚的玻璃制品相近。在年代与文化渊源上完全不同的是来自公元8世纪叙利亚的第47号玻璃盘，9世纪叙利亚或美索不达米亚的第48号盘，以及9到10世纪美索不达米亚或伊朗北部的第49号杯，它们在年代和特征上都具有伊斯兰文化的特点。

本书中不同类型和工艺的印章被认为主要跟萨珊世界有关，第14号金戒指出土于汉代早期墓葬（年代在公元前5世纪到公元3世纪）；第32号金戒指属于萨珊印章制品，而第18号玉髓印章其中有翅膀的男性形象也明显属于萨珊文化；第19号玛瑙印章属于中亚西部的匈人文化，可以追溯到公元5世纪上半叶或5世纪中叶。第39号石英印章最有可能来自于萨珊王朝的最东部地区。接下来的一组金器的年代在公元前2世纪到突厥时期之间。第8号金项圈属于西汉时期（前206—23）；第15号金饰品年代在公元前3世纪至公元3世纪（汉晋时期）；第20号金面具可能属于5至7世纪的西部突厥人，或者属于匈人—萨尔马提亚文化；而第40号鎏金铜覆面被认为与祆教信仰有关，且在匈人时期的吉尔吉斯斯坦有过类似发现。

21号金罐、22号金杯、23号金剑鞘、25号金饰件、26号编织金带、28号金指套和金护臂、37号金壶、38号鎏金铜盘等器物被认为属于公元5—7世纪的突厥—拜占庭文化、来自欧亚草原的珠宝、甘肃吐蕃与粟特地区的文化交流产

the basis of an archaeological *terminus ante quem* can be dated back to 874. Glass bowl no 33 presents clear Sasanian influences through the Roman-Byzantine world, and is datable to the 5th-8th centuries AD; glass bottle no 42 is, instead, certainly attributable to the late Sasanian/ early Islamic period, whilst glass cup no 44 is possibly coming from Iran and datable to the 7th century AD.

Rhyton no 45 finds comparisons with Egypt and the Hellenistic Bactria and the glass bottle no 46 with Mesopotamia of the 8th-9th centuries AD. Completely different are the chronological and cultural grounds of the glass dish no 47 of Syrian origin in 8th century AD, of dish no 48 of Syrian or Mesopotamian origin of the 9th century, and of cup no 49 of Mesopotamian or northern Iran origin of the 9th-10th century AD, all, seemingly, Islamic in period and character.

The group of seals within a different typological and technical ground have been considered mostly relating to the Sasanian world, as gold ring no 14 coming from an early Han cemetery (datable, nevertheless from the 5th century BC to the 3rd century AD); gold ring no 32, seemingly belonging to the Sasanian seal production, whilst chalcedony seal no 18, with winged male figure clearly belonging to Sasanian glyptic as well; whereas agate seal no 19 belonging to the Hunnish cultural environment of the western Central Asia, is datable back to the first half of the 5th century or mid5th century AD. The onyx nicolo seal no 39 finally, is probably of a provincial origin in the easternmost areas of the Sasanian Empire.

The following group of golden items can be located in a wide time span oscillating between the 2nd century BC and the Turkish period, as the golden torque no 8 belonging to the western Han period (206 BC-23 AD), and the gold ornaments no 15 belonging to the 3rd century BC and to the 3rd century AD (from Han Dynasty to Jin Dynasty). A gold mask no 20 is clearly belonging to the western Turks of the 5th-7th century, or even to the Hun Sarmatian culture; whilst the gilt bronze mask no 40 has been considered to be related to somewhat beliefs, Zoroastrian in character, and finds

物以及公元8世纪的本地产品。第24号银杯属
于公元5至7世纪的萨珊工艺，第43号银杯似
乎是公元7至9世纪的早期伊斯兰或粟特文化
（也可能是中国的仿制品），而第6号银杯套的
时代可以追溯到战国末期。

　　在陶器中，第5号釉陶杯的年代在战国晚
期，第29号来通属于公元4世纪到7世纪，而第
31号陶罐出土于公元3世纪至9世纪的遗址，
其本身带有佛教因素，年代不晚于公元7—8世
纪，展现了新疆西部、巴特克里亚地区与南兴都
库什的交往。30号梳妆石托盘跟匈人、犍陀罗、
萨珊和笈多文化传统有关，可能来自巴基斯坦
西北部的斯瓦特地区。

　　纺织品也有相当长的年代跨度。第10号
棉布（蜡染棉布）的装饰带有佛教美术特征
（人狮搏斗），这种纹样发现于贵霜钱币以及犍
陀罗地区。第11号染色的羊毛裤子的年代大
约在公元3世纪，在中亚的绘画中能找到相似
品。第12号毛毡长袖服（羊毛、丝绸）属于东
汉至晋朝（25—420）。第34号织锦的时代在公
元4至10世纪，第35号织物的特征并非源自萨
珊，而是公元650年至675年中亚地区的产物，
第36号织物的年代相仿。最后，第41号铜器可
能来自伊朗或北印度，年代在公元7世纪。

parallels in Kirghizstan of the Hun period as well.

The following golden objects among jar (no 21), cup (no 22), sword scabbard (no 23), plaques (no 25). woven band (no 26), finger and arm guard (no 28). pot (no 37) and tray (no 38) have been considered belonging to the 5th-7th century AD, to the Turkish-Byzantine culture, to Eurasian jewellery and to the cultural interaction between Tibet in Gansu and Sogdian region, and local productions in 8th century. Silver cup no 24 belongs to the 5th-7th centuries AD, and is of Sasanian craftsmanship, whilst silver cup no 43, seemingly, is pre-Islamic/Sogdian (or Chinese copy) of the 7th-9th centuries AD and silver cup sheath no 6 has been chronologically dating back to the late Warring States Period.

Amongst the terracotta items, glazed pottery cup no 5 is chronologically dating back to the late Warring States Period and Rhython no 29, to the 4th-7th centuries AD, pottery jar no 31, coming from a site of the 3rd-9th century, seems to be Buddhist in character, and is dating back to a period no later than 7th-8th Century and presents relationships with the western Xinijang, Bactrian region and south Hindu-Kush. A part should be considered the stone toilet tray no 30, which has numerous cultural connections with Hona, Gandharan, Sasanian and Gupta cultural traditions, and is coming from north-eastern Pakistan in Swat region.

The textiles also can be located within a very ample chronological time span with the cotton cloth (wax resist dyed cotton) no 10 whose motifs, Buddhist artwork in character (as a man fighting with a lion), are known from the Kusham coins and the Gandharan area. The trousers (wool, dye) no. 11 are approximately dating back to the 3rd century AD, having strong parallel with the Central Asian paintings. The felt caftan (wool, silk) no 12, belongs to the Eastern Han-Jin dynasties (25-420 AD); Brocades no 34 belongs to the 4th-10th centuries AD, no 35 (silk) not Sasanian but central Asian in character to the third quarter of the 7th century, no 36 (silk), to the third quarter of the 7th century AD. Finally the metallistic production of the bronze ewer no 41, coming probably from Iran or northern India, belongs to the 7th century AD.

图片出处
List of Illustrations

1. 对翼兽铜环 Copper Ring

国家文物局等编:《丝绸之路》, 文物出版社(北京),2014年,页84。

State Administration of Cultural Heritage *et alii* (eds.) (2014) *Sichouzhilu (Silk Road)*, Cultural Relics Publishing House, 84, Beijing.

2. 青铜武士像 Bronze Statue

国家文物局等编:《丝绸之路》, 文物出版社(北京),2014年,页83。

State Administration of Cultural Heritage *et alii* (eds.) (2014) *Sichouzhilu (Silk Road)*, Cultural Relics Publishing House, 83, Beijing.

3. 铜盘 Bronze Tray

新疆维吾尔自治区博物馆编:《新疆维吾尔自治区博物馆》, 文物出版社(北京),1991年,图28。

Xinjiang Weiwuer zizhiqu bowuguan (1991) *Xinjiang Weiwuer zizhiqu bowuguan (Xinjiang Uygur Autonomous Region Museum)*, Cultural Relics Publishing House, fig. 28, Beijing.

4. 竖琴 Harp

历史博物馆编辑委员会:《丝路传奇:新疆文物大展》,2008年,台北,页63。

Museum of History editorial committee (ed.) (2008) *Silu chuanqi: Xinjiang wenwu dazhan (Legends of the Silk Road: Treasures from Xinjiang)*, Exhibition Catalogue, Museum of History, 63, Taipei.

5. 釉陶杯 Glazed Pottery Cup

国家文物局等编:《丝绸之路》, 文物出版社(北京),2014年,页93。

State Administration of Cultural Heritage *et alii* (eds.) (2014) *Sichouzhilu (Silk Road)*, Cultural Relics Publishing House, 93, Beijing.

6. 银杯套 Silver Cup-Sheath

甘肃省文物考古研究所:《西戎遗珍:马家塬战国墓地出土文物》, 文物出版社(北京), 2014年,页110。

Gansu Provincal Institute of Cultural Relics and Archaeology (ed.) *Xirong yizhen: majiayuan mudi chutu wenwu (Splendid Treasures of Xirong: Cultural Relics Unearthed from Majiayuan Cemetery of Warring States Period)*, Cultural Relics Publishing House, 110, Beijing.

7. 有柄铜镜 Bronze Mirror

中国历史博物馆等编:《天山·古道·东西风——新疆丝绸之路文物特辑》,中国社会科学出版社(北京),2002年,页52。

National Museum of China *et alii* (eds.) (2002) *Tianshan gudao dongxifeng, xinjiang sichouzhilu wenwu teji* (*Mt. Tianshan·Ancient Roads·the Meeting of East & West: The Extraordinary Cultural Relics from the Silk Road in Xinjiang*), China Social Sciences Publishing House, 52, Beijing.

8. 金项饰 Gold Torque

新疆文物考古研究所:《交河沟西:1994—1996年度考古发掘报告》,新疆人民出版社(乌鲁木齐),2001年,彩版七.3。

Xinjiang Institute of Cultural Relics and Archaeology (2001) *Jiaohe Gouxi: 1994–1996 niandu kaogu fajue baogao* (*Jiaohe Gouxi: the archaeological excavating report from 1994 to 1996*), Xinjiang People's Publishing House, Colorful Plate 7.3, Urumqï.

9. 铅饼 Lead Ingots

甘肃省博物馆编:《甘肃丝绸之路文明》,科学出版社(北京),2008年,页96,图84.

Gansu Museum (ed.) (2008) *Gansu sichouzhilu wenming (Civilization along the Silk Road within Gansu)*, Social Sciences Academic Press, 96, fig. 84, Beijing.

10. 印花棉布 Cotton Cloth

新疆维吾尔自治区文物局:《丝路瑰宝:新疆馆藏文物精品图录》,新疆人民出版社(乌鲁木齐),2011年,页92。

Administration of Cultural Heritage of the Xinjiang Uygur Autonomous Region (ed.) (2011) *Siluguibao, xinjiang guancang wenwu jingpin tulu (Silk Road Treasures: Catalogue of Extraordinary Cultural Relics in the museums of Xinjiang)*, Xinjiang People's Publishing House, 92, Urumqï.

11. 裤子 Trousers

祁小山、王博:《丝绸之路·新疆古代文化》,新疆人民出版社(乌鲁木齐),2008年,页67图⑧。

Qi Xiaoshan, *et alii* (eds.) (2008) *Sichouzhilu, xinjiang gudai wenhua (The Silk Road: Xinjiang Ancient Culture)*, Xinjiang People's Publishing House, 67, fig. 8, Urumqï.

中国历史博物馆等编:《天山·古道·东西风——新疆丝绸之路文物特辑》,中国社会科学出版社(北京),2002年,页130。

National Museum of China *et alii* (eds.) (2002) *Tianshan gudao dongxifeng, xinjiang sichouzhilu wenwu teji* (*Mt. Tianshan·Ancient Roads·The Meeting of East & West: The Extraordinary Cultural Relics from the Silk Road in Xinjiang*), China Social Sciences Publishing House, 130, Beijing.

12. 红地罽袍 Felt Caftan

祁小山、王博:《丝绸之路·新疆古代文化》,新疆人民出版社(乌鲁木齐),2008年,页36图①,页38图①。

Qi Xiaoshan, *et alii* (eds.) (2008) *Sichouzhilu, xinjiang gudai wenhua* (*The Silk Road: Xinjiang Ancient Culture*), Xinjiang People's Publishing House, 36, fig. 1, 38, fig. 1, Urumqï.

13. 玻璃杯 Glass Cup

新疆维吾尔自治区文物局等:《新疆文物古迹大观》,新疆美术摄影出版社(乌鲁木齐),1999年,页199,0531。

Xinjiang Uygur Autonomous Region Cultural Relics Administration *et alii* (eds.) (1999) *Xinjiang wenwu guji daguan* (*A Grand View of Xinjiang's Cultural Relics and Historical Sites*), Xinjiang Fine Arts Photography Press, 199, fig. 0531, Urumqï.

14. 嵌宝石金戒指 Gold Ring

Wieczorek, A. und Lind, C. (hrsg.) (2007) *Ursprünge der Seidenstraße, Sensationelle Neufunde aus Xinjiang, China*, 295, fig. 179, Mannheim-Stuttgart.

历史博物馆编辑委员会:《丝路传奇:新疆文物大展》,2008年,台北,页63。

Museum of History editorial committee (ed.) (2008) *Silu chuanqi: Xinjiang wenwu dazhan* (*Legends of the Silk Road: Treasures from Xinjiang*), Exhibition Catalogue, Museum of History, 63, Taipei.

15. 金饰件 Gold Ornament

历史博物馆编辑委员会:《丝路传奇:新疆文物大展》,2008年,台北,页63。

Museum of History editorial committee (ed.) (2008) *Silu chuanqi: Xinjiang wenwu dazhan* (*Legends of the Silk Road: Treasures from Xinjiang*), Exhibition Catalogue, Museum of History, 63, Taipei.

16. 玻璃杯 Glass Beaker

新疆维吾尔自治区文物局:《丝路瑰宝:新疆馆藏文物精品图录》,新疆人民出版社(乌鲁木齐),2011年,页86。

Administration of Cultural Heritage of the Xinjiang Uygur Autonomous Region (ed.) (2011) *Siluguibao, xinjiang guancang wenwu jingpin tulu* (*Silk Road Treasures: Catalogue of Extraordinary Cultural Relics in the museums of Xinjiang*), Xinjiang People's Publishing House, 86, Urumqï.

17. 玻璃高足杯 Glass Goblet

国家文物局等编:《丝绸之路》,文物出版社(北京),2014年,页190。

State Administration of Cultural Heritage *et alii* (eds.) (2014) *Sichouzhilu* (*Silk Road*), Cultural Relics Publishing House, 190, Beijing.

18. 印章 Seal

《丝绸之路：大西北遗珍》编辑委员会：《丝绸之路：大西北遗珍》，文物出版社（北京），2010年，页89，图78。

The Editorial Board (ed.) (2010) *Sichouzhilu: daxibei yizhen (Silk Road: The Surviving Treasures from the Northwest China)*, Cultural Relics Publishing House, 89, fig. 78, Beijing.

19. 印章 Seal

新疆维吾尔自治区文物局：《丝路瑰宝：新疆馆藏文物精品图录》，新疆人民出版社（乌鲁木齐），2011年，页237。

Administration of Cultural Heritage of the Xinjiang Uygur Autonomous Region (ed.) (2011) *Siluguibao, xinjiang guancang wenwu jingpin tulu (Silk Road Treasures: Catalogue of Extraordinary Cultural Relics in the museums of Xinjiang)*, Xinjiang People's Publishing House, 237, Urumqï.

20. 金面具 Gold Mask

Wieczorek, A. und Lind, C. (hrsg.) (2007) *Ursprünge der Seidenstraße, Sensationelle Neufunde aus Xinjiang, China*, 303, fig. 190, Mannheim-Stuttgart.

21. 带盖金罐 Gold Covered Jar

中国历史博物馆等编：《天山·古道·东西风——新疆丝绸之路文物特辑》，中国社会科学出版社（北京），2002年，页62。

National Museum of China *et alii* (eds.) (2002) *Tianshan gudao dongxifeng, xinjiang sichouzhilu wenwu teji (Mt. Tianshan · Ancient Roads · the Meeting of East & West: The Extraordinary Cultural Relics from the Silk Road in Xinjiang)*, China Social Sciences Publishing House, 62, Beijing.

22. 金杯 Gold Cup

中国历史博物馆等编：《天山·古道·东西风——新疆丝绸之路文物特辑》，中国社会科学出版社（北京），2002年，页61。

National Museum of China *et alii* (eds.) (2002) *Tianshan gudao dongxifeng, xinjiang sichouzhilu wenwu teji (Mt. Tianshan · Ancient Roads · the Meeting of East & West: The Extraordinary Cultural Relics from the Silk Road in Xinjiang)*, China Social Sciences Publishing House, 61, Beijing.

23. 金剑鞘 Gold Sword Scabbard

中国历史博物馆等编：《天山·古道·东西风——新疆丝绸之路文物特辑》，中国社会科学出版社（北京），2002年，页57。

National Museum of China *et alii* (eds.) (2002) *Tianshan gudao dongxifeng, xinjiang sichouzhilu wenwu teji (Mt. Tianshan · Ancient Roads · the Meeting of East & West: The Extraordinary Cultural Relics from the Silk Road in Xinjiang*), China Social Sciences Publishing House, 57, Beijing.

24. 银瓶 Silver Vase

中国历史博物馆等编：《天山·古道·东西风——新疆丝绸之路文物特辑》，中国社会科学出版社（北京），2002年，页59。

National Museum of China *et alii* (eds.) (2002) *Tianshan gudao dongxifeng, xinjiang sichouzhilu wenwu teji* (*Mt. Tianshan · Ancient Roads · the Meeting of East & West: The Extraordinary Cultural Relics from the Silk Road in Xinjiang*), China Social Sciences Publishing House, 59, Beijing.

25. 金饰件 Gold Plaques

新疆维吾尔自治区文物局：《丝路瑰宝：新疆馆藏文物精品图录》，新疆人民出版社（乌鲁木齐），2011年，页270。

Administration of Cultural Heritage of the Xinjiang Uygur Autonomous Region (ed.) (2011) *Siluguibao, xinjiang guancang wenwu jingpin tulu* (*Silk Road Treasures: Catalogue of Extraordinary Cultural Relics in the museums of Xinjiang*), Xinjiang People's Publishing House, 270, Urumqï.

26. 编织金带 Gold Woven Band

祁小山、王博：《丝绸之路·新疆古代文化》，新疆人民出版社（乌鲁木齐），2008年，页

261图⑦。

Qi Xiaoshan *et alii* (eds.) (2008) *Sichouzhilu, xinjiang gudai wenhua* (*The Silk Road: Xinjiang Ancient Culture*), Xinjiang People's Publishing House, 261, fig. 7, Urumqï.

27. 金杯 Gold Cup

祁小山、王博：《丝绸之路·新疆古代文化》，新疆人民出版社（乌鲁木齐），2008年，页259图⑤。

Qi Xiaoshan *et alii* (eds.) (2008) *Sichouzhilu, xinjiang gudai wenhua* (*The Silk Road: Xinjiang Ancient Culture*), Xinjiang People's Publishing House, 259, fig. 5, Urumqï.

28. 金指套和护臂 Gold Finger and Arm Guard

祁小山、王博：《丝绸之路·新疆古代文化》，新疆人民出版社（乌鲁木齐），2008年，页261图⑧。

Qi Xiaoshan *et alii* (eds.) (2008) *Sichouzhilu, xinjiang gudai wenhua* (*The Silk Road: Xinjiang Ancient Culture*), Xinjiang People's Publishing House, 261, fig. 8, Urumqï.

29. 陶来通 Rhyton

新疆维吾尔自治区博物馆编：《新疆维吾尔自治区博物馆》，文物出版社（北京），1991年，图19。

Xinjiang Weiwuer zizhiqu bowuguan (1991) *Xinjiang Weiwuer zizhiqu bowuguan* (*Xinjiang*

Uygur Autonomous Region Museum), Cultural Relics Publishing House, fig. 19, Beijing.

30. 梳妆托盘 Toilet Tray

祁小山、王博:《丝绸之路·新疆古代文化》,新疆人民出版社(乌鲁木齐),2008年,页181图⑧。

Qi Xiaoshan, *et alii* (eds.) (2008) *Sichouzhilu, xinjiang gudai wenhua* (*The Silk Road: Xinjiang Ancient Culture*), Xinjiang People's Publishing House, 181, fig. 8, Urumqï.

31. 三耳陶罐 Pottery Jar

中国历史博物馆等编:《天山·古道·东西风——新疆丝绸之路文物特辑》,中国社会科学出版社(北京),2002年,页183。

National Museum of China *et alii* (eds.) (2002) *Tianshan gudao dongxifeng, xinjiang sichouzhilu wenwu teji* (*Mt. Tianshan · Ancient Roads · the Meeting of East & West: The Extraordinary Cultural Relics from the Silk Road in Xinjiang*), China Social Sciences Publishing House, 183, Beijing.

32. 金戒指 Gold Ring

宁夏固原博物馆:《固原历史文物》,科学出版社(北京),2004年,页129。

Guyuan Museum (2004) *Guyuan lishi wenwu* (*Historical and Cultural Relics from Guyuan*), Science Publishing House, 129, Beijing.

33. 玻璃碗 Glass Bowl

国家文物局等编:《丝绸之路》,文物出版社(北京),2014年,页217。

State Administration of Cultural Heritage *et alii* (eds.) (2014) *Sichouzhilu* (*Silk Road*), Cultural Relics Publishing House, 217, Beijing.

34. 对羊对鸟灯树纹锦 Brocade

国家文物局等编:《丝绸之路》,文物出版社(北京),2014年,页151。

State Administration of Cultural Heritage *et alii* (eds.) (2014) *Sichouzhilu* (*Silk Road*), Cultural Relics Publishing House, 151, Beijing.

35. 覆面 Brocade

新疆维吾尔自治区博物馆编:《新疆维吾尔自治区博物馆》,文物出版社(北京),1991年,图57。

Xinjiang Weiwuer zizhiqu bowuguan (1991) *Xinjiang Weiwuer zizhiqu bowuguan* (*Xinjiang Uygur Autonomous Region Museum*), Cultural Relics Publishing House, fig. 57, Beijing.

36. 联珠鹿纹锦 Brocade

新疆维吾尔自治区博物馆编:《新疆维吾尔自治区博物馆》,文物出版社(北京),1991年,图56。

Xinjiang Weiwuer zizhiqu bowuguan (1991) *Xinjiang Weiwuer zizhiqu bowuguan* (*Xinjiang Uygur Autonomous Region Museum*), Cultural

Relics Publishing House, fig. 56, Beijing.

37. 金壶 Gold Pot

甘肃省文物局编：《甘肃文物菁华》，文物出版社（北京），2006年，页160，图170。

Cultural Relics Bureau of Gansu (ed.) (2006) *Gansu wenwu jinghua (Collection of Precious Cultural Relics in Gansu)*, Cultural Relics Publishing House, 160, fig. 170, Beijing.

38. 鎏金铜盘 Gilded Bronze Tray

甘肃省文物局编：《甘肃文物菁华》，文物出版社（北京），2006年，页309，图326。

Cultural Relics Bureau of Gansu (ed.) (2006) *Gansu wenwu jinghua (Collection of Precious Cultural Relics in Gansu)*, Cultural Relics Publishing House, 309, fig. 326, Beijing.

39. 印章 Seal

宁夏固原博物馆：《固原历史文物》，科学出版社（北京），2004年，页215。

Guyuan Museum (2004) *Guyuan lishi wenwu (Historical and Cultural Relics from Guyuan)*, Science Publishing House, 215, Beijing.

40. 鎏金铜覆面 Gilt Bronze Mask

宁夏固原博物馆：《固原历史文物》，科学出版社（北京），2004年，页213。

Guyuan Museum (2004) *Guyuan lishi wenwu (Historical and Cultural Relics from Guyuan)*, Science Publishing House, 213, Beijing.

41. 铜壶 Bronze Ewer

国家文物局等编：《丝绸之路》，文物出版社（北京），2014年，页172。

State Administration of Cultural Heritage *et alii* (eds.) (2014) *Sichouzhilu (Silk Road)*, Cultural Relics Publishing House, 172, Beijing.

42. 玻璃瓶 Glass Bottle

杨伯达：《中国美术全集·工艺美术编·10·金银玻璃珐琅器》，文物出版社（北京），1988年，页120，图二二九。

Yang Boda (ed.) (1988) *Zhongguo meishu quanji gongyi meishubian, 10, jinyin boli falangqi (Complete works of Chinese art, Fine arts, vol.10, Gold, silver, glass and enamel wares)*, Cultural Relics Publishing House, 120, fig.229, Beijing.

43. 银带把杯 Silver Cup

陕西历史博物馆等：《花舞大唐春：何家村遗宝精粹》，文物出版社（北京），2003年，页88。

Shaanxi History Museum *et alii* (eds.)(2003) *Huawu datangchun: Hejiacun yibao jingcui (Selected Treasures from Hejiacun Tang Hoard)*, Cultural Relics Publishing House, 88, Beijing.

44. 玻璃杯 Glass Cup

陕西历史博物馆等：《花舞大唐春：何家

村遗宝精粹》，文物出版社（北京），2003年，页101。

Shaanxi History Museum *et alii* (eds.)(2003) *Huawu datangchun: Hejiacun yibao jingcui (Selected Treasures from Hejiacun Tang Hoard)*, Cultural Relics Publishing House, 101, Beijing.

45. 兽首玛瑙杯 Rhyton

陕西历史博物馆等:《花舞大唐春：何家村遗宝精粹》，文物出版社（北京），2003年，页92。

Shaanxi History Museum *et alii* (eds.)(2003) *Huawu datangchun: Hejiacun yibao jingcui (Selected Treasures from Hejiacun Tang Hoard)*, Cultural Relics Publishing House, 92, Beijing.

46. 玻璃瓶 Glass Bottle

韩生:《法门寺文物图饰》，文物出版社（北京），2009年，页289。

Han Sheng (ed.) *Famensi wenwu tushi (Ornaments of Cultural Relics from Famen Temple)*, Cultural Relics Publishing House, 289, Beijing.

47. 黄玻璃盘 Glass Dish

韩生:《法门寺文物图饰》，文物出版社（北京），2009年，页292。

Han Sheng (ed.) *Famensi wenwu tushi (Ornaments of Cultural Relics from Famen Temple)*, Cultural Relics Publishing House, 292, Beijing.

48. 蓝琉璃盘 Glass Dish

韩生:《法门寺文物图饰》，文物出版社（北京），2009年，页296。

Han Sheng (ed.) *Famensi wenwu tushi (Ornaments of Cultural Relics from Famen Temple)*, Cultural Relics Publishing House, 296, Beijing.

49. 玻璃杯 Glass Cup

韩生:《法门寺文物图饰》，文物出版社（北京），2009年，页291。

Han Sheng (ed.) *Famensi wenwu tushi (Ornaments of Cultural Relics from Famen Temple)*, Cultural Relics Publishing House, 291, Beijing.

图书在版编目（CIP）数据

异宝西来：考古发现的丝绸之路舶来品研究 / 葛嶷，
齐东方主编. —上海：上海古籍出版社，2018.10
ISBN 978-7-5325-8969-2

Ⅰ.①异…　Ⅱ.①葛…　②齐…　Ⅲ.①丝绸之路—出
土文物—研究—西北地区　Ⅳ.①K873.4

中国版本图书馆CIP数据核字（2018）第202105号

封面图片取自河南洛阳唐神龙二年（706）安国相王孺人唐氏
墓（《丝绸之路》，文物出版社，2014年）。

异宝西来：考古发现的丝绸之路舶来品研究
葛嶷、齐东方　主编
上海古籍出版社出版、发行
（上海瑞金二路 272 号　邮政编码 200020）
（1）网址：www.guji.com.cn
（2）E-mail：guji1 @ guji.com.cn
（3）易文网网址：www.ewen.co
上海丽佳制版印刷有限公司印刷
开本787×1092　1/16　印张16.5　插页4　字数158,000
2018 年 10 月第 1 版　2018 年 10 月第 1 次印刷
印数 1-3,300
ISBN 978-7-5325-8969-2
K·2540　定价：188.00 元
如有质量问题，请与承印公司联系